Debora

Through the Eyes of
100+ COLLEGE & UNIVERSITY PRESID....

COMMENCEMENT

Higher education
is better because
of you!
We hope you
enjoy the book.

The Beginning of
a New Era in Higher Education

Dr. Joe Sallust

Kate Colbert

Praise for *Commencement*

"Kate and Joe have masterfully captured reflections and insights from the industry's most innovative leaders, paired with their own unique voices that pull back the curtains on some of today's biggest higher ed challenges. Their conversational style and passion are infectious and draw upon the power of community to reimagine, (dare I say disrupt?), reinvent, and advance the future for students. *Commencement* weaves together first-hand accounts and industry research while encouraging readers to see new possibilities and opportunities for a better way forward. If you are looking for inspiration, this book is a must-read!"

Laura Ipsen, President and CEO, Ellucian

"Listeners of *The EdUp Experience Podcast* have come to expect a fast-paced conversation about topics relevant to higher education leaders with a range of perspectives. Colbert and Sallustio's *Commencement: The Beginning of a New Era in Higher Education* — the book born from the podcast — delivers exactly that kind of important conversation, but without the cool sound effects. A post-COVIDian age welcomes the insights of 100 university leaders curated in this book."

Frank J. Dooley, PhD, Chancellor, Purdue University Global

"*Commencement* is a must-read for all higher education leaders regardless of the size of their institution. The business of higher education is on the precipice of enormous transformation, and colleges and universities need to adapt to meet the changing needs of today's students and educators. Colbert and Sallustio succinctly capture the current state of the higher education market and offer real-world insight into what needs to be done moving forward."

Elliot Markowitz, Editor-in-Chief, Head of Content, *Fierce Education*

"Dr. Joe Sallustio, Kate Colbert, and Elvin Freytes have done us a great service. *Commencement* isn't a survey or a research study. The material comes from open, frank discussions with leaders from across the higher education spectrum. I think readers will be surprised and enlightened. This book is a torch to be passed in the long relay race of higher education."

Bill Pepicello, PhD, Former President, University of Phoenix,
and Author of *Leadership on the Field of Play*

"As HigherEd struggles with the questions of whether to change from traditional modes of operation to one enabling great access and connectivity through technology, Colbert and Sallustio eloquently bring to light the tensions, struggles, dichotomies and — most importantly — the opportunities ahead for HigherEd with examples of successes. Rather than a dry report of woe, this is an enthralling study of a bright future with examples gleaned from interviews and conversations with leaders. A must-read for anyone with an interest in the future success of HigherEd."

Vistasp Karbhari, PhD, Professor and Former President,
The University of Texas at Arlington

"In an ever-changing higher-education industry going through transformation at all levels, it is wonderful to discover a book where all the diverse voices within the ecosystem are elevated in a manner that inspires innovation, strategic partnerships, and social impact. *Commencement* is a must-read for everyone who works for, on behalf of, and in support of higher education."

Geoffrey M. Roche, MPA, Senior Vice President, National Health Care Practice & Workforce Partnerships, Core Education Services, PBC; MBA/MHA Faculty, Moravian University; and Population Health Faculty, Harrisburg University of Science and Technology

"The role of a college or university president has become increasingly more difficult. Hearing from these visionary leaders, in an organic and engaging way that only Colbert and Sallustio can pull off, gives me confidence that better times are ahead in higher education."

Jim Milton, Chairman and CEO, Anthology, Inc.

"Timely and insightful. Colbert and Sallustio unify influential voices from across the industry and around the world to examine the disruptive challenges threatening higher education and illuminate the exciting possibilities before us."

Erika Liodice, Executive Director,
Alliance for Innovation & Transformation

"This is an incredibly insightful book about the future of higher education and how higher education leaders responded to the COVID-19 pandemic, the most significant disruptor that we've experienced in our lifetime. The authors are witty and entertaining and do a great job exploring the future of higher education with presidential leaders. It's an excellent read that will be enjoyed by a broad audience ranging from higher education leaders, faculty, staff, policymakers, students, parents, philanthropists, and many other stakeholders."

Linda Garza Battles, Western Governors University (WGU) Regional Vice President, South; Chancellor, WGU Texas

"Higher ed is in a pivotal moment, with everyone looking for solutions to the many challenges we face. Reading this book is like sitting down with countless presidents and learning what they are doing to survive and thrive during these challenging times. Joe and Elvin brought us the podcast, and now Joe and Kate have done an awesome job bringing those stories to us in this book. *Commencement* is a seminal piece of work that allows us to learn from the best, the most innovative, and the most resilient leaders in the industry."

Amardeep Kahlon, PhD, Dean, Technical Institute for Environmental Professions, Unity College, Maine

"Higher education has needed this unvarnished conversation regarding radical transformation and innovation for a long time. Colbert and Sallustio deliver — over and over again — offering real-world examples and interviews with true leaders who know what needs to be done now. *Commencement* is truly the most relevant book on higher education innovation because it uses the collective voices of practitioners and industry veterans to help us re-imagine higher education. *Commencement* is an outstanding and insightful book, and a must-have for anyone interested in true radical change that will make higher education more responsive to the needs of students and those in the workforce."

Dr. Kurt T. Steinberg, EdD, President, Montserrat College of Art

"Colbert and Sallustio introduce us to the best minds in higher education. The relevant insights and practical advice offered through the more than 100 interviews have immediate application for all higher education professionals. *Commencement* is quite literally the equivalent of having an inside view of leadership discussions happening across academia, and an invitation to learn from those leading innovative institutions and programs. It's a must-read for anyone in the business of education."

Kerry Salerno, Chief Marketing & Communication Officer, Babson College

"Kate and Joe are right — what's worked for higher-ed in the past simply won't work in the future. We are at a historic moment. The institutions that are willing to take risks, to change the face of their mission, and who resolutely know — and act — on hard truths are the ones that will succeed. Kate and Joe brilliantly capture insights from leaders in higher education and dig into some of the most difficult challenges and realities the industry is facing. And they do it in such a way that is fascinating and thought-provoking. Whether you are an insider yourself or just curious about the state of higher education, *Commencement* is a must-read."

Lauren Shaka, Education Marketing Consultant, and Former Senior Director of Enrollment Marketing and Communications at Northeastern University

Through the Eyes of
100+ COLLEGE & UNIVERSITY PRESIDENTS

COMMENCEMENT

The Beginning of
a New Era in Higher Education

KATE COLBERT | JOE SALLUSTIO, EdD

With contributions by Elvin Freytes

With a foreword by
FRANCISCO J. MARMOLEJO
Higher Education President, Qatar Foundation

Dedication

For Gemma and Giulio, and Jackie and Olga — the future is yours.

With all our hearts, we hope that our efforts here — to shine a light on what you deserve and what you are capable of — will create the pathways to your dreams. Born into the information age, you represent a new kind of learner — with new expectations, new needs, and new ways of assessing whether higher education is measuring up. Demand more — a better experience and better outcomes. We promise to continue to enable and inspire evolutions and revolutions in higher education so, one day, you'll be able to gratefully say: "This is not my parents' college experience. It's so much better."

Contents

PART III
Resources, Acknowledgments, and Additional Information About *Commencement* 515

With Gratitude

When we began writing this book, more than 100 college and university presidents had already honored *The EdUp Experience Podcast* with their time and insights. As this book is released to readers, that elite cadre of leaders numbers nearly 200. To every single president whose insights made this book possible, thank you. Your candor, care, wisdom, and collegiality — because you were willing to share of yourself so freely and widely — leave a legacy with ripple effects that will improve higher education for decades to come.

A Note to the Reader: In the pages of this book, you will find the ideas, stories, and recommendations of dozens of college and university presidents, in their own words. More than 100 presidents were interviewed for this book, and even more were surveyed anonymously; while their collective insights inform the themes and arguments that Colbert and Sallustio lay out, not every president is quoted directly. See the book's appendix for a comprehensive listing of the 100+ presidents who contributed to *Commencement: The Beginning of a New Era in Higher Education.*

Foreword

By Francisco J. Marmolejo
Higher Education President, Qatar Foundation

There is no doubt that higher education is in the midst of a significant turmoil. But how profound is it? How do we differentiate between a set of short-term transitional events and a more persistent and profound change? And how might it all influence the way higher education institutions operate?

In trying to respond to those questions, we may become frustrated if we solely analyze the related research being conducted by field experts, as the pace of change is so rapid that the work of researchers — which may help us digest and dissect emerging new realities — is still pending.

Therefore, the interesting work conducted by Dr. Joe Sallustio, Kate Colbert, and Elvin Freytes is refreshing, informative, and timely. *Commencement: The Beginning of a New Era in Higher Education* provides readers a good grasp of up-to-date reflections shared directly by higher education's decision-makers as they cope with the challenges that colleges and universities face today. By virtue of sharing their experiences in and reflections on the management of complex higher education ecosystems, interviewees become both protagonists and, in some way, co-authors of *Commencement*.

I am sure that the task carried on so diligently by Sallustio, Colbert, and Freytes — the work of researching and writing this book — has not been an easy one. Identifying key trends and extracting significant lessons learned from the many conversations held during the past three years — with literally hundreds of higher education leaders who have shared their perspectives as part of *The EdUp Experience Podcast*'s President Series — requires objectivity, a systemic mindset, analytical rigor, time, and patience. The result of such dedicated work is *Commencement*.

But are we really witnessing "the beginning of a new era in higher education," as provocatively proposed by the authors of *Commencement*? I have been working in higher education — and seeing its evolution in many parts of the world — for more than 40 years, so this is not the first time that I have heard similar statements. (I have most probably said it as well). In fact, it can be argued that even though there are many changes experienced in the ways colleges and universities work — and in the contextual environments in which they strive and survive — at the end, the essence of higher education remains the same. But it would be naïve to assume that higher education institutions are immune to structural and circumstantial transitions happening around and inside them.

It would be naïve to assume that higher education institutions are immune to structural and circumstantial transitions happening around and inside them.

There are many transitions that, whether we like it or not, have a profound impact in our lives and in our institutions — like the significant societal shifts experienced in the world, the fascinating technological and scientific endeavors achieved in recent years (and expected to be achieved in the near future), the magnitude of huge challenges (such as climate change or the recent pandemic), and the realities of a complex, intrinsically interconnected and convoluted socioeconomic and political landscape. Because of these converging forces, colleges and universities can no longer be "ivory towers." In fact, it can be said that the "ivory tower" is just a rhetorical expression, because institutions of higher education stopped being isolated from the surrounding environment quite a long time ago. But also, as it is mentioned by many of the institutional presidents and other higher-education leaders interviewed in *Commencement*, resistance to change persists and internal dynamics of colleges and universities many times deter an appetite and urgency for fast adaptation. The paradox of higher education is that, on one side, it is the very institution that should be upfront *anticipating* and even *fostering* change and innovation, while, on the other side, it is highly *reluctant* to change or innovate in any way. The testimonies captured by the authors of *Commencement* clearly transmit this irony that is being faced by institutional leaders as they attempt to "move the needle" — not always successfully — which they accept with candor.

In summary, *Commencement* is a must-read to understand the complexities, contradictions, and key trends — narrated by institutional presidents, the very protagonists of what is literally a new era in higher education.

Preface

By Joe Sallustio, EdD

"Welcome back, everybody! It's YOUR time to #edup on The EdUp Experience Podcast, where we make education YOUR business."

I've said this introduction, or some version of it, more than 500 times in the past three years as *The EdUp Experience Podcast* has taken the higher-education industry by storm. As of October 2022, the podcast has been played nearly 200,000 times, in more than 163 countries, with an 85/15 split between domestic and international listeners. Our first episode, released on January 25, 2020, introduced the podcast to a non-existent listening audience. I did, however, negotiate chores with my wife for her listenership so I could say there was an audience.

I say "our" first episode because EdUp is a partnership between myself and the incomparable Elvin Freytes. Elvin and I met through Dr. Jean Norris, a mutual contact within the industry. Elvin was in discussion with Jean to purchase a product through her company, and Jean recommended he speak with me, as I had previously used her product. Elvin and I immediately hit it off on the phone call, then we connected through LinkedIn and began to follow each other's content. At the time, I was podcasting with a higher-education outfit, and Elvin had a podcast that was just getting off the ground. When I discovered that Elvin had a podcast, I pitched to him that I should be his first guest — up to that point, the podcast featured only his voice and perspectives. We had a wonderful conversation about kids, life, and higher education.

A few days after my appearance on Elvin's podcast, he reached out to me on LinkedIn messenger, and I still have the exchange — here it is.

December 20, 2019

Elvin Freytes (He/Him) 4:25 PM

Ok. I am thinking of a side business. Interested?

Joe Sallustio, EdD 4:27 PM

Yep. And I don't even need to know what it is!! Lol

Elvin Freytes (He/Him) 4:56 PM

Awesome! Will keep you posted! 😎 👍

And this is how *The EdUp Experience* was created. We spent the first six months figuring out how to podcast — what do we ask, how long should it take, can we get guests? Our first chunk of episodes was not awesome. Episode #9 was the first time we asked a guest some questions about the global pandemic and its (at the time) forecasted influence on the higher-education industry. One byproduct of the podcast we didn't anticipate was that we chronicled the entirety of the pandemic's effect on higher education in real time. More on that later. We ended the first year with 10,000 plays of the podcast and were stunned we achieved that level of engagement. Little did we know that interest in EdUp would move faster than a decision in higher education without a committee.

Fast forward many podcasts later, nearly 100 interviews with college and university presidents, and a big question: "What do we do with all this content?" Before we could answer the question, we ended 2021 with more than 100,000 downloads of the podcast, which included live recordings at a few higher education conferences and tremendous interest in EdUp from industry partners. It's important to note that Elvin and I started this podcast-turned-business in 2019, and we did not meet in person until our trip to Doha, Qatar, in 2021 for the World Innovation Summit for Education!

Just as 2021 turned into 2022, a guest on our show introduced us to Kate Colbert. Kate was a purple unicorn for us — she was a former higher-education employee, a higher-education consultant, a current advisory board member of an institution, *and* a best-selling nonfiction author. Then it hit us — let's write a book! We had all these amazing interviews with college and university presidents, and we had a connection to a best-selling author who, wait for it … also owns a publishing company!

And so, the stars aligned. We embarked on the journey to create this book, *Commencement: The Beginning of a New Era in Higher Education,* written by Kate Colbert and Joe Sallustio, EdD, with contributions from Elvin Freytes. Insights from this book come from the three of us and the more than 100 college and university presidential interviews conducted on *The EdUp Experience Podcast.* I never thought I'd write a book — but it became more apparent with each interview that we had to do something with this priceless content. So, we started listening even more closely, and we started writing.

We've had to persevere. I had a huge job change and moved my family from California to St. Charles, Missouri. Right in the middle of our writing process, Kate became very sick, was diagnosed with Tethered Cord Syndrome, and had to have risky neurosurgery in May of 2022. There are writing barriers, and there are writing full-stops — Kate's surgery was a full-stop moment. I remember emailing Kate after her spinal-cord surgery and asking if she thought she could continue writing (or if she was even *interested* in writing after her surgery). Unsurprisingly, Kate was more bullish on writing this book post-surgery than she was pre-surgery. She told me that writing this book — for all of you and an industry we both love — had given her the hope she needed to push her recovery faster so we could deliver on our promise. Blood, sweat, and tears have gone into the pages of this higher-education work. So, we give you *Commencement: The Beginning of a New Era in Higher Education* through the eyes of more than 100 college and university presidents.

Oh, and by the way, something unexpected happened at the height of the manuscript development. The relevance, affordability, and value of higher education became national and global news with the August 24, 2022, announcement of broad-based federal student loan forgiveness measures in the United States.

The stories told by the presidents in our book contribute to a passionate, ongoing national and international conversation. That conversation includes stakeholders of all kinds — current and prospective students, alumni, parents, higher-education employees, higher-education consultants and service providers, industry experts and workforce developers, economists and financial professionals, and even armchair economists. Our *book* is important and timely because — in new ways and old — the higher education *industry* is essential and is going through evolutions and revolutions whose time has finally come. This is a *moment* in higher education — a moment like no other — and we're honored to bring new insights, perspectives, and data to bear on an infinitely consequential conversation.

Introduction

By Kate Colbert

H igher education is no longer about "*or.*" It's about "*and.*" In the 2020s and beyond, it's not about higher-education decision-makers asking themselves: "Should we focus on serving traditional, 18- to 22-year-old students with coming-of-age educational and social experiences? *Or* should we emphasize the creation of value for the nontraditional student — the working professional looking to level up their skills, finish a degree they started many years ago, or earn a mid-career credential like an executive MBA?" It's not about "Should we emphasize on-ground *or* online instruction?" It's *and*. It's *both*. It's no longer about "Do we have academic excellence, *or* is this a lifestyle school, with hundreds of student clubs, winning athletic teams, and Instagram-worthy dorm rooms?" It's got to be about *and*. Today's learners want it all.

**The biggest mistake we can make in higher
education is continually choosing to operate
for the era in which we were founded instead
of the age in which we currently exist.**

Developing strategies and executing them in the world of higher education requires fresh mindsets and a willingness to build upon — and even abandon — the activities and offerings that were once central to our identities. Maybe your institution was founded 60 years ago or 150 years ago. What worked then won't work now. The biggest mistake we can make in higher education is continually choosing to operate for the era in which we were founded instead of the age in which we currently exist. Customers want options, and they want *more,* and they want it *now* (and yes, students and learners of all kinds *do* see themselves as customers and they expect to be served).

Think for a moment about how you choose to spend your time and money. I'm guessing you're relatively discriminating; you're willing to pay more for better quality, that you expect the product or service to be delivered expeditiously, and that when you're disappointed with the product or service, you vote with your feet (and leave a critical review online). I believe that we have collectively become savvy modern-day customers who want (and sometimes demand) more — when choosing the products and services of *any* industry — because we have finally learned that we can ask for "and" instead of "or." We believe we deserve more. We don't want to "settle" for less than what we need or want, and neither do your organization's stakeholders. Just as we desire with anything else we purchase, we want added value and speed. We want antilock brakes, heated seats, *and* a touchscreen heads-up display, and we'd like to take it home today. Your students are no different.

If a college or university purports to offer not just a learning experience but a living experience, a lifestyle experience, a credential, a brand connection, and a powerful career network — if it's going to promise to be *all* those things — today's customers are saying "bring it." *Be* all those things you promised students you could be. Are we ready to answer that challenge?

📝 Pop Quiz!

The choice for traditional colleges and universities — when it comes to delivering on the promise that we make to students — is a consequential multiple choice (*choose one*):

☐ **A. Figure out how to excel at everything you do.** Better programs, better activities, better student services, better overall experience with your current roster of degree programs and majors, all your non-degree offerings, your community partnerships, your residence halls, and more. Keep everything you've got ... and take it up a notch.

☐ **B. Reinvent yourself.** Get sharp about which students you want to serve, which programs you will continue to offer or offer for the first time, and which perks will define the overall experience. Be unapologetic about not being "all things for all people" and, instead, being the right things for the right people.

☐ **C. Keep on coasting and let the future of higher education have its way with you.** Choosing the status quo is an option; the truth of the matter is that it's the option that most institutions are currently choosing. But by operating in the 2020s the same way you did in the 1990s or the 1970s, you choose — at your peril — to let the waves of change in a drastically and quickly evolving industry wash over you in a way that might leave you fighting to come up for air. Whether or not the prognosticators are correct when they predict that dozens or hundreds of colleges and universities will be subsumed by larger, more stable institutions or will go out of business altogether, one thing is certain: Doing nothing as the tsunami of change washes over us is a sure way to splutter, get battered, or even perish.

All this is not to say that institutions of higher education must "be all things to all people." Quite the contrary. Think about it this way: When we're shopping for something (e.g., backpacks for our kids, a standup desk for the office, a pair of earrings, or a sledgehammer), we want Amazon to sell everything, and we're disappointed when they don't. But when a local coffee shop only sells coffee, pastries, and coffee mugs, we're not angry or frustrated that they don't sell hoodies. We don't *expect* them to sell hoodies; they never *promised* that they could. In higher education, on the other hand, the promise of "Come live on our campus — we'll change your life" is a big promise. And finally, students are saying, "Prove it." And when an institution says: "Our geology program is world-class," learners are saying, "But will it help me land a job with a family-supporting income upon my completion?" Delivering on the promise of higher education is an incredible responsibility. So, institutions must decide now: Do they want to be executing on everything, or do they want to figure out how to shut down many things and focus on doing one or two things well? And that's a big decision. This book, we believe, will help you make some of those fundamental choices or at least spark some crucial conversations on your campuses.

In higher education the promise of "Come live on our campus — we'll change your life" is a big promise. And finally, students are saying, "Prove it."

Drive the Change ...
Instead of Letting It Drive You

Perhaps I'm not giving higher-education leaders enough credit when I liken the evolutions and revolutions in higher education to a tsunami. While much of the attitudinal changes among learner populations are impossible to ignore, and while the pandemic's influence on communities and economies is impossible to escape, it *is* possible for colleges and universities to drive innovation right now — rather than simply reacting to the myriad forces at play. In this book, we share insights from several academic leaders whose institutions are changing the game, setting new bars, challenging the status quo, and disrupting the entire higher-education industry. If you find their stories and advice even half as compelling as I do, this book is poised to change your work, your career, your institution, and your stakeholders' experiences and outcomes in remarkable ways.

In this book, we share insights from several academic leaders whose institutions are changing the game, setting new bars, challenging the status quo, and disrupting the entire higher-education industry.

If you have listened to the 100+ interviews via the podcast (at the time of the writing of this book, nearly 200 college and university presidents have been interviewed), you no doubt will agree that the whole is greater than the sum of its parts. *The EdUp Experience Podcast* President Series is an audio masterclass on higher education's key issues. Unfortunately, few among us have the time or will to listen to 100 or more hours of podcast episodes; that's why we're giving you the highlights in a book (which should take about 8 hours to read! You're welcome.).

We titled this book *Commencement* because everyone who works in or serves the higher-education industry has a story or a connection to a "commencement" ceremony or a graduation ritual that they consider powerful. Commencement is the ultimate moment for the students we serve — a rite of passage, an initiation into the world that awaits them, the dawning of something new — one of the rare and precious moments in life that signifies an endpoint and the beginning in the very same time. I cannot be alone in admitting that nothing makes me well up with emotion and begin to weep happy, prideful tears like the first strains of "Pomp and Circumstance." As learners, we *begin* an educational pursuit with the purpose of *finishing* it so that we can *begin* something else — a job, a career, a transfer to graduate school or another degree program, a life in which our minds have been stretched and our personal and professional skills have been broadened. We all begin with the end in mind. And we end with new skills, new competencies, and new credentials.

I challenge you, as you read the sometimes shocking and downright mind-blowing stories of innovation and heart — presented by the 100+

college and university presidents who contributed to this book — to take note of what makes *you* well up with emotion. Take time to reflect upon what makes you pause and think: "That's exactly the mindset we need at our institution," or "It's never occurred to me to approach that element of our operation in such a way," or "That's the kind of leader I commit to being."

As a former higher-education insider and the proud recipient of four college credentials, I've walked across or stood at the podium upon many commencement-ceremony stages. While sitting in the *audience* during a commencement address, I heard a story that has stayed with me my entire career. It was humorous and the most honest piece of advice I've ever received. Speaking to a group of graduates from a renowned community college — individuals of all ages receiving associate degrees and technical certificates, and even high-school equivalency diplomas — the commencement speaker said this:

> If you want to be happy for an hour, go to lunch with a friend.
> If you want to be happy for a day, go golfing or go to the spa.
> If you want to be happy for a week, go on a vacation.
> If you want to be happy for a month, get a boat.
> If you want to be happy for a year, get married.
> *[Insert uncomfortable laughter from the crowd.]*
> **If you want to be happy for the rest of your life,**
> **get an education.**

Although we wrote this book primarily for the professionals who work inside or alongside colleges and universities across the globe, we purposefully crafted the chapters so higher education's consumers and supporters — students, learners, alumni, parents, donors, and community partners — can also benefit from the mindset reset that we offer. As this book headed to press, I had the opportunity to talk about it with a Gen X client named Chris, whose academic experience is now 30 years in the rearview mirror. When I shared an overview of the simultaneous evolutions and revolutions in higher education today, he said: "Most people don't know the things you just shared with me about higher ed — and that's a problem." A few days before that conversation, news about the 2022 student-loan forgiveness plan in the United States had gotten non-academics buzzing and offering up strong opinions about the industry, for better and worse. And it had become clear to me that the opinions and decisions being made today — whether to send a child to community college or a state school, whether to criticize or empathize with middle-aged professionals regarding their decades-old educational debt, and whether to build bridges between our companies and communities with educational institutions — were often based on old, outdated information about how higher education works today, and where it's headed tomorrow.

Higher education cannot be divorced from the communities and economies they serve. Even if you went to college or earned a career credential 30 years ago, have never worked inside a college or university, don't have children or grandchildren who are taking part in the higher-education ecosystem, or have never given much thought to what's happening online and on the ground at the colleges and universities in your region, the themes of this book impact your life. As Dr. Elsa Núñez, President of Eastern Connecticut State University, reminded us during her interview for this book, "If you want an educated workforce, you've got to invest in it." And if you're going to invest in it, you ought to learn a little more about the changing tides that are influencing it today. So, whoever you are and wherever you are, this book is for you.

What to Expect in the Pages Ahead

We hope that you might approach this book with curiosity and commitment. Perhaps you'll find a quiet space, put on some music, grab a pen and a highlighter and your favorite notebook, locate some sticky notes, and get ready for a reading experience that's equal parts candid conversation and eloquent academic motivational speech. We encourage you to let the presidents of some of the most incredible colleges and universities today take you "inside higher education" in a way that has *never been done before*. If you've participated in a conference with several chief executives from higher education and walked away feeling inspired, imagine what more than 100 presidents can do. It's about to get practical, pointed, purposeful, and poignant. Never has a book for the higher-education industry done what Dr. Joe Sallustio and I attempt to do for you here — bring to bear the voices of 100+ college and university presidents on the topic of the future of higher education, with the benefit of the by-the-seat-of-their-pants experiences and discoveries from the COVID-19 pandemic, arguably the industry's most significant and sustained disruption.

So, what should you expect from this book?

- ➤ **A love letter and a devil's advocate.** While Joe and I are bullish on higher education (as is our contributor, Elvin Freytes), we're willing to ask the tough questions about what's working and what's not. This book shines a bright light on the gems of the industry and challenges us to ask: "How else can we do better?"

- ➤ **Conflicting viewpoints.** We let the words of the presidents speak for themselves. Some argue for preserving residential coming-of-age undergraduate institutions; others suggest that an expensive four-year college experience no longer serves our communities and students. You might read something in Chapter 2 that gets torn apart in Chapter 7. We leave it up to you to apply the learning of this book to your life, your career, and/ or your institution without us positing that there's a single "right way" to think about the key themes.

- ➤ **Personal and institutional representation.** An original goal of the President Series on *The EdUp Experience Podcast* was to capture true diversity of thought by finding presidents of diverse backgrounds who were leading various institution types. Each president's personal and professional background shapes their leadership perspectives and deeply held passions for higher education. The presidents whose voices are represented in this book are individuals who lead (or have led) community colleges, state universities, private nonprofit universities, for-profit colleges and universities, trade/vocational schools, Historically Black Colleges and Universities (HBCUs), Hispanic-Serving Institutions (HSIs), Predominantly Black Institutions (PBIs), and Asian American and Native American Pacific Islander-Serving Institutions (AANAPISIs).

- ➤ **Quotable quotes.** The words of the presidents (and often my co-author, Joe, as well!) sometimes resonate like mantras. We hope you'll feel compelled to pop them into social media memes, dog-ear the pages, and quote the voices in this book — the brightest and most influential minds in higher education — at every turn. Please give credit where credit is due, and drive people to CommencementTheBook.com for full context.

➜ **A national perspective with international impact.** Most of the presidents interviewed on *The EdUp Experience Podcast* — which served as the source and inspiration for this book — represent colleges and universities based primarily or exclusively in the United States. We do have a handful of presidents based in places like Ireland and Qatar and many U.S.-based enterprises with global online campuses. Our survey research included academic leaders internationally. With few exceptions, the insights in this book are applicable and instructive for post-secondary education leaders worldwide.

➜ **Honesty.** We believe that higher education is at the precipice of unprecedented excellence. We also believe that when it comes to the industry's most tangled issues and complex challenges, it will get worse before it gets better. To belabor the obvious, "disruption is disruptive." It's unsettling not just for the industry but for the people and the stakeholders in its midst. Change is uncomfortable. Sometimes it hurts. In this book, we don't shy away from the tough stuff. Instead, you deserve an honest assessment of where we are and where we're headed. The pursuit of higher education is a time-honored tradition, but traditions change.

The Beginning of a New Era in Higher Education Begins with You

As for where we're headed, we believe that *commencement* (see what we did there?) into a new era in higher education has already begun and that seizing the opportunity to benefit from the changes starts with YOU.

Through this book — and through the eyes of 100+ college and university presidents — you have an opportunity to discover how you can seize the moment to change higher education forever.

Learn how you can:

- ➤ Put students first in all that you do.

- ➤ Embrace a new leadership skillset that will change your college and your career.

- ➤ See your mission through a modern lens that creates new opportunities.

- ➤ Innovate, create, reimagine, and evolve beyond the status quo.

- ➤ Adopt a mindset about the purpose and value of higher education that makes the unimaginable possible.

- ➤ Have impact far beyond your campus or your local community.

- ➤ Create relationships, partnerships, and conversations that break down walls, silos, rules, and bureaucracies.

The colleges and universities providing millions of degree and non-degree credentials each year are a vital backbone of communities and economies. These institutions elevate the critical-thinking capacities of students and learners, and they provide crucial job skills and life skills to emerging workforces. But the skills we need, the ways in which we collaborate, and the very jobs available to graduates are changing. So, it's time for higher education to start anew.

Welcome to a conversation like no other.

A conversation where the truth is told.

Where the future is examined.

Where the possibilities are endless.

Commencement was born from 100+ presidential interviews that first aired on *The EdUp Experience Podcast*. Our analysis of those interviews, combined with our international anonymous survey of higher-education leaders, form the backbone of this book. Unless otherwise specified, direct quotes, paraphrased ideas, and quantitative statistics are derived from the interviews and survey.

I think the future of higher education is one in which we are able to unlock and move to the 'next level.' We can't even imagine that leve right now because we're just so tied up in this narrative of higher education. And I believe that diverse communities are going to take us there.

Angélica Garcia, EdD
President, Berkeley City College

"Collectively, we need to affirm our belief in the power of education to change people's lives."

Marvin Krislov, JD
President, Pace University

PART I

EVOLUTIONS & REVOLUTIONS IN HIGHER EDUCATION

Trends to Watch and Waves to Ride as We Move the Industry Forward

CHAPTER 1

HIGHER EDUCATION IS NOT AN ISLAND

How Colleges and Universities Are Becoming Industry-Responsive, Community-Connected, and Real-World Relevant

---

"Hello! Who's This?": How You'll Interact with the Authors of This Book

Hello, friends! It's Kate Colbert. Just a quick note about the "voice" of this book, so you feel right at home and ready to engage in the conversation. Unless otherwise noted, the general narration of this book (the "I" or "me") is typically Kate speaking. The sections entitled "Making Education Your Business with Dr. Joe Sallustio" are written in the voice of — you guessed it — the incomparable Dr. Joe Sallustio. And throughout the book, you'll also find fun and practical sidebars called "EdUp with Elvin," in which *The EdUp Experience Podcast* co-founder Elvin Freytes takes you deeper into some of the book's ideas by offering tips and helpful observations. And, of course, the insights and stories of the 100+ college and university presidents interviewed for the book will always be presented in their own words, personally attributed at every turn.

If you've been a student within the higher-education system or have worked — at any level — at a college or university, you've undoubtedly used the term "real world" to refer to the life that learners enter only *after* completing their degree or credentialing program. The idea that higher education is juxtaposed with independent living and work as two entirely separate "worlds" is (and indeed was) a common default mindset. Especially if you have experience with liberal-arts curricula, where the considerations for how to parlay one's sculpting skills, poetry talents, or history acumen into a stable and clear "life after college" were often unexplored until after graduation. When I was finishing my first graduate degree (in English composition and comparative literature studies), the internet was in its infancy. There was no way to know I was entering a job market in which I had no way to compete. I was going to be an English professor, forever and ever, amen (I thought). It wasn't until I was chatting with my department chair at Loyola University Chicago — where I was teaching part-time — that I learned the ugly truth. In the United States, in 1996, there were 700 English-instructor job seekers for every single tenure-track position. Many of the bookworms and wordsmiths against whom I'd be competing for a job were more qualified than me (they had PhDs, and I had just finished my MA). Sigh. Alas, academia had educated me well but had not prepared me for the "real world." It's a story that millions of us could tell.

Alas, academia had educated me well but had not prepared me for the "real world." It's a story that millions of us could tell.

Fast forward to the 2020s, and it's clear that colleges and universities have stepped up their games. Almost without exception, the more than 100 presidents interviewed for this book told us stories about their industry and workforce connections. They build programs based on what employers ask of them and they connect their leaders, students, and alumni with employers, mentors, and the community at large. The two worlds that once spun each on its own axis have collided — sometimes abruptly, sometimes smoothly, and always in service to the greater good. Higher education has opened its doors to the "real world," and the results have been remarkable. In "college towns" across the United States, the townspeople claim the college as a vital partner or community hub. Sharp strategies bring the elementary, middle, and secondary education systems (K-12) together with their post-secondary education counterparts. And everyone is getting wiser about the opportunities that abound when businesses, schools, and civic organizations start asking one another: "How can we help? Where are there synergies between what you're doing and what we're doing? What's your vision for the future?"

Higher education is not an island. Instead, its adjacencies to every other part of society provide endless opportunities for impact and growth. When invited to speak on these topics during their *EdUp Experience Podcast* interviews, college and university presidents renewed our faith in the possibility of the true, seamless integration of higher education with the rest of our lives.

 ## Making Education Your Business with Dr. Joe Sallustio

From Higher-Education Naysayer to Idealist

Higher education naysayers — they're all around us. So many thought leaders, writers, journalists, social-media content creators, and those who work within business and industry bring the "doom and gloom" prognostications for higher education. Before co-founding *The EdUp Experience Podcast* with Elvin Freytes, and probably for a year after we began recording episodes, I was also one of these people. Why? Because the work was difficult and the industry was undergoing significant disruption.

We all know that COVID-19 disrupted higher education in ways that we are still recovering from (and ways that have changed us forever). However, conversations about new leadership profiles and updated financial models in higher education were happening for years before the pandemic became a factor. It was easy to see how declining enrollment, antiquated business models, changing student-buying behaviors, and conversations around mergers and acquisitions affected high-level decision-making. It was all front and center for me because I was working in an institution dealing with all these scenarios. So, I get it. It's easy to be negative.

It turns out that it's also just as easy to be positive. No one had spoken, at scale, to the leaders of institutions worldwide. What exactly were/are the problems? How would those problems be addressed, and by whom? How do a president's perspective and strategic leadership decisions affect how internal and external stakeholders view the industry? What is the current value of higher education, and what is the outlook moving forward? After scores of interviews — talking to incredibly innovative presidents at institutions from every sector of higher education — my naysaying perspective of higher education changed. I moved from naysayer to idealist. Why? Because these leaders *are not* out of touch with the problems facing the higher-education industry today. There is activity, innovation, and action to lower the cost of tuition, to increase services to assist students through their educational journey, and to improve outcomes that either (a) communicate a defined return on investment or (b) provide students with a more traditional experience they'll remember for life. The value of a college degree, while in question in the public sphere today, will prove, once again, to be the fastest and most effective way to advance in life. So, for me — and higher education at large — the glass is very much "half *full*."

Strengthening Connections with Industry Leaders and Adopting an Economic Development Mindset

Most people today will readily admit that the purpose of college is to prepare people for the workforce. However, there is still (and likely always will be) a segment of the college-going population headed off to higher education for a coming-of-age experience and opportunity to become more thoughtful, "well-rounded" individuals. So, it's no surprise

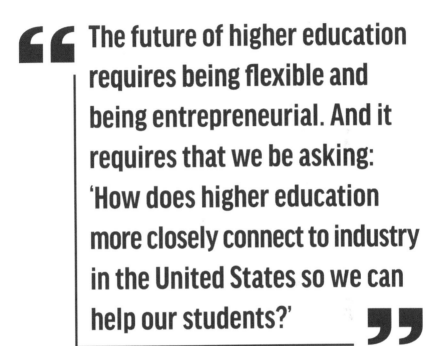

" The future of higher education requires being flexible and being entrepreneurial. And it requires that we be asking: 'How does higher education more closely connect to industry in the United States so we can help our students?' "

Bradford L. Sims, PhD

President, Capitol Technology University

that contemporary leaders at colleges and universities are increasingly focused on how they connect with, respond to, and serve the communities beyond the walls of their campuses or the firewalls of their online learning platforms.

Dr. Mel Netzhammer, Chancellor of Washington State University Vancouver, reminded us that not all strategic plans are "as strategic as we'd like them to be." He suggests that involving community leaders — from area businesses, nonprofits, and civic organizations — provides essential perspectives to college decision-makers. A crucial part of the WSU Vancouver strategic plan is a commitment to community engagement, and Dr. Netzhammer insists that the university try its best to measure up in the minds of its partners. "We had more than 150 people *outside* of WSU Vancouver who were engaged in helping us put this plan together and participated in that work," he told us. And he feels that if an institution is going to put itself and its broader community through a rigorous planning process, they must commit from the outset that when it comes to the strategic plan, "We need to *use* it and *fund* it."

While the WSU Vancouver campus is part of a larger, well-established system, the Vancouver campus is just 33 years old. Dr. Netzhemmer suggested that "Young universities have big expectations" because — unlike centuries-old institutions — young universities don't have operational malaise. He said, "The people who fought to get us here are, largely, still alive, and they have expectations of us." This is perhaps an essential difference between young and old institutions, with newer institutions offering greater transparency and seeing themselves as part of the larger community, wanting to prove themselves as the "new kids on the block." Conversely, older institutions are inevitably more insular (what Dr. Stephen Spinelli, President of Babson College, calls "walled communities") — large, established, well-resourced institutions can fend for themselves in many ways, especially if they have their own police force, dining options, bookstores, and multi-billion-dollar endowments. The challenge today is for *all* higher-education institutions to reach out to the organizations and people around them.

If area businesses and other organizations aren't helping drive your strategy through participation in your planning activities, they should — at the very least — be informing the programs you offer. For example, Dr.

Carlos Peñaloza, Chancellor of Leeward Community College in Pearl City, Hawaii, looks closely at the industries thriving in Oahu. Due to its natural beauty and island culture, Hawaii has a thriving movie/media industry to serve and a dominant tourism industry. "We continue to look at the workforce trends, and we align our programming that way," Dr. Peñaloza explained, then telling us about their academic strengths in culinary arts, education/teaching, and creative multimedia/film. Many savvy institutions operate similarly, choosing to bloom where they're planted. Colleges and universities surrounded by pharmaceutical companies, hospital systems, technology companies, and large financial institutions, for example, find themselves developing and strengthening degree and non-degree programs to serve those industries.

If area businesses and other organizations aren't helping drive your strategy through participation in your planning activities, they should — at the very least — be informing the programs you offer.

One such example is Southern Arkansas Technical University, led by Dr. Jason Morrison. His advice is to:

> "Know the community you are invested in, what's impacting its economic growth, and what's being pushed for. With probably 3,000 positions available, I see it as a responsibility of the college to go beyond what a typical [community college] service area is and attract students from all over who may want to come into the area and see a pathway to a career."

Educating your student body for the local workforce is especially important if your region is looking to retain more talent or if most of your graduates stay there. Dr. Netzhammer at WSU Vancouver sees his job as "serving a region" because 95% of WSU Vancouver students remain in the region after graduation. In serving an area, higher-education leaders are finding that they ultimately need to serve different demographics of students. In-demand careers often attract students of various ages looking for a chance to reskill or upskill beyond the first-time credential they may have already received. Daniel G. Lugo, JD, President of Queens University of Charlotte in North Carolina, explains:

> "In thinking about the jobs of the future, higher education has to adapt to bring a diverse audience in — to give them the training and to give them *access* to the career opportunities that all these employers need to fill."

But how do we know what the marketplace needs? We need to ask! According to President Emeritus of Norwich University in Northfield, Vermont, Richard W. Schneider, RADM, U.S. Coast Guard (Retired), a little market research goes a long way in helping a college or university offer the programs that the marketplace needs. He says we must ask ourselves (along with faculty and colleagues) when considering the development or continuation of an academic program:

> "Where's the market research that says we should start that program? Who does decent work and research to find out where there are 18-year-olds wanting to study that and whether their parents are willing to invest the money to send their kid to study that? And [we must ask ourselves]: Are there *jobs* at the other end? Because I'd like to hook up the businesses that are going to hire them before they come as freshmen. And then I want to have internships in those disciplines — at a place near their home, so they could live at home, and it'd be cheaper. I want them working on high-tech things in their community — or as close to their community as I can get. And if I can't make those things happen, why are we starting this program? What's the need for this program? That's the relevant part. Academic offerings must be relevant."

Ensuring academic-program market relevance is essential to delivering results and will help higher education reduce scrutiny regarding perceived academic/real-world disconnects. Says Dr. Christopher Roellke, President of Stetson University in DeLand, Florida:

> "All of higher education is under great scrutiny — in part because of the increasing and escalating costs of higher education. The return-on-investment questions are very, very real and my own take on that is that we need to provide an education that is going to be

absolutely rooted in a broad liberal arts education *and*, at the same time, we should not shy away from applying those understandings and that learning into a real-world context. We're giving our students who are working in a biology classroom the opportunity to apply what they're learning by providing service to a local community agency. Our students in education are learning how to become teachers, and they're doing extensive fieldwork in the community and applying what they're learning in the classroom in real-world settings. I think we have to be laser-focused on giving our students skills of critical thinking, being able to work across differences, being able to communicate effectively, and being able to use technology effectively. These are all the tools that our industries are requiring of our graduates. And I don't think we are at *all* sacrificing our rich history in the liberal arts to teach them to apply those skills in real-world settings. Again, it's a great opportunity there for faculty/student collaboration, action-research projects, asking ourselves: 'What are the needs in the local community here in DeLand, Florida, that need some assistance to figure out a particular pressing problem?' That is exciting work. I was certainly motivated by the work of a famous philosopher of education, John Dewey, who felt so strongly that experience plus reflection equals growth. I'd like to take that even further. And I would like to say that reflection ought to also include what students are learning in their disciplines. I think that takes it yet to another level in terms of the depth of learning and the value of an education. Listen, this group of graduates is likely to change their job five, six, maybe even seven times over the course of their careers. So, they must be able to think critically, understand data, and analyze data in a rapidly changing global marketplace."

Despite all the ways in which higher education is stepping up and connecting to local, regional, national, and international job markets, companies and communities are welcoming — and even demanding — more. For example, during a high-energy conversation with Salt Lake City, Utah's Ensign College's President, Dr. Bruce C. Kusch, Dr. Joe Sallustio teed up the following question: *"The demand for skills-based training and the question of degree value is happening simultaneously. This puts community colleges in a unique position. Yes?"* Dr. Kusch candidly assessed the situation and offered some powerful examples of how to challenge the status quo and offer new ways of learning that reflect the real world of work, where having the right skills matters infinitely more than having the right degree credential:

> "Higher education is not doing the job, generally, that employers want. There are a lot of employers out there that want to hire college graduates with skills, and they're finding that schools aren't delivering it. I kind of asked myself the question when I left industry and got into the college classroom: 'Why isn't college a little bit more like work?' Think about the first day on a new job, and then compare that with the first day of most college classes you may have taken. A new job doesn't come with a syllabus, and it doesn't come with a textbook, and it doesn't come with a reading list, and it doesn't come with a list of the papers that you'll be writing. And, by the way, when you come to work every day, you're not given a quiz to make sure you've done your homework. So, if work isn't that way, why is college that way?"

Frankly, it's a brilliant question that I've never thought to ask despite all my years as either a student, a faculty member, or a higher-education employee or consultant. Why *isn't* college more like work? And can it be? According to Dr. Kusch, the answer is yes — yes, it *can* be much more like real work. He explains:

> "At Ensign, we've created an instructional framework that is very immersive in terms of engaging students in a subject from the very first minute of the very first class on the very first day. Imagine walking into an accounting class, and you're given a shoebox full of receipts, and you're told: 'Welcome to your lives in the accounting department of XYZ Cookie Company. And, you know, we've been a little short on accounting help. So, we've been keeping all our receipts and bank statements in a box. So, now figure it out. You've got to create last quarter's financial statements.' And so, the students start looking through all this stuff. And before too much longer, they know what all the financial statements are, and they're creating those. They learn accounting by doing accounting. About a year and a half ago, we got a picture from one of our former accounting students who went to work, and on her chair was a great big box full of receipts. For real. And her boss said, 'Yeah, here's all this stuff. Would you please figure it out?' She knew exactly what to do because she'd already gone through the shoebox experience."

This approach to teaching honors the realities of the workplace and prepares graduates and employers alike for the relationships that await them. We asked Dr. Kusch for another example of how this real-world learning experience looks in their classrooms, and he replied:

> "Here's how it works in a leadership class. Students walk into a leadership class, and they're told 'Welcome to your life as a leader. You're going to immerse yourself in leadership this semester. What you become as a leader is up to you. And how you learn about leadership is up to you. How you demonstrate leadership is up to you. So, what are *you* going to do to create an immersive experience for yourselves to become leaders?' And then they're up on their feet. They're at a whiteboard, they're talking and taking notes, and they're crafting this experience. To be clear, we're very much in control of the outcomes. But in this class, there's no syllabus. Students create the syllabus in counsel and collaboration with the teacher. The outcomes are clear, and we don't compromise the outcomes, but *how* those outcomes are achieved is completely student-driven. And it's an amazing thing to witness."

While not all colleges and universities will be offering students the chance to role-play as accountants or leaders, most institutions are at least stepping up how they help students think about — and explore — the careers that they anticipate pursuing or continuing at the end of their educational experience. Dr. Michael A. Baston, Former President of Rockland Community College in Ramapo, New York,[1] offered some advice on how institutions of higher education can serve their learners and their communities in better ways in the future:

> "One of the things that I think we are doing particularly well — particularly over these last five to 10 years — is developing what we call 'guided pathways.' We are helping students engage at the *beginning* of their educational journey in the kind of career exploration and the

---

1   Dr. Baston began a new presidency at Cuyahoga Community College in Cleveland, Ohio, after his interview for this book and before the book's publication. Job titles and organizational affiliations referenced throughout *Commencement* typically refer to the interviewee's role at the time of the interview. A full roster of leaders whose insights informed this publication is included at the back of the book, where we — to the best of our ability — list both their titles and affiliations when we first collaborated with them and their titles and affiliations upon publication, if applicable.

career development process so that they can get into an academic program or onto a path that, when monitored and supported, they can complete and move into not just other institutions via a transfer, but for many, the world of work — in jobs that pay a family-supporting wage. So, it's very important for us not to build bridges to nowhere. It doesn't help if a person in poverty gets into an academic program that's going to keep them in poverty. That makes no sense. So, we are looking to develop academic programs linked to destinations and experiences that make achieving that destination possible. What does the economic situation in your region call for? What kinds of professionals are necessary for your region, and how are you ensuring that the educational experience, the in-classroom learning, is melded with the out-of-the-classroom experiences so that those students are competitive in the environment that they would be able to get to? It is very important for us to recognize that our colleges are models of this new, higher-level integration with community-based organizations and the business and industry folks."

Partnering with industry and creating strong linkages between a higher-education institution and the other organizations in its region, state, or even country can take many forms. For example, Don Kilburn, CEO of the University of Massachusetts Online (UMass Online), part of the University of Massachusetts System, addresses the topic of skills-based learning, "corporate education," and corporate partnerships. He suggests that employee tuition reimbursement was just the beginning — there is a unique opportunity for employers to co-create educational opportunities and sponsor their employees through meaningful experiences. He told us:

"I think at some point there will be, for certain students, more short courses. Certainly, you see it with MOOCs [massive open online courses], which have evolved into things like Coursera and edX. And I think there's a place there, and you'll see more partnerships with short-course programs and those credential programs for jobs. I also think you're going to see corporations playing a bigger role in the higher-ed space. They've woken up to the fact that just having educational tuition-assistance programs is not really strategic, per se. And I think they're looking at an increase in skills gaps and issues with retention and promotions. I think corporations are really going to start thinking deeply about educational partners who can deliver programs that can help their workers move ahead and help an institution or a corporation to fulfill its mission better."

Over and over during the interviews conducted for this book, we heard academic leaders talk about "partnerships." It was, without question, one of the most prominent themes (alongside access, affordability, and flexibility — all of which ostensibly can be achieved through the right partnerships). For example, we asked Dr. Mel Netzhammer at Washington State University Vancouver whether the pandemic — and all it taught us — might open up opportunities for collaborations between institutions and opportunities for offering learning in new modalities. He replied:

"I sure hope so. There is the possibility that we could rethink some of the ways that we provide education in a more collaborative way — a way that acknowledges that not every student is needing a degree (that some students may need and want us to take them down the path toward badges and certificates). Thinking about the educational experiences that students need, how do we partner to deliver those? I think the issues that will happen from coronavirus [the pandemic] may force some of these conversations even where we don't want to have them, but I would welcome them. These are exactly the kinds of conversations we need to have. We need to always be relevant for our students and for the communities we serve."

Dr. Netzhammer reminded us that, especially during crises and societal disruptions, sometimes competing schools begin to partner on behalf of the students they serve. He sees WSU Vancouver as part of a larger higher-education community, including the other five WSU campuses and local community colleges. At the height of the pandemic, WSU Vancouver — like many around the world — experienced unique demands when students from other colleges and universities (who were forced to leave their campuses) wanted lab experiences or other face-to-face experiences they were unable to receive from the school where they were enrolled. I remember this kind of cross-institutional collegiality from my time at Rosalind Franklin University of Medicine and Science in North Chicago, Illinois. Hurricane Katrina left New Orleans, Louisiana's Tulane University medical students homeless and without classroom and laboratory space in the fall of 2005. Suddenly, aspiring physicians from New Orleans were making their way to North Chicago. They were welcomed warmly and given unfettered access to the educational resources they needed. I remember thinking it was wonderful and odd because, to be frank, we'd been taught to think of the other 120+ American medical universities as our "competitors," not our friends or collaborators. It was an important mindset shift whose time has perhaps finally come.

Dr. Philomena V. Mantella, President of Grand Valley State University near Grand Rapids, Michigan, challenged us to consider the risks of competition — how isolation among institutions of higher education threatens to limit us and how connections across communities of all kinds can strengthen us:

> "I believe that higher education, many times, competes to its own detriment. And we hold close our cards because demographics are going down and financial pressures are up, and we have to compete. And the public is the big loser in this, because if you look at education and the needs for new competencies and the needs for adults to be engaged and who we're leaving behind, there is plenty of room for everyone."

Dr. Mantella makes a powerful point and offers what is perhaps a counterintuitive, if not altogether refreshing, approach to the looming demographic cliff. What if we stopped worrying about how to "steal away" students from other similar institutions when the crop of incoming 18-year-olds gets small (which is already happening in many regions) and instead looked at all the populations of prospective learners we can step up to serve? She went on to say:

> "I'm a fierce competitor for my own ["teams"] — I love to compete. But we can't compete at the public's detriment ... to keep narrowing our scopes to elevate our institutions. It's really about equity in education. It's about seeing the opportunity in this very difficult moment to move the things we need to. And I think there's room for many institutions to take that kind of broader frame and begin to work in new ways across higher education. That's what really excites me."

Presidents who are excited about doing new things, breaking the mold, breaking down walls, and creating new opportunities are at the helm of many intertwined evolutions and revolutions in higher education right now. Every interview for this book was conducted during a phase of the COVID-19 pandemic (i.e., between early 2020 and mid-2022), when higher-education administrators had every right to be exhausted, overwhelmed, pessimistic, and worried. Yet the way in which the crisis cracked open honest conversations and enabled innovation and teamwork was transformational. Dr. Tracy Y. Espy, President of Mitchell College in New London, Connecticut, shared the excitement of other leaders, saying:

> "I really love where higher education is. Not in the sense that I like the rollercoaster nature of what it's been, but the opportunity that we can go in directions and partnerships in ways that we have never thought about doing before. And it's like a completely open book, and we're learning in ways that we haven't thought about. So that excites me as an educational entrepreneur — that I'm not just doing the same old traditional thing that may have happened when I was an undergrad many years ago, but that there's so many great opportunities that we have before us. And, you know, technology is constantly changing. That's one thing to think about, and the opportunities to partner with corporations and organizations are unlimited."

Seeing a college president — and any higher-education leader, for that matter — as an "educational entrepreneur," to borrow Espy's term, is encouraging and inspires limitless ideas. I serve on the President's Leadership Council at Carthage College in Kenosha, Wisconsin, and recently witnessed this type of nimble, forward-thinking innovation on their campus. A local printing company with a niche customer base linked arms with the college to offer highly flexible part-time jobs to students who can earn a tuition buy-down (the employer literally sends checks to Carthage to contribute to each student employee's tuition bill!) in addition to a solid wage. Moreover, students who want to stay in the area during the summer to keep working don't have to take college classes to keep a roof over their heads. Students who work for corporate partners receive a housing waiver from the college to stay in their dorms while earning and learning at their job.

Indeed, the pandemic, for all the illness and loss it brought to the world, continues to be a dark cloud whose silver linings are hard to deny. Our collective humanity came into sharp focus when we all began struggling and suffering in unprecedented ways. The acknowledgment of that shared humanity has brought us closer together — within and across organizations and communities.

What we have learned the most is the need to be adaptable. Michell College's entire culture and curriculum are built around the Mitchell Ability Model, which "teaches the ability to be flexible, capable, and adaptable in the face of rapid change." Their staff, faculty, administrators, and students were hardwired for the 2020s because of their emphasis on adaptability. The Mitchell Ability Model is based on "7 Essential Abilities" — critical and creative thinking; communication; diversity and global perspectives; information and communication technology literacy; analysis and problem solving; values, ethics, and social responsibility; and social interaction. Some of these abilities are honed through internships; most — if not all — Mitchell students complete an internship. Internships are one critical way in which colleges and universities create meaningful connections with corporations, nonprofits, and community organizations. The ability to forge and sustain partnerships requires leaders to have an inherently collaborative spirit. When presented with 14 different character traits and asked to identify the six they believe to be most important in higher-education leaders, 48% of respondents to our survey research chose "collaborative spirit" as a top-6 critical trait for higher-education leaders.[2]

 of higher-education professionals say that **"collaborative spirit"** is **one of the most important attributes of higher-education leaders,** especially presidents.

In years past, the idea of college students, faculty, and others connecting with the community was often rooted in "service learning" requirements,

---

2   A crucial part of the research for *Commencement* was an anonymous survey of higher-education professionals conducted online and promoted to The EdUp Experience mailing list, to the authors' higher-education networks, to LinkedIn higher-education groups, and other social media platforms. Insights gained from 136 survey respondents are presented throughout the book. In Chapter 7, we reveal survey data about higher-education leadership skillsets of the future, leadership job satisfaction, what big moves higher-education leaders are planning to make, and much more.

" I think it's really vital that we, in higher education, are partnered with industry to understand not just their current workforce needs, but their economic development needs. **"**

Melody Rose, PhD

Former Chancellor of the Nevada System of Higher Education

whereby students volunteered or interned in various capacities with the "real world" outside their campuses. Dr. Bradford Sims, President of Capitol Technology University near Washington, D.C., often reminds prospective and current students: "Employers still value the four-year degree, and they love internships on top of your resume as well." Dr. Saúl Jiménez-Sandoval, President of California State University, Fresno (also known as Fresno State), talked to us about this very trend of internships and service learning and how it manifests itself today with his students:

> "The connection between the community and Fresno State is very strong. On average, Fresno State students produce one million hours of community work, service learning, or internships in our community. It was 1.23 million hours this past year. That's about $47 million worth to the economy Fresno State produces just through volunteer work, service learning, or internships. These real-world connections for students reinforce two main things. Number one, it reinforces our students' resolve to graduate faster. And number two, it really reinforces our students' resolve to find their passion in life and pursue that profession right after they graduate."

In all the many ways that the spirit of partnership will manifest for higher-education institutions in the coming years, we're sure to see creativity and connection that inspires us all. Dr. Stephen Spinelli, President of Babson College in Wellesley, Massachusetts, thinks that partnership is the future. He told us:

> "I think that the collaborative environment is the future of higher education. We've had social networking, which led to economic networking, which did *not* lead to educational networking. The future is the collaboration amongst and across institutions of higher learning with an ecosystem of learning organizations. People will emerge from this, and that's the big lesson I come away with. We have all the technology tools, and we have all the motivations, but do we have the gumption to say that we can grow better as an educational network rather than individual walled communities? I'm absolutely committed to a greater level of partnership and collaboration in education across all kinds of spectrums — other institutions, communities, government, social organizations, and companies. It's the way forward."

I think the future of higher ed is partnerships. I think it's creative outlets. I think it's the ability to see through to the new — to see what we haven't seen yet. Because everyone knows that higher education is constantly changing.

Emily J. Barnes, EdD

Provost & Vice President of Academic Affairs,
Sienna Heights University*

*At the time of this statement, Dr. Barnes was Interim President & CEO and Provost at Cleary University.

Many Ways to Blur the Lines Between Campus and Community

It is true that more and more colleges and universities live entirely in the ether — with global online programs and learning communities that eclipse the trappings of place-based education. That notwithstanding, thousands of brick-and-mortar higher-education institutions in the United States, occupying millions of acres of land, are situated within cities and towns of all sizes and cultural makeups. And the leaders of those campuses are finding powerful ways to make themselves welcome and even indispensable in their broader communities.

Dr. Philomena V. Mantella, President of Grand Valley State University, finds herself reflecting on the generosity and collegiality of the greater metropolitan area in which their campus is located:

> "Grand Rapids is, I think, the second-most philanthropic city in the United States, and that philanthropy has extended to the university. So, there's this really strong commitment as a public/private partnership for education. And so, it's not 'someone else's responsibility' — not, in the minds of our community, the federal government's responsibility to fund, or the people to pay their own tuition, or the state to fund. It is truly an institution that is *sponsored* in many ways by all those stake-holders. And Grand Rapids is a very 'change *able*' place."

When we are "able" to create change, as Dr. Mantella says, and able to create connection, the sky's the limit. For some institutions, this starts with understanding and embracing the region's history. We've all heard of the "college town" — that place where every resident feels somehow connected to the college or university in its midst. If you're not an alumnus, you're an employee. Or you're a big fan of the football team. Or you enjoy attending productions from the theatre department. Or you employ students and alumni. Or you just feel a warm affinity for the institution and its people.

Dr. Saúl Jiménez-Sandoval, President of Fresno State, reminds us that embracing the "college town" is being done and communicated better in some regions than others. All areas with colleges and universities need to have citizens who understand the impact of the higher-education institutions on their lives:

> "Many people don't realize that the region is fully and entirely permeated by the power of the disciplines of Fresno State. If you were to come to the Fresno region, and you would just go to any institution within the Fresno region, you will find alumni from Fresno State everywhere, upholding the quality of life of everyone in the Valley [San Joaquin Valley] within these institutions. And I think we need to be more front and center about how higher education, for the everyday person, concretely manifests in very specific ways, in very specific benefits to society. Not just to society in general but to someone specifically going to a hospital, for example, with the nurses educated here, or someone going to the supermarket where there's evidence of how our farming industry has really benefited from the research at Fresno State. Or you can look at the business sector or the engineering sector and on and on and on. I could give you a long list of disciplines that impact the everyday life of individuals in the Valley just because Fresno State has existed here for more than 110 years."

Think about the people in your region. Do they appreciate how your presence in the community impacts their personal lives? Many leaders mentioned the need to create a "college-going culture." There's much work to do to help young people believe, years before it's time to take their first college class, that they have what it takes, that they deserve post-secondary education, and that it can be accessible to them. We discuss this topic deeply in the coming pages, where we talk about dual-credit and dual-enrollment programs and various partnerships with the K-12 system. We can't help but also wonder: How do we become not just a college-*going* culture but a college-*appreciating* culture? What might it look like to more deliberately communicate beyond the institution's walls to help residents understand why your college or university is essential to them?

 # EdUp with Elvin

Practical Tips and Frontline Insights from Elvin Freytes

One of the best ways to build a deeper relationship with an institution of higher education's (IHE) surrounding community is to develop Program Advisory Councils (PACs). These groups are sometimes called Community Program Advisory Boards, Curriculum Advisory Boards, etc. Call it whatever you like, but no matter what you name it, please don't put the word "committee" in it!

A PAC consists of leaders from the community who can help each program within an IHE to, among many other things, continuously improve the curriculum.

PACs are not a new concept, but the trick is creating meetings that are attended by the right *people*, that are *action*-based, and that are *mutually* beneficial.

So how do you make this happen? Here's a step-by-step breakdown. Think of it as PAC 101:

1. Set quarterly meetings.

2. Make the meetings no more than an hour long.

3. Make these groups very niche. For example, don't try to put all the educational programs together — break them out.

4. Ensure that your attendance includes, at minimum, a current student, alum, faculty member, program chair, and three industry professionals.

5. Let the industry leaders do most of the talking.

6. Ask them pointed questions about your curriculum. For example, you might ask: "We are using this book, which talks about this method. Is that useful in today's market?"

7. Ask how you can help *them* with their businesses (perhaps with internships, board memberships, mentorship, research, employee tuition discounts, collaborative projects, hiring, retaining employees, etc.).

8. End each meeting with at least three action items that will be reported on during the next meeting.

9. Have the mindset (and then clearly convey that thinking) that the meeting is about *them* and not you. It's all about how you can help them; in doing so, they will naturally help you.

10. Remember, *do not* call it a committee, whatever you do!

All too often, universities know their "origin story" but don't communicate it well to the outside, while community leaders might know their history but don't see that regional story reflected in the higher-education strategy. Dr. Jiménez-Sandoval believes this is an area of distinct opportunity. Fresno State, which is one of 23 campuses in the California State University system, is in the San Joaquin Valley, where 85% of the world's almonds are produced, and which has a rich history of agriculture and immigration. He can speak credibly about different waves of immigration and who introduced the farming of different crops, like stone fruit and tree nuts. How does this connect to his university? Integrally. At Fresno State, their leading academic powerhouse is agriculture. He says that with experts predicting that the world will need to produce 60% more food by 2050, institutions like his must be looking at "hybridizing agriculture and engineering." How he thinks about regional history, economic trends, and his campus can be instructive to us all. He urges us:

"To the universities out there, I say the following: Know your history, number one, so you can determine your future. And then, number two, really know the impact that you have within your region. Really know the impact that you have within the student population who comes to you. Where are these students going [after their education]? Is it an international or a national impact? Then, home in on that and really move forward with a vision that speaks to your past in order to determine the future."

For institutional leaders who think their location and their founding story can and should guide their future, there are many ways to continue blurring the lines between campus and community. Not long ago, I heard Dr. Terri Goss Kinzy, the then newly minted President of Illinois State University in Normal, Illinois (one of my alma maters), say that "town/ gown partnerships" are vital to the lifeblood of a region. I happen to agree. And those connections can manifest in many ways.

Dr. Mary Papazian, Former President of San José State University in San Jose, California, shared stories about how her institution connects the campus with the community to address acute challenges — like the rising cost of housing (San Jose is the most expensive housing market in the U.S.). San Jose State is developing a piece of property that will provide under-market housing to faculty, staff, and students, with the hope of providing housing at 75% of market cost. This will also bring members of their campus community into the downtown area, creating more connections between the university and the city. Dr. Papazian told us:

> "The community walks through our campus all the time. We share a library with the city of San Jose, for goodness' sake. We are really *part* of the community. Our students do a tremendous amount of community service and service learning in the community as well."

Blurring the lines between "town and gown," "campus and community" has been meaningful in my own life. I grew up in Grayslake, Illinois, where the county's workforce development center (or what we thought of simply as "the unemployment office") is on the campus of the large, prospering community college — College of Lake County. They have a remarkable library that the community can use, and they have a small-business center where local entrepreneurs can avail themselves of services. So, whether your campus has a medical clinic, a business incubator, or a performing-arts center that serves people in the community, you can develop powerful connections that generate mutual benefit.

Making Education Your Business with Dr. Joe Sallustio

Building Community in an Online Environment

Community development doesn't happen exclusively on-ground or in-person, as I know you all realize. Today's learning environments are diversified and include hybrid and online — and *community* in an online environment is just as important as (if not more important than) building community in person. For all the obvious reasons, creating connection points for students to interact within their online coursework helps cement their online identity and voice. While online learning can be isolating, it can be designed to create community and connection. Unfortunately, it's not difficult to reach back in time and find the articles and content that crystallized the difference between emergency-response online learning and true pedagogically designed online learning. During and after the pandemic, institutions that had already invested heavily in online learning benefitted from the expansion of online interest and emerging technology. Western Governors University President Scott Pulsipher, early in 2020, said that "WGU was engineered" to serve students in an online environment. Developing a sense of community (for students, alumni, partners, and other stakeholders) in the online education environment takes imagination, involvement, online presence, and an active approach to service and retention. Static content delivery and multi-dimensional interactions leading to engaged learning and online community development are incredibly different.

The Power of the Pipeline

As we did the research for *Commencement*, it became clear that some topics and trends are so significant they could warrant their own book. Dual-credit and dual-enrollment programs with high-school students was one such topic. More and more, colleges — particularly community colleges — are excelling at giving local high-school students the chance to fast-track their education by taking dual-credit courses at their high school and/or simultaneously enrolling in some college courses before they receive their high-school diploma. Kishwaukee College (affectionately called "Kish" by their community) in Malta, Illinois, is doing this in a particularly powerful way. Kish President, Dr. Laurie Borowicz, says that 25% of the juniors and seniors in their local high schools have some credit from Kish. A quick visit to Kish's website demonstrates their commitment to this concept. They boldly tout "Two Degrees, Three Years." Students get dual credit for up to a year of their associate's degree while still in high school, spend a year at Kish finishing their associate's degree, then transfer to a baccalaureate program for two more years. In just three years after graduating high school, students will have an associate's degree from Kish and a bachelor's degree from the transfer school of their choice. And the process couldn't be easier to understand on a website that contains co-branded course listings from the top six high schools that serve as the college's primary pipeline.

**While pipelines are essential – getting
the learner to the front door is, of course,
how it all begins – getting those learners
through to graduation is equally important.**

While pipelines are essential — getting the learner to the front door is, of course, how it all begins —getting those learners through to graduation is equally important. In the case of Kish, which allows high-school students to earn as many as 32 credits through dual credit, students can save up to $22,000 by choosing the high-school-plus-Kish-plus-transfer pathway, which goes a long way toward improving educational access and addressing the educational debt crisis. Dr. Borowicz explains:

> "There is so much research on how beneficial it is for young people to have a college experience while they're still in high school. It helps them be college- and career-ready. The success rates, the retention

rates, the graduation rates are all increased when young people can have a college experience while they're in high school."

Dr. Michael A. Cioce, President of Rowan College at Burlington County in Mount Laurel, New Jersey, told us that high-school partnerships are crucial to their operations as a thriving public community college:

> "Dual enrollment has been huge for us. We've expanded the number of partners and that's because we want students in eighth grade to think about college, in some degree. And we try to be as agnostic as possible because there's legacy students who are going to attend 'Fill in the Blank U' and I know I'm never going to change their mind. But if they can start 'Fill in the Blank U' with 9, 12, 15, maybe 20 college credits, they're already going to be ahead of the game. So, I think partnerships between colleges and high schools are key. I think partnerships, long term, matter too. I think four-year and two-year institutions need to get out of each other's way and decide where there's enough students for everybody. So, I think 'gen eds' will have to be enforced somehow, but we can't be cannibalizing each other, knowing that there's a finite number of prospective students. And the third piece of partnership [after high schools and other colleges and universities] goes to the employers."

Dual-credit and dual-enrollment programs are proof that higher education needs identifiable pipelines. Dr. Carlos Peñaloza, Chancellor of Leeward Community College, shared:

> "One of the biggest lifelines that we throw out there is our work on the dual-enrollment side of the house. Leewood works with 14 different high schools within our region to get high-school students motivated, interested, and committed to working on their education. We know that that has been a major lifeline at connecting with these communities and getting them into the higher-ed pipeline."

Dr. Borowicz at Kishwaukee College says that dual credits in high school give students "a leg up." And Dr. Michael Baston, Former President of Rockland Community College, says that such a leg up starts with intentional K-12 partnerships that ensure that high-school upperclassmen don't slip through the cracks. Superintendents, he says, are key:

"One very important thing is working with the superintendents because we recognize that the challenges *they* have are *our* challenges too. And not deciding that 'That's their problem.' It's our collective opportunity to become much more seamless in our work together to keep the students within a pipeline of opportunities. So, I think that it is extraordinarily important to work with superintendents in your community."

Dr. Melody Rose, Former Chancellor of the Nevada System of Higher Education, agrees that the challenges of K-12 are the challenges of higher ed. She told us:

"We want to lean into the K-12 challenges and be good stewards and good partners to them."

There are many ways that higher-education institution leaders can partner with K-12 leaders. Wherever possible, they might be forming collaborations, forging friendships, and exploring initiatives. And whatever they do, those programs need to be equally successful across zip codes, with more affordable price tags for different communities. It's not enough to reach out to connect with high-schoolers in affluent communities; *all* high school students deserve access to the kinds of programs that give teens a head start.

Where pipelines are missing, there need to be bridges.

But what's a college or university to do if the pipeline stops flowing — if students coming out of high school are either not prepared to begin college or don't even see themselves as "college-going" people? Where pipelines are missing, there need to be bridges. At the beginning of the fall academic semester in 2022, California announced it would award $54 million in grants to strengthen the K-16 education-to-career pipeline, reducing equity gaps and creating new pathways to education and careers for young adults in three key regions of the state. With or without this kind of support, higher-education institutions are getting creative and generous about meeting high-school students where they are and helping to prepare them for degree or non-degree higher education. One of the most

I firmly believe that K-12 success is higher education's success. We're not going to get more students or better-prepared students without supporting our K-12 system. We're integrally tied.

Melody Rose, PhD
Former Chancellor of the Nevada
System of Higher Education

boldly ambitious chief executives we spoke to about bridge programs between K-12 and college was Dr. Akiba J. Covitz, CEO of Foundry College in San Francisco, California. His institution has partnered with St. Francis College in Brooklyn, New York, to develop a high-school-to-college bridge program for New York City public school students who are "dropping off" in astounding numbers, not showing up in the post-secondary education world at all. For Covitz, this is something that *can* be done and *should* be done across the nation, and he's willing to lead the way. He told us:

> "The St. Francis partnership is, I think, a nationally scalable model. The public-school systems in the United States are under tremendous strain, and we want to support them. We want to support public schools around the country, especially large inner-city public schools. And we know we can take those students, and we can continue them into college if they want, or if they want to jump off and get a job with the credentials we give, we can do that as well. So, we take that — [high-school-to-college bridge programs] — as one of our responsibilities to the planet to do that."

Championing hesitant or as-yet-unprepared high-school students has largely been the playing field of community and technical colleges. Dr. Borowicz at Kishwaukee College told us:

> "It's so important that we are connecting to our communities and that we, as community and technical colleges, are providing a local, skilled workforce."

It's reassuring to see that private and public four-year institutions are developing their own successful bridge programs. For example, the Thames Program at Mitchell College has a bridge program cleverly named for the river upon whose banks the college is located. The new Summer Bridge Scholars Program at Northeastern University in Boston, Massachusetts, helps incoming students adjust to the university environment and the many facets of being away from home. Many other approaches ease one's way into beginning the college experience for young adults.

Ultimately, colleges and universities need to become professional "bridge builders." They need to connect their institutions to other institutions, their classrooms to high-school classrooms, and the very idea of being "college-going" to people of all ages who currently lack the skills, access, or confidence to jump into a post-secondary educational experience.

Dr. Baston from Rockland Community College left us with what we believe to be one of the most important messages about bridge-building: These programs must be equitable. It's not just about shy students or students who are legacy students for your competitors or for working professionals who have the financial means for college. We can't just build bridges for the privileged. It's also about underserved populations, single parents on tight budgets, and youth who are in high school now and don't have a plan for college. To focus on equity in this regard, Rockland has a partnership with a Pathways in Technology Early College High School ("P-TECH school"), which provides high-school students from underserved backgrounds with the academic, technical, and professional skills and credentials they need for competitive STEM jobs. No matter what kind of institution you serve, there's one true thing: When it comes to students who aren't reaching out on their own for a college experience — who don't currently have the needed access, understanding, intention, or confidence — there's a lot we can do. And there are a lot of *people* counting on us. Dr. Baston said to us, during our conversation about creating pathways for all populations who need them:

> "Equitable dual enrollment is one of the ways that we have to think about this in very intentional ways. We also need to think about the possibility of boot camps and how we get people into the pipeline who are from the K-12 system. But we can't stop at K-12 because we have a lot of folks who have some college and no degree. We have a lot of folks who had an industry *before* the pandemic whose industry is no longer in existence, and they need to get a job. How will they get back into the stream of opportunity if they've been out of college for 20 years or 15 years or only picked up a few credits? How are we engaging them in 'credit for prior learning?' They have experienced things they should be able to get some kind of credit for — credit that then could get them into shorter-term credentials or get them back into college in a flexible arrangement so that they have a chance to change the trajectory of their life. So, I think that we spend a lot of time focusing on K-12, which is important, but we also must understand that there's a whole landscape of opportunity. And we've got to think about how we engage *everyone* in this ecosystem of opportunity in higher education."

We couldn't agree more.

CHAPTER 2

NOT JUST A PRETTY PIECE OF PAPER

The Many Ways in Which Higher Education Is Demonstrating Its Value and Meeting Its Mission

B ack when education was an island — divorced from the "real world" in the ways we explored in Chapter 1 — the way we defined its value was quite different from the way most people define its value *today*. For almost every key market that higher education serves in the 2020s and beyond, gone are the days of going off to earn a degree simply as a status symbol, a signal to the marketplace, or a way to kill some time between youth and adulthood. Yet in the past, with the exception of people who were singularly focused on pursuing professions that require a degree — like medicine, law, or finance — millions of people in generations of yore went to college or university as a coming-of-age experience and an opportunity to spread their wings, to mature emotionally and intellectually, to expand their horizons, to meet new people, and, yes, even to increase their social status and marriageability. About that coming-of-age experience, Dr. Arthur Keiser, Chancellor of Keiser University, whose flagship campus is in West Palm Beach, Florida, said to us: "Listen, some folks have said that college is 'a four-year extension of adolescence because the job market can't handle the 17- or 18-year-old yet.'"

Frankly, there's some truth to that. The K-12 system is coming up short when it comes to teaching life skills and career skills. Few teens are ready to "fly free" after finishing high school. So, they do what their friends are doing (and what their parents or aunts and uncles might have done) — they apply to college. But even those students — the ones looking to explore and to find themselves and to have an organic or even circuitous route to an endpoint — are questioning whether the conferred degree at the end of that experience will deliver the results they paid for. They want their time, money, and effort to count.

As I sit here writing this chapter, I can't help but glance at the frames on the wall above my desk — frames that contain several very pretty, very expensive pieces of paper. While I've managed to misplace my associate's degree somewhere along the way (but am determined to find it — probably in a box in my basement), my wall is carefully adorned with four framed "status symbols" — my bachelor of arts diploma, my master of arts diploma, my master of business administration diploma, and the logo of the company I founded 20 years ago.

Do you have diplomas and certificates on your wall too? My most recent degree credential is only 15 years old and, already, the way some of us feel about the "piece of paper" itself has begun to change. Back when the gold foil was *gold*, the seals were hand-stamped, and the calligraphy was hand-lettered, we couldn't *imagine* someone mailing it to us instead of handing it to us on a stage with lots of tassels and flowing robes and "pomp and circumstance." Those were the days when that piece of paper meant everything. There was a time when having gone to a university — particularly certain *types* of universities — was all that people needed to know about you for them to feel they had a sense of your character, commitment, and competence in the world. Today, we live in a society where those credentials mean less. I honestly can't even remember the last time someone inquired about my education — whether I pursued formal learning after high school, where I went, or what credentials I earned. They certainly aren't asking about my GPA.[3] Oh, the things we agonized over that have no bearing on our lives at all!

---

3   Case in point for how irrelevant a college GPA is once we're established in our careers? In attempting to type "GPA," I typed "GPS" — now *that's* something that's relevant to my day-to-day life. "Waze" more relevant!

Those of us who use LinkedIn might have noticed that where you put the degree credentials (the section called Education) is way, way down the page on your profile — near the bottom. What's at the *top*? Our headline — our brand and a summary of our career experience or interests. To our networks and future employers, that's what matters. Our skills and our accomplishments are important. Sure, our degrees and/or shorter credentials are important too — and they get lumped together equally in the "Education" section. But it's our expertise — what we know how to *do* — that counts. Whether we learned how to do those things at a college or university (on campus or online), at a vocational/technical school, through an apprenticeship program, or as part of on-the-job training from our employers, the actual skills and competencies are where the rubber meets the road. It behooves those of us who work in higher education to remember that.

Skills and competencies are where the rubber meets the road. It behooves those of us who work in higher education to remember that.

Students are demanding new things delivered in new ways. And sure, when they are mailed a diploma or a certificate of completion on a fancy piece of paper, learners often still frame it and hang it somewhere prominent. But that pretty piece of paper is no longer the end game. The end game is *outcomes* ... results, meaningful experience, return on investment. Savvy institutions today are focused on the way they deliver outcomes to all stakeholders, embracing the imperative that higher education (and all forms of post-secondary education) should first benefit the learner — in objective, measurable ways — while also benefitting the community (regions, families, industries, and economies).

While the world is changing, there's still a strong case to be made for multi-year degree programs that have a proven approach to creating the proverbial "well-rounded person" — graduates who emerge rich with confidence, critical-thinking skills, and open minds. Just yesterday, in fact, I was talking to someone with more than $200,000 in student loan debt who still believes a formal degree program at a college or university is critical for its ability to teach us to *think* critically. And she might be right. But if our conversations with the brightest and most influential minds in higher education — the people interviewed on *The EdUp Experience Podcast* and featured in this book — have taught us anything, it's that many things are simultaneously true in modern post-secondary education. Skill-building and critical thinking are not mutually exclusive. We stand at the forefront of an era in which we can deliver more options for more learners in more impactful ways. And the conversations we had about how education can deliver "more than a pretty piece of paper" are instructive and inspiring.

**Skill-building and critical thinking
are not mutually exclusive.**

Competency-Based and Skills-Based Learning

One of the largest barriers to education is the amount of time it can take to complete an academic program. Not until recently did we even entertain the possibility that time — when it comes to learning — might not matter all that much. In talking to us about the competency-based model at Western Governors University (a fully online university based in Millcreek, Utah), President Scott Pulsipher said: "We seek to allow the *learning* to be held constant, but let *time* be a variable." This model honors the long-understood truth that people learn at different speeds. Competency-based education challenges us to acknowledge that, when it comes to a meaningful learning experience, it's not about staying for 14-16 weeks (or 2-4 years) — it's not about "sticking it out" or surviving until final exams. It's about being able to *do* the thing you showed up to learn.

We asked Pulsipher why some people in higher education continue to resist competency-based education, and he told us:

> "Anytime change is happening — whether that's disruptive or even just evolutionary change — one of the biggest impediments to it is often the structural and cultural barriers that exist … the negative inertia, if you will, to the envisioned future. Because the reality is the future only takes the form of now. We never really live in it. We only live in the present."

Making Education Your Business with Dr. Joe Sallustio

An Industry Ripe for Disruption

Clayton Christensen, Harvard Business School professor and originator of the theory of disruptive innovation, succinctly notes why being so effective at delivering a product to a consumer repeatedly, over time (like delivering a college education to thousands of people across decades or even centuries!), makes an organization (or institution) ripe for disruption. However, organizational *structures* can literally prevent innovation from taking place because many internal structures are designed to sustain what is working well and prevent something new from upsetting the proverbial apple cart.

Isn't this a true picture of higher education in the United States? An institution, so good at doing something for so long (e.g., educating to degree), develops and maintains internal structures — like tremendous governance and bureaucracy at every level — to slow down innovation from taking place. In higher education, we get in our own way. Running an institution of higher education is like running any other business. Arguably, the customer and service relationship might be different from other businesses, but when the balance sheet is reviewed by a leadership team or board, the line items like revenue and expense read like any other balance sheet. Speaking of balance, one of the ultimate balancing acts of a university president is walking the tightrope between decision-making and shared governance. Let's just say it like it is: For a brief time, the COVID-19 pandemic gave many college and university presidents an environment they relished. Speed to serve students was the priority, and all the governance and bureaucracy had to take a back seat ... no matter how much any staff or faculty member disliked it. The student and their needs came first, and the speed at which they needed service was unprecedented. We spoke to many presidents on the podcast who were very clear about the disruption that COVID caused within their institutions but who were also full of gratitude and humility about how something negative could be turned positive for the industry. So where are we now — now that the pandemic is essentially over? Have we stepped right back into the quicksand?

Many institutions, to prevent the quicksand from taking hold, have specific "build or buy initiatives" to serve an ever-growing online student population that includes tens of millions of students with what we sometimes call "some-college-no-degree." What would prompt the University of Arkansas to acquire for-profit Grantham University? Why would the University of Arizona acquire for-profit Ashford University? Why would the University of Massachusetts acquire Brandman University, a nonprofit college with competency-based education pathways? The answer: Organizational structures are designed to sustain what is working well and prevent something new from disrupting it. Many within higher education have figured out that speed to market means going *outside* of what already exists in their institutions as they now know them, and "bolting on" something new — rather than starting it from scratch. It's easier to acquire an institution that specializes in the adult-student market than it is to reengineer your entire university to serve that market.

Consider this: When was the last time something significant and innovative was created and launched at your institution? How long did it take from inception to implementation?

If you're thinking "My institution is different. We don't need to think about mergers and acquisitions," take a look at the data we collected during the research phase of producing this book. In an anonymous survey of college and university leaders, we asked: "Are you currently exploring (or do you intend to explore) the possibility of a merger, acquisition, or significant strategic partnership to ensure your institution's viability and improve quality and access for prospective learners?" A resounding "yes" came from 27.12% of respondents and 17.80% said "maybe." Accounting for those for whom the question was not applicable (like leaders who have retired or who work in an education-industry role that's external to colleges and universities themselves), only 35.59% of collegiate leaders were a "no" when it came to the possibility of a merger, acquisition, or significant strategic partnership.

45%

of higher-education leaders were actively exploring (or beginning to consider) a merger, acquisition, or strategic partnership to ensure their institutions' viability and improve quality and access for prospective learners.

Living in the present makes it difficult for academic leaders to lead us into the future. Our current focus can make it hard to plan for the future (especially in recent years, when higher education was juggling the overwhelming challenges posed by the pandemic). So, what of that future that we need to be creating now? Pulsipher told us that:

"The future of education is apt to be more designed around not just the *first* opportunity, but the *next* one. So much of the construct we have now is about the 'one and done,' you know, the first-time, full-time [educational credential]; then you're done, then you're off on your lifetime of progress. I think that our future will be defined, instead, by this continual learning loop. I think that individuals will find that the skills and competencies they need, they will have to regularly kind of 'refresh' because the shelf life of them is shortening to 2-7 years.

"There *is* one wonderful thing about a bachelor's degree, though; it pretty much signals to everyone that you have the capacity for learning, and you have the capacity for dealing with ambiguity and new environments and everything else. It presents *optionality* in a way that some of the other short shelf-life credentials won't. However, even when I possess that, it doesn't mean that I don't always need to be advancing my skills and competencies as I continue up my ladder of progress. So that 'learning loop' to me says that the future of education is one that's going to be more 'competency and skills' as the unit of measure of learning. And that's going to allow us much greater flexibility in the credentials that are packaged together to deliver that. They will potentially be in shorter form with more rapid return on value versus a rather lengthy time to get your first credential."

Rapid return on value. I stopped in my tracks on those words from Pulsipher. In the past, we cared about *eventual* return on investment/value. But this emphasis on rapid return changes the game and truly takes a credential or educational experience solidly into the realm of "not just a pretty piece of paper." Imagine what is possible if we aim to deliver not just an educational experience and a broader mind, but actual skills that learners can apply immediately or in the very near future. One of the concepts that most attracted me to the MBA program at Lake Forest Graduate School of Management in Lake Forest, Illinois, was their brand promise of "learn it today, use it tomorrow." I started my MBA studies when I was 31 years old and serving as a communications director at a medical university. The idea that I could apply my classroom learning the very next day at work? Yes, please!

Emphasis on rapid return changes the game and truly takes a credential or educational experience solidly into the realm of "not just a pretty piece of paper."

Time and time again, our conversations with higher-education presidents confirmed that new learning "products" or experiences are transforming the industry — and changing the lives of the learners we serve. In talking to Jim Milton, Chairman and CEO of Anthology, Inc. (headquartered in Boca Raton, Florida), we explored this issue of choice and of the need for institutions to demonstrate value through its student outcomes. Anthology's positioning is built on the simple and powerful declaration that they have "Heart for education. Eyes on the future." So, we weren't surprised to hear Milton predict:

"When I think about the future of higher education, I think that the diversity of education types that we have in the United States is a strength, not a weakness. And I think we should continue to preserve that — to give people *choice* in the types of programs and institutions that they participate in. I think we need to add more *skills* into our degrees, or offer more certificates or stackable credentials, and increase the use of competency-based education or assessment-driven education."

With all the talk about competency-based education (CBE) among the leaders interviewed for *Commencement*, we wondered how chief executives were thinking about CBE, non-degree credentials, and other valuable offerings in the context of their institutions' viability and competitiveness. In short, can focusing on ROI and measurable outcomes keep colleges and universities competitive in a changing world? Many presidents say "yes." Don Kilburn, CEO of University of Massachusetts Online (UMass Online), whose flagship campus is in Irvine, California, explained it like this:

"In terms of the competitive landscape, I think we should continue to try to drive measurable outcomes. First of all, create courseware and curriculum that has measurable outcomes so we can see how we're doing. We should continue to drive those completion rates and those performance rates up.

I think we should continue to try to increase access. Part of increasing access is making education more affordable. One of the interesting things about UMass Global[4] is the offering of competency-based education courses, which are self-paced, which are very affordable. And we also have some programs with employers, such as Disney and Walmart, which, again, is driving the cost down for students, increasing access to education, and giving folks all the credit they deserve for previous work, which decreases the cost of education. So, you know, I don't think there are any magic bullets around competitiveness, but I do think if you focus on those kinds of measurable outcomes and metrics and build a brand around *performance*, you'll do very well competitively."

---

4 University of Massachusetts Global (UMass Global), formerly known as Brandman University, became part of the UMass system in late 2021.

Making Education Your Business with Dr. Joe Sallustio

All the Credit They Deserve

If institutions hope to attract working learners, having a robust transfer-credit policy is critical. Let's break down what these policies mean and why they are important. First off, when we hear "PLA" in higher education, it means "prior learning assessment." Another way to say prior learning assessment is "credit for prior learning" (CPL). PLA and CPL mean the same thing — we just love our acronyms in higher ed! Whatever we call it, the student cares about it. In fact, in today's world of student consumerism, the student consumer has an *expectation* that their work (i.e., their career accomplishments or military service) is recognized as college credit, which is why having an adaptive policy in place is essential.

> *The easiest example to illustrate the importance of PLA/CPL? The Army medic.*
>
> *Imagine a servicemember who has been trained as a medic in the military. Now this person comes to your college or university and wants some credit for that field training and for their expertise in crisis response and clinical medicine. Do you say "no" — that real-world field experience doesn't match up with our learning outcomes? Or do you say "yes" — that real-world experience satisfies this many courses and we want to honor what you've learned in the real world?*

In my 20+ years in higher education, I have seen incredible PLA/CPL policies that work in favor of the student, and I've also seen restrictive and subjective policies that favor the institution and create barriers for students. Today's student will literally shop their experience around and choose the institution that awards them the most credit for their skills and practical experience. Some institutions work to accept prior learning from students, and some schools take the easy road and just say no. Why? One reason is that the more credits a school awards or transfers in, the less they make in tuition dollars (and higher ed isn't a business?). Accreditation and learning outcomes become an easy excuse not to do something in service of the student. Maybe your policy makers say something like, "Accepting transfer credit or PLA credit into this program hurts the quality or integrity of the program or the school." Statements like that are a red herring, meant to stop the process in its tracks. Simply put, those who oversee these policies can literally *choose* whether or not to accept transfer credit or prior learning. Telling a prospective or new student that it's out of your hands or that there's nothing anyone can do for them is simply untrue. Institutions that are *proactive* in serving this student population — adult learners with employment or public service experience — literally advertise their PLA policy and the speed at which they can deliver an answer to a student. There it is again: speed to service ... the magic bullet in higher education.

I was particularly struck by Kilburn's word choice of "how *we're* doing" when he spoke about measuring academic outcomes. Far too often, the onus is placed solely on the students themselves — "failing" students bear the blame for their struggles and leaders fully expect there to be some "bad apples" in each batch of learners. In the past, institutions too infrequently operated on the belief that if the students aren't succeeding, the institution isn't succeeding. More and more, however, we've begun to hear institutional leaders clearly take responsibility for the academic outcomes of their learners. Kilburn also acknowledged that change is difficult and that our evolution — industry-wide — to a true focus on outcomes is going to take time.

When asked why he thinks so many leaders are hesitant or resistant to competency-based education or stackable credentials, Kilburn said:

> "First of all, there's hesitancy because it's not the traditional model that everybody's used to. And so how do you evaluate that and judge that with the systems and the review that we currently have set up? It's hard for people to get their head around these new concepts. For competency-based education and stackable credits, it's early days. I mean, everybody expects for the 'new thing' to come out of the box fully baked and performing well. And you know, just like anything you come out with new, it gets better over time. Think about the educational model of face-to-face — how many hundreds of years old is that? It had time to refine itself. And I think that's true also for things like competency-based or online education. These things are getting better. I do think that self-paced competency-based programs are not for everybody. I think there are particular students who need a different model, but, in general, the idea of stackable credentials, getting rid of the Carnegie units in time, allowing people to move faster, and assessing that ... well, you know, why not? *Why not?* It just seems to me the open access to education — to get people to move through at their own pace in a quicker way. I know it hasn't actually fulfilled its potential yet, but I *do* think it's one of those things that we should keep working at."

Practical Skills for a Practical World

Whether we're talking about competency-based education or skills-based curricula, we must be focused on student outcomes and making learning more practical and applicable in the real world of work. In Chapter 1, we shared thoughts from several leaders who are spearheading cultural and operational shifts to make their colleges and universities more responsive to the marketplace — more connected to other organizations and communities and shared priorities. Those shared priorities nearly always include a relentless focus on student success. At Western Governors University, President Scott Pulsipher says they measure everything:

> "In the outcomes bucket of our design, we obsess about improving the student's success rate. That's progress in terms of course-completion rates, persistence; that's ultimately attainment rates that also lead to job

placement and job-promotion gains, and economic returns. We measure all of it. We measure employer satisfaction. We measure graduate and student satisfaction. We measure everything because ultimately that's who we're serving, and we have to make the model work for them. If it doesn't work for *them*, then what do we do this for in the first place?"

Success, according to Dr. John J. Rainone, President of Mountain Gateway Community College (formerly known as Dabney S. Lancaster Community College) in Clifton Forge, Virginia, comes down to life skills *and* job skills. He challenged us to acknowledge that life skills matter as much as job skills because life skills *are* job skills. But how do academic institutions teach life skills? Sometimes they make connections for students where those skills and abilities can flourish, like through internships. Dr. Rainone says that internships can address what students need in this regard because, in the future, they're going to need to "be able to work in a true work environment" — how to sit in on meetings, how to maintain confidentiality, how to show up on time, how to communicate confidently. Internships are a proving ground and a practice field. And whether it's a single, short internship (which nearly every college or university now encourages and enables) or a series of full-time, paid "co-op" experiences (like the training offered at institutions like Northeastern University in Boston, Massachusetts), these early career experiences can create career readiness for students. Dr. Rainone himself participated in an internship when he was in college, and he credits that experience with teaching him how to express himself in a work setting.

When it comes to understanding how education enables not just initial career success, but also career *stability*, the pandemic was a masterclass for those who were paying attention.[5] We asked Marvin Krislov, JD, President of Pace University in New York, New York, about the future of higher education and he told us:

"In terms of the future, the pandemic has created an environment where the importance of education has been highlighted. Information workers — people who are using technology — are much more able to

---

5   When it comes to lessons from the pandemic, we're just getting started. We think you'll appreciate the in-depth discussion of the pandemic's impact on higher education in Chapter 5: Pandemic as Panacea — How COVID-19 Kicked the Academy's Potential into High Gear.

work remotely and have survived the pandemic. Those workers who are not in that position have had a much tougher time. And we need to take care of *everybody*. One of the things that we're talking about is what role can education play in providing the skills to *all* workers and all students so that they can have good careers and good jobs? And I think that there are going to be people who are going to be heading *back* to school. And I hope the government supports those efforts. The three jobs that I'm hearing — from our career services team — that are in high demand are health, technology, and digital marketing. And obviously things will ebb and flow, but I think that that gives you some indication of where the markets are. And so I think a lot of people are going to go back to school [in the next few years]. And, of course, we know that in economically tough times, many people do go back to school for *graduate* education. I think graduate education is going to be more varied. I think there's going to be more online [programs] and I think they're going to be more one-year master's programs and maybe even programs short of a full-on degree, like certificates or badges. And I think that Pace and other universities will need to step up and think about how to address the changing workforce, with the right skills."

Between the time that Krislov was interviewed on the podcast and the time that this book chapter was written, his prediction started playing out. I have already lost track of how many institutions are now marketing master's degree programs that take just 12-16 months to complete (and several of those degrees cost $11,000 or less). The academy is finally saying "we see you and we hear you" to busy adults who want to get in, get out, and get on with their lives — all without massive educational debt.

> **Pro Tip:** *One of the most sustainable ways to address cost and time to degree is to explore non-standard academic terms. Non-standard terms allow an institution to explore different course lengths and allow for the potential of increasing entry points to increase student enrollment. Think outside the traditional semester system!*

Krislov's words echo loudly: "We need to step up and think about how to address the changing workforce, with the right skills." There are many ways in which higher education can step up in a world in which learners are demanding (and deserving of) more than a piece of paper — more than just a diploma or certificate of completion. We need to do more than just get them through — we need to level them up. #EdUp

Focusing on skills, according to Pima Community College's Chancellor and CEO, Lee Lambert, JD, (whose institution is based in Tucson, Arizona) is a great place to put our efforts:

> "The future of higher education demands that we think in terms of *skills*, not degrees and certificates. And then, in thinking about the skills, you start to say, 'Okay, some of that should lead to a degree. Some of that should lead to a sort of certificate.' Maybe it's some type of micro-credential. Maybe it's a badge, but it's about the *skill*. We need to focus on skill attainment — in formal and informal environments.

> "We have to think about our degree programs in the context of skills. I'm not saying abandon degrees. It's not 'either, or.' This is an era of 'and, and, and' and not 'or, or, or.' Conjunctive versus disjunctive thinking.

> "We have got to get past this distinction between credit and non-credit. It's just skills, folks! Why does it matter if you did it non-credit or credit? That's a false distinction. Why do I need to sit in a room for X amount of hours to say I acquired a particular skill? That doesn't tell you if you acquired something or not.

> "These days, a degree better mean something. It should be a validation of the skills you've acquired."

Indeed. Again, if "credit" is about earning a piece of paper, it's simply not enough in the 2020s and beyond.

You might be thinking, "But what if learners are okay with the piece of paper? There are plenty of people who choose a college experience for the coming-of-age opportunity or the chance to become more well-rounded, better critical thinkers, and to develop more diverse world views." Yes, there are. And there's zero criticism from the authors of this book for collegegoers who have a holistic view of the experience — those who aren't clear about seeking specific skills for a specific job or career. The problem with giving today's young adults (or mid-career adults) yesterday's degree experience is that the world of *work* has changed. We can no longer count on employers to "train us up." It's no longer viable to be a generalist when you finish college, hoping someone will take you under their wing and turn you into an IT professional or a geologist or a professional writer. This sea change is powerfully explained by Dr. David Finegold, President of Chatham University in Pittsburgh, Pennsylvania:

> "Historically, large corporations invested a ton in training new graduates. So, companies like GE, IBM, Johnson & Johnson, others, they would hire just well-trained general graduates and train them to become leaders within their companies. I think what's happened over the last 20 years is that companies have really said, 'You know, we're getting out of that business, for the most part. And we're looking to you — colleges and universities — to do as much of this as you possibly can for us.' And that's partly because things have just gotten more competitive globally."

So, if you're going to need a job someday (and most adults will), it's important for higher education to accept — in big, bold, strategic ways — that college graduates are no longer expected to be just "well-rounded" when they show up for work. Graduates (of degree programs or shorter skill-based credentials) need to come out of college with burgeoning or even deep functional expertise — actual job skills in a particular discipline. Peter Cohen, then President of University of Phoenix, talked to us about the distinctions between knowledge, skills, and degrees:

> "As we look to the future beyond getting degrees, students — as they go back into their corporate [or other workplace] settings — need to have additional skills. Let's call it 'upskilling.' For example, today there's a lot of people focusing on both agile project and product development, as well as leveraging technology in the workplace; both of those things require new knowledge, but not necessarily new degrees. So, as we go forward here, we're looking at much shorter forms of learning. We call it 'short-burst learning,' but you can call it short courses, micro-credentials, or something like that, where students may go to class and may learn asynchronously or synchronously over the course of either weeks or months and pick up a credential that allows them to move forward in their career. As I look forward and ask myself: 'What is the role of a career university as we move forward in society?' The answer is that we have to move beyond our traditional approach of

> providing degrees and now provide those smaller bits of knowledge that people need in order to get that next promotion or in order to change careers and get that new job."

Many people who are looking to upskill are wanting to stay at the same organization but are seeking the opportunity to step into new roles or take on more responsibilities. And yet others are looking to higher education to help them change jobs or launch a new career altogether. Cohen says:

> "We're chunking out those competencies, skills, and knowledge you need into smaller forms of learning that allow you to demonstrate — through badging or micro-credentials — that you've mastered something, put that on your LinkedIn profile, and be able to demonstrate to your employer that you're ready for that next promotion."

A degree (particularly a two-year or four-year degree) has rarely been *proof of mastery* of anything. Now, however, by pairing industry credentials with academic credentials, higher education can offer its learners the credibility that comes with competence. In the 2020s, students can say: "Teach me how to do this specific thing and help me earn a credential that is recognized in the industry or the companies where I want to work." We need certain skills at the beginning of our careers and different skills at mid-career or career change; expecting working adults to come back for another full degree experience when their career is decades deep is unrealistic. Cohen suggests:

> "Career universities, in the future, need to do more than just focus on degrees. We have to think about the whole life cycle of getting your next job or moving into your next career field. And we have to support you all the way through that journey."

A degree has rarely been *proof of mastery* of anything. Now, however, by pairing industry credentials with academic credentials, higher education can offer its learners the credibility that comes with competence.

During our conversation with Peter Cohen, he spoke about practical, timely skills — like teaching people how to interview for a job via Zoom — and how it's a university's job to teach such skills to alumni, students, and the general public. He said:

> "People are going to need to be reeducated throughout their career. The idea that society is going to be as fixed as it was back in the '50s — when change was not quite as rapid, and you could go to school one time and learn everything you need to know to have a full career — is just long gone. The pace of technology has changed things so rapidly that every few years, you need to be reeducated in order to be able to use the tools that are available at that point in time. So, universities — if their mission is to help people succeed in *life* — have a responsibility to figure out how to come back and reeducate people over and over again."

At the time of his interview for *The EdUp Experience*, Cohen was able to share that University of Phoenix had just announced Career Services for Life®, giving their more than 1 million alumni and nearly 90,000 current students access to career exploration tools, career coaching, resumé building, interview preparation, personal brand development, job search support, salary negotiation, career blogs and video content, and networking and mentorships. He explained that their alumni will maintain access to career and academic counselors, the university library, and even math and writing services for the entire length of their careers. And yes, these significant perks are available to certificate alumni too, not just degree graduates.

I'll be the first to admit it — I was stunned by this offering. I could be wrong, but I'm quite sure no one in higher education is really doing this (at least not to this extreme). Schools love to brag about the "value of our alumni network" without backing that up with actual services and support for alumni; and by the time a student becomes a graduate and discovers that commencement is really "goodbye" at their college or university, it's too late. The institution has already cashed the tuition checks and moved on to *this* year's incoming and continuing classes. Today, academic leaders are using terms like "pre-K to grey" to talk about lifelong learning and their commitment to creating college-going cultures that begin long before high-school graduation and continue into our encore careers. But not enough are executing significantly on that vision. *Yet.* I find it refreshing (and a long time coming) to see an institution setting the bar for "lifelong learning" and career impact so high. Surely, the financial resources and scale of an institution like University of Phoenix allows them to do breakthrough things for their stakeholders in a way that a small institution cannot; but everyone can do something. What can *your* institution do?

 # EdUp with Elvin

Practical Tips and Frontline Insights from Elvin Freytes

Offering value to your alumni starts with being able to reach them. So, here's a not-so-sexy strategy to help create, maintain, and continue to improve alumni engagement: List management!

Before you can think of reaching out to your alumni, you must ensure your list is accurate, up to date, and has as much information on each graduate as you can gather. This will help you create extremely targeted campaigns to provide your alumni with as much value as humanly possible.

So how do you manage your list? Here's how:

1. If you haven't already done so, create or purchase a software/database platform to house all the data that will go into your alumni list.

2. Start at the beginning of the funnel when your future alumni (i.e., your prospective students) provide you with their information. Make it easy for people engaging with your college or university to provide their information.

3. Make sure the contact information is correct by contacting them as soon as you can after receiving it, even with a simple "Thanks for inquiring!" or "Thanks for updating your alumni record!"

4. If their email bounces, call them to get an updated email address.

5. If you discover that an alum's phone number is not working (not an uncommon issue in a day and age when many people are abandoning land lines in favor of their cell phone), email the stakeholder to get an updated phone number.

6. If they provide their mailing address and the mail is returned by the post office, email or call the student, prospect, or alumnus for an updated address. (As you can see, steps 4-6 require a relentless focus on loving your list or losing a whole lot of opportunity — and revenue! If at first you don't succeed, try, try again.)

7. As alumni, students, or prospects continue to interact with different offices at your institution, keep asking them if their contact information has changed. Training staff to do this will help students understand the importance of providing their updated and accurate information.

8. As your students continue through their studies, keep asking them permission to document their journey. Keep asking about how things are going for them so you can get as many data points as possible to help better target the services and resources you offer — services and resources and support that will help them become more successful.

9. Document this process and make sure all staff are continuously trained on it. Allow them to provide feedback and ideas on how to improve. List management is the critical first step to meaningful engagement, and meaningful engagement of your students (and alumni!) is what keeps the lights on at your institution.

10. Remember, too much complexity and too much over-thinking this will slow you down. Create processes that are strategic, simple, and repeatable. And remember what I taught you in Chapter 1: Whatever you do, *do not* create a committee to make this happen!

Regarding their massive commitment to career services and other evolutions underway, Cohen said:

> "I think you'll see more universities going down that road of recognizing that they need to change modality, they need to change timeframes, they need to change degree expectations into short-burst learning expectations, and they need to provide services and counselors to support graduates and students throughout what's going to be a career that spans probably five different areas (as we look at people who are graduating today and how quickly the world is changing)."

In speaking to college and university presidents about a new era in higher education — an era in which learners are calling for more practical skills, immediate application of learning, and a break from the ivory tower's theoretical roots, even the notion of "scholarly" faculty with tenure and little-to-no industry experience was repeatedly challenged. Cohen said:

> "There's theoretical knowledge, research knowledge, and practical knowledge. And we, as a career university, recognize that our students need *practical* knowledge in order to succeed on the job. Therefore, all our faculty are practitioner faculty. Our faculty are required to be working in the field in which they are teaching. Our faculty have, on average, 25 years of experience working in the field in which they're teaching. So, when you come in as a student and you're talking to the faculty member, they can say, 'Look, this is what I actually did on the job yesterday. This is why you need to learn this skill' or 'This is why this works that way, because I'm doing it in practice.' And our faculty, on average, have been working for us for about 12 years.

> "But when you think about the traditional university, on the other hand, most of the faculty there come straight out of school, getting their master's degree or their PhD, and rarely do they actually have practical application in the field that they're working in, as opposed to just theoretical knowledge. And there's a place for theoretical knowledge; I went to a traditional university myself and got that theoretical knowledge. But for most working adults who are already in the workplace, having that *practical* knowledge is going to be a faster path to getting them promoted."

Many moons ago, I chose an MBA program for myself based on a faculty model that cared very little about doctorate degrees and a whole lot about having the "heads of business head the class." I understood (as a marketing professional with about a decade of work experience at that point) that a "learn from experience" model was going to give me a leg up. I had already earned three degrees by learning from theoretical/scholarly faculty, and I was ready for some practical insights. Thanks to the practitioner-faculty model that was unique back then (but is thankfully taking hold in the higher-education world today), I took accounting classes from Fortune 500 CFOs, operations courses from manufacturing-sector COOs, and international business courses from instructors who showed up for class jet-lagged and with stories about something fascinating that just happened during a negotiation in Japan.

For a college or university to feel connected to the movers and shakers in their region — and to be connected enough to be attracting faculty from top companies — requires an articulated vision of the college or university as being an engine of the local economy. This is a topic we explored in Chapter 1 and bears further mention here. For higher education to be responsive to the needs of local businesses, conversations across and among different organizations need to be happening in an ongoing way. Dr. John Rainone, President of Mountain Gateway Community College, works to bring together job development boards and others to co-create opportunities that connect the students and alumni from his institution with the workforce in their region. "What I try to be is a convener," he told us. "In my last five years, half of my job was as an economic developer." Joe and I were particularly struck when he told us that the worst thing that could happen would be if a local company leaves the area and says, in explaining their departure, that the town/county/region didn't provide their workforce needs. Because, in his words, "that's on us."

I think it's a responsibility of higher education to get closer to the industries that are employing people who graduate from our universities to say: 'We need to work together to graduate people who have the skills, the competencies, and the knowledge that we are looking for' in order to make America much stronger than it is today.

Peter Cohen

President Emeritus, University of Phoenix

Making Education Your Business with Dr. Joe Sallustio

Creating Ties That Bind Between Your Institution and the Employers Around You

When it comes to area employers being able to fulfill their workforce needs, if it's truly "on us" as educators, there's so much we can … should … *must* do. How do we begin to blur the lines between "town and gown?" You start by doing. Ask yourself:

→ "What can my organization do to get closer to the companies in the region we serve?"

→ "How much time does our president and the executive team spend touring local businesses, manufacturing plants, etc.?"

→ "Do local business leaders know our chief executive's name — and vice versa — and do they know how to contact one another?"

→ "Do those of us who make decisions on behalf of our college or university really know how business is done (in healthcare, in agriculture, in tech, in education, in manufacturing, in pharma, etc.) in our region?"

→ "And are we building programs and supplying talent for these organizations?"

Business and industry move fast — faster, indeed, than higher education, which is why we see so many alternative pathways for learning beginning to emerge from brands that haven't historically provided post-secondary education. If higher ed can't deliver timely and relevant education, students (and the employers that provide tuition assistance) will look elsewhere. Fortunately, most higher-education institutions today are bringing together leaders from local employers and engaging them on their Boards, President's Councils, and even creating advisory boards to gather feedback on what is needed in the work world — locally, regionally, statewide, nationally, and even globally. The question we all must answer: Then what?

If we're going to build industry-responsive educational programs, what does the curriculum revision schedule look like? How fast your curriculum can be updated to reflect a new and emerging business need is a measure of success to meet employer needs. A great example of the need to update/revise curriculum is in the field of digital marketing. At the time of writing this book (and I say it like this because the landscape may change once again by the time you read this), one of the fastest-growing social media applications is BeReal. It's positioned as an "authentic" social media app that randomly notifies you and your friends to post unfiltered photos of what you're doing *right now*, in an attempt to help users share their lives with authenticity rather than staged "living my best life" videos and photos. Do you talk about BeReal within one of your courses if you have a digital marketing degree? Is the faculty member using BeReal? This might sound silly or extraneous, but real-world relevance of your curriculum is what employers and students need and deserve from you.

There is much to consider as we move toward being workplace relevant instead of approaching curriculum design in an old-school "set it and forget it" manner. Want to grow your enrollment? Tell the consumer that you are updating your curriculum every year to keep their learning modern and ultra-relevant in a crowded job market!

From Prestigious to Practical

For far too long, certain corners of higher education have been all about separating the proverbial wheat from the chaff as a way of making itself (and its students and alumni) feel special or chosen. The industry has a legacy of sorting through admissions applications and feeling elite and "selective" when we stamp thousands of hopes and dreams as "rejected." But how can higher education be the "great equalizer" we say we want it to be if all learners aren't set up for equal access and success? Letting go of the "prestige" imperative is a vital first step to improving outcomes, in a practical sense, as well as increasing access and reducing equity gaps. How many of you can relate to the following story, which has been told at institutions of all kinds, all around the world?

"Welcome to XYZ University! Look to your left. Now look to your right. One [or two] out of three of you won't be here next year."

This exact exclusionary speech was mentioned in several of the interviews for this book. And without exception, presidents told us that this outdated practice needs to be rejected. Cohen addressed it by saying:

> "The 'Look left, look right, two out of three of you won't be here going forward' [is rampant] — traditional universities think their role is to weed students out. But it *should* be 'Look left and look right. If one of you is struggling, I'm going to help you succeed,' which is what universities really should be doing. We should want everybody who wants to get a degree to be able to. We should strive to help them get that degree so that they can improve their lives and the lives of their families. And it just always makes me angry when I hear people who say, 'Well, you know, we want to be elitist. We don't *want* everybody to succeed at this.' That is *not* the American way. And it's *not* the American dream."

As a higher-education consultant, I used to benefit from this trend; it made me feel special when I was hired by the "elite" schools. But I, too, am finding myself more angered than impressed when institutions go out of their way to attract tens of thousands of applicants who have no shot at getting in because there aren't enough desks or dorm rooms. Is it ethical for a highly selective school to take $500,000 in application fees from prospects who were sold false hope (and additionally exhaust their underpaid admissions team in shuffling those papers)? One of my current clients just told me that their new VP of enrollment wants to keep driving hard on selectivity. And I'm left wondering if taking the reins of their brand-marketing research project just makes me part of the problem.

Incidentally, the "weeding out" in higher education can happen in many ways and at many junctures. It happens during admissions, and it happens as students experience the curriculum. During my MA program, my classmates and I were told there would be a 30% washout rate (that a third of us would not graduate) and I, young and arrogant as I was, took that as a challenge and a sign of prestige. Now, I think it's ridiculous. As students who bought into the narrative, we were all self-important in ways that didn't help us in the real world. We even had a first-term course called Introduction to Graduate Studies, which had assignments that were purposefully vague and impossible and headache-inducing, and the faculty had the nerve to tell us that the course was "the closest thing we can do to hazing you into the program." Welcome to scholarly life, where only the strong will survive. (So much for a commitment to helping all students thrive.)

 ## Making Education Your Business with Dr. Joe Sallustio

Moving Beyond Exclusionary Strategies and Tactics in Higher Education

Isn't it amazing that higher education is one of the only businesses where some celebrate the number of students *excluded* versus the number of people *included*? It's common — at the end of a recruiting cycle — to see a press release from an institution that notes their application numbers hit a record, up scores of percentage points, and admitted-student numbers were up 1%! Imagine this same scenario at a retailer. *Orders for widgets hit an all-time high, up 20% year over year, and we are celebrating that we only filled 1% more orders!* It's ridiculous.

During the pandemic, students were applying to more institutions than ever before. Test-optional and test-blind admissions practices gave students a pathway that was not previously available. But the student consumer (whether traditional student or working learner) is becoming more and more savvy. They are doing thoughtful research, and ed-tech companies in the space are providing resources that allow for cost comparisons, and histories of what other students were offered in terms of scholarships, what out of pocket costs are, and what discount rates were received. If I know my friend received X, why shouldn't I receive the same? Some sites even allow for students to see what their income might look like post-graduation and what cost of living expenses will be where they want to live when they move on from college.

Bottom line? The power is swiftly shifting into the hands of the consumer. Spend some time at www.TuitionFit.org and www.StudentDebtSmarter.org to get real about why your "selective" strategy might be outmoded — more a liability than an asset in today's changing world.

Let me say a little bit more about this tendency to "weed out" students by sharing some perspectives from my co-author, Dr. Joe Sallustio. He reminded me that though the practice of weeding students out may not be as obvious in today's higher-education environments, many institutions use barriers to entry (including admissions requirements) to create the same circumstances. Take a look at the program portfolio at your university. Is there any program that has a higher GPA requirement than another? Any program that requires students to take general-education courses before "applying for the major?" What about ACT/SAT requirements? There are two pathways for institutions to take: Educate the students we want or educate as many students as possible. It's the classic argument within higher education — create stringent admission requirements that ensure only the "best" students are in the program (ensuring easier teaching and reducing risk) or create a more open-enrollment situation that allows for greater access (but much harder work for faculty and staff).

Thankfully, today, most institutions are doing better. We have new mindsets and new skillsets — for students, faculty, and administrators alike. Dr. Mary Schmidt Campbell, President of Spelman College in Atlanta, Georgia, talked to us about preparing students for the unpredictable future of work, telling us:

> "What we want to do always is to be able to send our students out with some fundamental competencies, like writing. They have to write well. They have to speak in a way that is persuasive. They have to have computational skills. They have to have analytical skills. There are certain competencies we have to make sure that they have, but

the most important thing that we have to teach our students is *how* to learn and how not to be fearful of what we don't know. How to walk into a situation where we don't know anything and have the tools and the intellectual expansiveness and resilience to be able to say, 'Okay, I'm starting from square one, but I can do this.'"

"Intellectual expansiveness and resilience" — yes! We asked Dr. Campbell to say more about the reason why soft skills (also termed power skills, workplace-competency skills, or essential skills) and mindsets are critical to teach in higher education, and she told us:

"There's no such thing as preparing somebody for a job, because that job's going to be obsolete in five years, maybe less time than that. The way journalists, for example, do their jobs now is completely different and the *outlets* for journalists now are completely different from the way they were 10 years ago. So, we have to teach that resilience."

I loved this example. I was a magazine editor early in my career and we produced 12 glossy magazine issues per year. There was no "online" edition, and not even a website for the company. And there certainly weren't social media platforms and live videos. Anyone who trained to be a journalist a few decades ago has found themselves upskilling and evolving at a rapid pace, just to keep up. But with the intellectual expansiveness and resilience that Dr. Campbell says can be taught during a higher-education experience, professionals whose job descriptions keep changing are going to be just fine. (Well, maybe after a little upskilling!)

Fresh Perspectives on the Value of a College Education

In Chapter 1, Joe shared a candid account of how he went from a place of questioning the value of a college education to being downright bullish about the future of higher education. Because we know that various stakeholders are putting pressure on higher-education decision-makers to demonstrate that value in new ways, we asked some of the esteemed presidents featured in this book to talk about this very topic. Dr. Irma Becerra, President of Marymount University in Arlington, Virginia, told us how she answers people who question the value of higher education:

"This is one topic that I'm very passionate about because the single most important investment that any one person can do for their entire life is their college degree. It's the single *most important* investment. I want to repeat it again because I want everybody to capture that. Clearly, there is nothing that hurts me more than when I hear that 'Education and college degrees are not for everybody' because when I hear that, I wonder 'Who is it not for? Who is being left out?' You know, education is the great equalizer. There is no way that I could have entered the places that I entered in my career if I didn't have a college degree. There are so many jobs out there — great jobs — for which, if you don't have a college degree, you just can't have access to them.

"The college degree: that is the minimum requirement. [And when it comes to a college education], you need to finish … it's not enough to start. Because if you start college and you get through one year, two years, three years, and you don't get the college degree, it's not enough that you're halfway through or three-quarters through. You will not have access to that job that requires a college degree.

"And more so, you cannot even get a job that pays you three-quarters of the salary that the college-degree job will pay. So, it's an *all or nothing* game. So, with that, what I'm saying is when research shows that people who have a college degree will earn *minimum* $2 million[6] more over their lifetime than those who do not have a college degree, I said, my gosh, return on investment is *huge* over your lifetime. Then plus the opportunity to pivot no matter what happens in your life. So, I am a strong believer that people need to remember the real value of a college education. I think that students must make that the number-one priority, and parents need to make it the number-one priority that their kids get a college degree. And what they do afterwards, it doesn't matter. You know, I've had parents tell me, 'Oh my god. My daughter, she got this great degree and now she wants to be a ski instructor. I'm devastated.' And I'm saying to that parent, 'Let them figure it out. Later on, they may become a marketing expert for the resort where they were a ski instructor. But the fact that they have

---

6   This number is estimated by various sources as ranging from $1 million to $2 million. In the case of a president citing a different statistic from one presented by another voice in this book, please know that figures may be cited from various, reputable sources.

the college degree allowed them to pivot a year later into that great job where they can combine their passion for skiing together with their skillset in marketing.' So, what I'm saying is that a college degree is your ticket — in particular for immigrant families. Because remember that, for those of us who are really trailblazing through our journeys, you know, there may not be any *inheritance*. There is nothing that is going to help you kind of 'bootstrap yourself.' Education is your only inheritance. So, you have to be laser-focused on the college education, crossing the line."

In the introduction for this book, we told you that we'd be sharing differing, contradictory viewpoints and allowing you to be inspired and instructed by the lessons and insights that *you* believe are ideal for your institution or your career. And we hope you'll take time to consider the ideas that make you uncomfortable. As you can see, while some institutions are betting big on short credentials and non-degree programs, others are flourishing with traditional degree programs. As for the people (*outside* and *inside* academia) who are questioning the value of a higher-education credential or experience, many of them think that proverbial "old-school" education doesn't match up with "new-school" methods, but they don't really know what's happening to deliver on the promise of higher education in new ways. The people who doubt and criticize rarely have insights into the amazing work being done to improve student outcomes, increase retention, increase access, and generally "level up" what higher education means today. Ask anyone who earned a bachelor's degree in the 1970s to talk to someone who earned a bachelor's degree after 2010, and they'll quickly discover that while those pretty pieces of paper might look strikingly similar, the paths they took (and the skills and benefits they received) on the journey to those diplomas could not be more different.

But what do you do if the disagreements about the value of what we offer are happening on your own campus, and among your own leadership team? You get back to basics. Dr. Gregory Fowler, then the Global Campus President of Southern New Hampshire University and now President of the University of Maryland Global Campus, talked to us about getting a leadership team all on the same page. He shared:

> "One of the things I had the team do was say, 'We're going to go back to basics ... before we even have any further conversations. So, we all need to be in agreement on some very basic things around 1) what learning *is*, 2) how learning *happens*, and 3) the things that we're doing that either *help* or *hurt* what we know about how learning happens."

Dr. Fowler encourages higher-education leaders to question everything — to examine it all. He says that it's vital to question the little things about your operations, as well as the big things, like:

> "Are we using discussion-board posts just to take attendance? Because if that's the case, then we're not serving our students. [Then look at] far larger issues, like what's the purpose of general education? Is it really just a buffet of courses that we expect something magical to happen by students taking them? Or are we really preparing students for the skills and understandings that they're going to need to move and navigate a much more complex world? And if we're trying to do that *second* thing, how do we go about creating those experiences *deliberately*?"

It just so happens that *The EdUp Experience* had a conversation with a college leader that focused almost exclusively on this concept of creating impactful experiences for students and doing it deliberately —not just from day one of a student's enrollment, but from day one of an institution's founding. At most colleges and universities — especially those that were founded 100 years ago or more — making huge mindset shifts (like letting go of the "degree as holy grail" and investing in an outcomes-based strategy) is difficult. It's sometimes painful. Some leaders might tell you it's actually *impossible* to revolutionize an institution where time-honored traditions refuse to be broken. So, what about brand-new institutions? Is the easiest way to build an institution that blows up old assumptions actually to build a new school from scratch? At Foundry College, they're doing exactly that. And they're doing things that would create massive friction at schools that were founded decades or even centuries ago.

Our conversation with San Francisco, California-based Foundry College CEO and President, Dr. Akiba J. Covitz, was one of the first times we heard a higher-education leader come right out and say they are aiming to disrupt the industry as a whole. Dr. Covitz told us:

> "Foundry College aims to disrupt the traditional two-year college model. We're doing that by providing learners with 21st-century skills and knowledge that they need for the jobs of today and the jobs of tomorrow. We provide foundational courses that give broad skills that employers say are lacking and needed most. So those include oral and written communication, collaboration, and problem-solving. We call those 'durable foundational skills' and then using a stackable model through which you can then — based on that foundation — master knowledge specific to job pathways that are in high demand."

Less and less are we hearing people talk about "becoming a well-rounded person" — more and more, we're hearing about clear pathways to deliberate career and life destinations. As of the time of Dr. Covitz's interview, Foundry College offered two pathways — one in project management and one in Salesforce administration, built on top of those foundational skills Covitz told us about. Dr. Covitz explained:

> "We build those credentialed certificates in areas where learners can start a new job in about nine months and make $50,000+. And on top of that, the next thing that we're building is an associate's degree ... And then you can get your associate's degree from us ... and then again, from there, transfer it to a four-year college. You can step on and off the ladder whenever you want of this value chain. And that's what we're doing. We think this is an area of education that is in need of disruption."

He told us that Foundry only intends to develop programs that fit distinct and high-bar criteria: They want to educate people for jobs that will pay a family-supporting wage of $50,000 or more upon program completion, they want those jobs to not be ones that might be replaced through automation in the next 20 years, and they want those jobs to be ones that can be performed remotely. (So much for that poetry degree!) Within minutes of beginning our conversation with Dr. Covitz, we realized that Foundry College (which has as their tagline "Future-Proof Education for Working Adults") is not your grandfather's community college. In fact, it's nothing like the education I received at a community college 30 years ago. Dr. Covitz told us:

> "We're trying to see that learner as a customer who can start out from the beginning and do the foundational skills or those professional skills, then get a job in under nine months. They can be a Salesforce administrator, for example, and step off the educational ladder for a couple years and make real money as a white-collar worker. And then if they want to come back, we'll give you an associate's degree. And then you can just keep going up the ladder. I think learners now, especially in the wake of the pandemic, are looking for choice and they're looking for things in terms of *months* and not *years*. They don't want to commit to *four* years of one path or even *two* years of one path. They want to know that there are ways to step on and ways to step off. And that when you step off, you're ready to do something productive. And by that, I mean, you can very directly get a job, make $50,000 a year — those sorts of very direct things. Not 'be a better person,' which I *do* think education should do, but consumers want something very explicit in that they want to achieve in six months or in nine months. They want to know: 'I'll have *these* skills. I'll be able to get *that* job. It'll pay *this* much. And these are fields that are *growing*, so I know there are jobs out there.'"

While Foundry College is a venture-backed organization, it has its roots and inspiration in traditional higher education. Dr. Covitz and Foundry's founder, Dr. Stephen M. Kosslyn, met at Harvard University, where Dr. Kosslyn was Chair of the Department of Psychology and Dean of Social Science and where Dr. Covitz was Associate Dean for Faculty Development at Harvard Law School. Covitz told us:

> "What I've seen in my too-many years now in education — first as a professor and as an administrator — is that, in the past, I think we presumed (especially at places like Harvard and elsewhere, though not to say anything negative about my friends at Harvard) that we knew what students should learn. We were going to teach it the way *we* thought they should learn it. And it was up to *them* to figure out how to make it applicable to what they wanted to do in life. We just assumed that that credential, wherever it came from, because we were the experts, people should do what we told them to do. We professed

to know (and we *did* know — we had our PhDs or whatever). I think
what really changed about 10 or 12 years ago is sort of the flipping of
this perspective."

Flipping the perspective in higher education — no longer seeing faculty
as all-knowing "sages on stages" and starting to honor the learner in new
ways — creates almost limitless possibility for the industry as a whole. We
asked Dr. Covitz about the culture they're creating at Foundry College and
the prevailing mindset about the relationship between learner and institution, and he said:

> "First of all, just seeing learners as customers. I wrote about that
> about 10 years ago and got a lot of blow-back from my colleagues.
> I didn't mean it to suggest that we think of learners as someone
> buying any widget — of course, education is very specific. But once
> you see learners as customers, as *consuming* something, then they're
> just like any consumer, any customer. They're exchanging something
> of value — their time and money — for something that *has* value —
> a credential. And that altered mindset, I think, changes everything you
> do. Now, you have to figure out what the customer (what the *learner*)
> needs to get, and where they want to go. And that's a huge mind shift.

> "At Foundry, it's no longer 'You do what we say. And figure out what
> we said and tell it back to us in a couple of months.' Instead, it's 'Where
> do you folks want to go with this?' What Foundry College discovered at
> the beginning, and at the bottom of our stack [credential structure], is
> that employers want people to have these durable, professional skills
> that will last them for the rest of their career: oral and written commu-
> nication, collaboration, problem-solving. And I think in the past, you
> expected someone to take four years and a bachelor's degree and sort
> of learn those skills by osmosis. You were in a giant lecture class, and
> you saw how your professor made arguments, and then you went into
> recitation, and you made arguments in front of other people in the
> recitation, and then you went to seminars, and you sort of learned that
> stuff as a secondary, tertiary skill. What *we* do is we teach those skills
> absolutely *directly*."

I had to take a step back and think about Dr. Covitz's comment about
expecting students to learn soft skills by osmosis. And he's right. Nearly

every college or university I've attended, worked for, or consulted for has, of course, built communication and collaboration and problem-solving — at least to some degree — into their assignments or their cultures, but never offered multiple, ongoing, overt lessons on *how* to be an effective collaborator or a successful problem-solver. They just hoped the students would pick it up along the way, almost by happenstance. Some students do, and far too many don't. And when they don't master these foundational skills, such learners can flounder in the workplace — which contributes to value-based perceptions of the higher-education experience. Dr. Covitz told us:

> "We guarantee to employers, when they see a Foundry credential, that everyone who graduates has those professional skills, those personal skills, those foundational skills that will last those graduates for the rest of their careers."

And remember that Dr. Covitz leads an organization that offers credentials that take months — not years — to complete (and they're offering an associate's degree as well). I've been working in and around higher education for decades and I've never heard a college president say "We *guarantee* to employers ..." about any sort of outcomes at all. But perhaps it's time this becomes the rule, and not the exception. Incidentally, this was also the first time I'd heard someone refer to a certificate holder as a "graduate" and it sounded pretty good. It sounded right.

The way in which students, and their families, are defining higher-education value is shifting dramatically right now. Dr. Covitz suggests that academic leaders shift their own mindsets to keep pace with the change:

> "For higher education leaders, it's not enough to be thinking about how to 'impart wisdom' as a 'sage on the stage.' Now, it's incumbent on you to figure out how to see education from the perspective of the *rest* of the world. Not the 2% or 3% or 1% who get into those top schools, but *everyone*. And once you do that, you can't use that same old mindset, which is, 'Well, those people before wanted a *network* and they wanted *wisdom* and they wanted to be able to sound really smart at New York City cocktail parties.' None of that stuff's relevant to the rest of the

world. They might be interested in it, but it's not the coin that they can use to pay their rent or their mortgage. They need *job* skills."

This emphasis on being relevant to everyone is a theme we heard again and again, especially from community-college presidents. Dr. Anthony Cruz, President of Miami Dade College's Hialeah Campus, was among the first of the leaders who engaged in a conversation with us that absolutely shattered the stereotypes of higher education. He said:

> "There is no practical application of the 'ivory tower' in this community. We are here to serve the community. We *are* a community college, after all. So, while we do offer amazing educational opportunities for our students and we have great faculty and we have great staff and we do all the things that other higher-education institutions do, our mission is to really reach the *people* — to reach the community. And that's why, even though Miami Dade College no longer has 'community' its name, it still has it in its DNA."

A new emphasis on practicality in post-secondary education is taking many forms. Programs — at the graduate and undergraduate level — that organize their students into loose or strict cohorts are finding that doing so generates measurable results and teaches practical skills. Dr. Mary Schmidt Campbell, then President of Spelman and Kendall College campuses, made a strong argument for cohorts as an ingredient for long-term student success, telling us:

> "We recently realized (and validated with data) that our best-performing students — those with nearly 100% graduation rates and high GPAs — almost always were part of a cohort. They might have been part of our Women in STEM cohort or our WISDOM Scholars, (our Women in Spiritual Development of Ministry). They may have been our Social Justice Scholars. They may have been our Community Service Scholars. But they all belonged to a cohort of students who had a common purpose, who had — almost always — a faculty advisor and sometimes also a staff advisor. And inside those cohorts, they very often had research experiences, field experiences, and some kind of service learning or internship or something that gave them something *outside* the classroom to support what they had learned *inside* the

classroom. And these successful students came from cohorts that had continuity from one year to the next."

When students learn to rely on one another through cohorts or project teams or other collaborative experiences during their college courses, they're building teamwork skills that directly translate to their current or future jobs.

Someone who knows a thing or two about teamwork and collaboration — particularly about partnerships between higher education and Corporate America — is Lisa Honaker, former sales executive at FedEx Office and most recently director of expansion sales at Highspot, who has made multiple appearances on *The EdUp Experience Podcast*, as a featured guest and as a co-host. During one of those conversations, Lisa got us thinking about how higher education creates successful employees and how the confidence of college can prevent "imposter syndrome" in newly minted college grads. She suggested that college-educated employees bring a sort of confidence and resilience to the workplace that is critical, explaining:

> "That confidence that students develop, when that translates into the workplace, becomes the reality that you have somebody who has that kind of 'soft skillset' that's not readily trainable. You *do* see their confidence come out on day one. Even if they're brand new to the job or brand new to the industry, you can see them very quickly assimilate and connect the dots and figure out where they belong in the organization. This really then goes back to Maslow's hierarchy of needs. Because what is at the very bottom? *Safety*. At work, you've got to feel safe. You've got to feel secure. And that is that sense of *belonging*. And when you have somebody who doesn't have a developed sense of those soft skills — often someone who didn't go to college to learn these critical life and professional skills — they ultimately wander, and they meander and that confidence falters. And then they're like, 'Gosh, do I belong?' Then their performance suffers. And then it starts getting into really personal stuff, like 'Am I good enough?' 'Can I even do this?' And then just your personal self-worth can start to decline as well. So, it's weird to think about how the foundational college degree — which a lot of us *do* take for granted — how that translates to bigger, real-world topics about self-worth and about mental health down the road in the professional workplace."

Honaker's insights about "connecting the dots" are, in some way, the entire major takeaway of this book, because what the 100+ college and university presidents told us — in various interconnected ways — is that the future of higher education is an "and" imperative (i.e., compiling *this* and *that* and then *that other thing* for our stakeholders). We will succeed — together — by connecting the right dots in the right ways at the right times. The future of higher education, we were told again and again by institutional leaders, is about adding layers and connections to educational experiences until we arrive at a place where the lines are truly blurred between the things that used to be kept separate: classroom and laboratory, living and learning spaces, college and career, service learning and homework assignments, classroom experience and experiential learning, liberal arts and practical skills, degrees and certificates, faculty and students, higher education and the corporate world, campus and community. And the best way for us to blur the lines is to do it strategically, organically, and with clear purpose.

The future of higher education is about adding layers and connections to educational experiences until we arrive at a place where the lines are truly blurred between the things that used to be kept separate. And the best way for us to blur the lines is to do it strategically, organically, and with clear purpose.

How might we all build upon our strengths or skate in new directions, always doing so with *purpose*? Dr. Irma Becerra, President of Marymount University, referred to what they do at her institution as "purpose-driven liberal arts." She said:

> "We pride ourselves in having transformative experiences and this whole idea that we have a purpose-driven liberal arts. We are very focused on educating students for careers that really reflect their

purpose. And we want students to *find* their purpose in life, through their careers."

So, at Marymount, students choose careers based on their own life's purpose, get educated for those careers through a purpose-driven curriculum, and enter careers where their personal purpose gets further clarified, deepened, or changed. Dot to dot to dot … connected.

You might be thinking, "But can liberal arts really be practical and purposeful?" We believe the answer is yes. Dr. John Swallow, President of Carthage College in Kenosha, Wisconsin, talked to us about how his institution is evolving its liberal arts heritage in a way that honors the past and prepares for the future. They are looking to ensure they offer programs for what students and economies *need* right now. He calls it "critical thinking for critical need." It's an expansiveness in thinking that allowed them to add a thriving nursing program to an institution that previously didn't offer clinical healthcare degrees. As a marketer and an alumna of Carthage, I was equal parts impressed and bummed that I couldn't take credit for the tagline on the glass wall outside the nursing simulation lab, where the program's purpose is spelled out so aptly: "Where critical thinking meets critical need." Indeed.

Endgame: Thriving Career, Fulfilling Life

The more we engaged in this ongoing conversation with presidents about the value of a college education, the more we found ourselves discussing what the endgame — the goal or purpose — of higher education really looks like today. There was almost consensus on the fact that a changing demographic is increasingly looking for something different from (or in addition to) a coming-of-age traditional educational experience. For some students, the endgame is a job (and then another and another until it's a career). For some, it's a better life. For many, it's both. And what surfaced so clearly in this nearly three-year conversation that we engaged in on *The EdUp Experience* during its initial years was that "lifelong learning" is no longer a buzzword — it's table stakes. It's the new modus operandi; it's the path to institutional sustainability; it's the Golden Ticket; it's consumer expectation; it's a crystallized rally cry.

"Lifelong learning" is no longer a buzzword – it's table stakes. It's the new modus operandi; it's the path to institutional sustainability; it's the Golden Ticket; it's consumer expectation; it's a crystallized rally cry.

Dr. Michael Torrence, President of Motlow State Community College in Tullahoma, Tennessee, talked to us passionately about lifelong learning and his institution's vision, telling us:

> "If you intend on coming to us, we want to create spaces for you to thrive in, not just to be an input or throughput and output. We want for it to be *longitudinal*. Our expectation is that people don't come here for a job — they come here for careers. And our students don't come here just to learn during the timeframe they're with us. They'll be *back*."

Dr. Joe Sallustio, while hosting the conversation with Dr. Torrence, opined:

> "Dr. Stephen Spinelli, President of Babson College, said, 'We don't want you for two years or four years. We want you for 80 years. We want you to come back.' It strikes me that college and universities are perhaps the only business where we look at it as a 'one and done' proposition. Even if you're talking about people who go buy a car or a house, you'd think you want that customer back the *next* time they go make that kind of purchase. Higher ed doesn't typically look at things in that fashion."

Joe is, as always, right. His comment left me musing about the way in which all four of my alma maters saw my matriculation at their schools as a "one and done." The College of Lake County, where I earned my AA, never tried to recruit me for another credential and hasn't even had me back to deliver a guest lecture, despite my books and expertise in areas that might interest their students, staff, and faculty. (Fun fact: I also served on the English faculty there, but even that has not been enough to keep me in a database that gets offered some sort of new value once every decade.) Carthage College, where I received my BA, never offered me a graduate degree or a certificate, though they do a wonderful job of engaging me in other meaningful experiences. Illinois State University, where I earned my MA, never tried to get me back for a PhD (once I walked away from a PhD fellowship there to start my career — this girl needed a paycheck!) nor did they ever try to get me back for an MBA. And the school where I earned my MBA, Lake Forest Graduate School of Management (whose praises I have sung multiple times in this book), doesn't have anything to offer me at all — all their certificates are a sort of "101" to the degree learning (i.e., they're for people who don't already have an MBA), so they have nothing else to sell me. I have huge love for all four institutions and yet the truth that Joe alluded to is stark: those institutions left a *lot* of money on the table when they decided not to think of their graduates as "return customers" with the potential for repeat business. And with fairness to these institutions, they're in good company. The "one and done" stereotype exists for a reason — because most colleges and universities *talk* about lifelong learning but don't actually deliver it. But that is changing. And I predict that once this book has made its way to a 2nd or 3rd edition, hundreds or even thousands of institutions will have mastered the art of bringing their graduates back ... again and again, for mutual benefit.

 ## Making Education Your Business with Dr. Joe Sallustio

"Capture" vs. "Cultivate" Marketing and How to Balance Them in Higher Education

Brand equity, multichannel attribution, interest funnels, student archetypes, maturation rates, acquisition costs, search marketing — the beautiful (and sometimes daunting) world of marketing and communications. At the base of the 80-year lifelong-learning concept is the practice of *cultivation versus capture* marketing tactics. An institution *needs* students now, and they *want* students later. Distributing marketing expenditures (aka "spend") to effectively balance needs and wants is an exercise in restraint and responsibility. Spend money now to recruit students now or spend money now to recruit students later — it's a conversation within any marketing department and one that has implications on budget, job security, and results. How do I capture the interest I need now to help my institution meet my goals, and how do I cultivate interest, over time, to help meet my institutional goals later? We often feel forced to choose: capture current demand or cultivate new demand.

We have a hyper-content culture, where the most successful types of marketing involve different types of media experiences. Universities with robust data-analysis tools might deduce that a student experienced many different channels of their marketing before applying to the school. Therefore, attribution modeling (figuring what channel a student's interest came from or will come from) is critically important when considering the capture vs. cultivate marketing equation. Attribution modeling is particularly important in the capture versus cultivate framework because it can tell you what is effective both short-term and long-term. Unless a university has a brand that transcends the supply-and-demand equation, attribution modeling and capture versus cultivation marketing is a critical component of sound operational management; I call these lay-up drills — something you do *every day* because it helps to increase the efficiency of *future* performance.

So, if we are to imagine that a college or university might continue to serve the career and general intellectual and life needs of someone until they are 80, does that mean we should meet them long before they are 18? The presidents we spoke to said a resounding "yes." Dr. Torrence at Motlow State, for example, told us:

"Our engagement as a community college — and being really community-centric — is about engaging with third, fourth, and fifth grade. It's about addressing the pipeline to prison at the third-grade literacy rate and then asking the questions of the young folks about what they need and want. So, the fifth graders over the past several years have been the most influential for me in terms of thinking about

> our programming in the curriculum that we design, because they're asking questions about being Twitch coders and YouTubers. You know, I didn't grow up in that space. (I grew up with Donkey Kong and Atari and CalecoVision and Sega.) So, it's about making sure that we are creating a space where students are looking *forward* to coming, because they know we're prepared for *them*, just as much as they're prepared for *us*."

I love this, and I can't overstate how much. We, in higher education, used to think of "college readiness" as being an obligation of the learner. Yet to Dr. Torrence's eye-opening point, it can — and *should* — also be an obligation of the educational institution and the industry to be prepared for the students who are headed our way. *We* must be ready for *them*, not just the other way around.

We, in higher education, used to think of "college readiness" as being an obligation of the learner. Yet it can — and *should* — also be an obligation of the educational institution and the industry to be prepared for the students who are headed our way. *We* must be ready for *them*, not just the other way around.

Bloom Where You're Planted

When we think about what types of students are headed our way, and where they might land after they complete any credential with us, take a look at the corporate parks within a 25-mile radius. Is your institution surrounded by a hub of manufacturing? Or a technology and research haven? Or right in the middle of half a dozen pharmaceutical companies? Or just down the road from a healthcare/medical district? Dr. Torrence, whose college is near Nissan, Bridgestone, and Volkswagen, sees it as his responsibility to educate students about automation, robotics, manufacturing, supply-chain management, cyber-defense, and other fields that are thriving. Educating your students to be employable in the local region — especially if you're a college that attracts mostly students *from* your local area — is important. Dr. Torrence said:

> "We look at what we can offer to our students for careers here in our own region, because we believe in blooming where you're planted. I'm a staunch believer that you don't have to go to a Major Metro or a Micro Metro Area to be successful — that you can get the skills that you need right *here*. You can lead where you live, and you can thrive."

That's a nice mindset shift. So many college students (especially those from rural areas) for the past couple of generations have thought that their big "ticket" was to flee to big urban centers (Boston, New York City, Los Angeles, Chicago, etc.) and to leave their families and roots behind to have a successful career. If colleges and universities do better, they can be the reason why people stay where they grew up and why they are able to contribute to the local, regional, or state economy. "Bloom where you're planted," indeed.

No matter how you look at it, higher education has numerous new opportunities to prove its value — to the learners, to the partner organizations, to the employers, and to the community at large. Our ongoing conversation about value kept coming back to how the learning is packaged, and particularly about the value of a degree, these days, versus certificates or other non-degree credentials. Dr. Torrence weighed in by saying:

> "I see the dynamicism between the importance of having a skill as well as having a credential. I don't see them as mutually exclusive. I see them conjoined ... If there's anything that I've learned, it's that after you finish high school, *everything* is post-secondary education. You're learning something every day — most of us are, whether we realize it and put a 'stamp' on it or not. As for short-term credentials (STCs), we have an opportunity — as we're looking at this from the perspective of higher education as an *industry* — to not necessarily *compete* (because, can we take care of everyone anyway?) ... But that's what happens when you have an open marketplace. It's capitalism. An open marketplace that allows for students — or those who are in between jobs or in between skilled employment — to go out and find what they need.

"Now, what we're going to see happen is the expectation — from those who are taking our courses — they're going to walk in and say, 'Well, how long will it take me to complete this?' So, baking in those STCs or short-term credentials on the front end, as *well* as it leading all the way through to an AA or an AS or an AAS or through a transferable pathway. But at the end of the day, doesn't it all lead to a *job*? ... Really, it's about being able to create folks who are going to be gainfully employed who will positively impact their communities."

Bit by bit, our conversations with the 100+ college and university presidents who contributed to this book started to reveal that — while higher education works so hard to be competitive and differentiated — we have a lot more in common than we might think. The practical leadership mindset at Motlow State reminded us of the raison d'être of Foundry College. And reminder after reminder hinged on the common theme that "We're here for the students." Every decision should emanate from that. Dr. Torrence went on to say:

"I think it forces us to look at how we deliver and how we need to look at other models that are out there for the flexible delivery of programs so that we can *keep* students and get them where they need to *go* ... as *quickly* as possible with industry-recognized credentials."

As it turns out, traditional higher education isn't the only sector working hard to "be there" for people seeking an education or some sort of reskilling or upskilling. Now that big players, like Google and Amazon, are starting to offer educational experiences and credentials, it puts us all on watch.

Pivoting to Deliver What Students Want and Need

"The future of higher education will be not as complicated as people may think it is. I think that it will be more *open*. I think people will have the ability to engage at a broader range and it potentially could look like open source — meaning that students can take *whatever* they want from *wherever* they want at a higher clip. And that will be a way for institutions to connect, to provide the credential that learners need. Higher education has an opportunity right now to not *reinvent* itself, but to *evolve* itself.

And it is my hope that all those who are engaged with it are thinking along those lines." These were the parting words of Dr. Michael Torrence, President of Motlow State Community College, as we ended our interview. Evolutions, revolutions, reinventions — we think they're already happening, with more to come. And for the students and future students, the winds of change bring boundless opportunities.

It's not just the institutions that are changing — it's the students and the organizations in which they work. And they all want outcomes. Dr. Tracy Espy, President of Mitchell College, reminded us:

> "Employers are really looking for people who can adapt in any situation. They're looking for people who know how to communicate, people who have strong values and ethics, and who have had some social responsibility."

She told us that a focus on such lifelong skills, including adaptability and resilience, is "giving people the ability to shift and pivot, regardless of circumstance or situation."

If I had to coin a tagline for what it is that forward-looking, enterprising colleges and universities are trying to deliver today, it would be "Outcomes for Everyone." Because an outcomes-focused approach to post-secondary education is what we're all clamoring for. An emphasis on outcomes is not just a passing trend or an industry buzzword — caring about short-term and long-term results helps learners *and* it future-proofs higher-education institutions. It also benefits companies, partner organizations, communities, and economies.

If I had to coin a tagline for what it is that forward-looking, enterprising colleges and universities are trying to deliver today, it would be "Outcomes for Everyone." Because an outcomes-focused approach to post-secondary education is what we're all clamoring for.

It's a tall order and a heavy lift, but hundreds if not thousands of institutions are well on their way. Western Governors University President Scott Pulsipher took us down a thoughtful path when we asked him about this promising future. He said:

> "There are definitely institutions that are realizing that [big change is necessary] if you want to dramatically expand access to high-quality education and improve the outcomes — not just for the privileged, but for everyone — so that everyone's able to achieve at the same rate of attainment and put on that pathway of prosperity. There are definitely forward-thinking institutions saying, 'What we're doing isn't working and we need to find the next level of performance improvement.' And there are others who are in the camp of 'How do I survive to the fall term?' And if it's only, 'How do I survive to the fall term?' then there's not much of a motivation to change.
>
> "We are constantly thinking about 'What are the things that are going to occur (or could occur) that will disrupt our relevancy and efficacy in terms of delivering on the education-to-work opportunity and value proposition?'"

What a great, critical, so-obvious-that-it's-easy-to-miss question! Smart, resilient organizations are thinking about this — about what obstacles lie in the path ahead, and what they can and should do about it. And it's particularly impressive if colleges and universities can be thinking in this way when times are *good* at their institution. Rather than simply patting themselves on the back for being 150 years old or for their exponential enrollment growth, some institutions are focusing on what they can do to *stay* ahead of the curve and be ready for the changes and shifts that the future inevitably holds. The shifts can unmoor an institution if it's not clear on its purpose and its mission, Pulsipher told us:

> "If institutions aren't clear truly about their purpose and mission — and their endeavors to fulfill those purposes and missions — they could get themselves caught in the DMZ of disruption, where they basically get marginalized really quickly.
>
> "So, we're always worried about, 'What are the things that make us irrelevant 20 years from now? And how do we make sure that we continue to innovate on behalf of it?' Because I think if we keep

putting the student at the center of everything that we will do, then we'll be okay."

Strong institutions know — up, down, and across the organization — what outcomes they should deliver. Putting him on the spot, we asked Pulsipher: *"What results are you trying to achieve?"* His immediate, succinct answer? "At WGU, you could describe our primary outcome in four words: a happy, credible, employed, graduate. That's our measure of performance."

Many of the presidents we came to know had such clear senses of focus that articulating it took few words. The laser-focus on crystallized results was a common them amongst many of the presidents we interviewed. Queens University of Charlotte's President Daniel G. Lugo said of their emphasis on career results: "We are intentional, from day one, in getting a great professional outcome."

There are many kinds of outcomes that higher education can deliver for society, and we found it inspiring to engage in conversations about those results — the finish lines that await. Jim Milton, Chairman and CEO of ed-tech trailblazer Anthology, Inc., works with educational institutions of all kinds and, therefore, has a finger on the pulse of what's happening in the industry. He told us:

> "Improved outcomes, generally speaking, has been the focus. And retention and persistence is a key part of that. And the results, by the way — in aggregate across higher education in the United States — are not very good. I think we'd all agree with that assessment. And there's a lot more work that can be done when we talk about a five- or six-year graduation rate for a four-year program or a three- or four-year gradua-tion rate for a two-year program."

Milton's comment was a painful reminder that long programs (i.e., multi-year degree programs) often take even longer than prescribed to complete, which makes for ballooning expenses for students and their families. Everything we do in higher education, if we don't do it well, results in a cost to the learner. So being clear about where the rubber meets the road is essential. Milton said:

"Access, retention, driving outcomes, alignment of skills against the jobs that employers are seeking — these are all areas that we're intensely focused on."

It's no longer enough to let graduates and their employers figure out how to connect the dots between what the employee learned in college and how it plays out at work. John Farrar, Director of Education at Google, told us:

"I believe the time has come for the bridge between outcomes and education provider to be built more overtly."

What will continue to challenge higher education — and to push some institutions to create models that we can't even quite imagine today — is the idea of students or learners coming and going at their own pace, and of institutions of higher education (IHEs) learning to effect handoffs of graduates to workplaces not just once, but over and over again. It's easy to talk about "lifelong learning" but it's going to be hard to actualize. Fortunately, the brightest and most influential minds in the industry are busy thinking about it and starting to move forward. Dr. Tracy Espy, President of Mitchell College, talked to us about a mindset shift from "college as a few years of one's life" to a *lifelong learning* model:

"The future of higher education? It's going to continually be a challenge, but it's also an opportunity to have differences in the marketplace. As institutions in higher education, we're going to have to continually figure out how to adapt to this quickly changing nature of our society and what students want and need in their educational experience. I think that we're going to see a massive shift in the ways in which colleges have traditionally educated our students. I think we're going to see shorter time to degree, with more institutions also being able to provide people with badging and certificates of compliment their degree. I like to think about a move toward lifelong learning — this idea of 'cradle to career' — where our work really starts in the cradle and it continues on until people are into their first, second, or third career. I think we're just going to see a shift to lifelong learning, more and more, as education takes on a different phase than what we've seen before."

> "Our responsibility extends beyond handing you a diploma. Our job is to affect a good handoff of our students to the next chapter of their lives."

Martha Dunagin Saunders, PhD
President, University of West Florida

That new phase is going to challenge the industry to adopt entrepreneurial mindsets and more nimble cultures where people know how to take ideas and offerings to scale quickly. Laura Ipsen, President and CEO of Ellucian, an ed-tech innovator that specializes in delivering agile, scalable, and efficient solutions to higher education, postulates about the future by saying:

> "In terms of what's on the horizon for higher education, I think one of the most powerful things is that we haven't seen the capability to upskill at scale — you know, the future of online degrees and micro-credentialing, which is going to grow off the charts. It's going to go from $20 billion to $117 billion in 2025. We haven't seen the full force of those capabilities and all the institutions taking part of that. What does that mean? That means you're going to enable a world ... that includes cross-registration, so learners are going to know — before you go after a course online — if you're going to be able to get a degree from that, if you're going to be credentialed for it, if you're going to get credit from a job perspective and from your future job.

> "Look at so many tech companies now — Google, Twitter, so many others — that don't even require a degree for employment. So, I think we haven't really seen the power unleashed for upskilling for the jobs of the future and making sure that students get credit for *everything* that they're learning — whether that's a formal course, whether it's an apprenticeship. So, all that mashup is happening. What's been missing is the connection from higher education to the private sector and to the jobs of the future to make sure that we're educating the workforce of the future before the jobs are invented."

To deliver anything at a large scale these days requires the ability to meet students/learners where they are. Because, let's face it, if you can only serve the people who live within a reasonable commute of your campus or who are willing to relocate to your area, your ability to grow will always have an upper limit. When enrollments were high and 18-year-olds were plentiful, it was possible for many colleges and universities to turn a blind eye to online education. The pandemic offered them a glimpse of its possibilities. And now here we are, more enlightened in this regard than ever before.

" What I sense is really stirring in our nation is that education is going to shift from a conveyor of degrees to a talent-development agency mindset. And that's going to be a real win for students. It's going to be a real win for colleges that are able to make that shift. It's actually going to be a real win for employers too. "

Steve Rice

Faculty Member, Northwestern Michigan College

The awakening that the industry has been having — very slowly but very surely at this point — about the need to deliver education in multiple modalities was a topic that came up often in our interviews with our 100+ college and university presidents. Joe, Elvin, and I remember all too well the days when students and colleagues were in a tizzy about online education, insisting that delivering courses anywhere except a traditional brick-and-mortar classroom was somehow diluted or dangerously different. Now, we're finally acknowledging the fact that any delivery method can be excellent and that the outcomes are what matter most. Dr. Nathan Long, President of Saybrook University in Pasadena, California, said it succinctly:

> "If the delivery model is really secondary to the goals and outcomes you're seeking in the course, the model can help actualize those outcomes in really powerful ways."

Of course, there are some types of post-secondary education that simply can't be taught without a face-to-face, hands-on experience, like many of the core programs at San Diego Miramar College, a medium-sized comprehensive community college with deep roots in aviation, military, and police-and-fire training. Their president, Dr. P. Wesley Lundburg, told us about the many areas of excellence for which they are very well known in the region, pointing out that about half of what they do is in the career-and-technical-education (CTE) space:

> "We run the regional police academy here. We have the fire academy, EMT and search-and-rescue, lifeguard school. We have an aviation program that runs airframe mechanic, as well as the ground school for flight school — for piloting. We also have a very large auto tech program."

These practical programs — like all post-secondary education programs — must include an element of flexibility. Steve Rice, who co-hosted our interview with Dr. Lundburg, is a faculty member at Northwestern Michigan University in Traverse City, Michigan, and he said to us: "Students are crying out for flexibility." Dr. Lundburg offered his perspectives on what students need and want, by saying:

> "Mid-range students, older students, are retraining and there's shifts in career during your life. And one of the roles of a community college

is to be there for them. A couple decades ago, we weren't as good at recognizing that and being responsive. We were more reliant on being kind of the old 'junior college' sort of model."

The moment I heard him say "the old junior college," a lightbulb went off for me. Because that's interesting and it's big — the shift from a "junior college" positioning to a "community college" mindset; junior college is about 18- to 24-year-old students who will use their educational experience as a stepping-stone to transfer to another institution; community college is for *everyone*. In talking about all the big evolutions and revolutions underway in higher education right now, Dr. Lundburg said:

> "I've always been a proponent of modularized education, where we should be really focused on student *outcomes* and allowing students to stop in and stop out. I know this is not going to happen until way after my retirement and death, but that'll be the next great change."

Perhaps it won't take as long as Dr. Lundberg suggests. Big tech and employers are dabbling in the business of educating their workforce outside of the environment of higher education. The pressure on institutions to maintain a healthy pipeline of students for long-term financial sustainability may bring the next great change to higher education sooner than we all think. One of the most fascinating parts of the growth of *The EdUp Experience Podcast* has been a realization that many individuals from business and industry are listening to find out what higher-education leaders are saying and doing. So, is there a "model change" for higher education that is achievable now? When we asked Dr. Lundburg, here's what he shared:

> "I don't think we've found it yet. I mean, nothing's changed for so long. I think it's been well-documented that [higher education] is really based on an industrial-age model of an assembly line, you know, and if you think of the Carnegie model — three credits for an average of three hours in class per week, and it makes all kinds of assumptions. You know, my place in the classroom was as English faculty. And one thing I noticed was that students who were truly going to improve tended to have a decline in their performance toward the end of the semester, which means that if you're going to hold them to that old grading model, their grade would go down rather than up. So, I always

had a safety net in place. If I see that you're making an attempt to change and you're experimenting to improve, your grade is not going to hurt. I'm going to protect you from that. So, you know, be bold, make changes, do things that are risky. And that was kind of an early recognition in my career of the truth — that old model just doesn't work very well. It's a cookie cutter. It's an assembly line.

"So much has to change before we can adopt a truly new model. We've got union environments that are concerned about compensation and how that's handled, and if you have students popping in and popping out, how do you do that? How do you build a relationship with a student to help them grow and learn if you only see them for a few weeks out of your semester? And do we even *have* semesters or is it something different than that? Do we have learning environments and learning labs rather than traditional classrooms as we move away from the 'sage on the stage' and more toward the 'guide on the side' model? What does that look like?"

Leaders are asking great questions. *The EdUp Experience Podcast* became — almost by accident but in a powerful and organic way — the megaphone for asking these questions to an industry that is, finally, listening. It's not just the students (or the alumni, donors, or other "customers") who are crying out for change — the staff, faculty, and administrators are clamoring for something new as well. But are most colleges and universities courageous enough to be innovators, or disruptors, or even early *adopters* of new models? We all yearn for it, dream about it, wish for it. But when are we going to *create* it?

Important Work Ahead

Whether we're thinking about the work of higher education as a powerful one-time experience or a "lifelong learning" commitment (or both), it behooves us to take time each day for what I call "a moment on the mission" — to remember who we're here to serve and what our decisions mean for learners and their families. Don Kilburn, CEO of University of Massachusetts Online (UMass Online), articulated this perfectly when he said:

"I'm cognizant of how important this work is. I've talked to people who say, 'Look, if I get this degree, I get a promotion. And if I get a promotion, then I can do X for my kids.' And, you know, you hear enough of those stories, and you take the time to understand those stories, and you realize how important the work is and how important it is that we take responsibility for success as educators — and that we actually do *everything possible* to make sure that happens."

My incomparable and brilliant co-author, Dr. Joe Sallustio, built upon Kilburn's thoughts by saying:

"That's a dissonance. Sometimes I feel like, in higher ed, we are an industry that traditionally has looked at itself — the industry of higher education — as somehow not being about students at all. We were serving some *other* stakeholder besides the student — it was faculty, or it was research projects (and those things still happen). But I think the student is taking more center stage now. With the student at center stage, now it's about servicing the students — it's about providing for the student and it's about the institution being there when the student *needs* them to be there. That's one of the evolutions we are fumbling and bumbling through in higher ed — how do we make sure we're there when the student is ready for this education? How do we stay in front-of-mind for that potential student over time and balance that with the student who we need right *now*?"

Kilburn challenged us to get nostalgic about our own college experiences, and then consider what could have been better — and how we can deliver on a *better* promise for the students of today and tomorrow. He reminisced:

"When I graduated, you got a liberal arts degree and you kind of 'figured it out,' you know. And I think for certain student populations, the luxury of 'figuring it out' eventually isn't their reality. It's like, 'No, I need to figure it out *today*.'"

Today's academic leaders have a unique opportunity to create something better than what they had when *they* were students. Kilburn is just one of thousands of higher-education leaders who was offered little direction or opportunity or even agency at the start of his college experience. Dr. Philomena Mantella, President of Grand Valley State University in

Allendale, Michigan, shared a powerful story about gender and college advising that worked out well for her, but likely put countless learners on the wrong initial paths. She shared:

> "I was a woman of the late '70s. I went to school and I didn't consider a wide range of careers. Really, you went to your guidance counselor, and they said, 'Oh, you're college bound. You're a woman. Are you thinking of teaching, social work, or nursing?' And I didn't like blood and I didn't want to be in classrooms. So, I picked social work — but that was about how well-informed my early college path was. But it turned out to be a great opportunity for me, because one of the things about that particular field — social work — is that it does help both individuals *and* it's got a frame on community and society and it's really a systems-thinking approach. And so, it really worked well for me. Through that journey — with experiential learning and finding out what populations I enjoyed and where I wanted to be — I've found college students and vulnerable college populations as where my career started."

We all have stories like this — about how we stumbled into our college majors or became "accidental marketers" (I resemble that example) or lucked out when our paths came into clear view. But many of us meandered for a bit or had to make course corrections along the way, and far too many people find themselves at mid-career, needing access to education in various forms so they can begin new careers or level up or get reskilled in some way. The higher-education industry is beginning to understand this great need. And we're — finally — beginning to abandon that age-old "just figure it out" mindset in which we were supported (or not supported) when we were choosing majors or schools or careers.

Kilburn, whose institution recently acquired Brandman University (now known as University of Massachusetts Global) led his team through a massive "putting our money where our mouth is" initiative to marry their traditional roots at University of Massachusetts with a private online university in California that focuses on working adults — primarily on degree completers (i.e., people who have "some college, no degree"). Of UMass Global, he told us:

"Its primary focus is to increase access to education for those working adults who had difficulties completing their degree. Our basic goal is to help people advance their lives through education, get better jobs, and advance their family's lives."

We couldn't help but notice that UMass in now bicoastal (Massachusetts and California), which strikes us as a very smart strategic move. There are many, many "smart, strategic" moves being made across the higher-education industry right now, and a tidal wave of them headed for us in the very near future.

We asked Dr. David Stout, President of Brookdale Community College in Lincroft, New Jersey, to talk to us about the future of higher education, and he said:

"The future of higher education? What we're going to *need* to be doing — and this is an uncomfortable thing, I think, for most traditional faculty members — is starting to look at education as an experience that is spread across the [student or learner's] lifespan, but can be broken up into several smaller, digestible formats. We're going to need to allow for students to be able to enter into the educational experience, go back out into the workforce, and come back to us throughout a longer period of time. And that might mean that we take a course and we carve it up into modules, allow students to be able to come in and experience the module, and get a badge. Then rack up their badges into certificates, and even rack up their certificates into degrees. But whatever is the most valuable for that *student* at that *time*. But I think I can hear what, from the faculty perspective, some would be thinking: 'We don't want to dilute the value of education.' The value, though, is *beyond* just the workforce development aspects; [a modularized college education] *does* help to improve people's lives — their ability to think critically and things like that. So that's the challenge: How to deliver that content in a more digestible format that allows for people to move in and out of work but also retains the value of the overall experience of higher education."

Dr. Stout is absolutely correct — many institutions are struggling to figure out how to create and deliver non-degree programs that are meaningful, in-demand, and that consistently generate the intended outcomes.

During a conversation, with Dr. Anthony Cruz, President of Miami Dade College's Hialeah and Kendall Campuses, *Commencement* co-author Dr. Joe Sallustio got down to brass tacks on some of the discomfort that the industry is feeling about certificate programs, saying:

> "The certificate market is really blurry. It's like the wild west out there with the certificates. You get everybody and their brother offering a certificate — everybody *outside* of higher education. You can go find a *coach* for some coaching and leadership training and they have a 'certificate' offering. It's like everybody on LinkedIn's a coach or a leadership trainer these days. And they offer a non-credit certificate in Leadership 101, that's supposedly 'going to make you 10x what you make today!' I get those like 40 times a day, these messages of how these people in their online courses are going to change my life."

And perhaps that's what has got some higher-education professionals feeling uneasy about the certificate market — because some fly-by-night organizations are aggressively selling "certificates" and other so-called credentials without the kind of credible backing, thoughtful curriculum development, and outstanding instruction you would expect at a college or university. In short, what makes the realm of non-degree education so blurry — and what makes many education experts skeptical — is that, for the first time in our lifetimes, business firms and individuals are competing head-to-head with colleges and universities. Everyone offers a "certificate."

What makes the realm of non-degree education so blurry — and what makes many education experts skeptical — is that, for the first time in our lifetimes, business firms and individuals are competing head-to-head with colleges and universities. Everyone offers a "certificate."

Institutions of higher education are accustomed to long relationships with their stakeholders — two to four years, or even much longer. So, there's always been time to nurture those relationships and even to let the learner's path reveal itself slowly and organically over time. But with shorter credentials and learning experiences that are measured in months or even weeks, the relationship — and its goals and destinations — need to be clear from the start. We need to help learners understand the pathways in front of them when they choose to start with a certificate. Dr. Cruz at Miami Dade College addressed that issue for us, saying:

> "When we talk to students who are interested in a certificate program (particularly if it's a credit-bearing certificate), one of the things that we start off with is really talking about how they're stackable — showing them that pathway from where they are today (which may be that four-credit certificate) all the way through either to an associate's degree or even a bachelor's degree. And I think that students need to have that clarity at the beginning."

The Beginning and the End

So much of what we do in colleges and universities around the world focuses on beginnings and ends — matriculating into a program, starting or finishing an academic term, surviving finals week, crossing finish lines (in terms of a service-learning project or a thesis or "comps" or a dissertation), transferring to the next program or step, and — of course, receiving a degree or certificate credential. There's a reason we titled this book *Commencement*; starting and ending big initiatives, programs, and even personal relationships is what higher education does best. But even that — the way we "start and end" in higher education — deserves our scrutiny.

I recall a moment on *The EdUp Experience Podcast* when one of us called out an "old-school" mindset and practice that needs revision — industry-wide. We were reminded that, in the past (and, to a significant extent, still now), going to college was all about getting a degree, and if you left without a degree, you were a failure. Think about the language we use for students who take a break or who decide to end their educational pursuits before their college or university considers them to be done: We call them "drop outs." We talk about *graduation* rates as "success" and people who are infinitely more well-educated after having take some courses with us as "failures" if they don't walk away in the end with the pretty piece of paper.

During the past few years, I've been arguing (politely but passionately!) with one of my higher-education clients over a practice that I found unconscionable (and strategically and financially short-sighted). This college admitted to me — quite casually — that a former vice president of advancement had purged former students from their alumni database if those former students didn't leave with the fancy piece of paper in hand. In their mind, if you didn't "graduate," you're not an alumnus. Mind you, some of these former students who were scrubbed from the mailing list and never again engaged by the institution were individuals who:

- Had spent $30,000 or more on tuition and room-and-board.

- Had lived on campus and were involved socially and academically to a great degree.

- Were now successful and even renowned experts.

- Had grown up to have the luxuries of time and money to come back or otherwise support the school.

- Absolutely *love* the school and regard all their memories fondly.

- Miss the institution and don't understand why they're not being engaged.

- Stopped out without petitioning for graduation, usually because of extenuating circumstances beyond their control (e.g., financial limitations, illness, family emergency, job relocation).

Treating people who need to or want to stop out (forever or for a while) like "drop-outs" is a huge mistake. It's *human* to need a break, and the pandemic has illustrated how acute our mental health is to our overall well-being and ability to stay focused. Things happen, particularly for adult learners with responsibilities far beyond rolling out of bed and dragging themselves to class. Life happens. It's key for all of us to remember what a privilege it is for a student who has the support and resources to complete a degree without obstacles. The student is, more than ever, forcing the redesign of what institutions expect.

This idea of learners being able to "stop in and stop out" is a huge piece of higher education's future. A decade ago, Coursera arrived on the scene and promised its students that they could "Learn Without Limits." Udemy promised learners around the world that they would "be able." And the rest is history.

Don Kilburn of UMass Online talked to us candidly about the growing demand from the marketplace for higher education to let learners set the pace for how they stop in and stop out, and whether there should be embedded credentials or certificates inside degree programs. He told us:

> "We have this notion in higher education that there's a four-year degree or a two-year degree. And for many students who are what we consider 'degree completers,' they have spent maybe three months, four months working in a degree program, then life got in the way, and they didn't get through. So how do we begin to create competencies and shorter things within that educational degree that will allow somebody, if they have to drop, to still get a better job? I sometimes have been accused of making things too simplistic, but I frequently think that, for certain populations, if we got a person an interview, a job, or a promotion that they otherwise wouldn't have gotten, that's a pretty good measure of success for many. Because education *does* change a trajectory — for not just individuals, but families. So, I have also been thinking a lot about: 'How do we get milestones or gates along the path that actually allow somebody to achieve something that would be recognized as important going forward?'"

Kilburn reminds us that the degree is not everything — that what matters is social and economic mobility ... and that doesn't always require a degree. So here we are, contemplating the many ways in which higher education can (and does) demonstrate its value and meet its mission — in new ways for new learners in a new era. The moment we step back to consider post-secondary education as more than a path to a pretty piece of paper, we can clearly see where we have been and where we are headed. Alas, higher education — for hundreds of years — has been a one-trick pony. "We offer associate's degrees" or "We offer bachelor's degrees" (in different majors and flavors and formats) or "Come here for your juris doctor" or "We can give you a medical degree." The marketing has all sounded alike because the *products* were all alike. We have peddled degrees — typically in rigid two-year and four-year formats and delivered on campus for big sums of money and only to young people who don't have partners, children, jobs, or mortgages — for centuries. Conferring degrees was our only business. Higher education is a time-honored tradition; but traditions change.

So, here we are, in the 2020s, and the world (and the prospective learner) has changed. We can no longer sell them the same experience or product that we sold to their grandparents. And the good news is that many institutions don't want to; they have fully embraced the many evolutions and revolutions taking place in higher education and, already, what they're offering looks nothing like your mama's college story. Higher education is more adaptable than ever. As we all continue to expand our offerings — our menu of options for a broad range of stakeholders — we begin to "meet students where they are"[7] by providing the kind of practical education that fits their needs, careers, budgets, lives, and families.

I'll close this chapter with some wisdom I learned from an Uber driver who was (believe it or not!) excited to hear that I was visiting his city because I was conducting focus groups with prospective college students. He had nieces and nephews who were eyebrow-deep in the college choice, and he told *me* what he told *them*:

> "Selecting a college (or having them select you) is not a *prize* to be *won*; it's a *match* to be *made*."

And if that's true — and I think it is — the power dynamic shifts 180 degrees. With students no longer ingratiating themselves in admissions essays and praying to "get in," higher education is called upon to *serve* in a way that it never has before.[8] And the possibilities are endless.

---

7   Beyond a buzzword, "meeting students where they are" was perhaps the most commonly uttered phrase — totally unaided by the interviewers — during the conversations with 100+ college and university presidents. So keep reading; Chapters 3 and 4 dive deep into nuances of serving those students ... where they are, who they are, and how they are.

8   Wondering whether we'll discuss the idea of "student as customer?" Don't mind if we do! Stick around for (or jump ahead to) Chapter 4: The People Imperative.

" The blueprint for higher education is anchored in the blueprint for America. What will our economy look like? What skills will be required? How will we train, upskill, and retrain workers to function in a new economy? **"**

Sandra J. Doran, JD

President, Bay Path University

CHAPTER 3

WHERE DID ALL THE STUDENTS GO?

Redefining Programs and Preferences for a Changing Demographic

I n an industry where one of the biggest criticisms from its primary stakeholders is "I don't want to go to a school where I'm *just a number*," we have always been relentlessly focused on — you guessed it — the numbers. We count them all:

- → Inquiries
- → Applications
- → Admissions interviews
- → Attendance at tours and open houses
- → Acceptances
- → Packaged
- → Commitments
- → Yield rate

- ➤ Matriculations

- ➤ Melt

- ➤ Drops

- ➤ Headcount

- ➤ Retentions

- ➤ Returns

- ➤ Net tuition revenue

- ➤ Completers.

We *do* genuinely care about the students, in all their messy and beautiful humanity, but what matters — in the end — are "the numbers." The numbers are what keep the lights on ... what funds faculty and staff salaries, and what allows a college or university to offer new programs and supports.[9]

When I was the marketing director at a private graduate business school, we met weekly to review "the numbers" so that the entire admissions and marketing teams could — despite our best intentions — reduce the learners to buckets of data: to applications (not, interestingly, ever expressed as "applicants"), acceptances, RSVPs to "MBA Previews" (open-house events that, during my tenure, had a 50% chance of turning an attendee into an enrolled student), acceptances, and commitments. And, in the places where I have worked, there was a glaring disconnect between the efforts of recruitment and retention. I remember admissions managers working their tails off to convince busy working adults to take two MBA courses at a time (rather than the customary one course per term) only to find out that the business-office manager was telling students to "slow down" and maximize their employer tuition reimbursement by graduating in three or four years instead of two. And nowhere in those weekly "numbers meetings" were we talking about how much

---

9 Of course, there are those lucky few institutions whose endowments — and not just their tuition income — helps keep the lights on. And still, a burgeoning freshman class matters to them too. Being a "going enterprise" is the only way to keep fundraising. All that is to say that, arguably, everyone in higher education cares about enrollment/admissions numbers. Some of us lose *sleep* over the numbers ... and others, not so much.

tuition revenue we were losing when students slowed down or stopped out. It was all churn and burn to attract "the best and the brightest" ... and then to attract and win some more.

Not until Dr. Joe Sallustio and I sat down to write this book did I realize that 100% of the market research I conduct for colleges and universities comes down to those numbers — the surveys, focus groups, and interviews I conduct are all seeking to illuminate the stories and secrets behind an individual institution's ability to attract more applicants, how to use parents as retention partners, and how to engage alumni (so they'll refer more applications and be more generous philanthropically). It's all about the money flowing through the funnels and pipelines. (Yes, even for the schools that don't struggle to get *enough* applicants.) For every dozen or so institutions that must fight for each inquiry and application is a fortunately positioned institution that attracts, for example, 7,000 applicants for 200 available first-year seats. And guess what? Those schools care about driving up the numbers too; because their prestige comes, in large part, in being able to brag about how selective they are. In higher education, "selective" is code for "We turn away a lot of people and crush a lot of dreams."

Economics 101

At nearly every institution of higher education, the largest source of revenue is tuition income. Institutions are classified as tuition-dependent if the majority of their revenue comes from the tuition source, which is why schools work very hard to diversify revenue streams. Ultimately, the bills get paid by the students. And in those same institutions, the largest expense is human resources — the salaries, wages, benefits, and support expenses for faculty, staff, administrators, and consultants. While the students fill the coffers, the higher-education workforce empties them. And, in recent decades, this formula has worked well.

Yet a constellation of demographic and cultural crises are converging to upend this established cycle of "money in and money out," putting the higher-education industry on a potential collision course toward painful change that hurts the very people we care about the most: the students and the employees. You see, it's an impossible and vicious cycle when a drop in student population requires a decrease in human resources.

When and if enrollment rebounds, there may not be adequate staff and faculty to support bigger classes again. Getting this balance wrong — one way or the other — could lead to financial and operational disaster. One of the ways institutions are futureproofing against the see-saw of supply and demand is through technology. Using technology to enhance — and at times replace — some of the human resources does not come without significant consideration and conversation.

At one college, where I serve as a consultant, two dozen tenured faculty members were recently fired due to a lack of program demand. With savvy, practical students choosing majors that will make them employable upon graduation (STEM fields, healthcare programs, business marketing, etc.), many institutions simply can't justify — at least not on the balance sheet — an entire department for the Classics or for Art History or for Anthropology, Criminal Justice, or Creative Writing. I remember feeling surprised by the news at my client institution — saddened for those faculty members and for the students and alumni who love them — and simultaneously recognizing that we can't keep investing in programs that aren't (by quantitative, financial measures) succeeding. Program relevance has never been more important.

> **Reflection Question:** *Does your institution have one or more programs or entire departments that lack the demand to justify their existence? How much is it costing you to say and do nothing?*

We can't keep investing in programs that aren't (by quantitative, financial measures) succeeding. Program relevance has never been more important.

📝 Pop Quiz!

Where Did All the Students Go?

This book is being released in late 2022, as higher education seeks to recover from the bruises of the pandemic and as it hurtles toward stark demographic realities about a dwindling number of prospective college students — particularly those who are younger than 24 and are seeking a coming-of-age, traditional college experience. Some institutions have already seen their enrollments drop by 5-10% and others expect the losses to exceed 15% by 2025. The solutions, perhaps, lie in understanding the problem in a truly nuanced way.

So, we must ask ourselves: **"Where did all the students go?"** *Choose all that apply.*

❏ **They were never born.** With the Great Recession of 2007-2009 in the United States, millions of children who would have been 16-18 years old and headed off to college in 2025-2027 simply were not born. And the declining birth rate was not just a one-year blip. Since 2007, the birth rate has fallen precipitously, with no rebound in site. As of 2020, the birth rate in the United States had fallen 20%.[10]

❏ **They're part of the pandemic "lost generation."** When students or would-be students were forced to stay home to stay safe during the onset of the COVID-19 pandemic, a trend began that might be irreversible. Millions of young adults who would have otherwise enrolled at a college or university — in nearly every country in the world — simply did not. They had bills to pay, serious health issues to contend with, and family to care for. Some of the pandemic "lost generation" are now part of the workforce — without the benefit of a higher-education credential — and yet others are caretakers or coping with chronic illness as Long COVID becomes a crisis unto

---

10 Melissa Kearney, Phillip Levine, and Luke Pardue, "The Mystery of the U.S. Declining Birth Rate," EconoFact, February 15, 2022, https://econofact.org/the-mystery-of-the-declining-u-s-birth-rate.

itself. For far too many, going to college was, and is, a luxury that they can no longer afford (financially and logistically).

❑ **They're taking a "gap year" that's not pandemic-related.** There have always been high-school graduates who take some time off between high school and college. They take jobs at local restaurants and other shift-work places of employment. If they have the financial means, they travel. They spend time "finding themselves," which doesn't always mean finding their way to a college campus. And with remote work, students might be turning gap *year* into gap *years!*

❑ **They're training for the trades through union apprenticeship programs.** In the past decade, the number of people becoming apprentices — in professions like welding, electrical, HVAC, and plumbing — have increased by 64%.[11] Individuals getting such training typically bypass classroom experiences entirely.

❑ **They're earning their credentials from non-collegiate sources.** They're taking classes on Coursera and Udemy, and they're earning short-term credentials from Google Career Certificates or other providers.

❑ **They're trying their hands at entrepreneurship.** They're betting big on their own big ideas and are starting businesses — or working for start-ups — thanks to Kickstarter, Patreon, and private investors. There's an entire generation of young adults who look at success stories like Michael Dell, Mark Zuckerberg, Steve Jobs, and Jack Dorsey (none of whom completed a college degree before founding some of the world's largest corporations), and they think: "Why not me?"

❑ **They're firmly and happily working in the gig economy or the citizen salesforce.** With or without a college credential, there's a lot of money to be made — with flexible schedules and balanced lifestyles — by working in the gig economy for companies like Uber,

---

11 Preston Cooper, "Apprenticeships Have Risen 64% Since 2010. How Should Policymakers Support Them?," *Forbes*, May 7, 2021, https://www.forbes.com/sites/prestoncooper2/2021/05/07/apprenticeships-have-risen-64-since-2010-how-should-policymakers-support-them/.

Lyft, Instacart, DoorDash, GrubHub, Task Rabbit, and others, or in the citizen salesforce through direct-sales roles with multilevel marketing companies (MLMs), selling cosmetics, home goods, fashion, and more.

❑ **They're content creators and masters of making money on social media.** Passive income is all the rage. And why would a young adult "influencer" — someone who can make more than their parents by posting makeup tutorials or comedy/entertainment content to platforms like Instagram, Facebook, TikTok, Twitch, and YouTube — take a career break to invest in expensive tuition for a career that pays less than what advertisers and "collabs" (i.e., collaborators and paid sponsors) are forking over to them for their viral videos?[12]

❑ **They're freelancing their ways into flexible, "portfolio" careers.** Many potential collegegoers (in every age group, including mid-career professionals who might otherwise have chosen a program at a college or university to help them "upskill" or "reskill") are creating their own lines of business by partnering with established brands — like those who are selling insurance for Humana or getting trained as financial advisors with Merrill Lynch — and yet others are putting their handyman skills and natural "people skills" to use by getting into professions like real estate (as realtors, house flippers, and AirBNB hosts).

❑ **ALL OF THE ABOVE** (*Hint!* Check this box.)

---

12 At the beginning of the pandemic, our go-to photographer, Daniel LaBelle, was attracting clients from across the U.S. and beyond ... because nobody took better headshots or wedding photos than he did. (The headshot of me that appears on CommencementTheBook.com was taken by Daniel!) But lo and behold, Daniel is now a TikTok star — a social-media sensation whose videos rack up millions of views and are paying the mortgage. I recently asked him to travel to photograph a business-celebrity client of mine and he politely explained that there was no amount of money I could pay him that would make him say "yes." In 2022, I can't lure back my lost subcontractors and partners, so how in the world do colleges and universities lure back their lost students?

Welcome to the 2020s, Where "Traditional" is Nontraditional

Spoiler alert: The colleges and universities that — during their interviews with *The EdUp Experience Podcast* — did *not* express concern about "the numbers" when it came to their enrollment outlook were:

1. Institutions that serve (primarily or exclusively) the working-adult population.

2. Perceived elite institutions with guaranteed legacy enrollments.

3. Those that have bet big on non-degree programs and other short-term credentials.

Everyone else was talking about serving new learners at new junctures in their lives, and doing it in new, innovative ways. And it should be said that, while no one was completely dismissing the acute challenges of a changing demographic for higher education, everyone was talking excitedly about the *opportunities.*

During his interview with Dr. David Stout, President of Brookdale Community College in Middletown, New Jersey, *Commencement* co-author Dr. Joe Sallustio asked:

> "*Traditionally,* community colleges have played a key role in higher education, but we are not going to be in a *traditional* time anymore. There are going to be more students looking at gap years and interruptions in their education — perhaps not looking at going away to school in a four-year, traditional-university format as they have in the past. And so there's this opening for community colleges to play a more prominent role in educating people — whether it's through a skills-based training or a degree-based education — to people who maybe they wouldn't have reached before. Do you see that as a big opportunity?"

Dr. Stout, whose institution is ranked in the top 3% of community colleges in the nation, said:

> "There's no doubt. And we're seeing that right now. We have students — who might not otherwise have considered community colleges

— who are starting to at least ask questions, if not actually beginning the application process. They're beginning to engage with us. We are expecting to have a more substantial increase in our enrollment in the fall[13] than what we were previously expecting ... We have small class sizes so that the students will really get that supportive one-on-one care from a faculty member who knows their name. (Unlike what happens in many of these gigantic research universities, where there are 700 students packed into a seminar hall.) We have these advantages already with our smaller class sizes, even when the technologies *aren't* in place. We have highly engaged faculty members who know that they want to work one-on-one with students — who want to provide that support. So those are absolutely advantages.

"I think one other thing that we have as a major advantage on the community-college side is that most of our community colleges are comprehensive community colleges, meaning that we focus a lot on workforce development. And we focus on transferable pathways for people to get bachelor's degrees and beyond. So, most community colleges have built some sort of pathway system between their non-credit side of workforce development and their credit side of providing certificate programs and degrees. So, people who may not have been thinking about coming back to school — who may have been financially affected by this devastating pandemic — they may be looking to pivot in their careers. They can get an assessment done on their work that they've completed and how that might be able to convert into credits. They can come through the pathway of the non-credit division for workforce. And they may be able to get credits toward a degree where they may not have ever been *thinking* about that before, and now they have the need to do that."

Students who are still sure they need to go to college to earn a degree are signaling to the marketplace that they *need* to graduate in a reasonable timeframe. Suddenly, everyone seems to understand that life is short, and that time is money. Dr. Irma Becerra, President of Marymount University

---

13 Dr. Stout was interviewed during the summer of 2020, when the pandemic was at its peak and many institutions were seeing declines in fall enrollment.

in Arlington, Virginia, takes her responsibility of meeting the needs of students exceedingly seriously and personally, telling us:

> "This is a student-centered learning community that values diversity and focuses on the education of the whole person — this whole idea of a personalized education where we really focus on getting our students to success.
>
> "I have made a personal commitment that *every* student that comes to Marymount: We will do everything on our part to see that that student who is studying for their bachelor's degree will graduate in four years or less. That's a big commitment on our side — a big commitment. Because we need students who enter college to *graduate* from college.
>
> "I don't know if you've heard this, but when I went to college — and it's been quite a long time — I remember clearly hearing from the university president on the first week in college: 'Look to the right, look to the left. Only one of you will graduate from college.' And so, essentially, the president was saying 'Our graduation rate will be 30% ... only one of three will make it.'"

Dr. Becerra wasn't sure if we'd heard that awful expression — what amounts to a threat to students who are hoping to earn a degree if they put in the work. And sadly, yes, we've heard it far too often. I heard it at the beginning of my MA program, along with descriptors of our degree program as "cut-throat" — and I'm a bit embarrassed to admit that I was young and impressionable enough at the time to have been proud of it. My classmates and I thought that *we* had what it took, and we were looking around the room wondering who the 60-70% were who wouldn't make it to graduation (those poor suckers). Stories about higher-education leaders giving this cliché speech really remind us how this kind of selectivity and ruthlessness has dominated higher education in the past. We heard this same story from many of the presidents interviewed on the podcast, or versions of it. But it's time for something different. The workforce needs trained/educated people. We should *want* them to be successful — to learn, to complete the programs they've begun, and to receive the credentials they seek. A higher-education industry in which we commit ourselves to help learners achieve is *not* an industry that awards free passes or welcomes diploma mills. It's an industry in which we hold

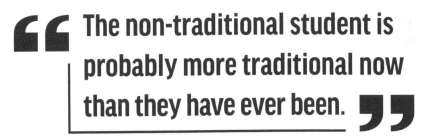

" The non-traditional student is probably more traditional now than they have ever been. "

Nathan Long, EdD
President of Saybrook University

ourselves accountable for being student-supportive institutions that — when the student does their part — helps ensure student success.

Student success and student services, which we'll talk about in greater detail in Chapter 4: The People Imperative, becomes increasingly critical in an era in which we're looking around and asking, "Where did all the students go?" When students are scarce, we can scarcely afford to lose even a small percentage of them.

 ## Making Education Your Business with Dr. Joe Sallustio

"What's All the Fuss About? We Have Plenty of Students!"

Is this resonating with you — all this talk of scarcity and lost or missing students? Maybe you are saying to yourself, "This isn't us. We just had a record enrollment at my university this past fall of 2022."

Any sentence that includes a statement about "this fall" screams traditional education. Large online mega-universities enrolled students the month before, the month of, and the month after "this fall." Anyway, back to my point.

Supply-and-demand elasticity during and immediately following a pandemic that kept people away from each other for multiple years is not surprising. The high-school student who didn't see classmates their junior and senior year was on a mission to go to college and have an experience. Working learners who spent a few years balancing a work-from-home situation with kids learning on Zoom were downright ecstatic to invest in themselves. Honestly, does the rebound in enrollment across colleges and universities in 2022 and 2023 surprise you? There are even institutions with CARES Act funds that bridged their financial gaps created from multiple years of lost students and retention issues. For some schools, everything is just fine right now. So now the question that should be resonating with you: *What happens next?*

Whether you have students in abundance or a shortage of students, they must be our relentless focus (not just counting them but serving them). We spoke to Dr. Arthur Keiser, Chancellor and CEO of Keiser University (with more than 20 campuses around the world and its flagship campus in West Palm Beach, Florida), about meeting the needs of today's students by being truly student *focused*. It was the late summer of 2020 and colleges across the world were still living through a global pandemic in a pre-vaccine world. Dr. Keiser told us about how they systematized "checking in" with their students in a truly powerful, personalized way:

> "If a faculty member calls [a student] when they're out (which we *require*), it shows the students we care and that gives them the strength to overcome the obstacles that they face. Because most of our students are adult learners. Most of our students have children: 64% have dependents, and 48% have a spouse. So consequently, they have challenges in their lives. Eighty-three percent of our students work. So not only do they balance work and balance family and balance the time and money, of course, they have to go to school — and *we* have to make it worthwhile for them.

> "And that's why we make policies that work for them. The one class at a time that we teach — rather than five classes or four classes at a time … the working adult can't deal with that. So, we do one course a month, four courses a semester, and we have courses all year round because summer vacations do not mean a whole lot. You know, the 'summer off' doesn't mean a whole lot to an adult learner who wants to get out of school as quickly as possible. Our programs and our policies have been designed to meet the students' needs, not necessarily the faculty or the administration needs."

One of the challenges that we face as an industry whose "traditional" student population is dwindling is finding ways to not only attract and serve new segments of learners, but also to do so with objective quality. Dr. Keiser is the chairperson of the board at the National Advisory Committee on Institutional Quality and Integrity (NACIQI), and like most college and university presidents, he's committed to maintaining and improving quality at every turn. As new segments of learners emerge, we'll be serving them in different ways — none of which are likely to be cheap.

When asked about the future of higher education and the students it will serve many years from now, Dr. Keiser said:

> "I think you will still have the need for those traditional campuses with traditional activities. However, I think you'll see the adult market is going to gravitate more to the online experience; the adult market has lots of responsibilities. And the one thing they will find, though, is the reality that online is not cheaper than on-campus."

Choosing Who to Serve, and Then Serving Them Well

Whatever you call it — the demographic cliff or the enrollment cliff or the admissions cliff, it's, well ... a cliff. Our collective numbers of enrolled college students the world over are beginning to fall off that cliff, and it's imperative that we don't also jump off the ledge, following those numbers to the bottom. Richard L. Dunsworth, JD, President of the University of the Ozarks in Clarksville, Arkansas, shared an inspiring and candid take on the looming cliff:

> "As we think about the demographic cliff that is coming at us in a few years and as we think about enrollment challenges, we've all wondered, 'How do all these schools *survive*, let alone *thrive*?' I think there's room for each of us if we get crystal clear about who we serve. And we must allow our mission to drive us. Sometimes cool new markets are great, but maybe some of us need to say 'no' to cool new markets and really *serve* the students we serve ... and do it as well as we can possibly do it."

It stands to reason that some institutions will absolutely need to go after those "cool new markets" in order stabilize, let alone grow or thrive. So, let's take a quick look at what those markets look like with — you guessed it — another Pop Quiz!

▤⃫ Pop Quiz!

Learner Populations of the 2020s and Beyond

If "traditional undergraduates" (i.e., individuals who begin college shortly after high-school graduation and remain in college until they are no older than 23) decrease by 15% in the near future, where can institutions of higher education (IHEs) make up for those losses? By serving:

❏ **Working adults who have some college, no degree** (i.e., "degree completers").

❏ **Learners of all ages who are seeking certificates or other short-term credentials**, who can be served on an open-enrollment basis or through corporate-education relationships between their employer and your institution.

❏ **More graduate students**. While graduate-degree programs sometime represent a smaller portion of an institution's enrollment than their undergraduate-degree programs, many institutions might thrive by turning more attention to recruiting and serving learners seeking master's and doctoral degrees.

❏ **Retirees or senior professionals** seeking encore-career upskilling and reskilling, or cultural and general-interest learning opportunities.

❏ **Employed executives** looking for rich experiences and expanded professional networks.

❏ **High-school students** who can engage with their local college campus or an online college program through dual enrollment.

❏ **Transfer students** who are unhappy at another institution and are ready to go elsewhere.

❏ **Incarcerated individuals** (nearly 2 million adults in the United States, the vast majority of whom will be released at some point and will join the workforce, in need of skills).

❏ **All of the above.**

No matter how you cut it, most presidents of colleges and universities are recognizing that a shrinking population of fresh-out-of-high-school students will have a notable impact on their organizations. As such, we heard a lot of thoughts from higher-education chief executives about how program delivery modalities expand the possibility of serving more audiences. Dr. Melik Peter Khoury, President of Unity College in New Gloucester, Maine, talked about this opportunity, saying:

> "Our new hybrid model says to prospective students: 'If you want to design an experience that mirrors the four-year traditional model of old, have at it. If you are a place-bound adult who really needs some outcomes-based learning to get a real degree, but you can't quit your job and move halfway across the country and just don't want the generic degree, we are here for *you* ... and for everybody else in between.'"

Whether a student is seeking an on-campus or online experience, and a degree or non-degree program, there are distinct sets of students within each of the larger categories. One of those subsets that gets a lot of attention of late are "first-generation students" or "first-in-the-family students" — those who are trailblazing through a college education without the benefit of parents who can show them the way. Dr. Joseph R. Marbach, President of Georgian Court University in Lakewood, New Jersey, told us that first-generation students from modest socioeconomic backgrounds — those who are receiving Pell grants and are the first in their families to go to college — are "a population that is both at risk and one that is buying into the American dream." He explained that:

> "These are students who understand that education is the way to not only prosperity and happiness and success, but to a better *life*, not only for the individuals themselves, but for their families."

In many ways, this is the challenge of the "Where did all the students go?" era in which we live: There are many student and learner groups needing and deserving to learn, but the groups who might benefit most from higher education — while they believe in the dream and sometimes even in themselves — don't always know the way and are often not even making themselves known to the institutions that would love to welcome them. These students and higher-education institutions often can't find one another. Dr. Marbach also spoke to gender equity, reminding us that Georgian Court was originally founded as a women's college and remained a women-only college for 105 years before becoming co-educational. To this day, empowering women is core to their mission. He said:

> "We want to show women that they can be empowered, and that education is the first step in doing that so they can not only *compete* in the world but can *win* in the world as well."

Throughout this book, we have several opportunities to talk about "silver linings" to difficult moments in recent history (and still at play right now or on the horizon). We explore how the COVID-19 pandemic revealed the higher-education industry's potential and we're struck by the way the enrollment cliff is already inspiring academic leaders to fully see unseen populations of learners so we can collectively step up and serve them. Dr. Marbach said it best when he said:

> "Education is the new Ellis Island. It's the new success story for Americans. It's the key to not only economic success, but personal enrichment and happiness."

The Ellis Island analogy is apt because it reminds us that higher education is about dreams and opportunities and a brighter future. When we spoke with Dr. Claudia V. Schrader, President of Kingsborough Community College at The City University of New York (CUNY) in Brooklyn, New York, she told us that those *student* dreams are *her* dreams, remarking that:

> "The future of higher education is bright. I say that not from thinking about a policy or a fiscal perspective. I'm thinking about the kind of young men and women who I encounter. We're raising a different generation of students; they're bright, they're inquisitive, they're quick, they're smart. They are ahead of the curve with technology. They're going to be the future *faculty* — the future leaders — and their kids are going to be the future students. Higher education is going to be a force to be reckoned with. These are the same students who have been in the streets, protesting social injustices. They're going to be the ones to lead our institutions in the future. The future is very bright."

We walked away from hearing Dr. Schrader's prediction feeling inspired and thinking "She's right." Today's students are tomorrow's higher-education workforce — the thought-leaders and the visionaries who will build upon what we're crafting today, believing in the continual evolutions and revolutions of the industry. We can't help but think that Dr. Marbach at Georgian Court University would concur, as his motivation is the students and what *they* are capable of. He told us:

> "Our vision is to empower students to transform the world, making it a more just and compassionate place."

Fitting the College Experience into Already Full Lives

As institutions of higher learning seize the opportunity to serve students who are 24+, the challenges will be many. A decent portion of today's college and university leadership teams were themselves educated when college was the only thing on their "to-do" list — when they were taking classes full time, living on campus, and free from the responsibilities of families or jobs. It was "all homework, all the time" (well, not *all* the time ... there were football games and frat parties and student clubs). Today's higher-education decision-makers can invariably relate now to the complex lives of adult students, but they rarely have a frame of reference for having juggled it all at once. Dr. Frank J. Dooley, Chancellor of Purdue University Global (based in West Lafayette, Indiana), told us how his institution thinks about flexibility for busy students. He said:

> "As an online institution of working adults, one of the things that we find for our students is that *sometimes life gets in the way*. And by that, I mean something could have come up at work. Something could be health related. And so, we're fairly liberal on our policy for withdrawals, with the notion, you know, 'Come back to us in six or seven weeks when life is going to work for you again.'"

I nearly wept with validation upon hearing those words. I was once a student for whom "life got in the way." And when an appeal all the way to the president's office during my own undergraduate experience got me nowhere in terms of compassion for my situation (a medical diagnosis in the middle of an academic term, and a need to have urgent surgery), I was forced to remain in classes and on campus in terrible pain for another seven weeks because my family could not afford for me to withdraw and pay to repeat the courses after my surgery. I put my college ahead of my health because there was no "medical leave of absence" policy to help me; it was an impossible situation and one in which I, as a student, had no control. Today, students have so much more control and garner so much more respect. Time and time again, as Joe and I conducted the research and participated in the conversations for this book, we discovered that higher education is so much more thoughtful, strategic, compassionate, impactful, and student-centered than it was when we cracked open our first college textbooks. For all the ways in which the 100+ presidents told us that the future is bright, I can't help but observe that even the *present* is a lot brighter than our past. The higher-education industry is evolving to serve students better than before.

Leaders at institutions of all kinds are talking candidly about — and developing new policies and processes around — gap years and breaks. Dr. Stephen Spinelli, Jr., President of Babson College in Wellesley, Massachusetts, told us:

> "I think understanding goes a long way in this and colleges and universities need to be very understanding. 'You need to take some time off? You need to take a lower course load? You need to come back in a year?' We've got to make this easy for you to do that, or as easy as possible for you to do that, and then open our arms and welcome people back and stay connected with them while they're away. It's not, you know, 'Goodbye and we'll see you in a year.' It's 'Can we check in? Can we have Student Life interface in this period that you're away so that you feel connected to what's happening?' And we need to ask ourselves if there are ways to make those connections more human."

How does your institution operationalize on such a promise? Does your admissions team have dedicated staff who oversee a sort of "win-back program" through which lapsed students are contacted and nurtured back into the fold? I worked for one institution that hired (as contractors) our own former admissions professionals — those who knew our school and our admissions requirements well, and who had left employment with us when they took a career break to raise family or to attend to other priorities. They understood, as well as anyone, that "life happens" and they were able to connect with lapsed students and bring many of them back. Truly savvy institutions will develop or maintain such a program in an *ongoing* manner, not just when they are desperate for tuition dollars. Frankly, *all* students who step away deserve to be nurtured, remembered, and communicated with — if those students have responded in the affirmative when asked whether they'd like the relationship with the college or university to continue. Busy people who have had a "college interrupted" experience often still hope to come back and are just looking for life to ease up — or for their college to find ways to make a return more flexible and achievable.

 EdUp with Elvin

Practical Tips and Frontline Insights from Elvin Freytes

Here's the thing about helping students who have taken a "pause" — aka Leave of Absence (LOA) — and who then come back to hit "play" and continue their studies: You need to have real-time and accurate data to make that work!

Having this type of information can even help you *prevent* students from pausing in the first place. If you use predictive analysis, your college or university can offer and provide services and resources to students before they need to pause.

If retail giant Target could figure out that a young woman was pregnant before her own parents knew it (based on a change in her buying behaviors — thanks to pregnancy-related health needs and cravings),[14] why couldn't an institution of higher ed figure out that a student needs a certain type of intervention at a specific time to lessen the likelihood of needing to put their studies on pause?

---

14 Sean Kernan, "Target Knows You're Pregnant Before Anyone Else — And It's Making Them Billions," *Better Marketing*, January 11, 2021, https://bettermarketing. pub/target-knows-youre-pregnant-before-anyone-else-and-it-s-making-them-billions-7c4972a9bfab.

Obviously, it might take a massive amount of data points for a platform to perform this type of function — but with students' permission and today's technology, that is definitely possible. So instead of focusing on how to get lapsed students back, let's focus more on how to help them not pause in the first place.

So how do we do that? Here's how:

1. **Gather as much data as possible about your students before they enroll.** A big key here is capturing information about who's in their support system. Make notes about emotionally and financially supportive family and friends (who, it should be understood, are also potential referral leads).

2. **During the first class of every course, focus on building a community of learners by developing webs of connections.** Make sure each student has at least one other student with whom they can connect on a social-emotional and learning-style basis. (Institutions that use cohort-based models have a leg up in this regard.)

3. **Inspire students to create accountability groups** that help hold each student accountable for being engaged in the course content.

4. **Ask students to give you permission to collect data during their enrollment.** There are many key data points to note regarding a student's academic and non-academic journey — all of which might help you serve them better and prevent them from struggling or taking a leave of absence.

5. **Train staff and faculty to input quantitative and qualitative data in a tracking system.** Ensure they know how to do this on a timely basis. Healthcare delivery has learned to do real-time documentation, and higher education can and should follow in those footsteps.

6. **Review student data trends on a daily basis** to spot the "potential pause" students.

7. **Reach out to these students** using various methods, explain the trend you're seeing, and find out if your concerns are warranted and how you can help.

8. **Work together with the students and their support team** to develop a detailed and time-sensitive plan of action to avoid the pause.

9. **Continuously follow up until the potential pause is cleared up** and measures are put in place to avoid a *future* potential pause (and make sure everything is documented).

10. **Remember the universal wisdom I have taught you:** No matter what you do to prevent students from pausing, don't call any of it a "committee!"

As we think about populations of students who are incredibly busy or committed to non-college endeavors, there is perhaps no other community more "committed" than those who are enlisted in the armed forces. And yet, there are higher-education opportunities even for this audience. Dr. Dooley shared that Purdue University Global has a program with the Army, through which new recruits can earn an associate's degree during their first two years in uniform, with half of their credits coming from the Army training they're already receiving and the other half coming from coursework with the university. He suggests, in fact, that the future of higher education might involve many colleges and universities wrapping their programs around the training that students are getting elsewhere (in the military, on the job, etc.). In this way, the university program becomes the wrapper or adjuvant to the primary activity, which is the job or the military training.

Older learners, working learners, lifelong learners — the presidents interviewed for this book told us that *they* are the future. Dr. David Finegold, President of Chatham University in Pittsburgh, Pennsylvania, said:

"I think the future of higher education is going to be informed by an intersection of several forces, like the huge growth in online education and the opportunity to serve older learners. We've invested heavily in online education, and we see that as a huge part of the future, particularly for older learners — people who are returning to education and juggling education with work. I'm a huge believer in thinking about education over the whole lifespan. As we're seeing people living 30 to 40 more years after they so-called 'retired,' there's going to be a huge future around thinking about 'How do we tap their full potential over that lifespan?'"

Dr. Finegold was one of several leaders whose word choices made us sit up and take notice. I continually observed that expansive thinkers and open-minded leaders are talking about "learners" instead of "students" and sometimes "post-secondary education" instead of "higher education." The opportunity to learn life skills and job skills after leaving high school is more likely to be embraced by diverse groups of people if the industry itself becomes more inclusive in its language.

Expansive thinkers and open-minded leaders are talking about "learners" instead of "students" and sometimes "post-secondary education" instead of "higher education." The opportunity to learn life skills and job skills after leaving high school is more likely to be embraced by diverse groups of people if the industry itself becomes more inclusive in its language.

> **Reflection Question:** *What comes to mind when you hear the word "learner" in place of "student?" If you think of 18-year-olds with backpacks when you use the word "student," isn't it possible that prospective students do too — and that a simple word choice is keeping adult, working learners from feeling welcomed at your institution?*

Making Education Your Business with Dr. Joe Sallustio

Choose Your Words Wisely: Language and Higher Education

Kate has asked us to think about word choices: learners instead of students, or post-secondary education instead of higher education. And isn't language everything?

On EdUp, I've frequently pontificated that there is incredible parity from institution to institution when it comes to "quality." Is the quality of a degree at one regionally accredited institution that much better than the quality of degree at another regionally accredited institution? Both degrees and institutions meet their respective standards — so what are the real differentiators? It all comes back to language and the way an institution communicates to their potential consumer. What is the true value proposition? Can you say it in a way that captures the hearts and minds of prospective students? And can those word choices turn your high-quality degree into something that seems more desirable in the mind of your target student than the *other* high-quality degrees they might be considering? Language can be powerful.

It can also be outdated. Think about outdated (in my opinion) language like "for-profit" and "nonprofit." How did an institution's tax status begin meaning something (or confusing matters) for stakeholders? Because people coined phrases and repeated them enough. Remember "essential-worker" designations from the pandemic? The CDC defined essential workers as "workers who are essential to maintain critical infrastructure and continue critical services and functions." Many vocational, trade, and career colleges train essential workers. It's easy to turn up our academic noses at the "for-profits" until we need HVAC units, aviation maintenance, medical assistant care, or automotive repairs (just to name a few). Community colleges are now expanding programming to educate in the trades, competing head-to-head with career colleges. "For-profit" and "nonprofit" are suddenly indistinguishable, as they should be. Because they all produce "essential" workers. Language changed the game.

Language can also change a culture — across an entire college or university or at least in the department where you work. Take, for example, a word with which you are all familiar: *melt*. Melt is a word that is intended to describe the number of students graduating high school that melt away during the summer before beginning college. The term has expanded beyond its original intent and many institutions use it to describe any student who doesn't start on time at any point in their educational journey. Melt is a passive term to describe retention efforts. Personally, I use "cancel." Cancel, to me, captures the student's active intent not to attend or continue at a university. And if they canceled, *why* did they cancel? What could the institution have done *better*? Higher education, in general, must look at shifting our language from passive to active if we're going to truly see our responsibility for the results we bear and if we're going to step up and *act* to improve the outcomes.

What other passive language do you use in your institution?

Up until now in this book, it has been assumed that the stakeholders in the higher-education industry all have, at the least, a high-school diploma. But what of millions of people in the United States who have become adults and never finished their high-school studies? We were fortunate enough to speak with Frank Britt, then CEO of Penn Foster Education Group based in Scranton, Pennsylvania.[15] He told us:

> "High school is one of these areas of our economy that gets so little attention. And yet with even a modest amount of expansion of thinking, [it's an area that] could be so profound. You have about 30 million Americans in the United States today who have aged out of high school and do not have a high-school degree. And if you were

---

15 After his interview for this book and before the book's publication, Frank Britt left Penn Foster to become the Executive Vice President, Chief Strategy and Transformation Officer at Starbucks Corporation.

asked to recommend a high school for a 25-year-old who didn't finish high school — for a variety of good reasons, medical and otherwise — it's difficult to even identify where you might propose they go. And that's even amongst people who are 'education people.' If you ask an ordinary person in a company, they'd have no idea. We believe that those 30 million Americans deserve a chance."

More than once in the pages of *Commencement*, you'll see us talking about the ROI that college graduates experience — the increase in career earnings made possible by having a college credential. And yet, we had not thought about the career-earnings potential for those who are given a second chance at finishing high school. Britt told us:

"The greatest increase in wage gains you can gain is going from 'no high school' to 'high school.'"

This is a huge opportunity not just for organizations like Penn Foster, which already operates a thriving high school for adult learners, but for all accredited colleges and universities. As the traditional-age undergrad student demographic becomes too thin, higher education should perhaps be looking to these 30 million Americans as a pipeline. If Penn Foster and others can get these learners to that first milestone, how might *you* take them further?

Britt helped us to put all the learning opportunities that aren't a bachelor's degree into a category of educational services called simply "the workforce development economy," saying:

"We think this workforce development economy that includes high school, micro-credentials, career diplomas, and associate's degrees — that's the place you're going to see a tremendous amount of innovation going forward."

From Prestige to Purposeful: Rethinking Elitism in a Changing World

For every college or university on earth, there is a shared and articulated sense of who you serve and how you serve them. And conversely, whether you'd ever say it out loud or not, it's understood at your institution that "We don't serve *those* students." Maybe it's students with a GPA or a standardized test score below an ambitious threshold that your academic leaders have set. Maybe it's local kids or international students or people who want to take a light courseload and don't care much about a pretty piece of paper at the end of the learning odyssey. No matter who you think you serve and what percentage of inquiries or applications you turn away, the headwinds are beginning to beat back those sometimes-arbitrary rules about selectivity. Dr. Hal L. Higdon, Chancellor of Ozarks Technical Community College System and President of OTCC Springfield Campus in Springfield, Missouri, told us that demographers predict that the admissions cliff will hit Missouri in 2026, just four years after the publication of this book. And he shared that:

> "We're already seeing the public and private universities who used to be highly selective are now simply selective. Those that were selective are becoming moderately selective. The previously moderately selective are basically becoming open admission."

ACT and SAT requirements are being dropped, and students who couldn't have gotten into a particular university five years ago can get in now. Colleges and universities are becoming more inclusive because too few of them can afford to remain exclusive; there simply aren't enough students to fill the classrooms and dorm rooms if they want to fill them with students who look like last decade's student body. Society is changing, and higher education is responding and adapting, even if begrudgingly.

Ask anyone in higher education, and they'll tell you that they need and want more students. But can they *define* those emerging categories of students, and do they know how to *find* them? Dr. Bill Pepicello, Former President of University of Phoenix (based in Phoenix, Arizona, and with a massive online presence), helped us think about student profiles and marketing. Reflecting on the early days of University of Phoenix's story, during its first 30 years of rapid growth and innovation in offering degree programs in a nearly fully open-enrollment fashion, Dr. Pepicello told us:

> "When Arizona State or Ohio State or any large university does their marketing, they already know who their student is. They have a profile of that student. And so, they know exactly how to market. At University of Phoenix, we were marketing to people who had no idea that education

was accessible to them. They were first-generation (or no-generation) students, at-risk students, and students who were not wealthy and didn't realize that there was an opportunity for them. So now what traditional institutions are faced with is the truth that there are students out there who don't know that they can access higher education at name-brand institutions online. So, number one, those institutions need to let people know they have an online presence, and, number two, they need to understand that marketing online is going to attract a different kind of student than they might have been used to attracting."

 Making Education Your Business with Dr. Joe Sallustio

Re-engineering Your Recruiting Efforts for the New Students You Seek

That point needs to be restated. "Understand that marketing online is going to attract a different kind of student than they might have been used to attracting." And, for those schools looking to expand through online education, attracting a different kind of student means creating and maintaining the appropriate infrastructure. More important than infrastructure is the appropriate mindset. Have you ever heard a staff or faculty member say something like the following? "We're used to serving *our* students, not those students." You know, *those* students — the harder-to-serve students, the ones who need more nudging, reminders, writing services, technology support, etc. The students who expect someone to answer the phone at 11:00 p.m. when they're doing their homework and have a question. You know who they are.

Those students just happen to also be students who represent a market that could save an institution because they come with employer tuition assistance, military benefits, and potential partnerships. Simply put, when you cast a wider net, you'll catch more fish. Are you going to throw the fish back or find a way to keep them all? (Yeah, yeah, yeah — students aren't fish, but you get the point.)

Dr. Pepicello hits the nail on the head by calling out the holy grail of "already knowing who your student is." Recruiting and retaining the types of students you've attracted and chosen to serve in the past is probably "old hat" to you. You know how to market to them. Your admissions team knows how to talk to them. Your student services teams know how to support and serve them. Your faculty know how to teach them. But as we collectively look around and observe our physical and virtual classrooms becoming less full, we must step into the unknown — to boldly go where we've perhaps never gone before. If you're good at working with traditional-age students, there's a lot to learn about the adult-student market. If you've always had a business-to-consumer (B2C) approach to recruiting individual learners, there's a lot to consider if you decide to bet big on a business-to-business (B2B) approach of building meaningful programs for the employees of large corporations. This is your time to flex, grow, and be nimble.

This is precisely what we talked about with Dr. John R. Porter, President of Lindenwood University in St. Charles, Missouri. One of his institution's top-six new initiatives as of the publication of this book in fall of 2022 is micro-credentials, and this builds upon Lindenwood's strengths in traditional degree-program delivery. When asked to speak about the value that today's learners place on the opportunities available to them through an institution like his, Dr. Porter said:

> "It comes down to two words: Discipline. Knowledge. So, I think a student coming to our university or to any university — talk about discipline! It's one thing to have discipline in high school. It's a different thing to have discipline in the college ranks, where the expectations are much higher. The rigor is much harder. I think this is an opportunity; hopefully, during your four years here, you're going to learn what discipline's all about: *how* to study, *when* to study, how *much* to study. And people have different intellectual levels and so some require more, some less. But I think that discipline is — when it comes to the value of a college degree — second to none. The other piece is the knowledge. Hopefully you walk away from a degree program with a lot of knowledge. Even though we're a liberal-arts college, we've got the life sciences, you got biology, you got ecology, you got the neurosciences, you got logic, mathematics, philosophy, the physical sciences, like physics, chemistry, geography. So, you're going

to be a well-rounded person. What better situation than to take the discipline that you've achieved and the knowledge that you've learned to those *employers* out there? So, I think there's always going to be a model for higher education.

"Now, second to that is the opportunity for micro-credentials. There is a market out there for what I call 'hit-and-run' learning for the student who says 'I just want to learn something quickly and then I want to run. I want to go and get my job.' Now think about skills gaps in corporations. Some employees have degrees, some don't have degrees, but the skills gap may still be there. How does a micro-credential fill that gap? An employer comes to us and says, 'Listen, here's where we'll give you the IP (intellectual property). We need you to build the infrastructure to give this to our employees.' Micro-credentials are going to do that for us. So, we're not trying to just look at the four-year degree, but we also want that continuing education.

"Incidentally, those credentials can be stackable. We just signed agreements with two companies that are going to really catapult us to that next level. These are one-year certifications and once these folks are certified, that's going to give them greater employment opportunities. It's not a four-year degree. However, they can probably plug that in and *earn* a four-year degree based on credit hours they've received for the certification. So, I think we're looking at it both ways, but it all boils down to *discipline* and *knowledge*."

Not only are academic leaders looking at the types of educational offerings they provide (e.g., degrees, certificates) and the modalities with which they deliver them (e.g., on-campus, online, hybrid), but they are looking at the *content* of those programs in fresh ways. And the admissions cliff — combined with the myriad after-effects of the pandemic — is driving that introspection and strategic curriculum planning. Dr. Michael A. Cioce, President of Rowan College at Burlington County in Mount Laurel, New Jersey, was the first president to use the phrase "lost generation" when we spoke to him. He said:

"We've all seen the numbers and they're quite scary when you look at this *lost generation* that opted to not enroll anywhere in the fall of 2020."

In looking just at the high-school Class of 2020, who received diplomas in the spring or summer of 2020, we saw that their college enrollment the next fall dropped by 6.8% over previous high-school classes, quadrupling the declines seen prior to the pandemic.[16] Dr. Cioce offered sound and pointed advice about how to respond to these serious changes, saying:

> "It is imperative that colleges and universities do serious deep dives on their program viability. You better be offering programs that lead to employment (or lead to transfer that *then* leads to employment) because otherwise we're all going to be dealing with a serious reckoning. There's already too many colleges and universities on my coast. And there's not — from a long-term birth projection — enough of the traditional 18-year-olds (this year and next year and the year after) who will support the sort of physical campuses that have been built over the past two decades.

> "So, if you are not seriously looking at the adult population or the underemployed adult population, you're going to have programs that have to be sunsetted. And then when you layer in all the bad things that higher ed has done over the past 25 years, there's going to be a lot of broken hearts and upset people — because we built things in the late 1990s and the early 2000s that are no longer needed."

As we forge ahead, endeavoring to be more purpose-driven with what we offer and how we operate in a changing world, it will be important not just to do things differently, but to do things that are *Meaningfully Different*™ (a term we use every day at my company). Because, while we know that modern learners want something different — more flexible, more bite-sized, more practical, more tailored, and more personalized — it behooves us to remember that these learners don't know how to *consume* the new, innovative offerings coming out of higher education right now. We must teach them how to navigate the new higher-education landscape. So, while hundreds of universities are jumping on the certificate-programs bandwagon, Dr. Thomas R. Bailey, President of Teachers College at Columbia University in New York, New York,

---

16 Dalia Faheid, "Fewer Students in Class of 2020 Went Straight to College," *EducationWeek*, April 6, 2021, https://www.edweek.org/teaching-learning/fewer-students-in-class-of-2020-went-straight-to-college/2021/04.

reminded us that not all certificates are created equally, not all "stacking plans" make sense, and very few students will understand how to leverage this opportunity. We asked Dr. Bailey for his take on certificates, and he started by saying, "Many of them aren't worth that much." As for how to stack them or use them as an alternative to a degree program, he said:

> "It's a lot to ask of students to ask them to put together a series of certificates that will eventually lead them to a kind of a coherent outcome … If you're employed in a job and something comes up and you need to learn a skill to do something, I think going to get a certificate or a non-credit instruction is useful. But if you're talking about certificates as a basic educational strategy, I think that's a different question."

Dr. Bailey went on to tell us about some research he did about the concept of "stackable credentials." In short, undergraduate students don't know how to "stack" certificates and create a pathway that adds up to something useful. He explained:

> "With stackable certificates or stackable credentials, the idea is that you get a credential now, then you can go out and work, and then you come *back* and you add to that. And we did research that showed that that's not a very common process to actually happen. We need to have a strong path for students — that they're helped to understand the skills that they get and how they can accumulate those skills in a coherent manner. I think it's difficult for students to do that on their own. And then if you really want to put certificates together, then I think that has to be organized in a way that helps students do that. One thing we found in community colleges is that students often got lost. Even when they were in a regular institution, they get lost. So, I think it's a lot to ask of them to put together a series of certificates that will eventually lead them to a kind of coherent outcome."

He makes an excellent point. Very few college students have been taught — by their high-school teachers and guidance counselors or by their family members — how to navigate the college experience: how to choose courses and register for them, and how to build one experience atop another. Fewer still will understand how to collect multiple credentials — degrees, certificates, or both — in a manner that serves them well and that means something to current or future employers. To be honest, most people within higher education don't understand it either. So, what can colleges and universities learn about their prospective students and the inner circles (e.g., coworkers, teachers, and family members) that influence the learners' perceptions, desires, and behaviors? This was a topic that came into clear focus when we were talking to Dr. Carlos Peñaloza, Chancellor of Leeward Community College — part of the University of Hawai'i Community Colleges in Pearl City, Hawaii. He talked to us about cultural considerations for institutional strategy and making higher education attractive and doable. He told us that:

> "Being culturally sensitive means involving families a little bit more in what we do than we would typically in the *continental* U.S. and there are practices that have really been quite successful. Something to know about communities like our native Hawaiian population, as well as Pacific Islanders and Filipinos, is that there is a huge tendency for being in a familiar environment — very tight-knit families and multi-generational homes. And so, to get to a student to commit to coming to higher ed (instead of maybe getting a job to support their families) can be quite difficult. And so, we have to find that balance. Whether it's finding major financial resources to cover their cost for attendance or working with opportunities where they have apprenticeship-style opportunities — where they're coming through the educational pipeline while getting some money — or even employing them on campus has been a major contributor to us having this large population on our Leeward campus.

> "The new mechanism that we're trying to build out for establishing pipelines is family enrollment — trying to get siblings or even multiple generations coming and signing up for college because they thrive more as a family. And everyone can benefit from the education."

Family enrollment! Picture me, listening to Dr. Peñaloza and having my mind absolutely blown. Because, honestly, I could not love this concept more than I do. Many moons ago, my brother and I were students at the same community college at the same time. I think I had a cousin there too, all three of us there at the same time. But no one was savvy enough to try to recruit us together. And because I come from what I lovingly sometimes describe as "my big, fat Irish family," I had relatives aplenty living in the same county, all of us with some degree of need for traditional education, upskilling, or reskilling. Asking one of us to talk about our family or to bring a relative to the first admissions meeting would have been such a smart strategy. This works at the graduate-degree level as well, where it's not unusual for spouses to both pursue an MBA together or for one to tackle a master's degree in computer science while the other finishes a PhD in English.

The trick is, of course, finding people in the right moment or mindset to even think that college is for *them* ... or that it's for them *right now*. Dr. Peñaloza reminded us that there is a prevailing perception by some people that they aren't college-bound — that they aren't "college material" or that they can't possibly do this. He said:

> "I think that there is a level of fear with higher education that shouldn't be there. And then, we in education unintentionally set out barriers that reinforce that feeling from the communities. We put out these pretty difficult applications for them to complete and we ask them to get together documents that probably don't even exist within their families. And so, the minute that they stumble into something like that, that's the minute that they feel, 'Okay, this is not for me — at the very least, not right now.' And so, if we could just focus a little bit more in reducing some of those barriers and doing good outreach and connecting with them in a nurturing way, we can show them that they *are* college bound."

This discussion reminded us that the little things are the big things. If people can't figure out how to complete the application, it's like running a college with no front door or a business with no cash register. To identify these barriers (and then to fix them), Dr. Peñaloza secret shops the various processes at his institution — including their application — periodically. Even the "What ethnicity are you?" question often has options/answers that don't fit for every applicant. And what's a prospective student to do when they hit a brick wall during the application process and when they don't have the name and phone number for a trusted individual who can help them overcome that hurdle? They give up.

Making Education Your Business with Dr. Joe Sallustio

How Student-Friendly Are You, Really? Getting Smart About Smart Phones and Higher Education

To put the reality of barriers into perspective (and to raise a point about processes you should be "secret shopping" at your institution), think about the important things you do on your phone.

➜ Do you check your bank account information on your phone? And, if you want, can you do important tasks, such as transfer money between accounts?

➜ Could you run a leading higher-education podcast from your phone, including all editing and graphic design? (Spoiler: The answer to this is YES!)

➜ Can you order lunch or a coffee, pay for it, and have it delivered just from using your phone?

➜ Can you book a flight, pay for it, choose your seats, and share your itinerary from your phone?

➜ Could you check your email, log into a meeting, and operate as if you were in the office — all from your phone?

➜ **Can you apply for admission, complete all paperwork, register for courses, and check your grades — all from your phone?**

You get the point. Today's students expect to do the majority of their tasks on their phone, and it's not just "traditional students," if that's what you were thinking. We literally can run our lives, right from our devices — and higher education is one of the industries that needs to catch up to this growing trend. Now, don't get me wrong, some institutions do things very well. Exceptionally, even. But too many are way behind in making their educational experience mobile-accessible and mobile-friendly. Never forget that it's part of the value proposition if a student can receive swift service from your college or university, without running into barriers. *Value*!

From "Comprehensive Colleges" to "Big Niches" and Everything in Between

For as long as most of us can remember, college students were a homogeneous group — fresh out of high school, invariably starry-eyed and full of angst, as impressionable as wet concrete, and so disinterested in the "real world" that awaited them in the next few years that you'd think that the world was their oyster and that they'd been raised to believe that anything is possible. They all carried heavy backpacks or messenger bags, dressed to blend in with the crowd, dated and partied with abandon, and took copious notes in spiral-bound notebooks that they bought at the campus bookstore. Their classes were taken during the day (hopefully not at 8:00 a.m.!), their part-time jobs were secondary to their schooling, and their closest relationships were with friends and parents (not with spouses or children).

In those old days, it was easy for a community college or a liberal-arts college or a public university to call itself "comprehensive" — which was code for "We offer lots of majors and a couple different levels of degrees, and we have a vocational or workforce-development division too." And we offered that so-called comprehensive experience to just one group of young people who were seeking a coming-of-age experience straight out of high school. If someone had asked us about diversity, we would have raised an eyebrow in confusion. And if we found out that one of our classmates was in her 30s, we thought it was quirky but cool — and we treated her like a mom instead of a peer. The "adult student" in decades past was branded a "nontraditional student" ... and any time you're labeled "ex" or "non," it's clear that you exist outside the norm in a way that's permissible but not desired.[17]

---

17 This paradox reminds me of my visceral reaction to the term "adjunct" instructor or professor. I've been a part-time or "contract" faculty member at several institutions and they all use the word "adjunct" to describe the capable, competent, qualified, and hard-working educators who aren't on the tenure track or receiving healthcare insurance and other fringe benefits. And because the definition of the word "adjunct" is basically "connected but not essential," I've always despised the term. Some institutions have more course sections taught by adjuncts than by employed faculty members; and yet, they still use a term that literally means "you're not essential."

" **The fact of the matter is there's just less students looking at college. And the new 'traditional student' is the adult student.** "

Joe Sallustio, EdD

Senior Vice President, Lindenwood
Global & University Strategic Enrollment
Management, Lindenwood University

Making Education Your Business with Dr. Joe Sallustio

Learning While Earning:
The Importance of Working Learners

"Working learners" is a category of learners that has emerged — and for some institutions, come to the forefront — over the past 20 years. For-profit institutions of the 2000s decided to serve this market of students in a way that nonprofit colleges and universities couldn't (or didn't want to). Free from state funding, faculty tenure, and slow shared governance, the for-profit colleges and universities leveraged speed, retention, and career services.

Still today, many institutions are just beginning to turn their attention to working learners, despite how long they have warranted our attention. One of the earliest references to "working learners" came from the Center for American Progress in a report by Louis Soares in June of 2009. In the report, Soares writes:

> "The increasingly dynamic labor market that all Americans face is further complicating the educational prospects of working Americans, and it is particularly challenging for those without college credentials. First, there are a dizzying array of college credentials — from occupational certificates to associate's to bachelor's degrees — that are either required for jobs or simply necessary to get a job that pays a decent wage and benefits. Second, with long-term jobs in large companies a thing of [the] past, workers are moving in and out of new jobs more often with little notion of how to get ahead.

> "What's more, our postsecondary education system of two- and four-year colleges is ill-equipped to address the needs of those who have already begun their working lives. In particular, the system is poorly designed to deal with the fact that, for most of these individuals, advancing their

education will mean juggling work and learning over much of their working lives. These 'working learners' face a college and university system designed for students entering a course of higher learning at a young age and completing a degree or other credential after a fixed, continuous period of education.

"Working learners can't do that. They are older, independent students who attend school in non-traditional ways, are less likely to apply for financial aid, get less financial assistance when they do apply, and are less likely to complete any kind of degree within six years. They are also more likely to drop out because they are trying to do all this while earning a living for themselves and their families. That's no mean feat, especially in a college environment designed for young, full-time students."[18]

More than a decade later, we are having this same conversation within higher education. Changing our language from "non-traditional" student to "working learner" helps to eliminate stigmas associated with serving a market that simply needs different types of resources. A college or university must be willing to serve this market — a market that now includes more than 39 million students with some college and no degree. Simply put, there is a different mindset and infrastructure needed to serve working learners.

But today, college and university classrooms can have a student age range of 17 to 77, and what Jim Milton, Chairman and CEO of Anthology, Inc., told us is undeniably true: "The new student has become what we formally called a nontraditional student."

One leader who knows the "traditional" student well is Dr. Summer McGee, President of Salem Academy and College in Winston-Salem,

18 Louis Soares, *Working Learners: Educating Our Entire Workforce for Success in the 21st Century*, Center for American Progress, June 2009, http://cdn.americanprogress.org/wp-content/uploads/issues/2009/06/pdf/working_learners.pdf.

North Carolina. Unlike most college presidents, Dr. McGee also oversees a boarding and day school of high-school girls. And while she's accustomed to serving stakeholders as young as 13, she's as committed as the rest of the industry to serving *college* students throughout their lives. She told us:

> "I think where we have to go in higher education is to find learners wherever they are, but also to be able to tell a clear story and a narrative about who we are as an institution and to really transform and to focus in a really *meaningful* way. And so, I think we're going to see more of that across the small, private, liberal-arts-institution space, but we *all* — whether we're larger or small — have to continue to meet and find those learners, those students, wherever they are, and to provide access and educational support and resources to meet them *wherever* they are on their educational journey. I think the institutions that master that across a whole range of lifelong learners will be those who are successful."

Dr. McGee was speaking my language here. Have a story; know how to tell it; be meaningfully different; put your stakeholders first in all that you do.

Some of the institutions that do a remarkable job of being student-centric and having a unique story that guides their operations are those colleges and universities that were founded long ago to serve distinct audiences with powerful missions — like Historically Black Colleges and Universities (HBCUs) and institutions that were founded to empower women. We had the opportunity to interview several HBCU presidents on *The EdUp Experience Podcast* and found their stories to be particularly insightful and instructive. HBCUs serve a niche but change the world. Dr. Wayne A. I. Frederick, President of Howard University in Washington, DC, told us:

> "Every time somebody poses the question to me about whether or not HBCUs are relevant, I tell them that the issue is not about relevancy, but it's about *excellence*. It's about: How can we ensure that these institutions are thriving because of how necessary they are to the fabric of America's success? And that is underscored by the fact that HBCUs represent only 3% of higher-ed institutions, but are responsible for about 22% of the bachelor's degrees that are awarded to African Americans. And then when you look in STEM disciplines; about 34%

of the African Americans who receive STEM degrees went to HBCUs. And institutions like Howard send more African Americans to medical school than anybody else in the country. We've graduated more black physicians than anyone else in the country. And over the past couple of decades, we've sent more African-American STEM PhDs into the marketplace than Stanford, MIT, Harvard, and Yale combined."

Let that sink in for a moment. Maybe your institution is small, or maybe it serves a niche audience, or maybe there's only a few other institutions like yours. When that's the case, it's easy to think you're a "small player" in the overall higher-education space or that while you might change a community that maybe you can't change the nation or the world. Dr. Frederick spoke to this, telling us:

"HBCUs represent 3% of the higher-ed institutions in the country. Yet still, we punch well above our weight. We are responsible for one in five African Americans getting their bachelor's degrees. And then look at other levels — at Harvard's MBA program over the past 50 years, for example. The number-one supplier of African Americans to that program (from their undergrad campus) was Harvard itself; and number two was Howard University."

How do we, as an industry, look at these success stories and commit ourselves to expanding upon them? How might we create a new crop of colleges to expand the HBCU mission (and the Hispanic-Serving Institutions, and women's colleges, and other institutions with meaningful niche focus)?

One leader who has a lot of perspective and a powerful vision when it comes to the populations most in need of and deserving of higher education's attention today is Dr. Anthony Cruz, President of Miami Dade College's Hialeah and Kendall Campuses in Florida. His Hialeah campus makeup is 95% Hispanic, and his institution does all their marketing and communications bilingually. While some might think of a Hispanic-Serving Institution (HSI) as serving a niche audience, the truth is that the Latinx audience represents the future growth opportunities for many colleges and universities in the United States.

Dr. Cruz told us that it's important to him to get into the community "in places where college is a mystery." He explained:

> "Our role as Latino leaders is to really show students (and their parents) that college is obtainable and it's something that they can do and they can accomplish their goals and really showing the necessity of it at this point, because we know how important it is for *everyone* to have some type of post-secondary credential."

I previously argued in this book that the future of higher education is about "outcomes for everyone" — about delivering measurable results to all learners who want to engage in some sort of formal post-secondary education. And by "everyone," we mean everyone. Dr. Amardeep K. Kahlon is a nationally recognized leader in competency-based education (CBE) who has joined *The EdUp Experience Podcast* as a guest host on several occasions. During a conversation with Dr. Saúl Jiménez-Sandoval, President of California State University, Fresno, Dr. Kahlon identified a large, at-need population of prospective learners when she said:

> "There is a class of learner which higher education seems to have kind of pushed to the side. And that is the massive, *massive* incarcerated population of the United States."

This population includes nearly 2 million adults in the United States, the vast majority of whom *will*, in fact, be released at some point and who will join or re-join the workforce, in need of skills. Recently, it was announced that inmates will become Pell-eligible in 2023-2024, ending a decades-long ban on the use of federal funds to assist people in prison who want to get a college education. Our local economies will be best served if higher education serves these citizens proactively, consistently, and well.

The wide availability of online learning is making it possible to serve new populations of all kinds. And the demand for high-quality education for these new populations is growing at Mach speed. Laura K. Ipsen, President and CEO of Ellucian, told us:

> "The need for upskilling is going to increase 2 billion by 2050, in terms of new learners."

The ability to meet that massive need will be aided by higher education adopting and embracing technology (finally!) at scale. Ipsen reflected on the work her firm is doing for the industry, saying:

> "We see the evolution and the transformation moving forward at a faster clip than I think any of us would have expected."

Different Strokes for Different Folks

While we titled this chapter "Where Did All the Students Go?" and have spent our time here engaging in an exploration of shrinking admissions pools and innovative strategies to throw the academy's doors wide open to serve a broader range of learner populations, the often unmentioned truth about "trends" is that they don't always affect everyone (or they're so fundamental for some folks that what's a trend to others is old hat to them). So, while community colleges are already getting hit hard by the dual impact of the demographic cliff and the pandemic's lost generation (Dr. Michael Torrence, President of Motlow State Community College in Tullahoma, Tennessee reminded us that community colleges have seen a 10% enrollment decline nationally, which adds up to 554,000 students across the nation!), other leaders told us that they're not seeing these trends at their institutions.

Dr. W. Kent Fuchs, Former President of the University of Florida in Gainesville, Florida, told us:

> "We have a specific context here in the state of Florida. It's a state where the college-age population is growing. The entire state is growing — and is growing through families that were already here, but also through immigrants from other states and from around the world. So, we're not being challenged as some colleges and universities are with just the demographics."

In addition to institutions that simply aren't seeing a contraction in their prospect pools were institutions that remain "all in" on serving traditional-aged students, come what may. Many higher-education leaders continue to talk about their students as being fresh out of high school and being "young adults." Dr. Tracy Espy, President of Mitchell College in New London, Connecticut, told us:

"We're really about helping young people to be their very best self — not what *we* think is the best, but what *they* believe is the individual best for themselves."

It's interesting that she describes their market as "young people" (as do many other colleges and universities in the 2020s) in an era when — at many institutions — the *non*traditional student is now the typical student. It just goes to show that different places serve different segments of the overall market for higher education.

Whether most universities undergo small *evolutions* or major *revolutions* in the coming years remains to be seen, but the changes are inevitable, they're already happening, and higher-education leaders are preparing for them in many ways. In an anonymous survey of higher-education leaders in the summer of 2022, 80.65% of respondents told us that the pandemic's impact on their institution and the industry had "changed their long-term outlook on their career stability." Nearly one third of respondents said their outlook on their career stability had changed "a great deal." We also specifically asked academic leaders about the demographic cliff and whether, as a result, they believed their institution was "in trouble." We heard an unqualified "yes" from 22.03% of respondents and 36.44% more told us that they believed their institutions were "potentially, but not entirely" in trouble. With CARES Act funding drying up, institutions will need to expand quickly to ensure revenues align with expenses.

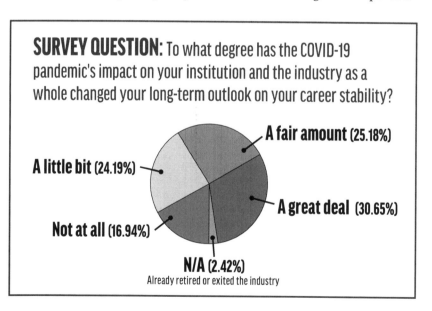

SURVEY QUESTION: To what degree has the COVID-19 pandemic's impact on your institution and the industry as a whole changed your long-term outlook on your career stability?

A fair amount (25.18%)

A little bit (24.19%)

A great deal (30.65%)

Not at all (16.94%)

N/A (2.42%)
Already retired or exited the industry

There are few prognostications we're apt to make strongly and unequivocally in this book, but one of them is this: Institutions of higher education that skate to where the puck is going in terms of developing programs and systems for serving learners 24+ or learners of *all* ages are the institutions most likely to weather the storms. During our conversation with Peter Cohen, President Emeritus of University of Phoenix, he talked to us about the university going "all in" on the adult-student market, saying:

> "Now we are exclusively focused on helping adult students succeed in their career by both getting degrees and now expanding beyond that into a lot of career services to help them, after they've gotten their first degree, to get that *second* job."

All around us is proof that universities can evolve and change. Arizona State, Western Governors University, Southern New Hampshire University, and a few others have taken the best of what the for-profits had from the early 2000, in terms of operations, and blended it with nonprofit status and regional accreditation to the tune of hundreds of thousands of students.

Right now, as we face major changes in the industry at large, what's perhaps most important about mega-universities is that they are proof that there are plenty of students ... if we're willing and prepared to serve them. I can't help but think that if schools that only serve 18-23-year-olds ultimately fail because of the demographic cliff and the changing needs and behaviors of young adults, those institutions will be *choosing* to fail through their refusal to serve the learners who need them now.

Institutions of higher education that skate to where the puck is going in terms of developing programs and systems for serving learners 24+ or learners of *all* ages are the institutions most likely to weather the storms.

Making Education Your Business with Dr. Joe Sallustio

Is Bigger Better? Higher Education and the Growth Imperative

How often is the size of the university population discussed as a part of the mission? Discussions of enrollment declines began years before the pandemic emerged in early 2020, but conversations of growth have only accelerated. If there is one blanket statement I could make about the entire industry, it's that no one wants to shrink. The evidence is all around us. There is, in fact, no doubt that most institutions of higher education across the United States have been striving to increase in size, importance, or both — the pandemic hindered the plans for many, but it has not *changed* those plans. Enrollment declines, shrinking endowments, brand distortion, and the decay of public trust in higher education due to increasing costs and mountainous student debt have led institutions of higher education to re-evaluate business models and rethink their budget-management tactics.

There aren't many ways for tuition-dependent institutions to drive toward financial sustainability other than increasing overall student population or cutting expenses. Once an institution accounts for their discount rate, overall expenditures, and lost tuition revenue via drops/withdrawals, the remainder is net tuition revenue. That net tuition revenue may be part of an institutional surplus or institutional deficit, but it is the single-most important financial number. Increasing student mass and net tuition revenue is always preferable to looking at expense cuts. The statement that an institution (*any* business, for that matter) can't cut its way to profitability is true. In higher education, expense reductions start in support departments but end up with the identification of low-performing academic programs, leading to the elimination of faculty. These types of decisions often put administrators (with fiduciary responsibility) on the opposing side from the academics who feel that budget cuts reduce overall quality provided by the institution.

Is "bigger" better? A pandemic consequence has been the shift and solidification of (for some institutions) online learning as a viable and scalable option for institutions to grow their overall student population. There are, after all, 39 million working learners with "some college and no degree."[19] These students, now known as the new majority, are specific about their preferred learning pathways and bring the "student consumer" mentality to the higher-education marketplace. Tapping into the working-adult student archetype can increase enrollment rapidly *if* the institution designs marketing, enrollment, retention, and support services for adults. This is a big *if*.

One of the best examples of online expansion and the desire to serve increasing numbers of learners comes from Dr. Michael Crow, President of Arizona State University, with the plan to serve 100 million learners by 2030.[20] Conversely, similar RI research institutions are deploying resources to enhance the on-ground experience and are using online learning to complement growth efforts (rather than online education *leading* growth efforts). Take Dr. W. Kent Fuchs, Former President of the University of Florida, as an example. On his episode of *The EdUp Experience Podcast*, Dr. Fuchs spoke about their online division's goal of meeting 10,000 online learners while they bring increasing numbers of students to campus. While the strategies are different, there is one undeniable similarity between these examples: these are super-brand universities that have

---

19 Todd Sedmak, "More Thank 39 Million Americans Have Some College, No Credential, According to New Research," May 10, 2022, National Student Clearinghouse, https://www.studentclearinghouse.org/blog/more-than-39-million-americans-have-some-college-no-credential-according-to-new-research/.

20 Michael T. Nietzel, "Arizona State University Announces Effort to Educate 100 Million Students Worldwide," *Forbes*, January 21, 2022, https://www.forbes.com/sites/michaeltnietzel/2022/01/21/arizona-state-university-announces-effort-to-educate-100-million-students-worldwide/.

the resources to accomplish their goals. For most institutions, incremental growth is a smarter path to sustainability — particularly for institutions that do not have strong or self-sustaining endowments. Understanding staff-to-student ratios to support a growing student population ensures that the learning experience isn't diluted as more pressure ultimately tests the academic and student-support infrastructure.

Given the different paths to increases in size and scope, intentionality is key. As the value of education continues to be questioned by certain segments of the public, there is an elevated sense of awareness for boards and presidents to ensure that physical expansion and technological innovation will be supported by increased numbers of students and their tuition revenue. The decision-making is complex when statistics point to overall declining enrollment. The desire to expand and the opportunity to do so are not always lining up for institutions. So ... is bigger better? It depends.

As the world keeps turning, higher education will — perhaps against all odds — remain a continued and significant force for good. It will do so through a wholesale mindset shift as we seek to redefine market segments, understand the various and changing preferences of different learners, and open the door to serving eager and worthy would-be students who push us outside our comfort zones. Whether there are too few students, too many students, or just enough will — in the end — be up to the institutions of higher learning themselves. Now is the time for honest reflection and deep resolve about where you go from here. Ask yourself:

➔ Will you find and embrace the new learners who need you?

➔ Will you improve your quality to improve your competitive edge among your current sweet-spot students?

➔ Will you look at the changing demographics and simply hold on tight, or will you charge into the storm, ready to push through the headwinds that threaten the status quo and determined to find and ride the tailwinds that will surely come?

What lies ahead is an odyssey, and a very human one at that. All you have to do is imagine the personal stories of the thousands of future students whose lives you stand to change, and — suddenly — all the pivots and disruption required for you to serve them well won't be so scary after all. (We promise.)

CHAPTER 4

THE PEOPLE IMPERATIVE

Treating Students as VIP Customers and Faculty and Staff as the Heart and Soul of the Institution

I n Chapter 3, we took a deep dive into the demographic and cultural shifts impacting the makeup and size of various current and prospective learner populations. We shined a bright light on the many students who need us and who will, as we move into a new era in higher education, challenge us to be our best. Now, it's time to talk about *how* to serve those learners in all the ways they deserve.

If I was ever to be the founder of a university, I'd want our mission to be "Outcomes for Everyone." In a succinct and ambitious way, it sums up my hope for the entire higher-education industry. I want us to deliver on the promise of post-secondary education for everyone who needs and wants it, and I want us to do so in a way that generates measurable career outcomes and other meaningful, tangible results. We've talked about the outcomes imperative in Chapter 2 and will address academic value again in Chapter 6, and we've just explored the various learner populations that make up the "everyone" in my imagined brand promise of "outcomes for everyone." But what of the *people* imperative? How should we prioritize those learners in all that we do, and build our entire institutions around serving them?

We start by welcoming them — by providing access to our campuses and communities, and by letting them know that we're here to support their goals and dreams. We start by creating opportunity for all.

If I was ever to be the founder of a university, I'd want our mission to be "Outcomes for Everyone." In a succinct and ambitious way, it sums up my hope for the entire higher-education industry. I want us to deliver on the promise of post-secondary education for everyone who needs and wants it, and I want us to do so in a way that generates measurable career outcomes and other meaningful, tangible results.

Creating Access to Higher Education

For all the millions of people who have asked themselves, "Where do I want to go to college?" there are millions more who have asked themselves, "Do I have what it takes to go to college at all? Am I welcome there? And where, exactly, is *there*?" For all the ways in which colleges and universities have provided social mobility, career opportunity, and financial fuel for their graduates, far too many of those institutions have kept their gates closed to the people who need and deserve a collegiate experience most. In the 2020s and beyond, there is perhaps no more important theme and call to action in higher education than improving *access* to education.

The reality is that we fundamentally need to reinvigorate the promise of education. How do we provide great post-secondary pathways that create ample opportunity for all of us in the U.S., especially for those who have been disadvantaged or disenfranchised? If we want individuals to have progress, we need to make education – and all of its pathways – work for so many more than those for whom it's currently working. ""

Scott Pulsipher, MBA
President, Western Governors University

🖊 Pop Quiz!

In the United States, there are millions of unserved would-be learners who have not inquired about or applied for admission to any colleges or universities. Which of the following phrases are they saying to themselves — and to their friends and family — when it comes to the possibility of college?

❑ I don't know how.

❑ I don't know where.

❑ I don't know if I can afford it.

❑ I don't know if I will fit in.

❑ I don't know anyone in my family who has gone to college before.

❑ I don't know if now is a good time.

❑ I don't know how I'll juggle it with the rest of my life.

❑ I don't know if I have what it takes.

❑ All of the above.

If students aren't coming to us — or if they're coming to us and then walking away (like when our website is discouraging or too complicated to navigate) — we must challenge ourselves to come to them. Dr. Carlos Peñaloza, Chancellor of Leeward Community College in Pearl City, Hawaii, told us:

> "We really do need to get to students where the students need us — as opposed to hoping that they come to us. It's about creating more accessibility, and COVID demonstrated how inaccessible education can be. *Access* in terms of finances, *access* in terms of know-how, and *access* in terms of geography are all major concerns."

Dr. Peñaloza leads a campus where serious traffic issues become serious accessibility issues for their students. Driving from Pearl City to Waikiki, he tells us, can take up to two hours one way during rush hour — to go less than 20 miles. "Traffic is a total nightmare on the island of Oahu," he said. So, with all jokes aside about how a president's biggest challenge is always parking, leaders of modern institutions of higher education are looking at everything — including traffic patterns — to identify places to improve educational access for current and future students.

Sometimes, access is about being able to get to class without a commute — and this is an area where higher education has begun to make break-throughs with engaging online courses. Dr. Jack Thomas, President of Central State University in Wilberforce, Ohio, told us that it's important to remember that:

> "Place-bound students probably would not have gotten an education or would not go to college, had it not been for online education. And I think that online is the way of the future."

Dr. Thomas's institution, which offers free tuition scholarships for quali-fying students from four large local high-school districts, is focused heavily on accessibility and affordability. Creating opportunity for everyone is important to Dr. Thomas; he himself was a first-generation college student, and now he's a college president. He told us that:

> "If not for institutions like ours, education would only be for the rich and famous."

For the industry of higher education to help the masses become a confident college-going culture that can avail itself of all the post-secondary education opportunities they deserve (when and where they need them) will require mindset shifts, infrastructure investments, cultural resets, and operational overhauls. Knowing that the "rich and famous" and the otherwise privileged and lucky already have a leg up when it comes to "access" to higher educa-tion, we spent a lot of our time during presidential interviews asking about disadvantaged students and what their institutions are doing to ensure improved access for these populations. What we heard was inspiring. When asked how to think about helping students who are disadvan-taged or marginalized in various ways, Don Kilburn, CEO of University of Massachusetts Online (UMass Online), told us:

> "I happen to think that life gets in the way for a lot of students. And I think that's true for many African Americans and Latino Americans. I think life gets in the way, especially when socioeconomic situations put you at a disadvantage to begin with. And therefore, I think education that is flexible and affordable — and then support that is proactive, not reactive — can help to change that."

Dr. Daniel F. Mahony, President of the Southern Illinois University System, talked to us about how the divide between advantaged and disadvantaged students became more acutely obvious when colleges and universities were forced to close their campuses in the spring of 2020 due to the onset of the COVID-19 pandemic. He reminded us:

> "I think a lot of people, when they said, 'Send the students home,' are imagining them all 'going home' to homes like theirs — homes that have good internet access, where the families are affluent enough to make sure that they're well fed, that they've got all the resources that they need and all the support that they need. But that's not the reality for every one of our students. And we have to *recognize* that fact and make a different decision based on that."

He further said:

> "Keeping the residence halls open [during the pandemic] was an important part of our social-justice mission. And I think that's an example as we go forward — when we look at the way we do things, our policies, our procedures, our processes: Are they truly fair? Are we considering how this may impact people who are 'different than me?'"

During the early days of the pandemic, many students were unable to take the SAT or ACT, and schools like Dr. Mahony's went (at least temporarily) "test optional" rather than relying heavily on test scores to make decisions about scholarships. We heard many presidents say that their grading scales, when campus-based students and faculty were forced into an online modality, became pass/fail.

We talked to Dr. Melik Peter Khoury, President of Unity College in New Gloucester, Maine, about a student-centric way forward for higher education as the industry rebounds from the pandemic. His candor was inspiring. He said:

"The future of higher education is right now uncertain. I think many institutions are clinging to an outdated model that is not being funded appropriately, hoping to find that major donor who is going to keep them afloat for a few more years. I think if we are serious about education and higher education, we need to put the students in the first position in every sense of the word. And I don't mean we do that by diminishing our rigor, but by really looking at *how* students want to learn, *where* students want to learn — by looking at what it is to be an educated society and rethink how we deliver this. We must really think about accessibility, affordability, and flexibility. Because the *world* has changed. (COVID has shown us that.) The *demographics* have changed. *Lifestyles* have changed. How students want to *work* has changed. How students want to *learn* has changed. And to assume there's only one way to learn (otherwise you are somehow not delivering 'education') is something that we, as a nation — and we, as colleges — have to look upon very, very carefully.

"Because if our job is to regurgitate information, then we are not an institution of education. We need to *generate knowledge.* We need to prepare students, not just to be career ready, but to be good citizens and environmental stewards. And you cannot do that if 55% of the population cannot finish what they started. And I think the graduation rate in this country — outside of the Ivy League schools — is pretty poor right now. And *that* is what we need to tackle. Because there's nothing more dangerous than an uneducated society."

Today, there are entire institutions — new ones and evolving ones — that are dedicated to enabling the kind of wide access that can create the broadly educated society Dr. Khoury alludes to. Foundry College, based in San Francisco, California, is one such institution that is newly minted and looking to disrupt higher education for the better. Foundry College CEO and President, Dr. Akiba J. Covitz, talked to us about how they address the equity imperative in post-secondary education. He was previously in academic leadership at Harvard Law School, and he told us:

"I left a very exclusive form of education in order to just throw the doors open."

Making Education Your Business with Dr. Joe Sallustio

Access and Quality: An "Either/Or" Proposition?

Is the quality of an educational program diminished by allowing more students to experience it? Barriers in the admissions/enrollment process only serve as a filter — to weed out "those" students who an institution can't (or choose not) to serve. Think about how the supply-and-demand conversation is forcing many institutions (maybe yours) to reframe who they are trying to serve.

Spending money in marketing for students to slam into a brick wall of admissions requirements is an exercise in financial irresponsibility. The industry has historically celebrated programs or institutions that create the air of elitism — you've heard it before. Is the higher-education industry really shifting to celebrate the risk-taking institutions? And by risk-taking, I mean those willing to admit and serve students who need more support and attention, even to welcome those who could be (financially) one fender-bender away from hitting the eject button. I mean the institutions that invest in robust and complex student service and retention infrastructure designed to help students persist.

We can only hope, because celebrating institutions that provide *access* and *affordability* is the path forward to regain the public trust in higher education.

While many institutions are achieving access by throwing the doors wide open — by becoming less "selective" and more inclusive — yet other institutions are doubling down on exclusionary admissions standards so they can improve their own sense (and, to some degree, the marketplace's sense) of their own prestige and so they can produce, record, and market impressive career and learning outcomes by only educating those who are pretty much guaranteed to "succeed." Most presidents we interviewed rejected that instinct to remain exclusive in a world crying out for inclusion.

President Scott Pulsipher at Western Governors University (a fully online university based in Millcreek, Utah) told us that you can't just change your admissions standards to get to the outcomes you want. He told us:

> "You have to be careful that you don't achieve outcomes by who you admit. We're trying to improve outcomes for *all* types of learners."

I've mentioned already in this book that I have recently been struggling with my own involvement in "exclusive" colleges and universities. I have played a notable role in helping the selective folks crack the code on how to become even *more* selective by attracting thousands more applicants who they can reject. In some ways, co-authoring this book is a sort of personal atonement. I have proudly put words like "elite" and "top-50 research" and "renowned" on my website, to describe my clients. Just like the students who win the admissions-and-scholarship lotteries at elite schools (and/or who have legacy connections and significant financial means), I felt like my association with the selective institutions made me special. More credible. An expert with an impressive client list. But the conversations that are taking place on *The EdUp Experience Podcast* have me asking (finally): "Why should we want higher education to be a lottery? Shouldn't we want *all* learners to win?"

> **Pro Tip:** *It's always important to look at yourself, and ask "Could I have gotten into the college where I work? And would it have been convenient to do so?"*

When was the last time you went through the entire application and enrollment process at your institution — soup to nuts — to assess the user experience?

Dr. Khoury at Unity College answered that question for me — and for all of us. He passionately asked:

> "Should education really be a *lottery*? Should education only be for those of us lucky enough to get that scholarship? The biggest danger we can have as a country and as a planet is an uneducated people."

The antidote to that danger is educational access. Dr. Khoury said:

"I've made it my life's mission to debunk this idea that education is only for those who have the perfect SAT scores."

Being truly student-centric requires that we improve access *and* affordability.

Other leaders got us thinking about what is lost for society if brilliant minds aren't given a chance at education. Dr. Gregory Fowler, Former Global Campus President at Southern New Hampshire University (now President at University of Maryland, Global Campus), asked us to think about people like Ludwig van Beethoven or Stephen Hawking. He reminded us:

"We don't know where the next brilliant person's coming from, but if we do higher education right, we open the door for so many more people."

But if we open the gates, open the doors, open the admissions requirements and do so without making educational programs *affordable*, we increase access only for those with financial means (or the willingness to take on crushing levels of educational debt). As such, being truly student-centric requires that we improve access *and* affordability.

Making Higher Education More Affordable

One of the most compelling conversations we had about affordability and access was with Dr. Julie White, President of Pierce College Fort Steilacoom in Lakewood, Washington. She challenged us to think about value and cost, saying:

"We are going through a huge transformation in higher education as people question the cost and the outcome: At the end of the day, is it worth it? I just can't even imagine not having gone to college — not having the degree. As a female, what would my world look like if I hadn't gone to college? This perception of value is, I think, situational and personal. And I'm sure that *others* who are not white men have

Higher education has historically been a beautiful system that only worked for a few. What I have been trying to figure out is how we make the system affordable for everyone.

Melik Peter Khoury, DBA

President & CEO Unity College

similar feelings, believing that if they're going to aspire to be all that they can be, or if they're going to *achieve* being all that they can be, they need a credential.

"My brother-in-law said something really interesting not long ago. He said, of a college degree, 'It's kind of like your insurance policy. It'll never be taken away from you and it will always help you.' But the cost, I think, is an issue that we in higher education *do* have to come to terms with. And I think we also have to look at what is *in* our programs. Is it still relevant? I think for too long, we've been very traditional in *what* we teach and *how* we teach. And it's time for us to really analyze: 'What are our outcomes? How are we assessing what our graduates know and can do?' And it's going to be really critical for us on our campuses to have these conversations. And you know what, though? It's at the macro level too; it's got to be *beyond* our campuses. It's got to be us as a *system* in higher education. All of us saying, 'How do we make this affordable for everyone?' So, *everyone* has the opportunities and is on an equal playing field, with the ability to be all that they can be — which I *do* believe you get from having a degree."

My co-author, Dr. Joe Sallustio, who works inside higher education as an administrator, has recently shared that he's disheartened and confused by people who question the value of a college degree. We're *all* disheartened, truth be told. But the naysayers are the vocal few and I think that Joe and I have both decided that we all need to ignore the noise from the naysayers. Because they don't represent the masses and because, according to Dr. Julie White, the naysayers are hypocritical critics (who are active consumers of higher education, despite their criticisms). She said:

"A lot of times, the people who are questioning the value of a college degree, (a) have a college degree themselves and (b) are sending their kids to college. So, I sometimes question the motivations."

Making Education Your Business with Dr. Joe Sallustio

Conversations with Our Children

I always wonder who the naysayer is — that person who is advising their children not to attend college — and what that conversation sounds like. Perhaps the conversation isn't a direct attack on the value of higher education, but rather the exploration of all options available for post-secondary education. That, I would believe. Or, perhaps, a conversation around how to assess the *value* of higher education, particularly a conversation around the skills economy.

As a parent, I know that I cannot look my children in the eyes and advise them against the pathway to an undergraduate degree. Now, how they *get* there may evolve from traditions past, but the ability to think critically, act professionally, and exercise empathy are developed from and through a college experience. So many other skills too: grit, responsibility, perspective. Can one achieve the same through alternative pathways? Certainly so, and that is okay for some. But, in the end, education beyond high school is infinitely valuable — to individuals, families, communities, and economies. I can't be a naysayer and I simply don't understand today's adamant critics — those who would deny the value of a formal post-secondary education. It's my hope that books like *Commencement* and public-access media like *The EdUp Experience Podcast* can provide more perspective to those who are questioning the value of higher education. Certainly, my *own* perspective has changed so dramatically after experiencing the brilliance of hundreds of interviews with innovative higher-education leaders. Do I want my children to experience that brilliance through an accessible and affordable education? Yes. That's why I work every single day!

Many of the more than 100 presidents who were interviewed for this book talked about the lifetime value of higher education, as measured by job earnings. Dr. White told us:

> "The APLU — the Association of Public and Land-grant Universities — released a document indicating that bachelor's degree holders are half as likely to be unemployed as their peers with a high school degree. And they make $1 million in additional earnings, on average, over their lifetime.[21] And for an associate's degree or other kind of post-secondary credential, of course, it's going to be in the middle of that. And so, we know that there are economic benefits. And we've got to do a better job of making that case of providing *access* to everyone."

Higher-education leaders know that most graduates will receive significant financial returns on an investment in higher education, if only students can find a way to begin. Getting students beyond that initial hurdle requires a multi-faceted approach to affordability: offering more financial aid, offering non-degree on-ramps to for-credit certificate programs that are a fraction of the cost of a full degree, helping students complete a program in a shorter period, and even (gasp!) lowering the cost of tuition.

Dr. Akiba J. Covitz, CEO and President at Foundry College, told us about their affordable certificates (priced at a total of $2,950 at the time of his interview for this book). Foundry offers a tuition freeze, guaranteeing that a learner's program price won't go up for six trimesters, and they offer four ways to pay (easily explained on their website), including a deferred payment option where graduates can wait until their credentialed certificate translates to a family-supporting wage so they can pay for it. Frank F. Britt, Former CEO of Penn Foster Education Group (home of Penn Foster College in Scottsdale, Arizona, and Penn Foster Career School and Penn Foster High School in Scranton, Pennsylvania), talked about affordability in a way that we rarely hear in higher education, saying:

> "Our notion is quite straightforward to the point of it being obvious, which is you should continue to pay for our service as long as you

---

21 Different presidents cited different sources for the lifetime-earnings gap. Estimates varied from $1 million to $3 million.

get value from that service. And if you stop getting value, you should stop paying."

President Scott Pulsipher at Western Governors University told us:

"We have tackled the affordability issue, not by making more financing and funding available for an ever-increasing cost. We just fundamentally believe that you could lower the cost."

The longer a student stays in school (especially if doing so involves room-and-board), the more it costs them — now and later.

Refreshing, isn't it? These leaders and their institutions are proving that higher education is an old dog capable of new tricks. Their new messages for learners? Pay in a way that's convenient to you (even waiting until you've got a better salary to do so). Stop paying if it stops being valuable to you. And pay less. *Yes, please!*

More and more, we hear students demanding a guarantee that if they do the work, they'll finish on time — that a two-year degree is really a two-year degree, and that a four-year degree is really a four-year degree. Some institutions are going so far as to let the students decide how long a program takes; Western Governors University charges tuition at a flat rate every six months, allowing students to take and complete as many competency-based courses each term as the student is wanting and able to complete (with no extra cost for taking more courses). Whether you pay tuition by the course or by the term, graduating "on time" isn't just important from an outcome perspective or a student-satisfaction perspective — it's an affordability issue. The longer a student stays in school (especially if doing so involves room-and-board), the more it costs them — now and later. Dr. Hal Higdon, Chancellor of the Ozarks Technical Community College System and President of the OTC Springfield Campus in Springfield, Missouri, explained it like this:

"I tell every student I meet, 'I want to get you *in* as quickly and as efficiently as possible. And I want you to get you *out* of here as quickly and efficiently as possible. Every semester you stay here longer than you should costs you money in terms of opportunity. It also costs you money in terms of cash. And if you're doing student loans, it's going to cost you money for a *long time.*'"

In the end, not cracking the code on affordability at your institution is apt to pull you further from your admirable missions and contribute to societal challenges that extend beyond the walls (or firewalls!) of your campuses. We already live in a world of the "haves" and "have nots" — but higher education, as an industry, can lift millions out of poverty, drive the engine of regional economies, and change the lives of individuals and families. Dr. Melik Peter Khoury at Unity College told us:

"Education is one of the most important elements that we can do as a civilized nation. Every human being in the *world* should be educated because it is those who are *un*educated who are most susceptible to any sort of subterfuge. Yet too often, education is only for those who can afford it; education is only for those who are lucky enough to get the [scholarship] lottery; education is only for those who are willing to risk being eaten up by the system and walking away with a burden of debt and a burden of displacement."

We have the power to prevent that displacement — to give students their rightful places in the classroom so they can one day seize their rightful places in their career fields. There is much work to be done. In addition to the ways in which we should be working to make higher education more accessible and affordable, we need to be making it more equitable.

Dr. Daniel F. Mahony, President of the Southern Illinois University System, tied these issues together for us by telling us a story about a discovery he made during a previous university presidency. He shared:

"I found that when I looked at our data at one point, the group that got the most merit scholarships were upper-class white males. So, when we were giving out our scholarships, we were over-giving them to people who come from more advantaged backgrounds, people who were white. But the SAT actually was a horrible predictor of success in college. So, we're using something we *know* is not a good predictor to give money to people who need it less. In my mind, there's something seriously wrong with that. So that's one of the things we're looking at right now [at the SIU System]. I talked to both chancellors actually just this week about: 'How do we do our scholarship decisions? And should we be changing that in a way that's more equitable?'"

Today, more and more institutions are asking themselves the tough questions about all their critical processes — and identifying equity gaps that need to be addressed. With some of the brightest minds in the world working at colleges and universities, surely these equity gaps can be narrowed or even closed.

The Role of Diversity, Equity, and Inclusion (DEI) in Creating a Student-Centric Institution

Five years ago, my colleagues and I had vague and differing notions about what "diversity" means and the role it can and should play in higher education. None of us were talking about "equity" nor were we talking about "inclusion." For lack of a better way to characterize the recent past, "diversity, equity, and inclusion" (DEI) was simply not a "thing." Serving our students better by *seeing* them and welcoming them and celebrating their *differences* was not on our radar — not as a basic responsibility of higher education and certainly not as a competitive differentiator.

Fast-forward to the 2020s, and nearly every college and university has hired or named a chief diversity officer, even the most homogeneous college cultures are being transformed by new faces and new voices, chief executives are speaking out on issues of social justice, and some of the most pride-inspiring projects I've been asked to tackle as a higher-education consultant now involve the development of visionary and actionable DEI plans. The tide has turned — powerfully and purposefully. As we know better, we do better.

DEI is not a trend. It is not an area of focus for *some* colleges and not for others. And it is not a strategic area in which any of us can afford to continue to get it wrong. Dr. Melody Rose, Former Chancellor of the Nevada System of Higher Education, told us:

"We *all* have to get on the inclusion bandwagon. Our nation is demanding it; our nation deserves it."

Not only do we all deserve it, we have the opportunity to participate in the various initiatives aimed at making college communities more equitable, inclusive, and diverse. Queens University of Charlotte's President Dan Lugo articulated this beautifully, saying:

"The motivation that *everyone* should enjoy about equity, inclusion, and diversity is that we *all* have a stake in it, and we *all* get better as a result of that work. There are equitable moments where we need to bridge people to get access to the full spectrum of opportunities, but once we *do* that, everyone gets stronger. Our whole entire experience gets better. Our decision-making gets better, and our outcomes get better."

Dr. Christopher Roellke, President of Stetson University in DeLand, Florida, cut to the chase in reminding us why everyone must participate in diversity, equity, and inclusion efforts — because failure to be inclusive and equitable causes human pain and because a critical part of educational access is ensuring educational access for *all*. Dr. Roellke said:

"This has to be a community effort, a *full* community effort. Everyone at the university needs to be a diversity officer and an inclusion officer because things occur on our campuses that are hurtful, that are painful, and frankly are barriers to our students learning if they have to confront the 'isms'[22] that are so present in our society."

The long history of higher education in the United States has largely been a story about a wealthy white majority availing themselves of critical-thinking exercises and liberal-arts lessons in advance of (or instead of, for many women) a career. With the exception of Historically Black Colleges and Universities (HBCUs) and long-standing women's colleges, the first 150+ years of higher education in America has paid little mind to learners of diverse ethnic backgrounds, learners from lower socioeconomic backgrounds, and learners with unique needs (like learners with physical disabilities or learning differences). But today, just as the "nontraditional student" has become the typical student,

---

22 Racism, sexism, antisemitism, etc.

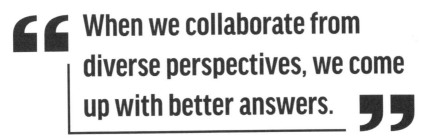

When we collaborate from diverse perspectives, we come up with better answers.

Stephen Spinelli, PhD
President, Babson College

the majority has become multicultural. In many regions, the groups we once thought of as "minorities" are no longer in the minority. And yet, many institutions of higher education are ill-equipped to serve the students of today.

John Farrar, Director of Education at Google, while co-hosting an episode of *The EdUp Experience Podcast,* said:

> "If you're under 18 in America right now, you're more than likely to be part of the multicultural majority. And as a result, every university's future student pipeline is reflective of that change. One of the things we're trying to do with our data at Google is provide some insight into what that looks like. That student population *does* value student services higher, sometimes dramatically higher. Things like career counseling, mental health, and academic advising are highly valued by today's multicultural majority. And this population leans into the online form of education at an even higher rate as well."

Ensuring that our campuses (in-person or virtual) are richly diverse and that all students are well-served and empowered in an equitable way benefits not just the "diverse" student, but also the student who feels right at home from day one (i.e., the white middle-class student). The commentary from Google's John Farrar was offered during an interview with Dr. W. Kent Fuchs, President of the University of Florida. Dr. Fuchs talked about the benefit of being intentional about diversity, saying:

> "You want, I believe, as a student to have maybe a dorm mate or a friend — or at least a classmate — who comes from a country you've never heard of or comes from a part of the United States you've never visited. Because that makes your own education richer."

Dr. Fuchs also challenged us to think about why "local" or "regional" colleges should seek to recruit students from across the nation and around the world — because geographic diversity matters in all communities. He gave us an I've-never-thought-about-it-that-way moment when he said:

> "If Yale only admitted students from Connecticut and if Princeton only admitted students from New Jersey, we probably would never have heard of those universities. It's because they have people from around

the world — and around the nation — that they provide that rich educational environment."

Good culture — an inclusive, diverse culture that is seeking to be equitable and fair — doesn't solve all the problems but it helps. It helps to have a good culture when students are underrepresented or when they had an experience with the campus police or if they're struggling academically. Good culture impacts everything. And Dr. Fuchs believes that part of creating an inclusive culture comes down to how we communicate. He told us:

> "I try to communicate that we *care* about each other — whether it's an employee caring about another person, or it's a faculty member caring about a student — and that it's okay to use the word 'love.'[23] It's okay to say, 'We want you to be successful and we're here rooting for you.' And so, I use that theme — that message, those words — a lot, and I think it really does begin to influence the atmosphere, the culture, of a university. And that's so important when you have a big place and people can get lost."

During the interviews that made *Commencement* possible, we often heard college and university leaders talk about their institution's unique take on a common theme — how women's colleges or HBCUs think differently about inclusion or how institutions with philosophical and curricular niches (like schools focused on healthcare or the environment or entrepreneurship) think differently about general-education courses and curriculum development. Dr. Stephen Spinelli, President of Babson College, talked to us about how the imperative to be more diverse, equitable, and inclusive plays out at his institution, which has boldly positioned itself as the premiere institution for teaching an entrepreneurial leadership mindset and skillset. He believes DEI matters during the student experience and once their graduates are out in the world, leading. He said:

---

23 One of the most personally profound themes that emerged from the 100+ interviews conducted for this book was the common thread of genuine, unconditional love for students and for colleagues. Many of higher education's highest-ranking executives began their careers in the faculty ranks, and we heard — again and again — how much they love the classroom, love the students, love the industry, and love playing a part in creating lifechanging experiences for learners.

"Different thinking embraced through passionate respect *emanates* from the development of a diverse, equitable, and inclusive community ... I think Babson has a special way of creating an entrepreneurial mindset that solves problems and increases social and economic value. And if we are doing the right thing from a diversity, equity, and inclusion standpoint, that wealth will be created *across* the society in more equitable ways."

Diversity, equity, and inclusion efforts aren't a one-time initiative or a single problem to "fix," but a way of being, operating, thinking, and feeling.

Perhaps one of the most important things for higher education to embrace about diversity, equity, and inclusion is that DEI efforts aren't a one-time initiative or a single problem to "fix," but a way of being, operating, thinking, and feeling — from here on out. It's something we should all be "constantly striving" to improve, according to Dr. Michael Horowitz, President of TCS Education System (which includes The Chicago School of Professional Psychology, Pacific Oaks College, Pacific Oaks Children's School, The Colleges of Law, Saybrook University, and Kansas Health Science Center). Dr. Horowitz told us that diversity and inclusion are "critically important" and that:

"Cognitive diversity — and ethnic, racial, and gender diversity — these all make a team stronger. They bring different viewpoints and perspectives and it's something we're constantly striving to strengthen."

When asked what advice he'd offer on diversity in recruiting staff, faculty, and leadership, Dr. Horowitz said:

"The best I can say is to have it explicitly in your consciousness. Some people might say there's a lag from graduation to achieving the numbers of professionals for recruiting. I feel, at this point, there are ample number of people to recruit. Just ensure that diversity is reflected in your candidate pool; make a point of it. We're finding that now, as we recruit for a new medical school faculty in Wichita, that the people we've hired thus far reflect a very diverse orientation. I think it's about taking off your blinders and maybe looking at places to post and advertise that address that audience specifically. But I don't think there's a reason today to not have that represented in staff, faculty, and leadership."

Dr. Horowitz's "no excuses" approach to recruiting and retaining a diverse workforce is one that many other leaders are actualizing. Dr. Elsa Núñez, President of Eastern Connecticut State University in Willimantic, Connecticut, told us that they have worked to ensure that their campus employee body matches the student body. Eastern Connecticut State is a Predominantly White Institution (PWI); they currently have 30% students of color, 30% faculty of color, and 30% staff of color "because students demanded people of color," Dr. Núñez told us. She shared:

> "I've been president for 17 years. And I've *worked* on those numbers because we're in a rural white area. And I didn't want to be *that*. I wanted us to have a diverse student body, faculty, and staff. We've changed the paradigm."

In seeking to maintain this representative balance of people on their campus and in navigating her university through the COVID-19 pandemic, Dr. Núñez found that the issues of diversity and mental health overlapped in a powerful and instructive way. Suddenly, their connections in the community were telling them about the mental-health counselors in the region who are minority people of color. So rather than just having counselors available, the university can match counselors to students in ways that honor a student's preferences. She explained:

> "So, when we refer a student now, it's not just a counselor. We make note of the student's preference. And that has helped a lot because a lot of Black men were saying, 'I don't want to go to a woman. I want to go to a man.' Or 'I don't want to go to somebody Caucasian. I want to go to somebody Black.' And we've been able to satisfy their needs and their wants in that regard. And I think that that's been a good thing. We have given more attention to mental health issues at Eastern

in the last five years than in my entire presidency, because it's really serious. The students are dealing with a lot in this generation, a lot of crises in their lives. Being proactive [about how we help them] really goes hand in hand with the diversity, equity, and inclusion table stakes that every single university has got (and corporate America, for that matter too). But when you're talking about an African-American male not wanting to talk to a Caucasian female because of relatability, that is a *real* deal. But for your institution to partner with outside businesses and bring the totality of that sphere of individuals [in this case, mental-health counselors] to a kind of menu, if you will, so people in need can be partnered up with providers who they can relate to … I really think that addresses two very relevant, current, big topics in the globe right now."

A key part of transforming academia when it comes to DEI is enabling a safe and respectful place for civil discourse. During the era in which our 100+ presidents were being interviewed for this book, the United States was in the midst of a racial reckoning. In 2020 and 2021, there were searing moments etched into history that go by the names of cities and people — George Floyd, Breonna Taylor, Portland, Kenosha. Individual victims and cities rocked by pain and violence. We interviewed several presidents who were vocal about police brutality and systemic racism, and we also spoke to some leaders who felt that their students' voices were more important than the institutional voice during these unsettling moments. We talked to presidents just weeks after their own cities were crippled by violence and riots and whose communities mobilized peacefully to declare that Black Lives Matter and to ask their colleges and universities to be unequivocal in their stance on the social injustices happening locally and nationally.

Dr. Ward Ulmer, Former President at Walden University, told us:

"That's one of the philosophies here, or one of our values here at Walden is we don't take a stance on every issue. We don't have an agenda. Our goal as a university is to build that toolkit for our graduates to go out and further their *own* agendas.

"As president, my first initiative was diversity, equity, and inclusion. And so it just falls right into our mission of affecting positive social change ... Walden is very involved in the diversity, equity, and inclusion conversations. We're talking about white privilege. We're talking about Black Lives Matter. We're talking about racism. In terms of what the future of higher education looks like, that future campus or that online campus or that university is going to have to be a place where civil discourse [happens] (and I don't mean protesting — anything other than peacefully). Civil discourse, the ability to disagree with someone and still not hate that person or want to fight that person. That's the environment that has to be created."

A key part of transforming academia when it comes to diversity, equity, and inclusion is enabling a safe and respectful place for civil discourse.

When it came to whether presidents were blogging about or speaking up about specific moments in history or about social justice, there was no "one size fits all" philosophy. For every institution that facilitated civil discourse without its faculty and administrators making bold statements about their own feelings or ideologies was an institution that was unequivocal about where they stood on such issues. Dr. Mel Netzhammer, Chancellor of Washington State University Vancouver, said during his interview in 2020:

"On many issues of national importance, I am inclined to express my feelings to our community. And so, I haven't shied away from that. Since the killing of George Floyd, I have written a bit, and one of the things that really struck me was an article in *The Chronicle of Higher Education* by two faculty members who were talking about how safe and tepid most of the responses were from higher education leaders about racial injustice. And this is so much a part of our campus community that I didn't want my statements to be perceived as equivocating or watered down. And I reflected on this a lot.

"Two weeks ago, I sent a letter out (that was a little bit more guarded, but not much) to our 13,000 alumni and donors. And I took some heat. I also expected it to be worse than it was. So that's not bad, you know, the six people who were very, very angry with my letter. We have to be on the right side of history — that's how I'm feeling right now. I'm in a unique position to be able to speak about racial injustice and have the platform to be able to call it out. And so, I do try to live that personally. And I have an incredible team of leaders around me who make it safer for me, and also push me in that direction."

Throughout this chapter, we address the many ways in which colleges and universities can better serve and honor their students. So, I found it particularly poignant to think about a student-inspired presential ethos after Dr. Netzhammer, when telling us about his students participating in protests and car rallies and coming to the aid of one another, simply said:

"My students inspire me, and I *want* to be inspired by them."

We, as authors — Dr. Joe Sallustio and I — are likewise inspired by the higher-education leaders who are inspired by their students. As I was organizing the content for the book you are now reading, it occurred to me that the above quotes — about leadership communication philosophies and student-inspired leadership styles — easily could have gone into Chapter 7, Leadership 3.0. In the end, Chapter 3 or Chapter 7 are both the right place for these conversations because if you're doing it right, *leadership* strategy and *student-focus* strategy should be the same thing.

> **Reflection Question:** *In what ways have your students inspired you? How was the courage or tenacity or heart of your students given you the strength and motivation to speak up or act differently in recent years?*

🔆 EdUp with Elvin

Practical Tips and Frontline Insights from Elvin Freytes

So how do you create an environment where civil discourse can take place without fisticuffs breaking out?

Here's how:

1. Make civil discourse a part of your culture by starting at the hiring process — ask candidates to tell you about a time when they disagreed with someone.

2. Train your staff and faculty on what civil conversations look and sound like, modeling ways to "address the issue" without "attacking the person."

3. Create frequent, structured opportunities for staff and faculty to engage in civil discourse.

4. Embed student programs into your culture — inside and outside the classroom — that promote civil discourse. Have these discussions facilitated by staff and/or faculty.

5. Invite students from a variety of backgrounds to attend these programs. Entice participation with food and beverages, if possible.

6. Lay ground rules at the beginning of civil-discourse exercises, and make sure the facilitator also participates with empathy and curiosity.

7. Get leaders from all levels — not only within the school but also the community — to participate, if possible.

8. Follow up with any students who need more time than allotted to work through their differences.

9. Promote these programs to prospective students (and invite them personally) so they can get a sense

of the school's culture and its values-based stance on civil discourse.

10. Do you know what I'm going to say here? You got it! Skip the committees.

The Diversity Component of Access

We've talked about educational access, and we've talked about diversity, equity, and inclusion. And like nearly every key topic in this book, the lines are being beautifully blurred between "access" and "DEI," all in service of the student. The story of HBCUs in the United States is a powerful example of how embracing marginalized communities created a richer society and created access to education for many more who deserved it. Dr. Anthony Jenkins, President of Coppin State University in Baltimore, Maryland, told us about how the origin story of HBCUs still guides their culture today. He said:

> "HBCUs, since their creation, have operated from a perspective of 'in loco parentis' — that is Latin for 'in place of the parent.' When free slaves and African Americans first entered our institutions, there was an agreement with the parents. They would bring their children to us. We would feed them. We would protect them. We would educate them. We would, in a sense, act in place of the parent.

> "And when the parent came back to get them, they would be scholars. They would be leaders. They would be change agents. HBCUs have never moved away from that. And so, being student-centered, operating from an 'in loco parentis' mindset is something that we do here at Coppin. And we believe here at Coppin that when our students are successful, we are successful."

All universities stand to learn a great deal from HBCUs and Hispanic-Serving Institutions as well. Dr. Dwaun J. Warmack, President of Claflin University in Orangeburg, South Carolina, told us:

> "HBCUs have been very intentional and strategic about embracing students for who they are.

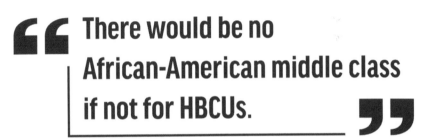

“ There would be no African-American middle class if not for HBCUs. ”

Anthony L. Jenkins, PhD
President, Coppin State University

"I fundamentally believe that every student has the ability to learn, but it has to be in an environment that *nurtures* them, that *challenges* them, and that *motivates* them.

"Until predominantly white institutions (PWIs) are intentional about diversifying the faculty, diversifying the staff, diversifying the student body, and diversifying the leadership, they'll continue to have distinct challenges."

As is the case with all the challenges that are highlighted in this book, the challenges posed by diversity deficits and equity gaps can be overcome. Even for institutions struggling to catch up when it comes to diversity, equity, and inclusion, the future remains bright — as long as they're willing to take the necessary steps to move forward. Dr. Anthony Cruz, President of Miami Dade College's Hialeah and Kendall Campuses in Hialeah, Florida, told us:

"For the United States to really have a bright future, it needs to continue to educate its people, in general, as much as possible — with *higher* education being a pivotal piece of that. And given the fact that the Latino/Latina population in the United States is increasing every time that there's a census, and given the fact that, unfortunately, completion rates for higher education for Latinos and Latinas is relatively low, I think for the future of higher education to be bright and for the future of the *United States* to be bright as an economic engine of the world, it needs to open its doors and its hearts and more opportunity to Latinas and Latinos. And that means starting early — in elementary schools — talking to kids about the importance of college and of higher education and continuing those conversations throughout their secondary education. So, by the time they're 18 years old, they are pursuing a post-secondary credential. And I think if this does *not* happen, we're in trouble.

"Just look at the numbers — how they're increasing in the country and how approximately one fourth of students in any school today (primary or secondary) are Latinos and Latinas in the whole country. These students will be moving into the workforce within the next 10 years, and if those individuals do not have the education that they need, we as the United States will not be the economic engine that we've been for the past 200 years. Maintaining our standing in the world is going to happen if we place more attention on this, not just at the higher-education level, but throughout the educational process for all Latinos and Latinas. Latinos and Latinas are now the largest minority group in the United States, and it will continue to be the largest and it will continue to grow. And for us to really be successful as a country, this must be one of our priorities."

While interviewing hundreds of higher-education leaders for *The EdUp Experience Podcast*, one priority for my co-author, Dr. Joe Sallustio, was to talk to leaders about the way their institutions market and position themselves. So, "I see that, on your website, you ..." was a common opener to vibrant conversations about doing the things we *say* and highlighting the things we *do*. In chatting with Dr. Michael Torrence, President of Motlow State Community College in Tullahoma, Tennessee, we couldn't help but mention that their website has a navigation menu drop-down for "Belong." Without skipping a beat when asked about this, Dr. Torrence told us that, as an institution, "Your values show up on your home page."

The more we talked about those values and, specifically, the concept of "belongingness," it became clear that belongingness is a key element of inclusion. Think of your own sense of yourself in certain groups and places in your life and career — where have you been simply "included" and where have you felt you truly "belong?" Dr. Torrence told us:

> "Belongingness is about the experiential component of coming to our institution and engaging with our faculty, staff, maintenance and facility workers, the office of the president, executives, et cetera."

I loved that he mentioned executives and himself last, and Dr. Torrence's was the first interview I reviewed for this book that mentioned interactions between students and the maintenance and facility workers as being meaningful. This is a president who, in my eyes, sees everyone. And everyone at a college or university — no matter your role or title or length of your tenure — has an opportunity to connect in vital ways with the students. While we often think of "student services" advocates as the people who work in offices with names like admissions, financial aid, student affairs, and residence life, Dr. Torrence reminded us that:

> "Students spend about 94 to 96% of their time with faculty members. So, we are looking at how to create better systems and better support structures for our employees, specifically our faculty, so that students can connect with them."

Connections matter. The student/faculty relationship can make or break the college experience, resulting in success or failure for the student. Are colleges and universities doing enough to train, inspire, and support their faculty to build strong, meaningful, multi-faceted relationships with students?

Belongingness was a topic that was surfaced in yet another interview, when we spoke with Dr. Saúl Jiménez-Sandoval, President of California State University Fresno. He told us:

> "There are two main pillars that really sustain student success at Fresno State (and I would say that, at many other universities as well). The one pillar, of course, is that sense of belonging. And the other is academic success. These two elements have to work together really, really well. Knowledge and belonging."

This is a powerful and simple call to action for Fresno State — how might we ensure that students learn and that they belong? Years ago, we spoke about belongingness by talking about "fit" — about whether a new student felt like a college or university was the right "fit" for them. I'm thrilled to see that institutions are beginning to recognize that it's not enough to be the right fit in terms of institution size or available academic programs, but that it comes down to culture and whether a student feels "at home" in every sense of the word. There is nothing quite so welcoming than to hear (and feel) "You belong here."

Pro Tip: *Back to those (sometimes pesky) admissions requirements. Do the admission requirements communicate "You belong here" or "You have to prove to us that you belong here?" Messaging will affect the top level of the interest funnel in positive or negative ways, and this is particularly important if an institution is looking to increase enrollment. Belonging isn't something you say — it's something you create.*

Another word that we added to our collection — layering upon diversity, equity, inclusion, and belongingness — was empathy. Dr. Tracy Espy, President of Mitchell College in New London, Connecticut, told us that her institution uses the phrase "diversity, equity, and empathy." She explained it this way:

> "Empathy and diversity go hand in hand. How do we sort of step back and reflect on what someone else's experience is? Or be empathetic to it? A lot of times, we focus on liking and acceptance, and some people may not be at that point yet. But they can have *empathy* for the path that someone else has either gone on or is trying to move through. It doesn't matter if you like or dislike someone, but it's trying to find some empathy within yourself to respect people and to give them the space that they need to become all that they can and want to be."

For students to become all that they can be, we need to move past DEI plans and statements to take big steps in achieving true diversity, equity, inclusion, belongingness, and empathy. Dr. Michael A. Baston, Former President of Rockland Community College in Ramapo, New York, spoke to this by saying:

> "At Rockland, we've engaged in what we call 'steps beyond statements.' And we are leaning very far in to ensure that we address structural racism through educational transformation. How do we use education to challenge unconscious bias — to challenge the unchallenged narratives in higher education and in society in general? And I'm really proud of the fact that we are improving our employee experience and doing it with an equity lens, by gathering people into the conversation and giving people a voice so that they can make our institution strong.

> "I encourage *all* educational institutions to look at their practices and determine what equitable reforms need to take place. Because when we, as institutions, make part of our mission preparing those educated citizens, we then will see how our world can get better, how our world can get brighter, how we can have a much more just union. And so, I believe it's incumbent upon every educator to participate in helping our country to get moving in the direction of appropriate, equitable outcomes for all students. And I hope that is a future we all believe in and will work hard to secure."

Dr. Baston's advice to ask ourselves about what equitable reforms need to take place echoed sentiments from other presidents interviewed for *Commencement*. Dr. Julie White, President of Pierce College Fort Steilacoom, told us:

> "We are building targeted supports for our most marginalized students. We are also looking at all our systems and processes to ask ourselves, 'How would this process feel for our most marginalized students?'"

That institution-wide introspection can yield powerful results. I'm particularly encouraged by the strides made in higher education during the pandemic; when times became unbelievably tough, colleges and universities stepped up in big ways. Dr. White talked about the ways in which the early 2020s lit a fire under the industry, by saying:

> "The dual pandemics of COVID-19 and a national racial reckoning offer a silver lining in that we have an amazing opportunity to reshape ourselves and to build anti-racist institutions. We know that that commitment is in a larger structure of a system of higher education that was built to *limit* access, not to expand it. That's just a fact; higher education initially was not meant for many of the students who come to our community colleges. We are trying to build a just institution in an unjust system. Yet if we do this right, we can actually make the *future* of higher education be anti-racist."

Creating Student-Centric Cultures, Environments, and Services

Putting students first is a way of being. It's a mindset. It's a commitment that never sleeps. So, while it's imperative that colleges and universities develop and fund the right departments, build and implement the necessary infrastructure, and offer experiences and services that support students at every turn, what comes first is a mindset reset. A students-first "mindset reset" is especially vital for institutions that have historically infantilized their students and maintained a culture in which students are expected to conform to existing power structures and comply with status-quo expectations. During the research phase of writing this book, Dr. Joe Sallustio and I were privileged to speak with several academic leaders who are embracing the opportunity to operate student-centric institutions. As such, we spent a lot of time learning from them about the power of culture and how to create an environment that puts the students first.

Putting students first is a way of being. It's a mindset. It's a commitment that never sleeps. So, while it's imperative that colleges and universities develop and fund the right departments, build and implement the necessary infrastructure, and offer experiences and services that support students at every turn, what comes first is a mindset reset.

If you've ever watched the television drama *New Amsterdam* — set in a New York public hospital with a medical director, Dr. Max Goodwin (played by Ryan Eggold), who is equal parts innovative leader and anti-establishment hero — you're familiar with the power of asking, "How can I help?" For Dr. Goodwin, all good things come from serving the patients in a "the customer is always right" manner and in constantly asking his colleagues at the hospital, "How can I help?" Sure, it's just a television show with a little too much drama and not quite enough science, but I'm not afraid to admit that the writers of *New Amsterdam* have changed the way I lead. In my conversations with colleagues and clients, I now try to default to an open-minded philosophy around my responsibility to serve. "How can I help?" It's amazing how much deeper my relationships have grown and how much my ego has diminished simply by employing this simple question wherever I can.

Why am I talking about my television-watching habits? Because pop culture mimics life at forward-thinking colleges and universities in the 2020s. Dr. John Porter, President of Lindenwood University, told us about his institution's "Q2 Philosophy" — a way of being through which everyone is encouraged to always ask employees and students two questions (Q2):

1. What do you need?

2. And how can I help?

Dr. Porter told us:

> "When you take that perspective, it's a service-oriented expectation. The Q2 sets the tone for how we want to drive and operate as an institution."

During our conversation with Dr. Porter, Dr. Sallustio shared his own thoughts on what such a student-centric institution looks like and requires of its workforce. Dr. Sallustio said:

> "If you always put the student first, you *have* to iterate and you *have* to ideate constantly because the student is moving faster than the institution."

The lessons for other higher-education institutions? Dr. Porter sums it up this way:

> "To succeed in the future, colleges and universities have just got to be more in tune with our students and the world around us. In higher education, you've got to have the critical thinking skills. And it's got to be pragmatic. And, bottom line, it's *got* to be student-centric."

Being student-centric is hard enough when you serve just one population of students, like institutions who exclusively serve students aged 18-23 through coming-of-age traditional degree programs. But for institutions who have students of many ages, lifestyles, backgrounds, and modalities of educational delivery, being student-centric gets complex (and ever more important). Dr. Summer McGee, President of Salem Academy and College in Winston-Salem, North Carolina, faces the daily complexities of having stakeholders of many types and ages. Salem College serves college students of all ages, and Salem Academy is a boarding and day school for high-school girls. She told us that, when it comes to being student-centric in a unique institution, communication is key. She said:

> "Being able to try to meet the needs and expectations of students ranging from 13 years old all the way through seniors who are joining us for our adult-education program really means you have to do a lot of *listening*. And you have to do a lot of *talking*."

Good communication with your students starts on day 1 and requires a nurturing approach to the student/institution relationship. I appreciated that Dr. Jack Thomas, President of Central State University in Wilberforce, Ohio, understands that there are phases of "onboarding" for new students and that students aren't up to speed on day 1. He said:

> "We want them to get acclimated to the university and have a successful transition from high school to college. And *then* we want to make sure that they have those skills necessary to be successful on a college campus."

Dr. Julie White, President of Pierce College Fort Steilacoom, is another leader who understands that students sometimes need a leg up when they're just beginning their college odyssey. While guest-hosting an episode of *The EdUp Experience Podcast*, Dr. White answered the classic EdUp question "What's your entrance music?" by talking about the song "Fighter" by Christina Aguilera. Dr. White told us:

> "I feel like it hasn't been easy. I'm a first-generation college student. I didn't have a lot of social capital throughout my higher-education experience. I feel like I've kind of had to be scrappy and work my way up and I have had some doubters, as we all do. And so, every time I hear that song "Fighter," that resonates with me."

This candid comment was a powerful reminder that the divide between higher-education leaders and their students isn't always that wide — many of today's academic decision-makers have walked in the shoes of students whose stories are not dissimilar to their own. In fact, that's why many people choose higher education as a career — because they've "been there and done that" and want it to work even better for the next generation of students.

The divide between higher-education leaders and their students isn't always that wide — many of today's academic decision-makers have walked in the shoes of students whose stories are not dissimilar to their own.

Knowing that time or age is sometimes the only thing that really separates academic leaders — faculty, staff, and administrators — from enrolled learners allows us to see the value of mentorship programs (formal and informal). Dr. Wayne A. I. Frederick, President of Howard University in Washington, D.C., told us:

> "Mentorship is such an important thing. Ultimately, I think one of the things that helps people succeed is instilling confidence in them early and often. Because there seems to be a generational divide, we sometimes fail to realize that young people want to be mentored. There's so much more to our humanity that needs to be explored between the generations and that should occur during mentorship. So, I urge all of us to play our role in terms of trying to mentor that generation."

Beyond formal mentorships and personal relationships, students deserve a certain amount of access to the leadership of the college or university where they are enrolled. In what other industry would we consider it acceptable for a customer to spend between $10,000 and $100,000 and not have earned the right to speak to "tier 2 support?" Dr. Emily J. Barnes, Former Interim President and Chief Academic Officer, and Provost of Cleary University in Howell, Michigan, talked to us about the frictionless culture that made her institution's leadership approachable and available, saying:

> "There are no rules of engagement here. If students want to come and talk to a VP or provost or the president, they can do so without any barrier."

I see that as a sign of respect for students, and a sign that has been a long time coming in higher education. A huge part of treating students well starts with how higher-education employees treat one another. Dr. W. Kent Fuchs, President of the University of Florida, talked to us about organizational culture and why it matters, saying:

> "Obviously we're working hard to be even more excellent and to achieve aspirational goals, but I say, in the midst of that, let's have fun. And so, I do things that hopefully communicate to the faculty and staff that you can have fun in the midst of working hard."

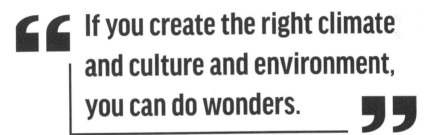

If you create the right climate and culture and environment, you can do wonders.

Mary Schmidt Campbell, PhD

President Emerita, Spelman College

What does it look like to have fun at a university? Every institution is different. At University of Florida, they take the work seriously but are careful not to take *themselves* too seriously. Every year, Dr. Fuchs told us, the president and his team play an April Fool's Day prank (and sometimes they get national attention for this bit of harmless fun). One year, they announced that they were merging with Florida State University (and they got Florida State to play along!). Another year, they said the president was switching jobs with the football coach. And another year, they said they no longer wanted to be the "Florida Gators" and were considering a new mascot. April Fools! "It's okay to have fun, as you work hard and as you love each other and care for each other," Dr. Fuchs said.

Higher-education professionals are stretched thin and need daily affirmation, inspiration, and respect to continue putting students first.

We wondered whether — across the entire higher-education industry — leaders were really having fun ... whether, on average, they were satisfied with their jobs. So, we asked 136 college and university professionals whether they really enjoyed their jobs as higher-education leaders. A concerning 28.22% were unable to answer in the affirmative. Some strongly disagreed with the statement "I really enjoy my job as a higher education leader," yet others simply disagreed, and the vast majority of dissatisfied academic professionals said that their job enjoyment "depends on the day (sometimes disagree and sometimes agree)." Knowing that higher-education professionals are stretched thin and need daily affirmation, inspiration, and respect to continue putting students first, it's crucial that decision makers at the highest levels focus on culture. Creating a culture conducive to supporting students as they deserve requires:

➜   Bringing humanity back to higher education.

➜   Ensuring your administrators are approachable.

- Reducing power distance (at every level — between faculty and students, between employees and administrators, etc.).
- Respecting your students as the adults they are.

We titled this chapter "The People Imperative" because we believe that putting the people first — the needs and humanity of the college or university workforce and its students always superseding a less-than-human adherence to status quo, history, policy, or tradition — ultimately benefits everyone. We can talk all we want to about traditions and history (and big, beautiful buildings and what have you), but a good experience that's created for students and other stakeholders really comes down to the employees — to the staff and faculty and administrators at an institution. As such, one of the things that most impresses me these days is when I encounter a higher-education institution that has addressed, head on, the limitations of a workplace structure that's built on silos and bureaucracy. I have worked in and alongside many institutions where faculty, staff, and administrators are using phrases like "That's not in my job description" or "That's above my pay grade" or "I'm sorry, but I don't have the authority to do anything about that."

We believe that putting the people first – the needs and humanity of the college or university workforce and its students always superseding a less-than-human adherence to status quo, history, policy, or tradition – ultimately benefits everyone.

Making Education Your Business with Dr. Joe Sallustio

Accredited and Innovative

In higher education, we have a bad habit of wielding our accrediting body as a red herring. Employees at all levels of an institution should understand that innovation is possible, and accreditation is *not* a barrier to innovation. No accrediting association *wants* to have institutions underperforming financially within their membership. I loved my conversation with Dr. Heather Perfetti, President of the Middle States Commission on Higher Education (MSCHE), in late 2020. She was adamant that institutions look at innovation and explore alternatives that keep them well-positioned for the future. Our discussion included the awareness of students as consumers and their ability to move between institutions, the importance of collaborations and partnerships, and about MSCHE being a *partner*, not the *punisher*, for higher education's future.

It's been refreshing for me to witness from afar the institutions where — from a student or alumnus's standpoint — it's impossible for stakeholders to even guess the job titles or reporting structures of the people they meet when they interface with college representatives. I love it when vice presidents roll up their sleeves to get involved in tactical work and when the athletics team is involved in fundraising while the fundraising team is involved in career services — and everybody is supporting alumni relations and admissions. An "all hands on deck" culture benefits everyone — especially the learner. We had the opportunity to talk about this with Dr. John Swallow, President of Carthage College in Kenosha, Wisconsin. We asked him about silos and bureaucracies, about job titles and department structures, and he said:

> "I just start with the idea that we have a lot of work to do on behalf of our students. And we should start with that. And that work might change from year to year. And that everything else should just follow from that. Why wouldn't you organize for the *work* instead of starting

"The heart of the university is not the business. The heart of the university is the students.

W. Kent Fuchs, PhD
President, University of Florida

with some arbitrary *organizational structure*, committees, or titles, and then try to fit all the work into it?"

While Dr. Swallow was speaking, I could practically hear EdUp co-founder Elvin Freytes cheering. Because, well, you know how much he loves committees.

At its core, college and university culture is about how leaders and decision-makers treat the students. Dr. Claudia V. Schrader, President of Kingsborough Community College (a CUNY campus) in Brooklyn, New York, told us:

"What makes us *special* is how we treat our students. And how we treat our students is what makes them *successful*."

Perhaps the best way to fully appreciate hundreds or thousands of students — and to create the organizational culture that sees and honors those students for who they are — is to regularly take time to imagine a few of the individual stories that make up your student population. Jim Milton, Chairman and CEO of Anthology Inc., told us:

"One thing I like to do when I'm talking to our Anthologists — our employees — even if it's a developer or somebody working in the back office who doesn't visit with our customers or see them or see the results of their work, is to ask them to envision two types of students especially. Envision a non-traditional student — maybe a single mother of two who's gone back to college to make a profound impact on her life and her family's life, or maybe a former inmate in a prison who has a chance through education to have a *second* chance at a successful life. Imagine the profile of *that* student. And that is what you are focused on, day in and day out, no matter what your job is within our company. That's the difference that we want to make."

Student as Customer

There are a lot of ways to talk about it: Meeting students where they are, being student-centric, treating students as customers. And while it's arguable that the words we use don't matter as much as the actions we take, Dr. Joe Sallustio and I feel strongly that the only way any business can succeed (and, yes, higher education *is* a business sector, no matter what you call it) is for you to first recognize that the learner is the customer. Because truly, how can "customer service" exist in your organization if you fail to acknowledge that your *customers* exist?

Making Education Your Business with Dr. Joe Sallustio

Student as Customer

Higher education is a business industry. The student is the customer/consumer of the product that higher education sells. Provide incredible customer service, or you will have no customers. That is all.

Honestly, anything else I could write on this topic — any detailed, eloquent, or long justifications of why the above paragraph is true — eventually distills down to what I already said above. There's a reason why we describe *The EdUp Experience Podcast* as the place "Where we make education your business."

If you don't think that higher education is a business and you don't think that students are its customers, you probably work for an institution with enrollment and/or retention issues.

We spoke with dozens of college and university presidents about the semantics and the strategies — about the big, polarizing topic of "student as customer." And what we heard was poignant and thought-provoking at every turn. Dr. Michael A. Cioce, President of Rowan College at Burlington County in Mount Laurel, New Jersey, told us:

> "There are pockets of higher ed that refuse to call students 'customers.' And I think that, at the end of the day, they're our clients."

Clients or customers, serving them better today than we did yesterday — and better tomorrow than we did today — is imperative. Dr. Cioce said:

> "I think continual improvements to 'meeting students where they exist' is going to help us as a sector writ large. Meeting students where they are is going to be vital."

We found, when talking to leaders about students as customers, those who have led in other sectors — especially business-to-consumer industries — were using different language and operating under vastly different principles than some leaders who have spent their entire careers in nonprofit higher education. Frank F. Britt, Former CEO of Penn Foster Education Group, had a lot to say about the topics covered in this chapter — about access, affordability, convenience, flexibility, and quality. That conversation led us naturally into a discussion of "student as customer." Britt told us:

> "We want to create a brand experience that works best for you and have, on the other side of it, high confidence that employment opportunities are available for you in whatever geography you exist. And we need to do so in a way that meets the criteria that I think all consumer products meet — which are a combination of convenience, affordability, and quality."

We asked Britt the question, "What do you say to people who bristle when we refer to students as 'customers' or talk about 'customer experience' and 'customer service' in higher education, as there are many people who think referring to educational customers only as 'students' or 'learners' is somehow more respectful or pure?" He responded brilliantly:

> "Firstly, what *I* think and what an *academic* thinks is not that primary — what matters is the way *consumers* are going to make choices. And I think we know, if you take a step back to think about it, consumer engagement is the most complicated, demanding industry in the country. And you have everyone from Disney to NBC, to CNN, to Spotify, all competing for one common thing, which is the attention of the consumer.

> "The reality is that education is a *choice* and you, by definition, have to *earn* the time, energy, and resources to embrace and engage a consumer to be upskilled, reskilled, and alike (AKA 'education'). That's a choice that the consumer has to make — along with all the other choices they're making in their lives — to allocate both their

Student demands are changing wildly.

Laura K. Ipsen
President and CEO, Ellucian

time, their attention, and their capital. And their reference point is not education. The reference point is a combination of all the *other* consumer products — both digital and physical — they consume in their lives.

"And so, what I *think* is not that important, but what I *know* (because we research this extensively — we're the largest provider in the United States of upskilling to the middle class, serving over 250,000 adult learners a year — so we have critical mass of understanding) is that they demand and *expect* a consumer experience that works for them."

Do you need a minute to let that all sink in? It's fascinating (and true) to think about higher education competing for a consumer's attention, as Britt suggests. If we can accept that fact, does it change our mindset on *when* we engage, *how* we engage, and *why* we engage students? Given all the ways students can engage in learning activities, and the premium on time, particularly for working learners, customer service becomes an operational imperative.

Some of our conversations challenged us to take our own considerations and outlooks and push them further. That's exactly what Foundry College CEO and President, Dr. Akiba J. Covitz, did when he said:

"Not only are learners consumers, they're also investors. They want a *return* on their *investment*. And they want a *rapid* return on their investment. They don't want to wait 10 years. They don't want to wait *four* years. In fact, they don't even want to wait a year. They want to know *what* they're going to get out of it and *when* they're going to get it. And I think in the past, some of my colleagues — and maybe even myself, 20 years ago — might have said, 'Well, that's just reductive.' My undergraduate degree is in something entirely impractical. There's nothing about my undergraduate degree, explicitly, that I apply. They taught me ways of thinking and I'll forever be grateful for learning that way. Not everyone can afford to spend the money and the time — the four years — I spent there to do that.

"If we can, at Foundry College, find ways to teach those skills to a wider range of people, I think *that's* where higher education is going. Learners want to know what they're going to get from their time and when they're going to get it. And the sooner that everyone can see that, I think the better everyone will be. It doesn't mean that schools shouldn't have a four-year program for people who are really willing to put in four years to do that, but *not* providing a shorter track for people who are not in that mindset, I think, really *does* limit access and it *does* limit equity."

Customer service. Access. Equity. Diversity. Inclusion. Belongingness. Empathy. Culture. Today's college students are asking us to step up the environment in which we deliver the products and services they seek. The ways in which we can do that are myriad and exciting.

Making Education Your Business with Dr. Joe Sallustio

Deconstruction of Brand Elitism and the Rising Importance of Speed

As the narrative changes from serving the few to serving the many, institutions are repositioning their brands to communicate openness, access, and service as opposed to exclusivity and brand elitism. Brand deconstruction and reconstruction — or brand clarification, if you prefer — moves a college or university to a position to serve more first-generation students, students from lower-economic backgrounds, and students of color. As universities across the United States see declining enrollment due to demographic and pandemic factors, the path to growth comes through serving the estimated 39 million students with "some college, no degree." This population includes working learners — those with responsibilities including balancing work life and home life, bills, and kids. This population of learners forces universities to reevaluate their target audience, which is not always in line with how the institution positions its brand. As this new audience is targeted, these brands walk the tightrope of balancing elitism for their undergraduate populations while opening themselves to students who need more support. That support, when done well, makes an institution "student-centric." Providing the right scaffolding and culture for degree completers or short-term credential seekers requires a customer-service mindset.

Many institutions vying for a new population of students saturates an already crowded marketplace. As we see higher education become more commodified, it cements the student-as-consumer operating model. Some institutions, which include online super-brands, are using Google pay-per-click advertising combined with a high-touch speed-to-service model that is edging out all others. If a company selling any product is the *first* product in front of the consumer, the likelihood of purchase is higher. In higher education, institutions have long sold their elevated quality as a differentiator, presuming that no matter when the prospective student finds them, the student will be willing to change their mind and choose the "high-quality" school. Accreditors, however, create parity regarding educational quality by holding institutions to certain standards of academic operation so that they are eligible for Title IV funding through the federal government. So, if we assume parity in educational experience and outcomes, doesn't *speed* to consumer become one of the most differentiating factors?

The student is buying goods and services on retail sites (sometimes delivered the very same day)[24], accessing their bank accounts on demand, and making offers to buy a house within minutes — all from their cell phone, which becomes the bridge between servicer and those serviced. This begs the question we've been asking for years in higher education: Can universities deliver on admissions, enrollment, registration, and support services as fast as a student can access their bank account? The answer ... not yet. Credit transfer evaluations, prior learning assessments, and other academic reviews (that include committees[25]) reduce the speed to service for the consumer. The student

---

24 Kate lives one highway exit away from an Amazon distribution center with 1.5 million square feet of warehouse space. If she orders something in the morning, it's not unusual to have it sitting on her porch a few hours later. "Waiting" for something to be delivered is often more convenient (and fast) than heading over to a department store on your lunch break. The game has changed. And students are expecting the same kind of service and immediacy from higher education that they receive from retail outlets.

25 If we played higher-ed word association, as we've done many times on EdUp, what would be your response to the word "committee?" Do not embrace complexity – great advice from my friend Dr. Bill Pepicello. Higher education is designed to slow innovation and shield from change. The committee actualizes complexity.

consumer is fickle, and more often than not, will go to the institution that serves them the fastest. Like it or not, in these moments, university brand becomes a secondary factor.

Most institutions know that speed is important, but there are internal barriers and general inertia that prevent change from taking place. Higher education is full of great oxymorons, like decision-making committees that champion shared governance while reducing the priority of "service to students." If we can't make quick decisions because of our bureaucracies, how can we ever take quick action in serving our students? The race to the top of a Google search demands speed in all facets of the institution. An institution of higher education doesn't just compete against institutions in its competitor set (i.e., "like" institutions); it competes with the general public perception that higher education doesn't have value *and* it competes with the alternative credentialing companies that are syphoning students from higher-education pathways. The problem of public perception is real. Think about taking a product, say sneakers for example, and placing it in the same context. Nike vs. Hoka is easy to understand when selecting a running shoe — but imagine if public perception of sneakers, in general, was that they weren't needed to protect your feet against the future weather, that sneakers weren't needed for running anymore, that they were too expensive, or that you should look at alternatives to needing shoes, like not running at all. Crazy to think about.

So, how does an institution win? We win with speed. With parity in educational quality, and the varying importance of brand depending on student type, the fastest path to differentiation is *speed*. When recruiting traditional students, be the institution that gives the first tour, not the third. When recruiting adult students, communicate about speed itself by relaying how quickly a student can complete their degree. In the 2020s, we can no longer assume that "if we build it, they will come." They will not.

We wondered, while conducting the research for this book, how different institutions thought about "customer service" or "student-centric" cultures — what it all means to leaders and to the learners they serve. And surely, not everyone is keen on using the actual words "customer" or "consumer," though many are unequivocal about their commitment to student-centric cultures. Don Kilburn, CEO of University of Massachusetts Online (UMass Online), told us:

> "I wouldn't say that education is moving to 'students as consumers.' But what I *would* say is that there is a lot of thought — especially around these degree completers and working adults — as to what it means to be truly student-centric and student-focused. I think that what you see in these wraparound services — in programs that do better by these students — is that they do financial aid advising, they try to get you as many credits as you're due toward your program (to reduce the cost and time toward your degree). They tend to have standardized navigation for the courseware. I mean, it's something as simple as the fact that you don't want to have a lot of variance in the experience every time you actually go into a course. Customer-centric institutions tend to be heavy on an assessment strategy that allows them to see when a student might have difficulty so you can actually intervene at that point and make a difference; whether it be a life event or an educational problem, you want to intervene before you find out the student has actually dropped the program. These are all, I think, examples of what you could say are 'consumer' focused, but I think that's really 'student' focused."

Not everyone is keen on using the actual words "customer" or "consumer," though many are unequivocal about their commitment to student-centric cultures.

As someone who is a self-proclaimed "word nerd" and "data junkie," I was interested to hear Don Kilburn talk about how being "data-driven" can make you incredibly "student-focused." He explained:

"When you begin to collect this data, you can continually improve the educational experience. The data reveals interesting things. I remember in my former days at Pearson, ... we did some research on an institution that wanted to find out why students were dropping out and the usual assumption was, 'Well, the students just weren't good enough or they weren't trying hard enough or something.' And lo and behold, we found out that 44% of the students in the institution who were dropping had GPAs between 3.0 and 4.0. So clearly, they weren't 'failing students.' Something else was getting in the way and something else was happening there ... Being truly student-focused is actually taking on responsibility — joint responsibility — for the success of those students."

Dr. Bradford L. Sims, President of Capitol Technology University in Laurel, Maryland, is a strong believer in doing the work to remain competitive in the students' eyes, moving quickly to make decisions, and constantly asking what they can do better for their learners. He told us:

"My goal is to keep our university up with what current market demands are. And we can do that because we're very entrepreneurial and we're always thinking about how we can make that happen. We're also customer-service focused. We understand that, whether you're an undergraduate or master's or doctoral student, you are our customer. And so, we're looking to the student and asking, 'What can we do to help support you?'"

The only way we, in higher education, can serve students as they deserve (whether you call them customers or not) is by putting them first in every consideration and decision and by building and nurturing cultures that are the ideal environment in which learners can thrive.

Pima Community College's Chancellor and CEO, Lee Lambert, JD, (whose institution is based in Tucson, Arizona), cares a great deal about the conditions that create student success. He told us:

"Student success; diversity, equity, and inclusion; and community engagement are our guiding lights. If we stay focused on that — regardless of what's changing in the environment — we're always going to be able to play our pivotal role as that hub within the community."

The business of higher education is a very personal business — one in which humanity should remain at the core. Lambert told us:

> "There has to be an organization that never gives up on the human spirit, that never gives up on people's potential. And that organization, thankfully, is the community colleges in the United States of America. We are a very, very unique innovation. And so, we should be embracing and continuing to invest in that because talent and human potential is a serious thing to allow to waste."

Creating a Smooth, Friction-Free Student Experience

We're certainly not going to close out a chapter about treating students as VIP customers without talking about the "services" themselves that make up "student service" and contribute to a smooth, friction-free student experience. We were particularly struck by an example provided by Dr. John Porter, President of Lindenwood University, who said:

> "Every experience a student has should be a *great* experience. If a student is in line for financial aid and they get up to the counter and are told, 'You're at the wrong place. You need to go two blocks down to the other building.' No, no, no. What *we* want to do is to come out from behind the desk, take the student over there, and let that student say, 'Wow, that was a great experience.'"

Are the employees at your institution empowered to create those kinds of above-and-beyond experiences for your students? How easy is your campus to navigate? How about your processes? Are there hoops to jump through or clear paths to follow?

Handholding takes a lot of forms in higher education, and most forms are crucial (but often overlooked by overwrought higher-education faculty and staff). Dr. Claudia V. Schrader, President of Kingsborough Community College in Brooklyn, New York, told us:

> "For many students — like first-generation students and students who stopped out and are coming back for a second try — it's necessary to do a lot of handholding. Because students are afraid to take that step

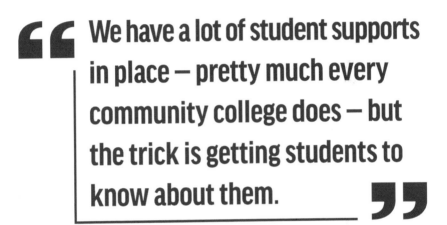

" We have a lot of student supports in place – pretty much every community college does – but the trick is getting students to know about them. "

P. Wesley Lundburg, PhD
President, San Diego Miramar College

into education. I think it's very scary for a lot of our students, but we grab their hands, we show them the way, and we tell them it's going to be okay. And we're there to support them and just root for them along the way."

Supporting students doesn't always have to happen outside the classrooms. Some institutions are building "student success skills" into the curriculum itself. Marvin Krislov, JD, President of Pace University in New York, New York, told us:

"I teach a class that we give to every first-year student called Introduction to the University. And we talk about how to handle your finances, how to take care of yourself, how to study, and how to manage your time. Time management is still, I think, the number one challenge for our entering students, for freshman undergraduates. And then at the end, we talk about 'Let's create a plan for you.' That first semester, we focus on a plan for the first two years."

Supporting students (and keeping them from year to year) has gotten a lot more attention of late. I'm a fan of the term du jour, "scaffolding" — because if we're doing it right, we're providing students with the external supports to feel held up and held steady, even during disorienting or stressful junctures in the academic experience. Providing that scaffolding, in the right ways and at the right moments, requires insights. And gathering those insights requires thoughtful processes and smart data-management. John Farrar, the Director of Education at Google, said to us:

"The amount of data that higher ed is sitting on in terms of understanding different student scenarios is huge."

And he's right. Why are we letting students flounder if we have data that tells us that the average marketing major starts to struggle academically when they take their first quantitative class? Why aren't we proactively offering assistance at predictable junctures? Not long ago, by virtue of my role on a liberal arts college's presidential leadership council, I had the pleasure of hearing Dr. Tim Renick, now the founding executive director of the National Institute for Student Success at Georgia State University, talk about how Georgia State eliminated equity gaps for their students by using data to guide an entire constellation of student supports — from what we call "intrusive advising" to AI-enabled chatbots to micro grants to keep students from needing to drop out. What Georgia State did, and what many excellent, forward-thinking, student-centric colleges and universities are doing, was answer the criticism from John Farrar by essentially saying, "Yes, we have tons of data (or we can get tons of data) and it's high time we used it to provide radical, game-changing student service."

Providing a better student experience — a journey that is frictionless and generates good outcomes — is an all-hands-on-deck proposition. Every department at a college or university needs to be involved. And, according to the presidents we interviewed, even families and external communities can become part of this experience.

Dr. Anthony Cruz, President of Miami Dade College's Hialeah and Kendall Campuses, told us that they are endeavoring to work more with the families of their youngest students. He said:

> "They're entrusting their children to us. We want to make sure that we're providing them the best experience possible."

Working with parents and families can be complicated, but the results can be remarkable. After conducting some focus groups for a private college a few years ago, I realized that too many institutions are letting FERPA get in the way. It's possible to have meaningful relationships with parents and families without compromising student privacy. At Viterbo University in LaCrosse, Wisconsin, where I held focus groups with parents who had previously never been communicated with (other than to receive a tuition bill), the work of family engagement was transformative. One of the big discoveries of this work — which many institutions are starting to appreciate — is that parents, other family members, and friends (the folks that the for-profit sector has long been calling the "buying committee" for a student) are a college or university's best "retention partner."

Hear me out. Imagine that Jordan is a first-year student at a liberal-arts college and she's living away from home for the first time. She's a first-generation student and she's not getting along with her roommate, she hasn't joined any clubs or made any friends, and her chemistry course is a lot harder than she expected. When Jordan calls her mom and dad and says, "I can't do this. I hate it here. I want to come home," Jordan's parents may have no frame of reference for what the onboarding or transition period looks like for a new student. They've never gone away to college. And if they don't know how to help their daughter, they might just say, "Then quit wasting our money, and come home. Maybe this isn't the right school or the right time for you to be there." But if Jordan's parents are properly engaged and educated about the support systems at the college, they might — instead of encouraging their daughter to drop her classes and move out of the dorms — tell her, "The student advising center is open until 7 o'clock tonight and I think it would be good for you to call them. Will you do that? And I saw that there's an open-house event for the robotics club this weekend, which sounds right up your alley. That sounds fun! Give it a chance, honey. There are a lot of people there to help you get acclimated and thrive. You've got what it takes. It's going to get better — we just know it."

It takes a village, as they say. And savvy presidents recognize that. Dr. Stephen Spinelli, President of Babson College, told us:

> "'Student life' people are going to have a bigger role in an integrated understanding of what education is. Frankly, I hate the thing about 'student life' and 'academic life.' Students have one life. I have one life."

Dr. Spinelli suggests a true mindset shift about "customer care" in higher education. Years ago, we thought of "student life" as the human part of education — the "Are they happy?" part — and it was entirely separate from academics. Today, everyone needs to be contributing to student service and student experience — and, in the end, student satisfaction. Faculty play a vital role. So do all staff members. And so do administrators. In thoughtful institutions, even alumni and community leaders are interfacing with students to enhance their overall experience.

No matter where you work or what your title is, student service is part of your job. I caught myself nodding and smiling when I heard Dr. Arthur Keiser, Chancellor and CEO of Keiser University (with a flagship campus in West Palm Beach, Florida), share:

> "My mentor in the career college sector said to me, 'If you take care of the students, the students will take care of you.' I've never forgotten that."

"If you take care of the students, the students will take care of you."

For all the ways in which higher-education institutions can better serve their students, it's important that students know how to also help themselves. Dr. W. Kent Fuchs, President of University of Florida, offered this advice to students:

> "Whether you're at a large university with graduate and undergrads, or whether you're at a small liberal arts college, you've got to find your community if you're going to thrive, if you're going to flourish, if you're going to actually be well-educated. Community is so important."

University of Florida puts its money where its president's mouth is in this regard; they have 1,000 different student organizations. There are groups based on common interests, personal backgrounds, ethnicities, and even religious perspectives. They also help create community where students might not proactively create their own by bringing them together through programs like their Machen Florida Opportunity Scholars — a program for "first in the family" college students. The university is intentionally creating a community of 1st-generation students (named for Bernie Machen, their former president). There is a ceremony for the students when they arrive and again at graduation, and being a "Machen Scholar" gives students a sense of community with one another. I'm reminded of our conversations with Drs. Torrence, Jiménez-Sandoval, and Baston about belongingness.

Even outside the walls of higher education (or perhaps *more* so outside the walls of higher education), at ed-tech corporations and other key players in the academic ecosystem, the need for improved student services and an easy-to-navigate relationship between student and college is clear. Jim Milton, Chairman and CEO of Anthology Inc., told us:

> "The need to put the student first and to provide more services and capabilities that put the student at the center is so vastly important. And I think that is probably one of the biggest cultural changes that I've

seen happen in higher education — not just *talking* about putting the student first, but actually *doing* it."

Even outside the walls of higher education (or perhaps *more so* outside the walls of higher education), at ed-tech corporations and other key players in the academic ecosystem, the need for improved student services and an easy-to-navigate relationship between student and college is clear.

One leader who spoke with great passion about putting the student first was Dr. Gregory Fowler, Former Global Campus President at Southern New Hampshire University.[26] He told us:

> "My work has been very much in trying to make sure we build the right *experiences* for the right *learners* at the right *time.*"

Like many academic leaders, Dr. Fowler often defaulted to the use of the term "learner" rather than "student" during our conversation. I personally believe that's more than a word choice, but a revolutionary mindset shift. Dr. Fowler said:

> "We are trying to get better at learning to *listen* more to our learners and what their needs are in the various types of situations they find themselves in. And that's certainly been accelerated by the pandemic, but we've been trying for a number of years now to get better at putting the learner at the center of this work — making sure that we think about what their needs are. And one of the things that I've said to some of my team members from time to time is, 'Remember that, particularly for our adult learners, we will never be better than their third top priority ... after work and family. So how do we take that

---

26 Between the time of his interview for this book and the book's publication, Dr. Fowler became President of University of Maryland, Global Campus.

knowledge — and rather than seeing that as a deficit — begin to see that as an opportunity for us to think about how we make sure every second they spend with us counts, and how we listen to what they're telling us? How do we build experiences that pull them in — that help them to be supported and needed — and to help us figure out how to get more of them to be successful? That includes a lot of things that aren't necessarily tied directly to content in an academic sense. Most of the reasons why students aren't being successful have nothing to do with their inability to learn.

"It has to do with all the challenges that they have to deal with in life. That 'life *does* happen.' ... The big challenge is trying to expand that consideration, that empathy, that ability to situate ourselves in the shoes of our learners. Given all these things they're facing and our desire to see more of them be successful, what do we need to do differently to help them?"

We interviewed Dr. Fowler at the height of the pandemic crisis, but it was clear to us that his student-centered philosophy of leadership predated and transcended acute moments of crisis. He challenged us all when he asked:

"How do we put students at the center? And then how do we move forward from there, as opposed to making this about us and our egos? How many people's lives can we change if we do what we do well?"

Staff and Faculty First: Changing Students' Lives Through the Company You Keep

The people who work inside higher education — whether they're faculty or staff, full-time or part-time — are the heart and soul of an academic institution. Without them, there would be no classes to teach, no systems for attracting and retaining students, no brand to promote, no centers of excellence, no ivy-covered anything.

The people who work inside higher education are the heart and soul of an academic institution.

I remember, when I was the director of communications at a medical sciences university, I would walk through winter snowstorms from a distant parking lot to my office, braving the elements all the way until I got to the little row of executive parking spots that was nestled warmly against the building. Ten parking stalls: Jaguar, Mercedes, BMW, Lexus, Mercedes, Porsche, Audi, Acura, Cadillac, Land Rover. By the time I was stomping my icy boots in the lobby and peeling off my scarf and hat, unable to feel my fingers or toes, I was seething with bitterness. The executives who I tried so hard to please had never once walked through white-out snow from the south parking lot (though the Jaguar driver once gave me a ride to the front door when the temperature was below zero — the leather seats were like butter). I had to wait 20 years before I met the counterpoint to the kind of leadership I used to serve — before I became acquainted with Dr. Christopher Roellke, President of Stetson University, whose respect for staff was apparent from the start. He had experienced the parking-lot pecking order from a different vantage point, and he told us:

> "I think there's some small symbolic things that leaders can do that can build teamwork. I've only been here for a few weeks, but one of the first things I did was I pulled out my parking sign, which said 'Reserved for the President 24/7.' I didn't understand why I had a reserved parking spot when my house is across the street. It's a small, symbolic gesture, but I must say that I think that makes a difference. I think people are perhaps observing, 'Oh, he understands. He's taking tangible steps to try to eliminate whatever real or perceived barriers there might be between those who are at the senior level of an institution and those who are serving the institution in a different capacity.'"

Big things and small things, they all matter when it comes to building a culture and shining a bright light on the talents and humanity of your people. Dr. David Harpool, Former President of Northcentral University in San Deigo, California, told us:

> "How you treat your faculty and staff is directly proportional to how your students will be treated.
>
> "It all starts with culture. And if the culture you build is that 'We're not a *president*-centric university. They're not here for me. It's not about glorifying me.' And that 'We're not a *faculty*-centric university. It's not about the faculty.' And that 'We're not *just* a *student*-centered university, but we're a *learning*-centered university.' Then that culture is built."

Dr. Harpool shared that, at the beginning of the pandemic, it was rather easy for Northcentral to make major changes in service of the students because they were able to simply ask themselves: "What's best for students?"

As we'll discuss in depth in Chapter 5: Pandemic as Panacea, the COVID-19 pandemic revealed us as a higher-education industry, for better and for worse. Among the most inspiring stories shared on *The EdUp Experience Podcast* were accounts of the ways in which the immediate response to the pandemic helped institutions move more quickly, more efficiently, and more effectively as they put students first. Dr. John J. Rainone, President of Mountain Gateway Community College (formerly known as Dabney S. Lancaster Community College) in Clifton Forge, Virginia, talked to us about how those initial days and weeks played out, saying:

> "We immediately asked faculty to talk to their students to find out which ones did not have access to computers. And beginning the second week, for every two weeks that we were online, we had staff call every student to ask questions about 'How are you doing? How's your internet? Are you able to access your classes? Do you have food insecurity issues?'"

Like many institutions, Mountain Gateway operates a food pantry and worked tirelessly to care for the students who were hungry and struggling in 2020 and beyond. And as all institutions are apt to learn eventually, recent years have taught us that the only way to take good care of the students is to first take care of the staff and faculty. In a conversation with Richard L. Dunsworth, JD, President of University of the Ozarks in Clarksville, Arkansas, we explored the myriad ways in which empowered, confident, supported employees can take good care of students. President Dunsworth shared with us:

> "We made a few decisions when we went online in mid-March [2020] and took that pivot. That was when we publicly said that we were committed to our employees. That was one of the first commitments that we said. And some folks go 'Hold it. Your commitment should have been to your students first.' We said it the other way around to our employees. 'We got you. You've got a job. Know that that's secure. Now let's focus on our students.' Because part of it's just human nature — that if I'm fearful that I might get furloughed or laid off, a part of my mind is focused on contingency planning for my spouse, my children, my home, my mortgage, whatever. So, we first said, 'Hey, we got you. It is our commitment to treat this as a challenge, as a blip, and we're going to be more resilient. We're going to be a better organization on the backend. We have a 186-year history that suggests we know how to do this.'

> "So, we started there and then we started working with employees and saying, 'Okay, your job's going to change. Your job over the next couple of months is just checking in with students. You're working the phones, and you're working whatever media platform is available to you. Check in with our students; make sure they're okay. See how you can help them.' And what we did is we tried to enlist everybody in the 'Let's find solutions for whatever hits us today. And if it's too big for you to solve, push it to someone else.' And what we found is almost every week, we were giving people more authority, saying 'You've got authority to do this' — whether that's student employment, whether that's how people change majors or minors, or how people get registered for classes."

As it turned out, an empowered, supported workforce can take very good care of its stakeholders. Students were largely okay because staff and faculty were okay. But during the first year or so of the pandemic, nobody in higher education was really "okay." Our limits were tested. And when we did our best to focus on our common humanity, we were our strongest, most resilient selves. Dr. Laurie Borowicz, President of Kishwaukee

College in Malta, Illinois, talked to us about loneliness, stress, and mental health through the pandemic. She, too, believed in a "staff and faculty first" approach to leading her institution. She told us:

> "We're only good for our students if we're good for ourselves and each other. So, our HR team is working hard right now on professional development opportunities. We're doing a series of Zoom workshops on feeling good about your job, finding joy in your work, and navigating through these challenging times. We're just really trying to put resources out there to make people feel good about being a part of our college and being able to serve our students."

Kishwaukee College, like many others, began prioritizing staff and faculty so staff and faculty could prioritize students. The college even began encouraging their people to take an extra hour a week for wellness — like structured activities in exercise, mindfulness, etc.

Treating faculty and staff as the heart and soul of the university — not just in exigent circumstances, but always — is the root of a student-centric culture. As Dr. Joe Sallustio and I have watched many evolutions and revolutions take hold in higher education, we've been particularly concerned about how "The Great Resignation" has impacted the industry (and we're quite confident that the impact has only just begun). Keeping track of leadership job titles for this book was a moving target — day in and day out, someone was leaping from College A to University B, or another president or chancellor was retiring. And easily one third of my friends and colleagues who are (or were) staff or faculty in higher education have had their careers disrupted in the past three years — many laid off with little explanation.

As a higher education consultant, I find myself in a strange predicament lately, as the institutions that need my help need me so badly that there aren't qualified or available (i.e., not entirely burned out) employees to be my point of contact for the market research or brand strategy work that needs to be done. We titled Chapter 3 "Where Did All the Students Go?" And we easily could have added an entire chapter on where all the alumni-relations professionals, the IT leaders, the finance experts, the administrative support teams, and even the presidents have gone. We asked, in a survey of higher-education leaders in mid-2022, how many college and university professionals are planning or considering an exit from higher education in favor of greener pastures in a different industry. The answer? More than 40%. You may ignore that statistic at your peril. If 40% of your workforce is ready or nearly ready to move on, how will you take your institution forward? Remember that the mass exodus on the horizon is an industry-wide phenomenon — you can't replace your lost talent if comparable talent from other colleges and universities has jumped to another industry altogether. Just like the 18-year-olds who don't exist in ample numbers for incoming freshman classes, mid-career and senior higher-education professionals are becoming scarce. The only option? Home-grown talent that takes a long time to ripen. Last time I had occasion to be on campus at one of my alma maters, two key departments were understaffed by 60%, and all the new hires were junior — full of potential but with almost no experience. The offices were a ghost town, and it had nothing to do with remote workers.

For a variety of reasons, faculty tend to be a more stable workforce than higher-education staff and administration. Leaning into a respectful, well-resourced relationship with faculty is more vital than ever in the 2020s and beyond. Dr. Stephen Spinelli, President of Babson University, spoke with great admiration of his faculty, saying:

> "The vast majority of academics have heartfelt expertise and commitment to their discipline. They're *great* at what they do. And so, I get blown away every time I go to a class. They've lived their lives in this deep understanding (and this continued understanding) of their field. You have got to respect people who do that. And that's one of the reasons I love being in academia, because I'm surrounded by absolutely brilliant, committed people who care desperately to have that knowledge blossom and feed other people and grow great minds and be a part of that."

 Making Education Your Business with Dr. Joe Sallustio

People-Focused Decisions, Financial Realities

Running a university is not easy. Presidents are caught between a rock and a hard place, especially when expense reduction becomes the necessary evil. The largest controllable fixed expense (generally speaking) for a college or university is the payroll. Institutions with unions or large numbers of tenured faculty are less flexible than institutions that operate with non-tenured faculty or large adjunct faculty numbers. The alarm bells go off when a college declares financial exigency — allowing them to make sweeping cuts to faculty numbers for institutional rightsizing. It is critical for an institution to create margin for its programs, which only comes from managing the revenue and expenditures in the most flexible way possible. I learned a lot of lessons from my time in for-profit education:

➜ Hire by staff-to-student and faculty-to-student ratios.

➜ Explore different faculty compensation models.

➜ Don't run a course with less than the number of students needed to pay the faculty member.

➜ Eliminate underperforming programs quickly (easier said than done if you have a lot of committees).

➜ The raise you give now is less than the amount to rehire for a position later.

➜ Don't raise tuition when you are building enrollment momentum

➜ Ultimately, control what you can control.

Dr. Spinelli went on to talk about the powerful relationships between faculty members and students, telling us:

"I think most professors believe they're in partnership with a student — that the hierarchy is more and more breaking down and that this is an *ecosystem* of learning and that we can learn from each *other*."

That continuous, virtuous cycle of teaching and learning is what higher education is all about. Dr. Felix Matos Rodriguez, Chancellor of the City University of New York (CUNY), reminded us that:

> "Teaching matters. And sometimes we forget that at universities. Improved teaching also can lead to very big changes in student retention and success."

I loved the clarity of that statement. In higher education, we can get so wrapped up in thinking that what makes a college or university special are great dorms or good scholarship opportunities, an awesome meal plan or a beautiful campus. But in the end, it's about content and the learning experience vis à vis instructors with solid pedagogy.

If taking good care of faculty and staff is imperative, and if championing diversity is imperative, it stands to reason that hiring and maintaining a diverse employee body is also critical. We asked Dr. Michael Torrence, President of Motlow State Community College in Tullahoma, Tennessee to talk to us about diversity among faculty and staff, especially in terms of hiring strategy, and he told us:

> "We're looking at ability as much as we're looking at ethnicity. We're looking at strengths as much as were looking at gender. We're looking at where we can help someone fill a gap in themselves — whether that is holistically or pinpointing something — as much as we're looking at their socioeconomic status and whether they went to a public or a private institution or if they hold a PhD or a baccalaureate degree and they're going to come and work with us.

> "It begins and ends with those who you hire, because they're going to determine the character, the culture, and the openness that needs to be created to move through these efforts that support diversity, equity, inclusion, and belongingness. So, it can move *away* from the cyclical conversations that have been going on for almost 70 years to 'This is just who we are.' I'm not an idealist, but I *am* a dreamer and I do believe in architecting and creating spaces by looking for people, personalities, and skillsets that benefit what you're trying to get accomplished.

" **Faculty members are the heart and soul of the university.** "

Jack Thomas, PhD
President, Central State University

"And we don't want to be *good* here. We want to go beyond being *great*. We don't want to be perfect; we simply want to be permanent. And that's what I want people who come here to realize — that when you walk through the door and you talk about diversity, equity, and inclusion, it's more than the taglines that'll be discussed in different pockets of politics and bureaucracy. This is about being human. This is about being a people's people. And that's important to us. It's important to *me*."

Dr. Torrence's words here made me tear up — the first time I heard him speak them, and again multiple times as we selected quotes for this book and began stitching together the manuscript into what you now hold in your hands. (So, if you teared up a little, you should know you're not alone.) As it turns out, college and university presidents are among the most compassionate, thoughtful, empathetic, and introspective leaders we have ever had the honor of meeting. To many presidents, the faculty, staff, students, and alumni are *family*. It's personal. It matters. And it's so much more than a job.

College and university presidents are among the most compassionate, thoughtful, empathetic, and introspective leaders we have ever had the honor of meeting. To many presidents, the faculty, staff, students, and alumni are family. It's personal. It matters. And it's so much more than a job.

Dr. Hal L. Higdon, Chancellor of the Ozarks Technical Community College System and President of OTCC Springfield Campus, told us:

"The faculty have to know that I will fight as hard for them as I would for any student. And I would fight as hard for them as I would if it was my family member."

Dr. Higdon also told us that he trusts and respects that "faculty family" inherently. He said he doesn't get involved in academic affairs appeals or student affairs appeals — that it's his job to trust the faculty, the provost, etc. — and to not get involved in overruling their decisions.

So very much about the culture of a college or university — the environment in which students will either struggle or succeed — is rooted in the decisions about hiring, development, and treatment of faculty. Dr. Bill Pepicello, Former President of University of Phoenix, talked to us about faculty development, saying:

> "There needs to be an ongoing faculty development program. It needs to be not just by discipline, but by degree level and, importantly, by what kind of student you have. If you have an at-risk student, that student has to be dealt with in a much different way than a student who goes directly from high school into the university and has the means to pay tuition. Contrast that with a student who is heavily burdened with financial aid, who probably has to work, maybe is a single parent. That kind of student just doesn't relate to that more 'traditional' kind of student and, more to the point, faculty have to understand — in ways they haven't before — that these students need a completely different kind of approach if you're going to retain them and help them get through the curriculum, whatever it may be (whether it's a certificate or a degree program or whatever) and become productive numbers in their communities and society."

Over and over again, we were heartened to hear just how much presidents revere and respect the faculty at their institutions. Many presidents, of course, have been faculty members (and many still are) — and many have also served in the staff ranks. And while plenty of leaders share a vision that's all about programs and products, enrollment numbers, and brand elitism, so many are stepping up to answer the people imperative, serving the students by supporting the faculty and staff. Dr. W. Kent Fuchs, President of the University of Florida, reminded us that the expertise of your faculty is what allows you to create programs, and to create and nurture cultures. He told us:

> "We're creating the university of the future primarily through hiring faculty ... The way I, as a president, and the college deans can influence

the future is not by creating a product that we're going to focus on (apart from the students and the research), but it really is an investment in the recruiting of the kinds of faculty who have interests and a commitment to the mission of the university that creates opportunity for the students."

How Can We Help?

In some ways, higher education really isn't all that complex. It's about people seeking to be treated well while acquiring skills and knowledge, and it's about institutional leaders working together to improve communities, lives, careers, and economies. It's about people, and it's less about us than it is about them. There are a million reasons why I am honored to have co-authored *Commencement* with Dr. Joe Sallustio, and one of those reasons is his good old-fashioned civility and humanity. While interviewing Dr. Claudia Schrader from Kingsborough Community College in New York, New York, Joe said:

> "There are so many excuses that we use as human beings to justify why we can't do something. And I think that our jobs as educators is to infuse students with a level of self-confidence — to say to them, 'Yes, you can, and we're going to help you. And we're going to give you resources.'"

That hospitality mindset — the "Welcome; come on in; we'd love for you to stay awhile" — is precisely what today's learners need and deserve. And when we can give them what they seek — when, where, and how they need it — we will have achieved something quite remarkable.

To connect with and serve our students best will require a balance of high-touch and high-tech approaches, remembering that data drives our best decisions and technology used in service of people is the best technology of all. Laura K. Ipsen, President and CEO of Ellucian, said:

> "The future of higher education, I think, is a world that's powerful. A big part of that new world is going to be around the digital transformation to enable *any* student *anywhere, anytime,* to learn *what* they want, *how* they want to learn, and to learn across any *institution* they want

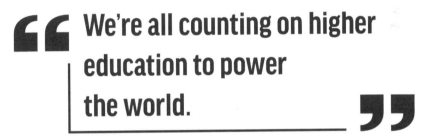

" We're all counting on higher education to power the world. "

Laura K. Ipsen
President and CEO, Ellucian

in the world, either on campus or online. The capabilities exist *now* to do that."

To connect with and serve our students best will require a balance of high-touch and high-tech approaches, remembering that data drives our best decisions and technology used in service of people is the best technology of all.

What does the future of higher education look like? It's the question that every president was asked during their EdUp Experience interview. The answers have filled this book. As for me, I think the future of higher education looks like a collaborative ecosystem of brilliant, thoughtful, multi-layered institutions that understand and embrace the people imperative — where students are treated like VIP customers and where faculty and staff are celebrated and supported as the heart and the soul of their institutions.

> "How do we disaggregate data to truly understand what we are missing — what are the gaps — for our students? How can we prepare our students — who are first gen, underrepresented, from marginalized communities — to be successful? We want to take an equity lens and apply it to every facet of the organization. "

Larry Johnson, Jr., PhD
President, Guttman Community College

"The aperture has got to open for higher education. We must be open to new ways of thinking and doing things. We see the speed at which corporations move, and there really is no reason why higher education can't move at that same speed. We can't be the laggards. We can't be afraid to make moves. We can't be afraid to fail."

John Porter, EdD
President, Lindenwood University

PART II

UNTANGLING THE TASSEL

Making Sense of America's Academic Predicament — What It's Going to Take to Reimagine and Rebuild Higher Education for a Promising Future

CHAPTER 5

PANDEMIC AS PANACEA

How COVID-19 Kicked the Academy's Potential into High Gear

We all have "COVID stories" — about our own illnesses or people we lost, about the toll that universal fear and long-term isolation took on our mental health, about jobs lost and transformed, and about children of all ages whose schools closed and whose teachers were asked to master online instruction (some with very little training). We have stories about dreams deferred, and about the day-to-day expectations and activities that changed so dramatically that we could barely keep up with the pace of crisis and transformation. This book is headed to press in November 2022 (nearly three years after the crisis began) and it still feels a little too soon to use terms like "post-pandemic" or "post-COVIDian." After all, I received my bivalent vaccine booster at the end of October 2022, and about half of the places I visit (pharmacies, doctor's offices, shops) still require that I wear a face mask. The crisis still looms large as we move from 2022 into 2023.

Whatever your stories look like, one thing is for certain — everyone's lives changed after the World Health Organization declared a pandemic in March 2020. The coronavirus (SARS-CoV-2) and the often-deadly disease caused by the virus (COVID-19) rattled us, scarred us, and permanently changed us. In higher education, it changed us for the better. The pandemic taught us that change is possible, that committees aren't entirely necessary, and that there are no legitimate reasons (and frankly never have been) why higher education can't make fast-paced decisions to immediately and positively benefit students, staff, and faculty. Literally overnight, the higher-education industry became all the things we've always wanted it to be: agile, collaborative, compassionate, vulnerable, nimble, and profoundly less bureaucratic.

The pandemic taught us that change is possible, that committees aren't entirely necessary, and that there are no legitimate reasons (and frankly never have been) why higher education can't make fast-paced decisions to immediately and positively benefit students, staff, and faculty. Literally overnight, the higher-education industry became all the things we've always wanted it to be: agile, collaborative, compassionate, vulnerable, nimble, and profoundly less bureaucratic.

 ## Making Education Your Business with Dr. Joe Sallustio

Previously Immune to Speed: The Inertia Problem That the Pandemic Solved

Committee – the one word in higher education that makes me start sweating. One of the questions leaders within higher-education institutions should ask themselves is:

Why were we able to move so quickly when we were *forced*, but can't move as quickly when we have *choice*?

At some point during the pandemic, institutional focus moved entirely to the student. Each student who disappeared from the population count was a nudge to move faster — to add student services, 24/7 access, WiFi hotspots, mental health and tele-health resources, and food pantries. When the pandemic tried to interrupt a student's educational journey, higher education — maybe for the first time as an industry — delivered amazing customer service. To continue their education, the student needed something, and institutions filled the gap.

The lesson, though thrust upon us, is now clear: Shifting from effective emergency response to strategic foresight will be a determining factor for long-term institutional success.

Looking back to 2019, it's hard to believe how much has changed so quickly. For literally hundreds of years, the academy was bound by its traditions, stuck in its ways, wrapped up in status quo. Then, suddenly, a crisis created opportunity. For weeks, then months, then years. And, like it or not, the truth is that there is no going back.[27]

It's uncomfortable to talk about "silver linings" to a crisis that killed millions of people, upended economies, and left the world reeling in almost every respect. And yet, here we are, admitting that the pandemic turned out to be a panacea for some of higher education's biggest failings. It put everything in perspective, and it put all the people — finally — on the same team.

The founding of *The EdUp Experience Podcast* created a profound and unique opportunity to chronicle what was happening at colleges and universities across the United States and around the world. From March

---

27 Surely, there are some institutions that rolled back some welcome changes once campuses reopened. In our survey research, we received several anonymous comments from higher-education professionals whose institutions chose to "go back" — back to offering zero online courses, back to complicated processes for students and prospects, back to slow decision-making and bureaucratic entanglements. Those professionals told us that they were disheartened by those short-sighted choices and that they were seriously considering leaving their institutions as a result. One survey respondent told us: "My online administrator position at my former institution was eliminated because the institution believes there is no longer a need for online learning as the pandemic has waned."

2020 through the end of that first terrifying year, the initial questions asked of the presidents and other leaders interviewed for the show were, "How are you and your family? Are you healthy? Are you safe?" Getting down to brass tacks during a leadership interview — pre-pandemic — was about jumping into discussions about mission and vision, strategic initiatives, enrollment numbers, and campus news. Suddenly, none of that mattered nearly much as human health and safety and institutional viability in the short- and long-term. No sooner had Elvin Freytes and Dr. Joe Sallustio launched the podcast did they realize that no matter how impressive a guest's title, resume, or university brand might be, we were all in this together. The playing field was leveled. Whether an institution was prestigious or practical or both, its leaders were all worrying about and scrambling to address the same problems at breakneck speed. As such, everyone brought their raw humanity to the microphone. The candor with which college and university presidents talked about their people, programs, and priorities was startling and refreshing. Their unvarnished commentary and their passionate candor made this book possible.

Everyone brought their raw humanity to the microphone. The candor with which college and university presidents talked about their people, programs, and priorities was startling and refreshing. Their unvarnished commentary and their passionate candor made this book possible.

Shining a Bright Light on a Range of Careers and the Need for Skills-based Learning

Traditional, coming-of-age undergraduate education has long been insulated from the pressures and disruptions of the outside world. "College life" and "real life" were entirely separate phases of human maturity. Enter the coronavirus pandemic. It was pure chaos — and opportunity — from the start. Dr. Akiba J. Covitz, CEO and President of Foundry College, based in San Francisco, California, talked to us about wholeheartedly embracing the evolutions and revolutions in higher education, some of which were accelerated by societal change in the face of the pandemic. He told us:

> "There's a lot of chaos — *beautiful* chaos — in education right now."

Much of that chaos was seen first in the workforce, then reflected to higher education, forcing us to think about whether we're educating for careers that are future-proof and pandemic-proof. Frank F. Britt, Former CEO of Penn Foster Education Group (home of Penn Foster College in Scottsdale, Arizona, and Penn Foster Career School and Penn Foster High School in Scranton, Pennsylvania), told us:

> "I think that the dislocation of 30 or 40 million people from retail, hospitality, and transportation has been kind of a once-in-a-generation moment to ask, 'What am I going to do next in my career?'"

Those displaced workers were suddenly looking to post-secondary educational institutions for upskilling and reskilling opportunities of all kinds. Whether the educations we provide in the future are shorter-form and skills-based or degree-length and holistic, the provision of those educational credentials is going to continue to matter to students and graduates — and they'll matter in new ways because of what the pandemic taught us. Dr. Anthony Jenkins, President of Coppin State University in Baltimore, Maryland, talked to us about delivering value and expanding the possibilities of an institutional mission by looking at trends outside our institutional walls. And as for what's coming in the months and years ahead, as we apply the lessons of the pandemic, he said:

> "The need for education and post-secondary education is stronger today than it has ever been. And it's only going to get stronger, because what we also saw is that the individuals who were in the type of credential-driven careers during this pandemic fared better than those who were not. And *that* is a glaring example of what the future is going to look like for our nation and for our world."

Workforce development used to be the domain of vocational schools and technical schools. Now, stakeholders are recognizing that everyone needs to have skills that are applicable to multiple job opportunities and that nearly every one of us will need to be educated multiple times in our lives as we make career changes along the way. So how do colleges and universities capitalize on this opportunity? By having a clear purpose and holding themselves to high standards in terms of the outcomes they enable for students. Dr. Covitz at Foundry College told us:

> "I think the true north of higher education and the workforce development system is as pertinent today as it's ever been, which is you should be purpose-driven and you should help elevate people to achieve their highest and best potential."

Much of what we learned through the pandemic were lessons we already knew but were comfortably ignoring. It was easy to ignore the importance of training auto mechanics until you couldn't find one to fix your car.

Much of what we learned through the pandemic were lessons we already knew but were comfortably ignoring. It was easy to ignore the importance of training auto mechanics until you couldn't find one to fix your car. It was easy to ignore the nursing shortage before the hospitals were over-crowded. And the many people with a broad range of skillsets to run and support your local grocery store — the refrigeration mechanics, the technologists who maintain the cash registers and online-ordering applications, the farmers, and the inventory specialists — never crossed your mind, until the only way to feed your family was by acknowledging these workers as "essential" and exploring how to educate and train more of them. Dr. Anthony Jenkins, President of Coppin State University, said:

> "The future of higher education is more important, I think, than ever before. Going through this pandemic, we have been able to illuminate

needs and gaps in our society that will require various levels of education and training to address. Our world needs diverse intellectual strength — more than ever before. We need greater tolerance. And I think institutions of higher education, K-12, and post-secondary education can play a significant role in that. So, the future of higher education I think is very bright."

Surely, the needs that accelerated during the pandemic are a trend worthy of our attention. How many of the following systems or processes did you take advantage of during 2020 and 2021 (and perhaps still now)?

- Instacart and other grocery-ordering and grocery-delivery services

- Retail websites (like Amazon and Wayfair) that maintain millions of square footage of warehouse space, where products are picked and packed — often by robots

- Meal-ordering and meal-delivery services, like GrubHub, Uber Eats, and DoorDash, or the online app for a favorite restaurant, like Pizza Hut

- Online meeting software like Zoom, WebEx, and GoToMeeting

- Use of the Calendly application for scheduling appointments with other professionals

- Virtual appointment-setting systems with your doctor and other professionals

- Contactless pickup at department stores and other retailers, where your purchases were brought directly to your car

- Self-check cash registers so you didn't have to interface with someone else up close

- Automated check in/check-out at hotels

Making Education Your Business with Dr. Joe Sallustio

Meeting the Expectations of a Marketplace that Expects Immediacy and Ease

Immediacy and ease — the overwhelming degree to which these concepts are now considered essential is a consequence of the pandemic. The expectations of our customer (the student) have changed to include frictionless experiences and expedient delivery. When I think about the expectation of "right now," it immediately brings to mind the classic movie from 1971, *Willy Wonka & the Chocolate Factory*. As she cries out to her father to buy her a golden goose, Veruca Salt says: "I don't care how, I want it NOW!"

You may think that I'm trying to compare today's students to spoiled children. Nope, I'm comparing *all* of us to spoiled children — our expectations as consumers are closer to Veruca Salt than we would like to admit. Recently, I ordered something online that I thought would be delivered within 24 hours. Those 24 hours lapsed, and I received an email saying that my order was delayed due to fulfillment and shipping complications. Like a spoiled child, I cancelled my order and re-ordered the same item from a different online store that would deliver my golden goose when I wanted it – NOW!

I know what you are thinking: that's not you. Right? You are the most patient person you know and would never dream of switching your buying habits due to poor customer service, slow delivery, or cumbersome buying processes. (Uh huh.) Recently, I tried to explain to my daughter why a show we were watching on streaming video only released episodes once a week. She's used to watching *Doc McStuffins* whenever she wants, so how dare these streaming services give you one episode at a time and not allow binge watching? Honestly, it *is* annoying.

Expectations and reality. Are the *realities* of your institutional processes meeting the *expectations* of the student? If not, what are you going to do about it?

Don Kilburn, CEO of University of Massachusetts Online (UMass Online), reminded us that these innovations and conveniences have become societal trends that impact higher education. He told us:

> "There's going to be increasing numbers of automated jobs through robotics and artificial intelligence (AI). And so, the hope is that there will be *new* jobs and you'll need to retool and train people for new jobs. I hope that's true. And if that's true, you — as an institution — need to continue to be nimble and quick enough to actually *develop* those programs so that people can make that shift as automation takes place. And you can be, by the way, entirely pessimistic or entirely optimistic on that issue, depending on your worldview going forward."

New Jargon, New Priorities

Whether we're pessimistic or optimistic about the trends taking off because of the pandemic, there's no denying that we're all using different words and putting our attention to different priorities. Or we should be. Because anyone still running their college or university like it's 2019 is going to get crushed.

It was on *The EdUp Experience Podcast,* during an interview with Pace University's President Marvin Krislov, that I first heard the term "de-densifying" to describe the process of removing or repositioning chairs, desks, tables, and cubicles from higher-education campuses so employees and students could maintain "social distance." Dining halls and learning spaces were transformed. Countless classrooms were moved outdoors or into big lobby spaces or giant auditoriums where more than two thirds of the seats were rendered unusable. Some institutions added second doors to classrooms to create a one-way traffic flow of students entering and exiting the rooms. Facilities teams were innovating and demonstrating their long-held (but previously unsung) roles as essential workers. And campuses where perhaps just a few employees previously had responsibilities for student health (like a campus nurse or campus security officers with first-aid training) suddenly found themselves assembling small armies of health-and-safety workers, responsible for COVID testing, for managing student quarantine arrangements, for distribution of personal protective equipment like masks and hand sanitizer, and for managing referrals to physicians and hospitals. In 2020 and 2021, working at a college or university whose student population was not already 100% online required a mindset shift; instead of focusing on educational mission with student satisfaction, it was necessary to focus *first* on keeping the students alive and healthy, and then on educating them. Institutions that did all this while keeping students happy became instant case studies worthy of our attention.

There was, surely, no universally perfect approach to the early days of the pandemic. Some campuses in remote areas or small towns, and especially those serving large percentages of Pell-eligible students, worried that closing their campuses would put their students at risk of hunger and would cut students off from the computer and internet access typically available to them through the college's library and computer labs. And other institutions whose coursework involved a great deal of hands-on experience or team collaboration worked diligently to stay open or to re-open as quickly as possible. Residential colleges and commuter colleges alike faced unprecedented challenges.

Dr. Michael Horowitz, President of TCS Education System (which includes The Chicago School of Professional Psychology, Pacific Oaks College, Pacific Oaks Children's School, The Colleges of Law, Saybrook University, and Kansas Health Science Center), reminded us that their average student is a 35-year-old working woman who is looking to become a nurse, psychologist, teacher, or lawyer and that the stories of such "nontraditional" students being sidelined by the pandemic weren't covered much by the media. And some of the challenges faced by students in professional schools were initially impossible to predict. Dr. Horowitz told us:

> "Our students are very focused on getting a bachelor's or graduate degree toward achieving a professional credential ... And so, what we have found is their focus [during the pandemic] is 'What can you do to keep my education on the move?' The *most* frustrating thing, for example, has been at our law school because the California bar postponed the bar exam. So, we had graduates ready to go and take the exam [and they couldn't]."

During the earliest months of the pandemic, so much was out of our control. When it came to the decisions *within* the control of college and universities leaders, it helped when an institution's internal leaders could quickly share best practices and support one another through the difficult and consequential decision-making that was necessary of them. I was struck by the degree of gratitude and confidence expressed during this era by leaders who were part of large university systems or consortiums, where there were multiple peer leaders to support one another. Dr. Horowitz told us:

> "I lead our overall system. Each of our colleges is led by a terrific president in his or her own right. And then they each have a leadership team as well. Since the lockdown started in March [2020], we've been meeting multiple times a week as a 14-person leadership team. My group of eight (myself and the people who report to me) and our six college presidents and, at the nursing school, the lead title is dean. This has been such a pleasure of our model that, rather than feeling isolated, we're there together — sifting through the information, which is ambiguous.

> "And we certainly don't live in a country with a common approach [to the pandemic] and we're cutting across communities all across the country. So, we've been able to share best practices, make decisions together, share our anxieties. That, in itself, has been phenomenal."

Even in institutions that were objectively very strong from a student-focus perspective before the pandemic, the degree to which the global crisis motivated colleges and universities to step up their game with student services, flexibility, and rapid decision-making was drastic. Dr. Hal Higdon, Chancellor of Ozarks Technical Community College and President of OTCC Springfield Campus in Missouri, spoke for the vast majority of the industry when he said:

> "The pandemic has put a jet pack on change and has meant that what we were hoping to do in *five* years, we've done in *one* year. And I think it's paying off for students."

Higher education has always had a sense of the nuanced differences between hands-on education and "classroom" education, but the pandemic allowed us to prioritize experiences that can't be replicated in an online fashion. The pandemic taught us to be thoughtful about delivery method and student engagement, and the crisis allowed students to have a voice in providing feedback about what was working well and what could be done better. Clinical healthcare training didn't work effectively in a remote setting, nor did robotics or chemistry class. Suddenly, geology professors were singing the praises of art professors who were shipping out kits of art supplies to students, and those who taught business were looking to the music department for inspiration because — let's be honest here — if the wind symphony could figure out how to practice and perform via Zoom, many other departments could get creative too. And they did.

Leaders, educators, and instructional designers all started sharing information and technology. Academia became truly "collegial" and interdepartmental collaborations became commonplace. The pandemic shined a bright light on what had been possible for higher education all along.

 # EdUp with Elvin

Practical Tips and Frontline Insights from Elvin Freytes

So, here's the million-dollar question: **How do you create an engaging online leaning community at your institution?**

Here's how:

1. Hopefully, by now, you know where I am going to start — at the beginning. Make sure to create opportunities at the very beginning of the funnel with your marketing and recruitment communications and experiences, so prospective students (i.e., your students and future alumni) can start to make connections among themselves first on their preferred social-networking platform (e.g., Telegram, SnapChat, Facebook).

2. You read that right. Prospective students need to start making connections with one another before you place/force them into a formal online community as matriculated

students. One way to encourage such connection is to engage them in ice breakers (believe it or not, they still work wonders). Get the prospective students sharing interesting and humanizing information and stories, so they can discover commonalities among themselves — like who likes to learn via video and are the big YouTube junkies in the midst, how many of them have winter birthdays, who grew up in Puerto Rico or Wyoming or Germany, who's interested in the same academic programs, who the athletes are, etc. You get the idea.

3. You can take this a step further and break the prospective students into groups to have them find 3 or 4 things that they all have in common on a deeper level. I've done this exercise many times and one memorable group found out that their grandfathers were all left-handed! These activities should also be embedded during the first class session of every online (and in-person, in my opinion) class. Once you begin engaging the learners in a community, it's important to keep the connection and communication going.

4. The key to the success of these programs is the facilitator. As such, training is pivotal for the students, staff, faculty, and/ or alumni who will serve as the facilitators. This training should be ongoing to help continue engagement once these students are enrolled.

5. Part of the training should involve mastery of the platform where the programs will take place. We say "meet students where they are" all the time, so this is exactly the time to do that. If the students want to meet via Telegram, your facilitators need to be masters of that platform. Be sure to meet prospects where and when they have the time (mornings, afternoons, evenings, weekends) and start to get them creating webs of connection with each other.

6. After each community-building program, thoughtful follow-up is imperative. But again, you must follow up via

their preferred method (phone, email, text, online forums, social media, metaverse, etc.), and follow-up should involve more opportunities to expand and deepen their connections. Keep the party going!

7.   You have to create a balance between programs that are prepared in advance and others that are created based on what's going on in the world. Could an online forum to discuss a news or pop-culture topic be helpful to create more engagement?

8.   Make sure you remember to have fun whenever possible, as that allows further engagement — this could be as simple as taking a quick poll on whether people like cats, dogs, or neither. (What's key is to make sure everyone can see who voted for what, so they can then start to reach out to like-minded folks. You can literally say "Make sure to connect with others you agree with you.")

9.   Now that your prospective students have connected with each other, you can focus on having them connect with your students, staff, faculty, and alumni by inviting them to programs designed for current students. Let them participate in forums and in an online class — and make sure to involve them in the course as if they are currently enrolled students. Let them feel what it's like to have a voice in the classroom and in the community. Nothing says "welcome" better than treating everyone equally.

10. Dare I say it again? #NoCommittees

All these online programs aimed at prospective students will start to create designed and organic connections between your future students and your existing community, which will translate into an engaged online learning community when they enroll! Waiting until they're already students to start community-building means you're already behind.

Leaders, educators, and instructional designers all started sharing information and technology. Academia became truly "collegial" and interdepartmental collaborations became commonplace. The pandemic shined a bright light on what had been possible for higher education all along.

Student support services stepped up their game in massive ways. I remember having a conversation with one of my coaching clients, who is an associate dean at a large state university. In the initial days of the pandemic and immediately after her institution's campus closure, she volunteered to "map" all the textbooks and resources used by the faculty in her college (an engineering, math, and sciences college) to match them up with equivalent free resources available on the internet. Within days, thanks to that book list, students whose books were abandoned in dormitories and libraries that were closed for the foreseeable future were able to learn and participate in their courses from anywhere with an internet connection.

But what of the millions of students without an internet connection? Dr. John J. Rainone, President of Mountain Gateway Community College (formerly known as Dabney S. Lancaster Community College) in Clifton Forge, Virginia, told us:

> "We created — on our website — a resource guide. The resource guide included all the Wi-Fi options in our service area — a service area about 1,800 square miles. We listed every public library and every school. And we had a couple of people contact chambers of commerce to find out where there were places for students to come up and sit outside and access the Wi-Fi from parking lots and sidewalks.
>
> "We were certainly learning as we were going, but I would say that we reacted pretty quickly, and it also told me that we had a number

of resources that became even *more* important. For example, our
24/7 tutoring. Of course, we have a writing center and we have
a tutoring center for face-to-face. What we had to immediately do was
purchase more hours of the *online* tutoring to make sure we didn't run
out. So, there were little things and we addressed as many as we
could, and we continue to call students, even students enrolled in the
summer. We're calling them every two weeks to find out, 'How are
you doing?'"

Augmenting, accelerating, and innovating when it came to student
services was a tall order during the first year of the pandemic. Many institutions really rose to the challenge. Dr. Michael A. Baston, then President
of Rockland Community College in Ramapo, New York, offered a tip to his
peers at other institutions, suggesting:

"One of the key things is to engage in the kind of comprehensive
virtual support services that students need. Before the pandemic, we
didn't have a 24-hour tutoring center. We didn't have 24-hour mental
health. We didn't have virtual testing centers. We didn't have academic
and career advisement — in a *significant* way — in virtual environments. We didn't have *any* of these sorts of things. And now, as a result
of the pandemic, not only do we *have* them, but they will remain
with us long after the pandemic is gone. That provides demonstrable
support to these populations who can't necessarily engage in support
services between 9:00 a.m. and 5:00 p.m. — who ultimately don't have
the luxury of turning on their camera in their home while the class is
going on. Because you have to make sure that dinner is getting cooked,
and your child's homework is getting checked while your spouse is
trying to do the work that *they* have to do while *you* still need to do your
schoolwork and do the job that *you* have. And you're all working in
a remote environment with one laptop. So, it's all those kinds of things
that we've got to be thinking about in terms of 'How do we reset expectations around a more 24/7 on-demand access to support?'"

Entire books will be (and probably have been) written about how the
pandemic accelerated the development and acceptance of high-quality
online learning opportunities in higher education (and in K-12). Surely,
a shift to online instruction (at least temporarily) was discussed in nearly
every presidential interview conducted for this book — especially those

interviews that took place before the development of a COVID vaccine. So, without being exhaustive on the subject, it's important that we share a few comments from academic leaders on this topic. Dr. Richard W. Schneider, Rear Admiral, U.S. Coast Guard (Retired), President Emeritus of Norwich University, talked to us candidly about the difference between educators who embraced online learning and those who resisted it, saying:

> "A lot has changed in America since the onset of the pandemic. And I think we're still all learning a lot. We have to be light on our feet. I think all the schools in America *will* do a better job in the future, but we had a bunch of faculty members in America for whom the thought of online education was abhorrent to them, and they didn't believe in it, they didn't want to do it, and yet they were *forced* to do it. When we look back 15 or 20 years from now, and when we do the research about what we learned and achieved, it may turn out to be one of the most interesting, innovative, creative times that higher education has had at the undergrad level."

Regarding the resistance among some faculty and administrators to deliver undergraduate education online, Dr. Schneider told us:

> "There's an arrogance, I think, on the part of *some* undergraduate faculty members who were taught in a didactic way, just the way many of us were taught before online was even created. And there is this sense of 'Well, this could threaten me. It doesn't look familiar. I don't like it. I'm not good at it. And [when it comes to my students], I'd rather have them sitting at my feet.' And they were forced to change. And, you know, it wasn't about 'seat time' anymore. There's been an issue coming forward over a long period of time; Southern New Hampshire University is right across the border from us, and people are paying attention about competency-based education.

> "And then, of course, everybody's complaining about our prices in higher education, but you know what? It costs a lot of *money* to deliver high-quality instruction in a residential model. A perfect storm is what's happened right now and the schools that have the financial resources to be able to pivot and invest will make it just fine.

> "For the ones that were struggling before — and we had tons of them in America, struggling, just teetering on the brink of financial ruin — this

is just like the final nail in the coffin. If they aren't investing in online instruction and making sure their students are having a good experience, those students won't stay with them. They'll jump ship.

"So, there's a lot of shakeout going to happen. I think the projections before COVID about the number of schools closing in America are going to be well exceeded now because of COVID. I think it's just going to be incredibly difficult."

When it comes to who is "jumping ship" (you've got to admit that we all smiled when Dr. Schneider drew upon his Coast Guard heritage with that analogy), it's not just the students. It's the faculty and staff too. Only 57% of the higher-education professionals surveyed for this book indicated that they intend to keep working in the industry for several more years or until their retirement. A concerning 19% of college and university employees intend to start looking for opportunities in other industries, and 22% remained unsure about their career futures, indicating they were waiting to see what opportunities might arise. But for now, the number of people working in higher education who remain committed to this work slightly outnumbers those who are feeling burned out. And what we don't know is whether a more innovative, creative academic industry might start attracting brilliant minds and dynamic leaders from other sectors. Surely, we couldn't help but notice how many presidents we interviewed had previously been business leaders or military leaders, technology innovators, and even physicians. So, while some dyed-in-the-wool academics were disenchanted with the rapid adoption of online instruction and support in the early 2020s, many others were thrilled. Dr. Stephen Spinelli, President of Babson College in Wellesley, Massachusetts, talked to us about COVID-era lessons and opportunities, saying:

"The rapid conversion to a more technology-enhanced delivery system has forced people to be more creative in their design ... and in their response to students. The level of creativity that is happening in the delivery of education is mind blowing."

The ways in which faculty and technologists took brick-and-mortar courses online within 10 days or sometimes less — plus the ways in which facilities and maintenance, business offices, security and safety teams, libraries, student services, and others reinvented their processes and stepped up in huge ways at the beginning of the pandemic (and for a sustained period) — are proof that higher-education employees can do anything. Now imagine what we can do if we're not fighting for our lives but instead are fighting to evolve and even revolutionize higher education in the way that stakeholders deserve. Anything is possible if we have the will and if we have the leadership.

As we step tenuously into a "post-pandemic" world, many of our priorities have changed. Health and wellness are now top of mind. Flexible delivery of education is paramount. Student services are no longer a 9-to-5 commitment but evolving to a 24/7 model. And the big issues that were once whispered about — like major partnerships and even mergers and acquisitions — are proudly on the table. Five years ago, if Dr. Joe Sallustio and I had written a book such as this, our survey research never would have contained the question: "Are you currently exploring (or do you intend to explore) the possibility of a merger, acquisition, or significant strategic partnership to ensure your institution's viability and improve quality and access for prospective learners?" Of the higher-education professionals who responded to the survey, 27% said "yes" to that question and 18% said "maybe." Dr. John Porter, President of Lindenwood University in St. Charles, Missouri, told us that he has assembled a mergers-and-acquisitions team. And that kind of design thinking and partnership exploration is happening at multiple levels and in many ways. Dr. Porter told us:

> "I want be on the lookout for something that's going to be great for Lindenwood University and is going to accelerate things — maybe some of the programming is going to accelerate, maybe some of our numbers and enrollment can accelerate."

This is perhaps the most exciting part of the industry's emergence from the emergency — challenging ourselves to identify all the ways in which colleges and universities can improve, evolve, and even transform. All the while we've been focused on teaching lessons to our learners, the world has been serving up lessons for us all.

Making Education Your Business with Dr. Joe Sallustio

M&A in EDU

To your knowledge, how many universities have dedicated a team to the exploration of mergers and acquisitions? While the CARES Act funding and shared-service agreements have prevented institutional closures, for now, there is still a reckoning coming for institutions that have flat or declining enrollment combined with tuition dependency. Consortium or shared-service type models — such as TCS Education and Core Education — are providing umbrella services to help smaller institutions access resources at a greater scale while reducing expense. Those familiar with the merger and acquisition (M&A) world within higher education will tell you that many institutions wait too long to explore a merger, acquisition, or strategic partnership. Closure is never a positive experience for students, even with appropriate transfer pathways in place. Merging or being acquired may be a path to sustainability that deserves attention by the board and president at your institution.

A Dual Pandemic: A Health Crisis and a Social-Justice Reckoning

The early 2020s posed challenges that sometimes seemed simply "too much." Because it wasn't "just" a pandemic that was taking our campuses to their knees, but political and social catastrophes had our stakeholders hurting and hopelessly distracted. Dr. Christopher F. Roellke, President of Stetson University in DeLand, Florida, said to us in the summer of 2020:

> "We're really fighting two pandemics at the same time. One is COVID-19, and one is the structural racism that we have struggled so mightily to try to overcome. The faculty are where the rubber hits the road in any institution of higher education and supporting their work, making sure that they have the tools and the wherewithal to teach effectively, to work effectively, with an increasingly diverse demographic of our students."

We spoke with Dr. Roellke about the ambitious goals to diversify the student body *and* the faculty body, making college communities more inclusive. These are goals that many institutions share, though many struggle to allocate ample resources. Colleges and universities have been attempting to step up in terms of diversity, equity, and inclusion, but many critical initiatives have gone unfunded because "life happens" to colleges and universities too — not just to our students. In fact, many institutions were just finally recovering from what the Great Recession did to their balance sheet when, out of nowhere, the pandemic struck. Dr. Roellke told us:

"I do think, a lot of times, this is about resources. We've got to make sure that we recruit and retain the very best faculty of color in a variety of disciplines. I also think it's important in a higher education community that we know that the job of diversity and inclusion is not in the form of one or two or three or four people who have those words in their titles. Everyone at the university needs to be a 'diversity and inclusion officer.'

"I think this is a critical moment for higher education to embrace this challenge, given what's transpired in the nation with police brutality and the like. And I think that there's no better place to be, frankly, than an institution of higher education — where we can have the difficult conversations and where we have the opportunity to try to meet the needs of particular communities to provide ample opportunities for multicultural exchange ... So that's kind of the way I think about our challenge and diversity ... meeting the needs of particular communities, providing ample opportunities for multicultural exchange, with the hope that we can move ourselves forward into an engaged and pluralistic society."

So how does an institution maintain that sense of "community" during an era of social distancing because of a rapidly spreading virus? Dr. Roellke told us, as his campus was preparing to welcome students back in the fall of 2020, that:

"One of the things we're going to do is pitch a tent outside the president's home during this time of COVID-19 because I so eagerly want to meet folks other than just virtually. And we can do this in a safe and responsible way — in a physically distant way. We're going to be outdoors. I think those little gestures turn out to yield big dividends in terms of building trust, building transparency and openness, and building community. These are *not* difficult decisions to make — they're easy ones to make, but I think they're also quite important."

I'm an alumna of Carthage College in Kenosha, Wisconsin, and a member of their President's Leadership Council, so it's fair to say that I visited their campus often prior to the pandemic. And during 2020 and 2021? We had tent parties on the bluff overlooking Lake Michigan. Tents were erected for commencement ceremonies and traditional celebrations that had previously been held indoors. Donor events and business-leader events were no longer offered in ballrooms or auditoriums or even the campus chapel, but under gigantic open-air tents on the president's lawn. There were many ways in which the great outdoors brought us together in the early 2020s and, like most things that got beta-tested during the pandemic, many of the new traditions stuck. Carthage purchased one of the big tents and has left it up perpetually in the president's back yard. And I'll be the first to admit that, when it came to the annual President's Recognition Dinner, attending a summer garden party instead of an indoor winter black-tie event was a pleasant change of pace. (Anyone who has ever walked the shores of Lake Michigan in December has sympathy pains and frost bite just thinking about it!)

My co-author, Dr. Joe Sallustio, recently reflected on the dual crisis of the pandemic and social unrest, reminding us that beyond the public health crisis and the social unrest was also an economic crisis, saying:

> "COVID presented the perfect storm — a financial disruption and the health and social disruption. And as we become acclimated, at least in some degree, to the disruptions of COVID, the social disruptions continue."

Academic leaders continue to struggle (and innovate!) as they work to keep everybody focused on the important educational missions that guide their institutions. But in a world of rapidly changing news cycles, community violence, protests, riots, social unrest, political division, and other painful and legitimate distractions, decision-makers are now somewhat better prepared than they were in 2019. We know how to disseminate information quickly, how to be transparent and candid when we don't have all the answers, and how to prioritize what really matters. And we expect the unexpected.

Against our own wills, we all became crisis communicators and crisis managers during the early 2020s. I feel like telling everyone "Welcome to the club!" — because, as a former communications director inside higher education, the high-stakes work of responding to and talking about crises was literally in my job description. And I hated it. In my own career in higher education, I've faced angry protestors pushing their way into campus buildings, a "pignapping" (seriously, someone broke into a medical school's research labs to steal some pigs), a college being put on probation by its accreditors, a real-estate scandal, outcry from current students opposed to a new degree program that provided educational access to "those" students, and an entire board of trustees being asked to step down when at least a few of them were implicated in a million-dollar embezzling scheme. But I'd never imagined a pandemic.

Now, as we approach different trials and tribulations — including the admissions cliff — institutions better understand the importance of being prepared for crisis and difficulty. One of the most important lessons learned during the pandemic — and especially from schools near riots or social unrest or where there was a crime on campus, etc. — was that no one is immune to crisis. If you work at a small college or university somewhere and you have previously said, "Oh, well, you know, it's kind of a sleepy town" or "Not a whole lot happens here" or "We never have crises," you're forgetting that *everyone* has crises.

→ If a riot happens six miles from your campus, it's your crisis.

→ If there's a shooting at a tavern a block or a mile from campus and three of your students are there, it's your crisis.

→ If your county's case count for an infectious disease is skyrocketing even though the virus is well-contained on your campus, it's your crisis.

→ If the public-figure spouse of one of your faculty members posts something salacious on Twitter and a screenshot makes the rounds to people who care, it's your crisis.

A crisis is *always* a possibility and having a leadership team that's prepared, structured, trusted, and empowered to be able to work together (and sometimes alone) to be able to make really important decisions — even *impossible* decisions — really quickly is something that every institution should prioritize.

📝 Pop Quiz!

Crisis-Ready and Pandemic-Proof

Check all the items below that deserve time, effort, and funding at your institution in the next six months.

❑ Put all key spokespeople through media training so you have 100% confidence that your leaders will be camera-ready and on-message when the next crisis occurs.

❑ Establish or nurture relationships with key partners, like the local health department, industry councils and associations, attorneys, and elected officials.

❑ Address any governance issues or internal rules standing in the way of liquidating assets in the case of major emergencies in the future.

❑ Update your institution's crisis-response protocols and templates with new lessons from the pandemic.

❑ Implement all technology that is missing at your institution but that has become table stakes for the efficient and safe operation of a college or university (e.g., mass texting systems, data backup and redundancy systems, etc.).

❑ Transform any 9-to-5 operations that deserve to be 24/7, through increased scheduling, hiring, chatbots, and other means.

❑ Gather and safeguard updated emergency-contact information for all students, staff, faculty, and contractors.

❑ Provide continual training for staff and faculty related to crisis communications.

❑ Other _____

_____

Leading Through a Pandemic

Listeners of *The EdUp Experience Podcast* learned a lot about leadership during the show's first two years, while institutional presidents and other decision-makers were interviewed about the problems they were solving in real time. Within the first few weeks after the pandemic was declared by the World Health Organization, I received a phone call from a state-university dean; she asked me a question I'd never been asked before: *"I need to assemble my faculty tomorrow and talk to them about what's going on. What do I tell them? I don't know when the campus will reopen or what any of this means for anyone. What in the world do I say?"*

My answer to her: "You tell them the truth."

And you do it confidently, compassionately, and candidly. You admit that the answer you give today might turn out to be wrong by tomorrow, and that you appreciate their faith in you as you attempt to lead the organization through something that none of us have ever endured. You acknowledge their fear and confusion. You look them in the eyes and say, "We're going to get through this. I'm not sure exactly how. But I know that, together, we will."

What the presidents interviewed for this book told us about leadership (and demonstrated before our very eyes) will inspire us for years to come. President Scott Pulsipher at Western Governors University (a fully online university based in Millcreek, Utah) talked to us about leading during the pandemic, and he told us:

> "My primary role during this time period is to provide stability where in so many other places there is none."

We asked Dr. Philomena V. Mantella, President of Grand Valley State University near Grand Rapids, Michigan, whether her leadership vision changed with the onset of the COVID-19 pandemic, and she told us:

> "The *vision* is the same. The *pace* is accelerated, and the *stakes* are higher."

Making Education Your Business with Dr. Joe Sallustio

Heroes Work Here: A Salute to Pandemic-Era College and University Presidents

One of the conversations on *The EdUp Experience Podcast* that sticks out to me as an example of pandemic leadership is episode #306 with Dr. Christine Mangino, President of Queensborough Community College. She stated:

> "I started in a two-dimensional world, so for many, many months I hadn't met another person on campus. It was all through Zoom. And how do you build trust, right? Does the campus trust me through this process and how do I get to know who they really are and the culture of the campus? The was my biggest fear of taking this [college presidency] on."

The pandemic forced us to grow as leaders in ways we would have never expected. It is so important to realize the immense pressure that was placed on college and university presidents — to manage the myriad and vital health, social, and financial concerns of an entire, complex ecosystem of stakeholders. Yes, there is no doubt that the financial models of higher education must change to create long-term stability. It's far too easy to look past leaders who helped hold higher education together during the pandemic, but it's important to remember that if they *hadn't* held us together, we'd never have safely arrived at this new inflection point, where we have the luxury of the opportunity to engage in a conversation about change for the future. Without the efforts of pandemic-era leaders, we wouldn't have a future at all.

Even the most seasoned and confident leaders found that leading during a pandemic required a new set of leadership muscles. Queens University of Charlotte's President Daniel G. Lugo reminded us that, pre-pandemic, we weren't necessarily looking for crisis managers when we selected higher-education leaders. He shared with us:

> "I knew that — taking on the role of being a chief executive on a campus — there were going to be episodic crises to manage and to get through that were going to test the mettle of the leadership team. I don't think *anyone* ever anticipated the *perpetual* crisis that we went through with the COVID-19 pandemic."

Lugo's team answered the unexpected call by focusing on values and priorities. He explained:

> "We decided as a leadership team and a board and a community that we were going to put our values and priorities out front. And we said, from the get-go, that health and safety were going to drive our decisions. That was going to be number one. And behind that was going to be our academic mission. And then even behind *that* was going to be our financial choices and needs."

How was that prioritization of values and that focus on integrity received by their stakeholders? It was a mixed bag. Lugo said:

> "We erred on the side of health and safety and that wasn't always popular. That didn't make my inbox always the most enjoyable. But I felt like I was fully supported by our trustees. There was great alignment with our faculty. Yet as I looked across higher education, that lack of clarity really damaged a number of institutions and their experience. There were several reputational dings to the academy. And, you know, people could be mad with me, and they could be mad with our decisions, but at least we were clear and at least our values were out front. We didn't compromise on our values, and I think we're stronger as a result of it today."

For decades — perhaps millennia — higher education has been a bastion of mysteries and secrets ... processes and decision-making philosophies that remained safe-guarded, behind closed doors. But the demystification of higher education was a reckoning whose time had come. President Lugo told us:

> "It's important for institutions of higher education to be thinking about how we manage the communication and transparency with which we make our decisions, and how we bring those decisions — in the most agile and accessible way — to our community."

During the pandemic, transparency became currency. And it will matter, now, forever.

Stability, vision, values, integrity, honesty, transparency — during the pandemic, they mattered immensely. We asked other presidents to tell us what mattered — and what kept them above the fray — when times were rough. Dr. Arthur Keiser, Chancellor and CEO of Keiser University, said that, in a post-pandemic world:

> "Everybody needs to be patient, and everybody needs to work together."

But not every institution or internal department was being led by an experienced or battle-tested leader when March 2020 came knocking. Dr. John J. Rainone, President of Mountain Gateway Community College, told us that crisis and change let new leaders lead. He explained:

> "I think the pandemic was an opportunity to bring some new leaders in the institution up, where they have really led a lot of initiatives and a lot of development, and it didn't necessarily fall on the executive team or certain key people. This was really a great opportunity for new leaders to emerge."

No matter how confident, eloquent, or experienced an academic leader is, there will be moments where the decisions are exceedingly difficult. Dr. Robert O. Davies, President, Central Michigan University in Mount Pleasant, Michigan, spoke to the EdUp team in the early fall of 2020, when higher education was facing the second chapter of the crisis. He told us:

> "There are no right decisions — no definitive, easy calls. And every decision will be faced with immediate criticism and immediate praise."

We talked to Dr. Davies about the way in which the pandemic thrust us all into the VUCA (i.e., volatile, uncertain, complex, and ambiguous) environment that most of us have studied in classrooms but rarely operated within for any length of time or extreme fever pitch. He told us:

"We are in ambiguous times. Things are changing rapidly. The key is constant communication with clear messaging."

That clarity, he told us, needed to be constant and leaders needed to lead from the front at all times. Dr. Davies said:

"Visibility matters — just being there and being clear about what you're trying to achieve."

It was a tall order and, by and large, higher education met the moment. For the rest of my career and my life, I will remain inspired by the kind of leadership I witnessed in the early 2020s, when we were all desperately seeking stability, normalcy, and hope.

 Pro Tip: *Take to heart the lessons from higher education's pandemic leaders. What you need — almost to the exclusion of everything else — during your next crisis is a shared commitment to the following:*

- *Stability*
- *Vision*
- *Values*
- *Integrity*
- *Honesty*

- *Transparency*
- *Collaboration*
- *Visibility*
- *Clarity*
- *Speed*

Can your institution deliver on all that? If not, how can use these leadership characteristics to guide your post-pandemic planning so that, next time, you'll be ready?

A World Forever Changed

There are a million ways to say it, but just universal one truth: The pandemic changed us. It changed our institutions and our teams, our communities and our families, and it changed us personally in ways that we have yet to fully realize or appreciate. And if we were paying attention and if we remain open to the kind of "lifelong learning" we espouse for our students, we are walking away with lessons aplenty. When we talked to college and university presidents about the current state of higher education, as we contend with the post-pandemic "Now what?" they reminded us of all the ways in which we collectively succeeded, improved, expanded our thinking, and positioned ourselves for a brighter future. Dr. David Harpool, Former President of Northcentral University, told us in the spring of 2020, when the future was uncertain and the crisis was at its scariest beginnings:

> "If you watch the response to the COVID-19 crisis, it is not an indictment of higher ed. It is actually proof positive that what we teach is the right thing: how to research, how to study, how to problem solve. And so, I'm very optimistic about the future of higher education."

Dr. Harpool's optimism about the future reminded us of something that Dr. Christopher F. Roellke, President of Stetson University, said to us when he told us that during moments of crisis and change, disposition matters — and that the best disposition is one of optimism. Dr. Roellke said:

> "If our community can maintain the disposition of optimism — of moving forward together, collaboratively, honestly, transparently — we're going to have a better outcome than if we don't practice those things as we move forward."

Optimism about the future of higher education is not about wanting things to go "back to normal" or to revert to the standard operating procedures that predated the pandemic. A bright future is about embracing the ways in which the pandemic gave us the impetus to *be* better and *do* better.

Optimism about the future of higher education is not about wanting things to go "back to normal" or to revert to the standard operating procedures that predated the pandemic. A bright future is about embracing the ways in which the pandemic gave us the impetus to be better and do better. Dr. Mary Papazian, Former President of San José State University in San Jose, California, suggested that the offerings that cropped up under exigent circumstances during the pandemic have already set the expectations for what stakeholders want in the future —like virtual orientations and 24/7 tutoring. Dr. Papazian said:

> "There's been a real commitment to meet students where they are, and I think that's what you have to do in this moment in time. And I think we're going to have to do that going forward, too. I think some of the things we're doing now will become part of what we do going forward. We can't emerge from this looking like we were when we went into it."

We agree with Dr. Papazian — we can't go back. But by the time we'd conducted most of the interviews for this book, we were starting to see some institutions return to their pre-pandemic status quo, which might as well be a step backward (not just "back") because the institutions that leapt forward —with the pandemic serving as a tailwind instead of a headwind — are going to lap the others. Dr. Gregory Fowler, Former Global Campus President at Southern New Hampshire University, told us during the summer of 2020:

> "There is still a tendency and a desire, I suspect, to go back to the way things were and I'm using those terms broadly to make the assumption that whatever happens in the fall [of 2020] will be very much like what was happening last fall. None of those things are true. This [the rush to remote/online learning and other areas of focus since the onset of the pandemic] is a genie that's out of the bottle in a lot of ways. And it will transform things. I don't know that the pandemic put us in a different *direction*. What I think it did was accelerate a number of items and issues that higher education was already beginning to deal with. And you began to see that with some of the school closures and mergers, but also with some of the places where people were asking questions like 'Is college worth it?'

> "I still do believe very much that college is worth it, but the experience and what we put in front of students is going to continue to develop. And we've got to be *prepared* for that without being in denial about what *was* and what *will be* moving forward. So, I think that a lot of colleges are going to have to think about how they do things differently as they move forward."

Making Education Your Business with Dr. Joe Sallustio

Online Learning and the Fortnite™ Generation

So much has been written about the difference between emergency-response remote learning and pedagogically designed online learning. Even though we have all read articles about students' negative perceptions of online learning as a pandemic response, there were an equal number of articles championing the flexibility and community of quality online learning environments. You'll still hear it though — maybe in your institution or in your professional community — "online learning is of lesser quality than its face-to-face counterpart."

In my humble opinion, I find that such criticisms are said most often by faculty who have not taken a fully online program themselves or by students who've experienced emergency-response remote learning during the pandemic (but never before and certainly never the kind of online learning that was pedagogically designed). It's interesting that the accrediting bodies don't provide any discussion around quality by modality — only that learning outcomes are realized. The Fortnite™ generation is coming, and there is a massive expectation of online access and community building within the online environment. Designing and implementing an online strategy not only serves the adult student in a critical way, but it gives options to the 18- to 22-year-old student who covets ease and flexibility.

Each modality — residential, hybrid, fully online — comes with advantages and disadvantages. If you aren't offering the modality the student wants or needs, they *will* go somewhere else. To think the student will choose residential when they are looking for online is naïve at best and ignorant at worst. If we are truly looking, as educators, to meet the student where they are, then we must be equipped to do so.

While online education and many of the changes and trends that took hold during the pandemic are proverbial genies out of the bottle, as Dr. Fowler suggested, most traditional colleges and universities are still finding their footing and are talking about hybrid delivery models or high-flex models rather than fully online options. Dr. Daniel F. Mahony, President of the Southern Illinois University System, told us:

> "As far as the future of higher education is concerned, I think it's going to continue to evolve ... where we're doing some things online, some face-to-face, and some hybrid. I think that model will be our model for a long time. I don't think we're moving entirely to a remote-education model. Because I don't think that works for every program and it doesn't work for every student. But I think having more diversity and more opportunities is a good thing. One of the only good things that has come from the coronavirus for higher education is that we now have more faculty who feel comfortable using technology. And so even if they're teaching face-to-face, this whole concept of 'face-to-face is just a lecture and that's all it is' will change pretty dramatically over the next several years. I think they have found lots of opportunities to enhance what they do educationally from the technologies available to them — technologies and approaches they may not have explored otherwise. And to me, that's the one positive of a really, really negative situation. I think it has pushed us to maybe innovate more on a faculty-by-faculty basis than I think would have happened otherwise, which, over the long term, will be a positive thing for higher ed."

Fully online or mostly online colleges and universities, of course, didn't experience the kind of disruptions felt by campus-based programs during the pandemic. When we spoke with President Scott Pulsipher at Western Governors University in the middle of the pandemic, he said:

> "We were designed and purpose-built for these types of scenarios so that we could continue relatively uninterrupted for all the students we serve."

Pulsipher spoke with us about two leadership schools of thought during and after the pandemic, when it comes to lessons about online learning and competency-based learning. He cut right to the heart of it when he said:

> "The distinguishing difference between the leaders who are thinking about it and those who aren't is really a question of whether they think this is a short-term disruption, or a catalyst for long-term change."

As I think about the ways the presidents articulated to us the many paths available to colleges and universities today — and the way it often boiled down to just two paths of "Embrace change" or "Avoid change" — I keep thinking of Robert Frost's "Two roads diverged in the woods ..." How might academic leaders — years or even decades from now — look back and talk about how the decisions they made in the early 2020s "made all the difference?" Dr. Robert O. Davies, President of Central Michigan University, talked about this moment of choice, saying:

> "Higher education is at a watershed moment. There is no question in my mind that, through COVID-19, we are dealing with the issues that higher education needs to deal with: the funding mechanisms, the cost mechanisms, the issue of how to pay for higher education. We're dealing with the cost of tuition and with higher education's use of technology in more and more advanced ways. This era is also forcing higher education to look at how we think about our role in terms of preparing individuals for truly lifelong learning ... and understanding that the bachelor's degree is a measure, but not necessarily the *only* measure."

Indeed, the past few years have been frightful and eventful, exhausting and exhilarating. And hearing higher-education leaders talk about the risks and rewards of their work was perhaps the most consistently exhilarating part of the experience for me and my co-author, Dr. Joe Sallustio. We'd sometimes ask a question we thought would be answered optimistically, and we'd hear pessimism and critique in response. And sometimes we'd ask a question that we thought cut to the heart of the scary stuff, like "What keeps you up at night?" and we'd get unadulterated optimism. Dr. Thomas R. Bailey, President of Teachers College at Columbia University in New York, New York, reminded us that even when leaders are burning the candle at both ends, the experience can be exciting and motivating. Dr. Bailey told us in 2021:

> "I can also stay awake at night, thinking about the opportunities that we have from this."

The pandemic gave higher education an opportunity to change. We don't need to go back to the way we were. We should ask ourselves: 'What's the world we want to see?' — then use this as an opportunity to make the change we probably *should* have made before, but just didn't.

Martha Dunagin Saunders, PhD

President, University of West Florida

I am drawn like a moth to a flame when I hear this kind of thinking. I was a director of marketing at a graduate business school when the Great Recession buckled our knees. And I have never forgotten how our president, when he gathered the entire staff together every few weeks, cheerfully urged us: "Don't waste the crisis." What can we learn? What can we do differently? What relationships and partnerships can we forge? What new mindsets can we adopt? Since 2007-2009, I have looked at every personal and professional crisis from that vantage point — with a commitment to learn from it and never waste the experience.

Sometimes a crisis — like a global pandemic —reveals us. During a conversation with Dr. Bill Pepicello, Former President of the University of Phoenix, *The EdUp Experience Podcast* co-founder Dr. Joe Sallustio said:

> "Great competition and weak financial models in higher education were already there and already coming. The pandemic just moved things along faster."

Dr. Pepicello agreed, describing the industry's less-than-graceful recent past but also pinning his hopes on a bright future, saying:

> "Higher education was sort of chugging along and chugging along and suddenly coronavirus hit and they went 'Whoa, man! We better get moving!' And it's painful.

> "The future of higher education is going to be bumpy for maybe a decade. We're going to see fewer institutions of higher education; we see that happening already. I think in the long run that will lead to a smaller number of institutions that will be *stronger*; they'll not only have a better business model, but also a better take on what they need to provide students — a better understanding of what the link is between students and the workforce. Because for better or worse, that has to be one of the driving forces of higher education now. So, I think we'll see turmoil for a good part of the next decade. But when we come out the other side, I think it's going to be pretty exciting."

Making Education Your Business with Dr. Joe Sallustio

Moving Mountains and Carving Out a Sustainable Future

College and university presidents have become more innovative than ever. There are many examples on *The EdUp Experience Podcast* where I reference the lack of urgency and the "sickness of slowness" embedded within many institutions today. However, there are just as many examples where institutions have moved, and will continue to move, quickly to serve students and adapt their business model. And for all those efforts, the public hasn't fully taken note or provided recognition where it's due.

When faced with the adversity of a global pandemic, higher-ed mountains were moved. The hard work of higher education is to continually imagine what the future of learning is for students and what the future sustainable business model is for the business of education. And higher education *is* a business.

As we wade into the uncharted waters of post-pandemic higher education, I think we can all agree that the changes will impact everyone — the students, the staff and faculty, the surrounding communities and employers, the alumni, the donors, the partners, and more. Dr. Wayne A. I. Frederick, President of Howard University in Washington, D.C., told us:

> "I think the future for higher education is bright. For a long time, as high-education leaders, I think we've sat back and kind of given up a bit of our role to be leaders in our communities and our society. And I think the pandemic has forced us to regain that and to really step up and step in. And there's so much for us to contribute. If we step up as we should, I think the future is bright. I also think the future is bright because I think young people are amazing. And I think what young people have been through right now is going to prove very, very useful. You know, there's an African proverb that says, 'Doesn't matter how long the night is. Dawn will come.' And these young people have seen

> a very dark moment in our history — as a world and as a humanity. And I think what they will get from that is the interconnectedness of all of us, the fact that when they get an opportunity to attend a higher-education institution like Howard University, they must fulfill Howard University's motto of truth and service. And as we say, you don't come here to get a degree. You come here to get an education and it comes alive when you go out and serve others."

Dr. Frederick was perhaps the only leader who talked to us about how the pandemic might prove to have changed the hearts of our students — inspiring them to serve others and connect in more meaningful ways. For the students, the pandemic showed them our collective humanity, a new kind of will and service-mindedness of faculty and staff at the institutions where they are studying, and new paths forward in a forever-changed world. And the students showed us how determined, creative, and generous they are too. Through a new lens, we all saw each other more clearly.

Dr. Mary Schmidt Campbell, President Emerita of Spelman College in Atlanta, Georgia, reminded us that what started out as pain was a pathway to a troubled industry's panacea, and that from chaos can come creativity to move us forward. She said:

> "COVID was so disruptive so quickly that we in higher education had to be responsive and improvise and really get things going without a lot of prior thought and planning. That experience accelerated most of us to think much more creatively and much more innovatively about how we can deliver that education most effectively. We now have the sense that we have more options — there are more things that we can do to support our students, to make ourselves affordable, to open up higher education for *lifelong* learning. I think the best institutions are going to take advantage of that. And higher education is about to become a very exciting place."

Are you ready for the ride?

CHAPTER 6

WORTH YOUR TRUST AND WORTH ITS WEIGHT IN GOLD

Redefining the Value of Higher Education in the 2020s and Beyond

I "shopped" for my first college degree (an AA) in 1992, my second (a BA) in 1993, my third (an MA) in 1994, and my fourth (an MBA) in 2005. Even back then, when I wasn't as savvy as I could have been, I blindly assumed that most accredited colleges and universities deliver parity in terms of academic quality — that I probably couldn't make a bad choice (and that was true). I didn't stress out about my options, I trusted the institutions and the industry at large, and I applied only to a few places for each degree experience. My "college choice" criteria were about convenience, location, affordability, perceived prestige, and unique experiences (like getting to study with professors who were renowned, published authors). There was less noise in the marketplace back then (and no internet, which was a blessing and a curse). There were no boxes of fancy brochures, nor overflowing email inboxes full of information. There was no social media. As a first-generation college student, I didn't have parents or other family touting the merits of their alma maters or urging me to apply at "Institution A" vs. "Institution B." And none of my friends were wearing collegiate sweatshirts, making me feel pressured and overwhelmed or triggering me to second-guess my plans (we were all Esprit and Benneton, thank you very much).

Today, it's so much more complicated (at least for students in the United States). How do students (and their families) know which institutions to trust, and which ones offer the kind of value they seek? How do you know how to approach a college choice when you're 18 versus when you're 38? Is the vetting process similar when you're shopping for an undergraduate degree versus a graduate degree? And what about certificates and other short-term credentials? Where in the world do you *start*? It's all a lot to consider, but there is good news. There *are* some ways to cut through the marketing clutter — to simplify the choice and to ensure you end up in a program that is worthy of your time, intellect, and resources. We're here to help.

Students and Families: We See You!

If you're on the hunt for an academic credential or post-secondary education experience — for yourself or someone you care about — this chapter is for you. The candid conversations we had with college and university presidents about value and trust will inspire you and instruct you. So, listen up!

BIG BONUS: *This chapter also contains an actual "shopping list" with tips and ideas to help you check off all the right boxes when doing your pre-college homework about who to consider and where to apply. Enjoy!*

The Role of Trust in Higher Education

In Chapter 4, we shared a story about HBCUs acting "in loco parentis" — in the place of the parent — when young adults were sent off to receive an education. Those relationships, by their very definition, were based on trust. The role of trust in higher education is as important now as it was 150 years ago or even 75 years ago. Without transparency, there is no trust. And without trust, there is no honesty, no loyalty, no safety, and no shared commitment to ensuring that learners receive the education (and sometimes the lifestyle experience) they bargained for. When we talked to Dr. Melody Rose, Former Chancellor of the Nevada System of Higher Education, she told us that across the state's entire system, her areas of focus were transparency, trust, and inclusion. She said:

> "I think the transparency issue is so vital to the national higher-education conversation. There's a lot of mystery about our industry. And the notion that we're the ivory tower and are somehow distant from our communities is, in part, a critique around transparency. Transparency builds trust. If we're open and honest about the places where we need to improve, folks are more likely to trust.
>
> "Our nation is at a low point in terms of trusting its institutions — trusting its political institutions, trusting its social institutions. And in higher education, we want to be an industry that has high levels of trust and understanding. So, we must hold ourselves accountable."

Dr. Joe Sallustio and I both believe so much in the importance of trust and trustworthiness, at every level in higher education, that we included questions about it in our anonymous survey of higher-education leaders. Among our survey respondents, 49% selected trustworthiness as a top-6 critical trait of next-generation higher-education leaders, and nearly 10% identified trustworthiness as the single-most important character trait for higher-education leaders, particularly for presidents.

Among our survey respondents, 49% selected trustworthiness as a top-6 critical trait of next-generation higher-education leaders, and nearly 10% identified trustworthiness as the single-most important character trait for higher-education leaders, particularly for presidents.

Making Education Your Business with Dr. Joe Sallustio

Developing Trust with Key Stakeholders

Trust — or, more specifically, the ability to develop it with key stakeholders across the higher education ecosystem — is a critical trait for next-generation leaders in the industry. Developing and sustaining an environment of trust goes beyond what immediately comes to mind — beyond the bond of trust between leader and board, leader and employees, or leader and faculty. These trust relationships must first be cemented before a leader can get to *external* trust relationships that help to define future institutional success. What, then, about *brand* trust, *social-media* trust, and *customer-service* trust?

Brand, social, and customer-service trust shape audience perceptions of the institution. As institutional leaders, many of the college and university presidents we interviewed understood that their personal brand and/or activity external to the institution humanized them as a leader of the sometimes mysterious higher-education institution. No one said it better than Dr. Daria Willis, former President of Everett Community College (and current President of Howard Community College), when I asked her about her accessibility and authenticity on social media, where she shares photos of her dressed up for her birthday or Halloween and where she is transparent about her personal life and her humanity in a way that students and other stakeholders really appreciate. I asked her "Is this part of a strategy for you or is this just unapologetically you and 'what you see is what you get?'" She immediately and confidently replied:

> "This is Daria. I keep it 100 as much as I possibly can. I think it *is* a strategy to *use* social media so that people see who I am … I don't have to be three different people — one person at work, one person at home, one person when I go to the grocery store. I need to be Daria 100% every day, all day, no matter where I am. And I also like people to know

I have a family just like you do. I hurt when I bleed. And when you bleed, I bleed the same color."

Wow. This is someone who understands how authenticity and transparency help craft a personal brand that helps to develop trust for the institutional brand. External trust-building (or lack thereof) will have a powerful impact — for better or for worse — on your institutional heft. It'll also translate well internally when your employees see that their leader — this real person — is trustworthy!

Trust flows in many directions when there are ideal relationships among a higher-education institution and its key stakeholders. The institution itself must do the difficult, daily work of earning (and maintaining) the trust of its students (and their families), the faculty, the staff, the alumni, the local and larger community, and industry leaders/employers. The faculty and staff must trust one another (which often requires outstanding leadership at all levels, and human resources leaders with expertise in connecting various internal groups around a shared mission). And something that no one really talks about — but that we think bears mention — is the fact that *we*, in higher education, must trust the *student* and their influencers (e.g., friends, family, guidance counselors, teachers, other members of their "buying committee") and believe that *they* know (better than we do) who they are and what they want. It's not about *selling* them something but about *revealing* ourselves to them and discovering whether we match up with what they're looking for — and what they're looking for right *now*. Far too often, higher-education professionals are unabashed about their distrust of the prospective and current student's own instincts. We try to tell them, "No, you don't want a certificate; you want a degree," or "I know you loved your tour at the big university on the other side of town, but what you *really* are going to value is *our* small class sizes and quaint campus. Trust me." Maybe you've even heard something like, "You may really want to rethink your focus on affordability, because — in the end — your future employers are going to be impressed by a college brand like ours. Trust me on this." Again and again, we ask students and others to trust us, while we do little or nothing to demonstrate that we trust *them*. How might your enrollment processes change if you were honest with yourselves about the ways in which you diminish the instincts and desires of your would-be student? What if you started honoring their needs, interests, and demands, rather than hoping they'll overlook the way in which your institution doesn't check their boxes?

A NETWORK OF TRUST

How it works now
with the institution at the center:

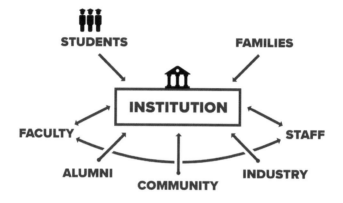

- -

How it needs to work in the future,
shifting the students to the center:

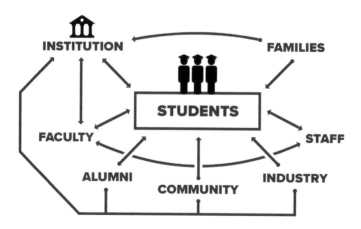

If trust is so important in higher education, shouldn't we be measuring it? Yes, yes, we should! At the risk of coming off as a broken record with what — for people who know me — is a very predictable argument (because I'm constantly saying, "A little market research goes a long way" and because readers of my last book, *Think Like a Marketer*, know that Principle #2 of thinking like a marketer is "Live and die by your customer insights"), here it comes: In higher education, a little (consistent, meaningful, well-timed) market research goes a long way. Want to know if the marketplace trusts you? Ask them! The answer to your trust quotient isn't a function of your enrollment growth or decline. Lots of untrustworthy folks have mastered the art of attracting (and then disappointing) new customers. But if your current and past customers are willing to *recommend* you to others, then you know that they trust you.

In higher education, a little (consistent, meaningful, well-timed) market research goes a long way. Want to know if the marketplace trusts you? Ask them!

Enter the net promoter score (NPS) measurement, one of the most reliable leading indicators of an institution's future health. By asking one simple question — "How likely are you, on a scale of 0 to 10, to recommend us to a friend?" — you can discover what percentage of your stakeholders are detractors (those who are actively hurting your brand and your reputation), how many are promoters (wearing your sweatshirts, singing your praises, encouraging others to apply for admission), and how many are passives (those who aren't really helping *or* hurting you right now, but who could easily be turned into promoters if you found out what it would take to delight them). Savvy colleges and universities are using the net promoter score to measure and improve just about everything. Your "score" will be calculated by subtracting the percentage of detractors (those who answered 0-6 on the scale) from the percentage of promoters (those who answered 9-10), and your score will be between -100 and +100. (Passives don't count in the score calculation but are a treasure trove of insight for future focus groups.) A good NPS "score" is typically between 0 and 30. Below are a few examples of how to apply NPS to your efforts at your institution, quickly and easily.

Six Ways to Use the Net Promoter Score to Improve Your Decision-Making

1. **Events:** Every time you host an event — a public lecture, a musical performance, a town-hall meeting, a holiday celebration, a donor recognition event, even a commencement ceremony — send an email within 24 hours to thank your attendees for joining you and to ask them, "Based on your experience at the XYZ event, how likely are you to recommend such events to fellow students, alumni, or community members?" Set a standard for your team and agree that no matter how much you enjoyed planning and executing the event (and no matter how important or traditional it is in the minds of your leaders), you will immediately discontinue the kinds of events that fall below your score threshold. Focus only on resourcing events that are so good that your stakeholders are moved emotionally in a measurable way by those experiences. Be ruthless.

2. **Website and communications:** Not sure whether your new website is resonating with target audiences? Heatmapping and visitor statistics aren't enough. Ask people who fill out an online form or enter your enrollment experience, "Based on your experience with our website, how likely are you to recommend us to others?" Or if you're not sure if you're wasting money on your expensive alumni magazine, ask the alumni, "Based on your experience with the past few issues of this publication, how likely are you to recommend that other alumni subscribe to the magazine?" A low score means you have work to do (not next fiscal year, but now).

3. **Leadership insights:** If you wait until people are speaking up publicly in outrage about your leaders, making it clear that confidence has been lost, it's too late. Ask (anonymously) your board members and other stakeholders, "Based on your observations of and interactions with the president and the executive team, how likely are you to recommend that colleagues and fellow leaders participate at the board level with our college?" You might not like the answer to this question, but you need to know.

4. **Recruiting and hiring:** The only way to care for your students is through your faculty and staff, so recruiting and hiring the best (and then preventing excessive turnover) is key. Ask, perhaps once a quarter, for all employees hired in that period (and all job applicants who did *not* begin working for you) to tell you, "Based on your experiences as a job applicant, how likely are you to recommend that others apply for employment at our college or university?" And your annual HR survey should always include the question, "How likely are you to recommend our institution to others who are looking for a new job?"

5. **Student satisfaction:** Many colleges and universities are good about conducting surveys of new students and new alumni, for accreditation requirements, but most institutions get complacent about checking in with second-year or third-year students. Be asking, every single year, "Based on your experiences at XYZ College, how likely are you to recommend us to a friend, acquaintance, or co-worker?"

6. **Alumni engagement:** As discussed in the event example and the leadership confidence example, there are a lot of ways to measure "intent to refer" among your alumni. In an annual alumni-engagement survey (yes, do one every year!), be sure to ask the big, general NPS question: "Based on your overall experience as an alumnus of XYZ University, how likely are you to recommend us to others?"

Frank Britt, Former CEO of Penn Foster Education Group, talked to us about trusting the prospective and current student — taking at face value that they know what they want and need. He said:

> "If there could only be one metric for the future of the education system, to me, it's the net promoter score. It doesn't literally have to be the net promoter score, for those who are a little wonky like me and who understand the calculus of net promoter scores, but the *principle* of the net promoter score says that the consumer is the best person to evaluate whether they got value from that experience — and value comes in many forms. It can be the convenience, it can be the quality, it can even be figuring out what they *don't* want to do ... And so, what we hope for the sector is that the measure, over time, of outcomes will be through the lens of the consumer, not through the lens of all the traditional systems that exist.
>
> "The consumer knows — better than we do — as to what they need, what they value, and when they got value from an experience. And our hope is that as the market continues to become more consumer-driven, so will the way folks evaluate the [educational] providers and evaluate whether they're honoring their brand promise."

In higher education, there are categories of institutions that have, historically, been granted a large dose of public trust based solely on brand. Ivy League institutions, Big Ten institutions, Research I (RI) institutions, Southeastern Conference (SEC) institutions, HBCUs, and others. If you're big, if you're old, if you're well-funded, if you have competitive college football, and if you have famous alumni, it's not unusual for prospective students, families, employers, and others to equate "brand" with "value." Some people are going to blindly trust a well-known brand; but even the big brands can admit (maybe in private, if not publicly) that brand is not the same thing as "value." We talked to Don Kilburn, CEO of University of Massachusetts Online (UMass Online), about the future of higher education and what all the evolutions and revolutions in higher education mean for institutions that, by and large, feel confident about the future because they have incredibly recognizable brands (like the University of Massachusetts) — brands that are associated with quality. He said to us, about institutions with brand recognition, that:

"You're also really responsible for making sure that after you've got that recognition that you do deliver a really high-quality education that lives up to that brand."

If you're big, if you're old, if you're well-funded, if you have competitive college football, and if you have famous alumni, it's not unusual for prospective students, families, employers, and others to equate "brand" with "value."

Demystifying the College Choice

Most people who are shopping for a college or university — whether for a degree program or a short-term credential — don't know where to begin. So, they default to brand recognition. Or they look around their local region for an educational provider that's nearby. Or they ask their friends, "Is this a good school?" Or they sleuth around on the internet, using helpful resources like Niche.com or the *U.S. News & World Report* Best Colleges rankings. We thought it would be helpful if we stepped up to offer a practical, holistic "shopping list" for our readers — something that could help any prospective learner or their influencers (family, friends, teachers, guidance counselors, tutors, and others) in making sense of a complicated and consequential decision about an even more complicated industry.

> **Pro Tip:** *You don't have to be "polite" or demure when shopping for a college program. Ask all your questions. Express all your thoughts and concerns. Speak up if something an admissions rep said doesn't make sense to you. You're in the driver's seat. Choosing a college and going through the admissions process isn't a prize to be won. It's a match to be made. Make sure they check all your boxes.*

7 Mighty Tips for Making the Right College Choice

A Candid Tutorial for Prospective Students, Parents, and Influencers

1. Reputation is Not Equal to Value

➜   Maybe you're a parent (or other mentor) guiding your child to choose the best university fit. Or maybe you're a prospective student yourself, ready to take the plunge into an undergraduate, graduate, or certificate program. If you're like most people, you probably start the conversation or the exploration by thinking about colleges and universities that you believe to have a good reputation. Reputation is not equal to value; they are also not mutually exclusive. For every high-quality institution with a strong reputation there are dozens of similar high-quality institutions you've never heard of (or heard much about). Sending a child where their parent went to school to create "legacy" may be important to some (or choosing the same school where your parents, spouse, or colleagues went might seem like an easy, logical decision), but *fit* is the most important criteria of all. Where do you or your student feel like they fit in? Finding your fit is everything; therefore, visiting colleges and taking the tours is of the utmost importance.[28]

---

28 If you're looking at a fully online program where a campus visit is irrelevant or not even possible, be sure to ask for a "tour" of the online learning platform and access to the kinds of virtual communities where the institution's students are interacting with one another. And check out Elvin's sidebar in Chapter 5 about what's possible for prospective students who want (and deserve) to meet other prospective students.

➜ How critical is *brand*? In the end, when the graduating student heads off to apply for jobs, there are very few careers where the hiring manager will eliminate candidates because they did or did not attend a particular college. In countries like the United States, where accreditors ensure that all higher-education institutions deliver similar outcomes, a college is a college is a college. Is paying for the *brand name* and for a particular college experience worth the debt?

➜ The kind of reputation that should matter to you is what you can find on Google and not on the college or university's website. With all due respect to higher-education marketing professionals, they're always going to tell you that their institution is a great place. A great website doesn't always equal a great college experience. What are local and national media outlets saying about the school? Are you impressed by what you read? And does the president of the institution — as evidenced by their blog posts, media appearances,[29] and social-media content — strike you as trustworthy, friendly, approachable, ethical, and focused on the issues that matter to you?

2. Understand Cost & Negotiate

➜ How much does the education cost per year (or academic term), and in total? Price can be confusing. There is the *sticker* price, and then there is the *actual* out-of-pocket cost. Parents and prospective students should understand that they have negotiating power to bring down the out-of-pocket cost through the application of various scholarships. (Just like buying a car or a house, buying a college education involves offers and negotiations.) According to NACUBO[30], the discount rate for the 2021-2022 academic year for first-time undergraduates at

---

29 Don't forget to take advantage of the opportunity to hear the president of your possible future college speaking candidly about their school and their values. Hundreds of presidents have been interviewed on *The EdUp Experience Podcast.* Find the presidents on podcasts, in television interviews, and on YouTube. Do you like what you hear and see? With few exceptions, the president is a great indicator of what the rest of the culture looks like.

30 The National Association of College and University Business Officers

private colleges was 54.5%. That means if the annual "sticker price" is $40,000, the student may only pay $18,200. (Check out TuitionFit.org for some helpful intel in this regard.) Colleges won't automatically apply reduced rates; parents and prospective students must ask. It's kind of like calling an airline and trying to convince them to waive the change fee when amending a reservation. Talk to a manager (if necessary), plead your case, and don't be afraid to mention the out-of-pocket cost (i.e., the real cost after application of discounts or financial-aid packages) from the *other* college(s) you are considering.

3. Look at Multiple Pathways

➥   There is a reason why many traditional and adult students (and their families) decide on a community college for the first two years, to knock out the general-education requirements and explore different majors. Your nearest community college typically has lower tuition costs while also being accredited by the same entities that accredit the Power 5 Conference[31] school down the road. Community colleges offer high-quality education at an affordable price. Check out companies like Unmudl, which allow a student to access a marketplace of community-college courses.

➥   If a student amasses credit at a community college and wants to transfer to a four-year university later, make sure to explore and understand the credit-transfer policy. Colleges can accept as many credits as they want to, up to a threshold dictated by the accreditor — but every credit accepted is less revenue for the university so, by and large, colleges have muddled this process in favor of the institution rather than the student. The community college may have "bridge partnerships" with four-year schools, meaning that articulation agreements allow for 100% credit

---

31 The Power 5 Conferences are the most prominent and highest-earning athletic conferences in college football in the United States. The schools in the Power 5 — the Atlantic Coastal Conference (ACC), the Big Ten Conference (B1G), the Big Twelve Conference (Big 12), the Pacific 12 Conference (Pac-12), and the Southeastern Conference (SEC) — are popular for reasons that eclipse athletics, as these schools are well-resourced and have the kinds of campuses and amenities that many students appreciate.

transfer to this institution or that institution. Be sure to explore this as early as possible.

➜   In the end, if an institution is not taking 100% of a student's credit from another institution (and perhaps even some credit for work, military, or life experience), move on. There is an institution out there that will. Your time, hard work, and financial investment should count.

4. Why College?

➜   Before getting wrapped up in the complexities of the college search/selection process, take time to get clear on why you or your loved one are choosing to pursue a degree or non-degree credential in the first place. Ask yourself whether you're seeking a financial return-on-investment in terms of earning potential (i.e., do you want to go to college so you can get a "good job?"), the expansion of thought (i.e., do you love to learn and want the chance to do that formally and expansively?), a pathway to a career that interests you (i.e., do you have a dream that you can only achieve by first going to college?), and/or finding yourself and growing into a contributing citizen (i.e., do you want a coming-of-age college experience to help you mature and become a "well-rounded" person?). The "why" of college has never been more important for a student and their family to understand. There is a tremendous amount of noise that can be confusing and distracting for students and their families, including naysayers about the value of college, and alterative-credential providers offering pathways directly to a job without a formal college experience at all. Understanding the "why" — for yourself or your family member — is critical for the college choice and, ultimately, important for retention and graduation. Starting with "why" allows you to finish (graduate!) with the kind of "how to" and "so what" that you're seeking.

5. Is There Help?

➤   Institutions provide tremendous amounts of resources to their
students. Many times, those resources are tailored to specific
groups of students depending upon who the institution serves.
Understand what is offered by the institution in terms of "wraparound services" to fully understand what the experience
will be like.

➤   Mental-health services are becoming increasingly important
for students. Ask what mental-health and wellness services are
provided, and don't be afraid to ask about what the institution is
doing to expand these services in the future.

6. Flexibility & Access

➤   The student wants flexibility in all facets of their learning and
living experience with a college or university. Spend some time
investigating the choices available to students and whether they
can really "have it their way."

➤   On campus?[32] Online? Hybrid? It's great that many colleges
and universities offer all three options, but how easily can the
student switch from one modality to another without losing
financial aid? This is a critical question to ask *before* enrolling.

➤   How "hard" is it to get into the institution? Many colleges and
universities remain selective, meaning that they are more
exclusive than inclusive. There are institutions in the United
States that receive 90,000 applications for just 6,000 seats in their
incoming class. Applying to those schools should involve your
full understanding that you are much more likely to be rejected
than accepted. If the institution has a difficult process for entry
— with frustrating barriers, excessive requirements, lots of
admissions-counselor meetings, expensive application fees, etc.
— look for an institution that demonstrates that their enrollment

---

32 Some institutions that offer multiple learning modalities refer to "on campus" learning as
"on ground." The terms are synonymous.

process was designed with a user experience through the eyes of the student. This will ensure a more positive experience down the road. Complicated admissions experiences tend to foretell complicated student experiences in your future.

7. The Student Is a Consumer

→ The student has purchasing power in this equation, and the institution is expected to deliver a level of services at or above expectations of the student and their family. Consult reviews of the institution, just like you would do for any other product that you might purchase. What are other people — especially people you know and trust — saying about the colleges and universities on your list?

→ Leverage your purchasing power by asking savvy questions and inquiring about how the college or university can best meet your needs. Institutions need enrollment, so understanding your points of leverage to decrease cost, increase services, or create better experiences is part of the process. Never be afraid to come right out and say, "This is what I'm seeking. Can you help me get what I need?"

🔆 EdUp with Elvin

Practical Tips and Frontline Insights from Elvin Freytes

It's impossible to write a book about higher education without talking about "wraparound services for students. So, what does "wraparound services" actually mean? In higher education, it refers to a holistic approach of support to ensure a student's needs are fully met, well beyond the classroom.

The key to developing effective wraparound services is *customer service*! And how do you provide a remarkable customer-service experience?

Here's how:

1. Start at the beginning of your relationship with the employees who will be providing that customer service. Customer service has to be embedded in every job posting.

2. It needs to be in the "qualifications/requirements" (e.g., "candidates must be obsessed with providing a remarkable customer-service experience") and in the "job duties" section (e.g., "provide a remarkable customer-service experience for all constituents") in every job posting — from board members and presidents to faculty and staff.

3. It has to be embedded as a question to all potential hires: "Tell me about a time when you provided someone with remarkable customer service."

4. It has to be embedded in your professional-development training strategy — not as an online exercise but rather as small groups with lots of role playing.

5. These training opportunities have to be consistent (ideally, once a month) and refreshed with the latest case studies and research.

6. Whenever possible, hire outside professionals to facilitate these customer-service trainings, which will increase engagement.

7. Develop a system of timely and anonymous feedback from consumers (e.g., parents, students) to provide crucial information on the quality of their customer-service experiences.

8. Train those in your college or university who are leading others (i.e., managers and supervisors) to approach employees who have received complaints from multiple consumers. Do this as soon as possible to create a plan of action to change the behavior and improve stakeholder satisfaction.

9. Reward those who have received multiple compliments for providing remarkable customer-service experiences and provide opportunities to have them share their tactics with others.

10. Goes without saying. (No committees!)

The reason why I use the word "remarkable" repeatedly in this tip list is because the goal is to have consumers remark to others on how wonderful their interactions have been with everyone at your institution!

Redefining the Value of Higher Education

Long before prospective students and their families go "shopping" for a college education, some of them question whether they should go to college at all. In a world in which some people love to hold up a handful of examples of wildly successful individuals who didn't attend or graduate from college — saying, "But I want to be an entrepreneur ... I don't need a degree!" — the truth of the matter is that high levels of overall well-being among people who did not avail themselves of some form of post-secondary education are the *exception*, not the rule. Meaningful education past high school creates opportunities that snowball and expand. Dr. Emily J. Barnes, then Interim President & CEO and Provost of Cleary University in Howell, Michigan (and subsequently Provost and Vice President of Academic Affairs at Siena Heights University), talked to us about the value of higher education, today and tomorrow. She said:

> "There's a lot of discussion about the value of higher education and if it's worth it. And if we're looking at, 'Well, I spent *this much* for college and now I make *this much* since I've graduated,' that's not the formula. Over a lifetime, over generations, what difference has that education made for your entire family? How impactful is it *everywhere*?"

Dr. Barnes was one of many higher-education leaders who spoke to us about the impact of a college education on entire families across multiple generations. Dr. David Finegold, President of Chatham University in Pittsburgh, Pennsylvania, agreed, saying:

> "One of the best investments any individual and family can still make is in getting a good college degree. If you look at the lifetime returns for college graduates versus high school graduates, you see that it tends to be over a million dollars greater for the college graduates."

Indeed, when we get a college education, it changes us, our children and grandchildren, spouses, parents, siblings, grandparents, and sometimes our entire community. Opportunity creates change, and it's important for higher-education decision makers to always remember the social, far-reaching impact of the opportunities they create. Why wouldn't we want to create more opportunity for more people? At every turn, the issue of accessibility looms large when we think about the future of higher education.

Why wouldn't we want to create more opportunity for more people?

If we had to simplify the complex research questions we explored in preparing to write this book, Dr. Joe Sallustio and I would tell you that we were seeking to find out just two things: 1) How is the value of higher

> **Changing generations of families permanently – that's what a college or university is all about.**

W. Kent Fuchs, PhD
President, University of Florida

education currently evolving? And 2) What will the future of higher education look like?

When we chatted with Francisco Marmolejo, Higher Education President at the Qatar Foundation and author of this book's foreword, he talked about the value of a degree and about people who are challenging degree value. He said:

> "Well, first of all, we need to listen and pay serious attention to those voices and the point they make about the limitations of higher education — and I believe a good chunk of that criticism is valid. There is also a little bit of a significant exaggeration in many things, as there is still no substitute [for a degree]. The value of higher education is not only about the knowledge of the profession, but also the capacity and development of the social skills that are equally important or even more important for successful citizens and professionals of the future.

> "What they say is a significant wake-up call. We need to pay attention. But we also don't need to diminish the value of the educational experience. First of all, because the educational experience is not only in the classroom but also outside of the classroom. We do have to challenge assumptions and recognize deficiencies, and also recognize the different ways higher education institutions have truly adapted to cope with those deficiencies."

In a global economy, value will always be delivered in different ways by different institutions. During the interviews we conducted for this book, we were fascinated to learn about the distinct cultures and niche differentiators at colleges and universities across the United States and around the world. Leaders at HBCUs shared uplifting stories about the sense of community at their institutions, while other presidents told us about their focus on key societal themes, like the environment, healthcare, or entrepreneurship — across their institutional culture and throughout their curriculum. During our conversation with Dr. Dwaun Warmack, President of Claflin University in Orangeburg, South Carolina, we talked about the difference between colleges that are actively trying to fail their students (e.g., those who are bragging at orientation: "Look to your left, look to your right — only *one* of you will be here at graduation") and those that are actively trying to help their students succeed. Dr. Warmack told us that, at Claflin's orientation, they say:

> "'Look to your left. Look to your right. You are your brother's keeper; you are your sister's keeper. You are only going to be as successful as that person to your left or right. So, if that person fails, you fail. So, it's imperative that when commencement comes four years from now, you're sitting right next to that person because you did what was necessary to uplift your brother or your sister to ensure that they reached the finish line as well.' It's a whole different narrative."

As higher education becomes more inclusive, its aims become more admirable. Dr. Thomas R. Bailey, President of Teachers College at Columbia University in New York, New York, reminded us that higher-education institutions — despite, and sometimes because of, the many evolutions and revolutions simultaneously at play in the industry — have bold, altruistic goals for the many stakeholders they serve. Dr. Bailey told us:

> "Our goal is to make a smarter, healthier, and more equitable world."

As higher education becomes more inclusive, its aims become more admirable. Higher-education institutions – despite, and sometimes because of, the many evolutions and revolutions simultaneously at play in the industry – have bold, altruistic goals for the many stakeholders they serve.

Because access to higher education has been so divided in the United States, it has been unrealistic for employers to expect all employees to show up with a degree in hand. And because industry hasn't been able to entirely influence higher education to provide equitable experiences for everyone, many employers have done the only thing they can do — they've reduced their hiring requirements and attempted to provide better on-the-job training. But some experts argue that the lack of a formal post-secondary education impacts individuals and teams in palpable, negative ways. Lisa Honaker, former sales executive at FedEx Office and subsequently the director of expansion sales at Highspot, was co-hosting an episode of *The EdUp Experience Podcast* during which she had a powerful conversation with Dr. Elsa Núñez, President of Eastern Connecticut State University in Windham, Connecticut. Lisa, drawing on her experiences in corporate America, shared:

> "Over time, you have seen big organizations drop that degree require-ment or lessen that requirement for a degree. But one of the key drivers of why a higher-education degree is so critically important is how that lack of degree translates in the real world. Those critical-thinking skills learned during the college experience become a *gap* on the job — and those aren't things that you can readily train as a leader, as a manager, even as a trainer in a corporate L & D [learning and development] department. And so, when we have team members in any functional area who can't problem-solve because they don't have critical-thinking skills or they can't work in a group because they haven't done group projects [in an educational setting], that's a problem. What also comes out of group projects is conflict management and conflict resolution. All those different things that are critical life skills — those happen on college campuses because of the curriculum."

Dr. Elsa Núñez said of Ms. Honaker's assessment:

> "I agree with that. I think that systematic thinking, analytical skills, critical-thinking skills, quantitative reasoning — you can't teach that on the job. Instead, you develop that over a four-year period, course by course, and those courses are rigorous, and they demand that of you ... in speaking, in writing, all of that as you reflect that you're growing from freshman year to senior year, and that those skills are being developed."

At Eastern Connecticut State University, freshmen and seniors are asked via survey to assess their own critical-thinking skills and analytical reasoning skills. By the time students are preparing to graduate, Dr. Núñez explained, surveyed students say, "Yes — I have stretched

— I have learned — I have grown." This is just one of many ways in which students and alumni repeatedly tell colleges and universities that they have found value in the higher-education experience. Surely, a college degree is far more than a pretty piece of paper. The value is there — from almost every objective measure. The challenge, then, is how higher education can continue to change and evolve, in lockstep with students who are nearly always moving faster than we are, to provide more value ... and to provide it to more learners in a more accessible way and a more affordable price point.

A college degree is far more than a pretty piece of paper. The value is there – from almost every objective measure. The challenge, then, is how higher education can continue to change and evolve, in lockstep with students who are nearly always moving faster than we are, to provide more value ... and to provide it to more learners in a more accessible way and a more affordable price point.

Reflection Question: *What skills, knowledge, attitudes, and habits did you develop during* your *post-secondary education experiences that serve you will in your day-to-day life and work?*

Making Education Your Business with Dr. Joe Sallustio

Value. For whom?

One of our bad habits in higher education is that we make blanket statements about "students." When we make statements about students and connect them to topics, such as value, affordability, or access, those statements become broad and, at times, incorrect. For example, you've probably heard someone say something like, "Students don't value higher education as much as they used to." Who, exactly, are these students? Are these traditional residential students rethinking the two- or four-year degree? Are these transfer students forgoing an additional phase of the educational journey to enter the workforce and become gainfully employed? Are these the some-college-no-degree students? Or are these working learners who are choosing to only work instead of to work *and* learn? I've soapboxed many times on *The EdUp Experience Podcast,* asking these types of questions. When we talk about the value of higher education, and specifically reference higher-ed detractors, I always ask who the parent is who tells their child *not* to go to college. Can you imagine having that conversation with your child? What does it sound like?

When we're talking about the perception of value, it's critical to crystallize the student demographic so we don't grossly oversimplify the challenges of working with a diverse student population. For every student or adult influencer who questions the value of higher education, there are many more who do value it. There is no doubt that those in higher education have to challenge the status quo and innovate — but I challenge us all to define the "who" when we talk about value. It can change the entire conversation when you do.

Giving Students — and Communities — What They Want

Earlier in this chapter, we offered our *7 Mighty Tips for Making the Right College Choice* — a cheat-sheet for prospective students and families looking for insider ideas on how to approach the college-shopping experience. We did this because, time and again, we see that the higher-education customer isn't equipped with the right information to make this complicated and consequential choice. And what's more is that sometimes one generation of influencers is confusing matters for the would-be student by inadvertently devaluing higher education through the things they say and do.

Sometimes one generation of influencers is confusing matters for the would-be student by inadvertently devaluing higher education through the things they say and do.

Let's talk community colleges for a moment, because community colleges are doing incredible work to redefine the value of college right now. What follows on the next few pages are insights from community-college leaders that reminded us how much of the industry is held up by the foundation laid by community colleges. I was particularly struck by the candor offered during a conversation with Dr. Michael A. Baston, then President of Rockland Community College and subsequently President of Cuyahoga Community College. We were talking to Dr. Baston about the power of a community-college education when he said:

> "The community college continues to become the college of first choice for families who want their young person to get a quality education at a price they can afford."

We agreed wholeheartedly. Personally, the community college was my ticket to a phenomenal future. I earned my associate's degree, then three additional degrees, availing myself of the kind of education that would have been financially out of reach had I chosen to attend a private liberal-arts college, for example, for the first four years. My local community college *was* my college of first choice, and it was a choice my mother and I both agreed upon. But not all parents (or friends or other members of a student's "buying committee") espouse the merits of community colleges. During his *EdUp* interview, Dr. Baston heard the hosts share a story about a mother who was initially disappointed when her daughter chose a community college instead of moving to a large university with a residential experience (an experience like the one the mother had chosen). When asked *"What needs to be done to help more students understand the value of a community-college education?"* Dr. Baston pulled no punches. He said:

> "Well, I have to tell you, the issue is less *students* and more *parents*. There are lots of parents who like to go to the cookout in the summer to tell your friends where Johnny and Janie are going off to school, and you put the pressure on them to go places that are not necessarily *good* for them. And you do it for *your* friends. But for those young people, they *do* need a place that has smaller class sizes. And many of the students, particularly if some parents are requiring the student to pay for their own college, are going to be thinking about how they can get credit while they're at high school so that they don't have to pay big bills, and how they can get in honors programs so that they can get to the higher-tier colleges without the higher-tier college price.
>
> "People who dismiss the value of a community college-education are forgetting about the fact that more than 40% of folks who are baccalaureate students *started* at a community college. So, what happens is that parents don't really recognize how many of your neighbors' children actually started at the community college. So, I think that we've got to get the message out to *parents* — not so much the *students* — because more and more students are making the community college the 'college of choice' because they *don't* want the loans and because they *took* the classes in high school and now they can complete more quickly. The students are starting to see the value of the value proposition in ways that the parents haven't caught up with."

I remember taking a deep breath and smiling when I heard Dr. Baston say this. It was a "mic-drop moment," if I'd ever heard one. As a former student, former staff member, and former faculty member of a community college, I couldn't love the model more than I do. Some of my favorite professors were those I learned from at my community college, and even after earning two graduate degrees, I can look back and say that some of the brightest, most worthy classmates I ever had the privilege of sitting next to were my classmates at the College of Lake County in Grayslake, Illinois. But even then, people loved to make snarky, self-deprecating jokes about being a student at CLC ("college of last chance," they'd call it) while their friends were off at the University of Illinois or Augustana College, spending a lot of money and hating their roommates. The community-college students and the university students had one thing in common — their beliefs about their own education (its value and their own worthiness) were colored by the very biased and sometimes ill-informed opinions of their parents. The role of parents in devaluing a college education cannot be overlooked, and yet Dr. Baston was perhaps the only president who had the gumption to address it head on during a podcast interview. We're grateful to him for his comments, which sparked this larger conversation with you, the reader, here in this book.

 ## Making Education Your Business with Dr. Joe Sallustio

Why "Unbundling" Is the Most Overused (and Wrong) Word in Higher Education

"Unbundle higher education!" "The unbundling of higher education!" You've heard it and probably read dozens (maybe even hundreds) of articles/books advocating for higher education to become "unbundled." I think it's the most overused and incorrect descriptor in the industry. The implication is that higher education, through its tuition and fee structures, forces students into groups of classes and services they may or may not need. I always wondered — for traditional students or adult students? At online universities or residential universities? I've been in higher education over 20 years and have never known an institution that forces students to accept services in a bundle without having waiver policies, opt-out policies, etc. In fact, an entire sector of higher education has been unbundled from the very start — our U.S. community colleges.

Community colleges have always been unbundled, but somehow, in many of the articles/books written about unbundling higher education, the community college sector isn't mentioned. One of the greatest consequences of doing *The EdUp Experience Podcast* has been our ability to highlight incredible leaders in our community colleges. They discuss how they tailor to their student's needs by only offering what the student needs, only charging the student by what they experience, and how they create flexibility based on the student's financial or living situation. Matching programming to the workforce need has always been there, particularly as community colleges literally serve their community through business and industry partnerships.

I will say, though, that the biggest bundle that higher education forces upon its students are through the confines of credit-hour requirements and prescribed time to degree (e.g., four long years). Then again, institutions like Western Governors University have been busting those bundles for years. While thousands of higher-educational professionals have been busy *talking* about "unbundling," many have been busy showing us how it's done.

In families with second-generation or third-generation college students, college is a biased tradition; young people are pushed to do what their parents or grandparents did — to choose the same schools (or same kinds of schools) and even to replicate the majors and careers of the generations that preceded them. And in families where the prospective student is a pioneer — about to become the first person or one of the first generation of their family to attend college — sometimes their parents, grandparents, aunts, and uncles, don't have the lived experience to inform an excitement about college or underpin an understanding of the value of higher education. If I could offer a piece of advice to young adults beginning to shop for a college program, I'd tell them: "Listen to your parents, but not too much. Find adults whose careers and lives you admire and ask them what they'd do if they were about to graduate from high school now."

In families with second-generation or third-generation college students, college is a biased tradition.

At the end of the day, what it takes to earn the trust of students and communities is up to those students and communities. And the degree to which your institution is valuable is defined by them, not by you. So, listening and responding to the needs, desires, and demands of higher-education stakeholders is the only path forward. Dr. Felix Matos Rodriguez, Chancellor of the City University of New York System, noted a few areas that are a priority for CUNY. First, he said:

> "One of the areas is career. CUNY has been known as a university system that has done an incredible job of moving individuals from the lower socioeconomic percentile to the middle-class and above. We do that through affordability, great faculty, and academic experience, but the career side has been uneven. When you have 50% of your students who are first-generation college students, that obligation to be the place where the students begin to think about their career possibilities and explore them, we must do better at scale — our social mobility power would become a lot more dramatic.

> "It became apparently vital to the city now about the commitment to create jobs and think differently about the relationship between employers and us, and to think differently about the way that we can structure classes and courses so the students are prepared to get better-paying jobs."

Thinking differently — this was the message that Dr. Rodriguez relayed during his episode of *The EdUp Experience Podcast*, and it's the ability to think differently that enhances the recruitment and retention of students. Retaining students to graduation and bringing them back for future educational endeavors are two of the greatest issues facing higher education today.

Retaining students to graduation and bringing them back for future educational endeavors are two of the greatest issues facing higher education today.

As this book goes to press, it's the fall of 2022 and my higher-education clients are telling me that their retention statistics are downright terrifying. Even at schools with previously very high retention rates (90% and higher), the number of students returning after a first year are as low as 72%. Understanding what students need and want — and then finding a way to give it to them — has never been so critical because the impact of doing *nothing* is dire.

Today, it's as important to be aware of and responsive to the needs of the wider community as it is to be focused on student needs. Pima Community College's Chancellor and CEO, Lee Lambert, JD, (whose institution is based in Tucson, Arizona), told us:

> "Community colleges are the hub of the wheel. What other organization in a community has more of a 360-degree touch to every facet of the community than a community college? We are where hopes, dreams, aspirations, and goals intersect."

He also reminded us that the work they do is often immediate and practical. He said:

> "We are the training arm of small business enterprises in our community."

We heard similar sentiments from other presidents when it comes to serving the needs of the community. Dr. Hal L. Higdon, Chancellor of

Ozarks Technical Community College System and President of OTCC Springfield Campus in Springfield, Missouri, said:

> "We've got to be plugged into our local economy. We can't have programs that don't have jobs on the other end."

Dr. Higdon also shared, when we asked him to opine about the future of higher education:

> "I predict that in the future, there's going to be fewer of us — community colleges, universities, higher ed, K-12. We will all be more technology-invested; there'll be more online. I think that even the *traditional* class will be hybrid and there'll be less public support. We will all be running much more like a for-profit did as far as the way we operate. In terms of states, we used to be state-*supported* and then we were state-*assisted*; now we're just state-*located*. So, we can't depend on the state. We have to behave in an entrepreneurial way. 'Entrepreneurial, public higher education' is what we have to be. We must be entrepreneurial, and then focus on the success of the student."

Being entrepreneurial as an institution is something that one of our other guests, Dr. Stephen Spinelli, knows a lot about. Spinelli is President of Babson College, located in Wellesley, Massachusetts — the institution widely considered the world's best college for entrepreneurship. Dr. Spinelli talked to us about the future of higher education, saying:

> "Everybody talks about the increased need for learning. My feeling is that higher education plays a key role. And if we don't evolve, we will abandon that; someone else will take that role because education is too important. And indeed, I think a lot of different kinds of competitive forces are filling a void for education. And *higher* education has to be more flexible. That *doesn't* mean there isn't an intimate, important role for credentialed education. I believe that we need to have solid underpinnings to how we deliver education. Bachelor's degrees and associate's degrees, master's degrees and doctoral degrees *are* important, but they are *not* the sole deliverer of learning.
>
> "If higher education can expand the thinking around 'How I deliver units of learning, how I help you and everyone else to self-curate your learning and I become a learning *partner* with you,' then I think the

role of higher education becomes more expansive. We don't have to *abandon* what we're doing. I think we can *grow* and do a lot of things in education. And indeed should. If we don't, I think we become diminished. I think we shrink in our impact, and I think the impact on society will be negative. We have this huge opportunity to do something really special. I think we have to just think differently and leverage who we are in more expansive ways."

Perhaps one of the best ways to serve learners in expansive ways is to get back to the basics — to focus on high-quality, accessible education without some of the modern distractions that have muddied the waters of the higher-education value proposition. Dr. Michael A. Cioce, President of Rowan College at Burlington County in Mount Laurel, New Jersey, sang the praises of a "back to core" or "back to basics" strategy, telling us:

"I think you're going to see changes to the physical locations of campuses because not every student is interested in a lazy river or a rock-climbing wall. What we've prioritized overall is going to change. We're in the business of *education*. So, I'm confused where five-star meal plans became the norm. And I get it — it was competitive because you don't want to lose a student because you have an inferior meal plan. But I think we need to worry about the basics because there are definitely people who want to be *educated*.

"*And* they want to enter the workforce and do amazing things. And that's what we in higher education all exist for. So that's where I think that — as a starting point — higher ed needs to make some serious investment."

Incidentally, getting back to basics changes everything about value and price. No matter how you look at it, the value of higher education is there. The constructs around the ecosystem, however, need to be transformed to let students and institutions thrive. Imagine what we all might think and feel about higher education, in general, in the wake of meaningful transformation when it comes to student loan reform, tuition costs, state and federal funding, new models for investors in higher education, and increased participation from donors and grant-awarding institutions. Already, we're beginning to see changes realized more quickly than expected due to the pandemic: federal student loan forgiveness, an improved loan-forgiveness program for public servants, venture-backed educational institutions, and colleges and universities that are diversifying their revenue streams so they can take the cost burden off the customer. You don't have to look far to find master's degree programs for under $11,000 and large universities introducing $10,000 MBAs and other high-value, lower-cost offerings. The tide is beginning to turn.

A More Valuable Future

Bolstering the value of higher education — and reforming higher education for the better — takes active, dedicated, ongoing commitment from many players. We chatted with Laura K. Ipsen, President and CEO of Ellucian, about what her company is doing to make a difference. She told us:

> "Sometimes during the toughest times is when you see the greatest need to step up and give back. I am personally very concerned about the state of diversity in education, and we know — from what we saw across the country and around the world [during the pandemic] — that diverse students suffer the most in terms of economic impact and dropout in those underserved communities. So, I was super proud as a company that we stepped up; we invested a million dollars in our PATH Scholarship (which stands for Progress, Accomplishment, Thrive, and Hope). We dedicated the first half a million to community colleges; we gave 20 community colleges $25,000 each to give to students directly. This was based on criteria that was from a third party. So, I didn't get a vote. I made a personal donation, and my executive team and many employees did as well. And you know, we're just seeing amazing things — 650 students received funding, and we're about to give another half a million out …

> "We had a student, who is an international student at Bronx Community College. He was receiving a 4.0 GPA and did not qualify for financial aid because he was international. [Because of the scholarship,] he was able to purchase his textbooks and get moving on spring semester. So, when you see these stories of 'How impactful is $500? $1,000? A little bit more?' you see how important just staying on track really is. I know this is just a drop in the bucket, but I'm really excited also that others in the ed-tech community — and some of my

competitors — are doubling down and doing the same thing that we led with, which is giving back to our community, making sure it gets to students in need, and doing our part."

Bolstering the value of higher education and reforming higher education for the better takes active, dedicated, ongoing commitment from many players.

As we move forward, we need to be looking both inward and externally to find all the ways in which we all can "do our part." We opened *Commencement* by talking about partnerships and connection to community, and it's important that we remind readers that when you think about all the things you need and want to do at your institution, you don't have to go it alone. How might the right collaborations — at your institution and across the entire higher-education industry — move you forward? Dr. Nathan Long, President of Saybrook University in Pasadena, California, talked about collaboration being key to the industry's forward momentum. He said to us:

> "I love this industry so much. Most of us in higher education do. But we have been so entrenched — for decades — around 'tradition' and 'the way things used to be' … and the way things *used to be* is not working.

> "Higher education is on the precipice of something pretty amazing if it can get out of its own way. I think the power of what we offer the amazing students and people who work for our institutions really has the potential of unleashing what I think is our country's greatest asset. We just need to get out of our own way. What do I mean by that? I mean, our focus has to be on greater collaboration that leads toward innovation."

Make Big Plans, and Execute on Them

There is no shortage of good ideas in higher education today, but it often comes down to institutional will and capability. As it turns out, it's not just learners who need competencies, skills, and tools — our institutions need them too. Laura K. Ipsen, President and CEO of Ellucian, told us that, when it comes to colleges and universities facing the opportunity to *do* more and *be* more:

> "It's really about the innovative *capability* to be the institution that they want to be today."

My co-author, Dr. Joe Sallustio, often talks about the fact that "our students are moving faster than we are" — that we need to harness a willingness to change and evolve, and then get busy doing it. Innovation is not an intellectual activity; it's an actual *activity*. It's something we must *do*, not simply *consider*.

**We need to harness a willingness to change
and evolve, and then get busy doing it.
Innovation is not an intellectual activity;
it's an actual *activity*. It's something
we must *do*, not simply *consider*.**

Innovation today needs to be broadly relevant in ways that were not at issue when most colleges and universities were founded. Today, the world is flat in terms of geographic access — students are enrolling in academic programs far from home (especially online and low-residency programs) and that should be a signal to us all that inclusivity today is a global imperative. I recently listened to the audiobook edition of Malcolm Gladwell's *I Hate the Ivy League* and was struck by the resonance of his arguments about global value and relevance. Institutions must be more than just a great option in their city, state, region, or country — because some institutions are being considered by learners around the world. Does what *you* offer to prospective students measure up to what those same individuals can get in the UK or Dubai or Toronto? In an industry full of self-proclaimed "best-kept secrets," no one can afford to be a secret anymore, and no one can afford to be too insular. The world is watching. Why *not* be attractive to students on the other side of town, the other side of the state or province, or the other side of the globe? Offer value and students will notice.

In an industry full of self-proclaimed "best-kept secrets," no one can afford to be a secret anymore, and no one can afford to be too insular. The world is watching. Why *not* be attractive to students on the other side of town, the other side of the state or province, or the other side of the globe? Offer value and students will notice.

Savvy students are sitting up and taking note especially when colleges and universities offer *new*, novel kinds of value, like when Foundry College promises to provide working adults "with the intellectual and emotional tools they need to adapt as the labor market changes." Customers love a lifetime guarantee. They also hate paying today's prices for yesterday's product. More and more students are asking themselves, "If my school isn't *charging forward* to innovate on behalf of learners, why am I letting them *charge me tuition*?"

Dr. Emily Barnes, then at Cleary University and subsequently leading at Siena Heights University, spoke to us about the institutional will to keep innovating, saying:

> "As higher education professionals, it's key to have an overwhelming intention that we're going to keep charging forward, knowing every moment that we may have to continually innovate until we get through the next piece. That's just the innovator's cadence; we know that the end is never near and that we'll never 'calm down' or it will never 'get

easier' if we continue with innovation — from here on out — in higher education. We are very committed to that notion."

Such innovation requires organization and planning. Dr. David Finegold, President of Chatham University, reminded us that just as we seek to help students develop new competencies, we must be building and exercising our own. He said:

> "The essence of any good strategic plan is a combination of understanding the organization's own *core competencies* — its strengths and weaknesses, and what can make you distinctive in the marketplace — and then understanding the key external forces that are shaping the competitive environment you're in."

Community and Industry Connected

Just as *Commencement* was headed to press, *The Chronicle of Higher Education* held its 2022 "Chronicle Festival," in which one afternoon was dedicated to "Reconnecting with Students" and the second day was all about "Reconnecting with Community." In their own way, the *Chronicle* and its featured speakers explored some of the very issues of importance to our 100+ presidents, reminding us that student-centric cultures are the way forward and that we'll only get to our destinations by partnering across communities. Dr. Wayne A. I. Frederick, President of Howard University in Washington, D.C., talked to us about the glaring inequities in the community and about the role that Howard, as an HBCU, is taking to reduce those equity gaps. Dr. Frederick, whose career prior to becoming a university president was as a cancer surgeon, has had a unique opportunity to see equity gaps in healthcare and in higher education. We asked him to talk about these gaps and about social justice in general, and he said:

> "When you look at outcomes for so many cancers, they disproportionately impact African Americans in particular. And a lot of that has so many root causes behind it. So, I've really tried to focus my career around 'How can we close that gap?' The social determinants of health are a big factor, but I'm not sure that we always realize as a society just how wide the gap is. Right here in Washington, D.C., which is a very small place, the life expectancy of an African American male who lives

in Ward 7 and 8, where the population is 95% (predominantly) African American, is about 67 years. If you come across the city to Ward 3, the life expectancy of a white woman, where the population is 95% (predominantly) white, is almost 87 years. That's a 20-year gap."

Awareness around these significant societal issues allows Howard University to be a force for change. Dr. Frederick told us:

"Howard is going to continue being at the forefront of trying to bring what I think is a social-justice issue to the forefront. This healthcare issue — and the disparities that exist — is really a social justice issue at the end of the day."

As more institutions of higher education start shifting, evolving, and growing, they're finding that it behooves them to get clarity on their institutional story and how to tell it. Dr. Summer McGee, President of Salem Academy and College in Winston-Salem, North Carolina, talked to us about how to evolve an age-old strategy (e.g., liberal-arts strategy, women's college strategy) for a student population that cares about career outcomes. Dr. McGee told us:

"The first priority was getting our narrative straight, being able to tell Salem's story in a compelling way. And that is something that we have spent a lot of time and effort on. We've engaged with partners because telling that story is important for enrollment management and it's important for our alumnae base and our advancement office. Especially for an institution that is undertaking a major curricular shift and a pivot, being able to explain and tell our story and how we still are committed to the liberal arts has been important. And we'll still *be* a liberal arts college, but we're reframing that as 'liberal arts for leadership development.' We have been working to translate that into something that really conveys value and meaning to prospective students, while remaining true to the values that our alumnae and others hold."

The tricky thing about creating and conveying value to the marketplace is that the marketplace is constantly changing its definitions of value. Long before the pandemic, the research I was conducting with thousands of prospective undergraduates (and their parents) was revealing a major shift in attitude. In 2014, prospects were looking for a college experience that left them "well-rounded" and that included a comfortable, enjoyable on-campus experience. By 2018, prospects were telling us — in no uncertain terms — that they were looking for return on investment (ROI), measurable by way of career/financial success. Did they still value the concept of liberal arts? Yes. But they wanted it to be liberal arts that led to career outcomes, not liberal arts for liberal arts' sake. At Salem College, they're evolving to "liberal arts for leadership development" and at Carthage College, they're evolving to "critical thinking for critical needs." This is what the future looks like — colleges and universities building upon their traditions and finding new, relevant ways to deliver upon the promise of education. History and heritage matter, but our students are hiring us to create the *future*.

History and heritage matter, but our students are hiring us to create the *future*.

That's why so many colleges and universities are being so deliberate about bringing the "real world" into their campuses and sending their learners into the real world. Daniel G. Lugo, JD, President of Queens University of Charlotte in North Carolina, told us that, from day one, their students are required to be engaged in real-life learning experiences. And being situated in Charlotte — a U.S. banking and finance capital — allows for many campus/community connections. President Lugo said of those connections:

> "We have sightlines into the world of business that are just unparalleled."

Those connections are worth their weight in gold to prospects, students, and alumni, for whom value is being measured in very practical, immediate ways. Between a student's *investment* and their *return* on investment comes the first wave of value, through their interactions with faculty, staff, and fellow students who open their minds and change their worldviews. Dr. David Finegold, President of Chatham University, reminded us that the human mosaic that is American higher education is, in and of itself, a treasure trove of value. Dr. Finegold said:

> "I think one of the historical huge advantages we've had in the U.S., compared to many countries, is how international our higher-ed system is. You know, the number of faculty members and the number of students we historically attracted at all levels, internationally. That's been a great strength of both our higher-ed system and — through that — our whole country in terms of attracting great talent."

For institutions to continue to attract outstanding educators and serve ambitious, capable students, today's colleges and universities must move quickly, connect personally, and take big strides.

For institutions to continue to attract outstanding educators and serve ambitious, capable students, today's colleges and universities must move quickly, connect personally, and take big strides.

Quick Moves, Big Strides

The negative quips are, at least to some degree, true: We move too slowly. We've made mistakes. We have a lot of work ahead of us. But the positive prognostications are true as well: We have endless opportunities in front of us. We have all the data we need to make wise decisions. We have access to prospective learners who need us. We are at a critical moment, in which higher education can become what it's always been capable of being — a great equalizer, a step up, and a promise for a brighter future. President Daniel G. Lugo at Queens University of Charlotte talked to us about the current value of higher education, as well as the future that awaits. He said:

> "When anyone questions whether there's still value to a college degree or whether higher education is still the great equalizer, the question doesn't require much opining. It's *fact* that's backed up by *data*. There are still incredible premiums on the differentiation of what

an undergraduate (and even what a two-year) education will result in — from a financial sense — over a lifetime. At every level, there's a premium and a return on investment. So, we have to articulate that without any shame, and use data, and get away from this kind of mealy-mouthed apologetic sense. I think that the academy must *own* this moment — to stop being such a victim of what the public and the media may say and start *owning* our message.

"We have to get back on the soapbox and demonstrate the public good that we are. Education is the miracle of modern America. It has brought us to where we are as one of the most diverse societies. Travel a little bit around the world and you'll see that we are an incredible 'city on a hill' in terms of what we've been able to achieve. And when we think about *how* we've achieved it, let us not *ever* be complacent on the true narrative: that higher education has been the difference maker at every turn."

President Lugo went on to deliver the kind of pep talk that higher-education professionals have long needed, saying:

"What would the United States be if it wasn't for the Morrill Act of 1862 that set up land-grant institutions all over this incredible country — that turned us from a family-farm-based, agrarian place into an agricultural and industrial power? What would the United States be if, after World War II, the GI bill hadn't educated millions of professionals who transformed us into the headquarters of global business for eras to come? Higher education is what did *all* of that and brought people along. And we're at another one of those moments. The whole world has changed again.

"We're turning into a technology-based society, full of opportunities and challenges. And let's not ever forget what institution has been the best answer-provider to society's questions — for not only our country, but the entire world — during each of these transformations ... It has been American higher education that's done this. We forget that at our peril. We forget — at our peril — that there hasn't been a better system in the world for leveling society, for advancing society, for innovating in society, and for really bringing incredible return on investment for our great country. I'm unabashedly proud to be a part of the academy and will not stand by without getting on the soapbox to remind folks of who we are and who we still need to be. What do I think about the future of higher education? I'm bullish."

On your hardest day, rereading President Lugo's words might renew your own faith in higher education. And with that faith, all you need is the energy to keep charging forward. Moving quickly, with high energy and big strides, isn't always easy — but doing so as a team or an entire institution (or someday as a whole industry) will make the hard work more exciting and will embolden us with the confidence to do *more* and do *better* for our students.

But how do we actually move forward swiftly in an industry that is known to move so slowly? Dr. John Swallow, President of Carthage College in Kenosha, Wisconsin, says we do it by getting comfortable with following one big initiative with another and then yet another, not letting the desire to over-study or over-analyze during a post-launch phase keep us from doing — right now — the next big thing that our stakeholders deserve. Given my personal connection to Carthage, I had the chance to watch them move quickly in recent years and I found their string of accomplishments to be inspiring. In short succession, they changed their athletic team names and mascot (no small undertaking), implemented a tuition reset (a huge undertaking), restructured some departments and added new academic programs (again, big), and developed an anti-racism program (big and important). Meanwhile, Carthage has been busy attracting new students through new academic programs and sports teams. We asked Dr. Swallow how they have achieved enrollment growth while most other Wisconsin colleges and universities have seen enrollment declines, and his explanation was a lesson in nimble operations. He said:

> "The facts are that, in 2020, our first-year class grew 6%. And then for fall of 2021, the first-year class grew another 5%. And it's really a combination of a lot of things. And, and I'll say at the outset that sometimes schools want to do *one* new thing a year and then study it. And I don't think there's time to do that anymore. I think we all need to be serving our institutions and serving our students as well as possible and get on with the good ideas that we know are out there. And that's really the approach we've taken.

"In 2019, when we did the tuition reset, we didn't just stop and wait. We also added three new sports. We added men's and women's wrestling. We added women's bowling. Recently, we added eSports. We've added new academic programs — everything from engineering science to a bachelor of music in composition or piano performance. We've added master's programs in music theater, vocal pedagogy, and ... sports management.

"I want to name this too. It's not all about the *front end*. It's about keeping the students that you *have* so that they succeed. So, we've really jumped in and I'm really proud of the faculty and staff here for undertaking all these initiatives at the same time. And what we should be excited about is that more students are coming, and more students are graduating. We don't need to undertake the deep research project, perhaps, to know exactly how to attribute the success. But our approach here is to try to launch the programs that we *know* are in the benefit of the students — 'critical thinking for critical needs.' I think that's the recipe for why we've had more students come each year."

Untangling the tassel is all about listening to the learners, responding to the needs of the marketplace, partnering where it makes us stronger, and innovating without fear. The only direction is forward.

As we look at the lessons that we've learned from academic leaders these past few years, it's clear that the future of higher education will involve the creation of *more* value from *fewer* institutions. The marketplace will continue to let us know how we're doing, and the colleges and universities that will grow and thrive will be those that heed the feedback. We are currently facing countless simultaneous evolutions and revolutions in higher education, and it can sometimes feel daunting to look around and ask ourselves, "What does it all mean? And what should we do next?" Untangling the tassel is all about listening to the learners, responding to the needs of the marketplace, partnering where it makes us stronger, and innovating without fear. The only direction is forward. Dr. Swallow said:

> "The future of higher education in the United States in the next decade will be one of significant change in industry consolidation. And the institutions that thrive through this will be serving their students better and better and better."

We're all ready for the better days ahead.

CHAPTER 7

LEADERSHIP 3.0

Trends in Higher-Education Leadership and
Words of Wisdom from 100+ Presidents

L eading an institution of higher education is both a power and privilege. It's also a nearly impossible job in an era of massive industry transformation, changing demands from learners and other stakeholders, and increased scrutiny from every angle. Despite the pressure placed on higher education's chief executives today, we heard nothing but passion and resolve when we spoke with more than 100 college and university presidents in preparation for bringing you this book. Presidents and other top leaders at campuses across the United States and around the world absolutely *love* their jobs and are more committed than ever — especially since the unprecedented disruption of the pandemic — to innovate, serve, create, repair, nurture, build, reimagine, and reinvigorate in an industry ripe for wholesale transformation.

We asked, in an anonymous survey taken by 136 individuals in the summer/fall of 2022, for higher-education leaders to tell us how much they love their work. We heard from presidents, chancellors, C-suite leaders (e.g., chief information officers, chief marketing officers, chief financial officers), provosts, deans, board members, department directors, faculty members, top consultants, and others, and when asked whether they *enjoy their jobs as higher-education leaders*, 71% said yes. It's easy to believe in leaders who believe in the value of the work.

Leading in higher education is an arduous but beloved job. It's not difficult to see why it's so hard ... and also why it's still worth it. Dr. David

Harpool, Former President of Northcentral University, talked to us about the way in which leading in higher education is as much a passion as it is a career. He told us:

> "I want to be remembered as somebody who was in it for the right reasons. I care about students. I care about faculty. I care about staff.
>
> "The only two things that have ever changed anybody's life are education and faith, and I want to be known for having promoted both."

Leading in higher education is an arduous but beloved job. It's not difficult to see why it's so hard ... and also why it's still worth it.

How higher education's leaders will be remembered varies from institution to institution and from one era to the next. What was enough to create a meaningful legacy in a post-WWII land-grant university might not come close to making a difference in a liberal-arts college in the 2020s. As times change, the demands upon (and opportunities for) leaders in higher education change as well. While this entire book, in so many ways, has been about higher-education leadership, we wanted to dedicate a special chapter to those of you who lead — providing a space to reflect on the cultural and governance issues at play, offering some new contexts for redefining leadership and identifying the ideal skillset for tomorrow's higher-education leaders, and sharing inspiring words from current presidents about what it means to lead in an industry you love.

Reflection Question: *What has been the most rewarding part of your work with (or connection to) higher education? If you could do it all over again, would you? And what would you do differently?*

📝 Pop Quiz!

In your experience, which of the following best describe the "job" that a college or university president is hired to do? At some institutions, the impossible job of president requires every item listed here, and more.

It is a president's job to:

- ❑ Get or keep the institution ranked by *US News*, *Princeton*, and other college reviews.

- ❑ Attract research funding and other grants and earn institutional accolades for everything from "Best Places to Work" lists to professional certifications, demonstrating "centers of excellence."

- ❑ Ensure the proper infrastructure and talent management to enable student success with measurable outcomes.

- ❑ Grow enrollment and increase retention to maintain a healthy balance sheet.

- ❑ Set the tone for institutional culture.

- ❑ Bolster the brand by performing well as the face and voice of the institution, improving or sustaining a strong reputation among key stakeholders.

- ❑ Put out fires, smooth out the wrinkles, and reduce noise; keep alumni, students, faculty, staff, and parents happy.

- ❑ "Friend raise" and fundraise to welcome the right people and the right gifts to the institution, creating a culture of support and philanthropy.

- ❑ Keep the accreditors happy and not make unnecessary waves.

- ❑ Be the "bad guy" when it comes to big changes that need to be made, like leading the institution through a name change, a reorganization or reduction in force, a campus relocation, a merger or acquisition, a come-back after a scandal, or a big announcement regarding the curriculum, tuition, or general operations.

❑ Improve the physical plant by building new structures and renovating for changing needs.

❑ Create and bolster community, workforce, and political relationships.

❑ Diversify revenue streams to create a sustainable financial future.

❑ Manage the levels of involvement of the Board of Directors/Trustees.

❑ Keep students safe (e.g., physical health, mental health, Title IX, etc.).

❑ Balance the academic mission and athletic aspirations.

Organized for Success: Governance and Culture in Higher Education

Leaders are not born — they are made. And when you put a bunch of leaders together and ask them to collaborate for common (and sometimes competing) causes, then cultures and bureaucracies, hierarchies and factions are made. Running any institution is challenging, and the students/customers are rarely the challenging part. Governance structures and team dynamics turn complex organizations into complicated ventures.

One of the most critical ongoing efforts underway at an institution of higher education should be the continual work of identifying and mentoring future leaders and supporting current leaders. We asked Dr. David Harpool, Former President of Northcentral University, *"How do you make sure that you have the proper leaders in place?"* He replied:

> "It has to be intentional. You have to put in a program to really identify — very early — people who you think have the potential, and then give them the opportunities. I think the most important thing is you've got to give them a safe place to fail. People have to be given a chance to demonstrate they can do it."

Mentoring and growing leaders is not just the domain of the human resources department, and it's not a once-a-year exercise when the meeting agenda says it's time to talk about "succession planning." Leaders are educated, inspired, supported, empowered, and tested through daily, incremental opportunities afforded them by their superiors and their peers. We talked to Richard L. Dunsworth, JD, President of the University of the Ozarks in Clarksville, Arkansas, about this and he said:

> "I want to invest in others and help them grow their leadership skills — help them grow their management skills. And in many ways, I want to try to build an organization that distributes as much responsibility and as much authority as possible."

I know what it feels like to have a manager who trusts you enough to distribute responsibility and authority. During my early years as the director of marketing at Lake Forest Graduate School of Management, I had a boss (the chief marketing officer) who used to joke that his career goal was to "delegate absolutely everything" and grow his directors and managers in such a way that he didn't have any real "work" to do. We'd laugh and roll our eyes when he made this joke, but I absolutely loved being trusted to make critical decisions and to do my job with authority and zero micromanagement. He once told me that his "bias was toward action," meaning that he'd much rather that his team get the work done — and maybe do it differently than how he would have done it — than to find out we chose *inaction*, not accomplishing key work on behalf of our stakeholders because we were worried about repercussions or because we lacked the confidence. His confidence in *me* allowed me to be confident in *myself*. And when he left the organization — to become a leadership coach — he was replaced by a leader who didn't share his bias for action nor the "distribute responsibility and authority" mindset of leaders like President Dunsworth. I left higher education to serve it from the outside as a consultant.

Leading is often about exactly that — motivating, inspiring, and empowering others. Western Governors University President Scott Pulsipher, who oversees a team of 7,500 faculty, staff, and leaders, told us:

> "My primary responsibility is to *motivate* and *inspire* the people that are part of WGU to do great things, to be a positive influence for the

change in the future — change that exists not only within higher education, but within our families, communities, and societies at large. That's the thing I hope to be remembered for."

If you're a higher-education professional looking to grow into your *first* leadership role or your *next* leadership role, there's much to consider. Maybe you're an admissions counselor on track to become a manager or director. Maybe you're a faculty member interested in becoming a department chair. Maybe you're a director looking to be sought-after for a vice presidency. Maybe you're a dean or department chair with interest in the provost position or the presidency. People at the top, during our research for this book, talked to us candidly about what leadership is all about, and offered practical advice and words of wisdom at every turn. Dr. Dwaun J. Warmack, President of Claflin University in Orangeburg, South Carolina, said:

> "My advice to folks who are seeking leadership is this: 'Don't seek it for the title or the position; seek it for the real work.' Because *getting* a position is one thing but *standing* in it is another."

Dr. Warmack alludes to the relentless devotion — the tireless commitment — required of strong leaders. Many of the presidents interviewed for *Commencement* demonstrated and talked about that type of devotion. In speaking with Dr. Emily J. Barnes, then at Cleary University and subsequently at Siena Heights University, we explored how this tireless commitment sometimes gives rise to a sort of leadership imposter syndrome. She suggested:

> "For leaders, when you feel self-doubt creeping in, instead of running away from it or getting rid of any sense of sadness or anxiety, try instead to *lean into it*. Snuggle it a little bit and say, 'Oh, I know. I know you're feeling insecure. We're familiar with this. We know this feeling of self-doubt.' Having that sense of presence with yourself is important."

We found it particularly inspiring when we'd meet a college or university president whose ascension up the leadership ladder was clearly motivated by their desire to do more for students. Dr. Daria J. Willis, Former

President of Everett Community College in Everett, Washington,[33] told us about her climb, saying:

> "When I was teaching classes, I would have five classes of 30 students each. And then there would always be some students who needed something a little bit extra, and I would have to go to the chair or dean and beg to get XYZ. And I was tired of begging. So, I said, 'You know what? Maybe I need to get in those positions so I can have a broader impact and so people don't have to beg me to do things for them.' And so, then I became a dean and said, 'Ah, I don't have enough power. So let me go be a provost.' And I said, 'Ah, I *still* don't have enough power, and let me be a president. Let me be at the top of the food chain so that I can make the broadest amount of impact on a group of students.' So, for me, that's what it's all about — transforming lives."

All this talk about identifying and mentoring new leaders assumes that colleges and universities promote from within when looking to fill key leadership roles (which is not always the case). There are many higher-education professionals who spend their entire careers inside higher ed; nearly 52% of academic professionals surveyed for this book have worked in higher education for 11+ years, and 16% have been in higher-education leadership for more than 20 years. What's more is that when we asked academic leaders how they envision the future of their careers, more than 57% said that they intend to stay in higher education for several more years or until retirement. You don't have to be a math professor to see the flipside of these statistics: 43% of higher-education professionals have been in the industry for 10 years or less (i.e., they're newcomers, at every level of the hierarchy) and, according to our research, 41% are actively planning to leave the industry or are on the fence about staying in academia. And the leaders who aren't in these numbers just yet are the ones who are currently working *outside* higher education — as learning-and-development leaders, as retail CEOs, as ed-tech innovators, as academic consultants, and in myriad other leadership positions — who will be soon tapped to become leaders inside colleges and universities. Higher education has a competing balance of "insiders" and "outsiders."

---

33 Between her interview on *The EdUp Experience Podcast* and the release of this book, Dr. Willis became President at Howard Community College in Columbia, Maryland.

Dr. Irma Becerra, President of Marymount University in Arlington, Virginia, told us about her fascinating journey to the presidency. She was the first woman to earn a PhD in electrical engineering from Florida International University and worked for several years with NASA, the National Science Foundation, and the Air Force Research Lab before serving on a university faculty, then rising through the ranks (professor, director, vice provost, provost, and vice president) at multiple universities before being recruited from St. Thomas University to Marymount University as president. We asked her about her career path and whether being a university president was something she long aspired to do, and she said:

> "If you would have asked me, when I was a young PhD student, if I want to be a university president one day, that was so far from my radar. I would have never imagined that would be my path. And a lot of times when people ask me, 'What advice can you give me in terms of careers?' I never think about doing a job as a steppingstone. But I *do* realize that every job that I've done in my life has prepared me to do the job that I'm doing now. So, I'm a big believer in not *jumping over* steps, but *enjoying* every step — not just taking a step because you want to take a step, but doing it because you're going to enjoy that next step."

Dr. Becerra went from being a research scientist at places like NASA to being a university president. The academy is full of unique leadership-trajectory stories like hers. We couldn't resist exploring the question of "How did you go from *there* to *here*?" during our interview with Dr. Wayne A. I. Frederick, President of Howard University, because it's not often that a cancer surgeon[34] caps off their career by becoming president of the university where they were educated. Dr. Frederick told us:

> "To be quite honest, I'm a reluctant university president. This was never an ambition of mine. I don't describe myself as a very 'ambitious' person. I think ambition is about oneself. I like to see myself as an 'aspirational' person and I think aspiration is about trying to do better for others and aspiring to a higher calling ... My role as president of

---

34 Dr. Frederick is still a practicing cancer surgeon at Howard University Hospital, where he continues to see patients and perform surgeries.

Howard is really an attempt to pay back a debt of gratitude that I know it would be impossible to repay."

> **Reflection Question:** *These days, we hope alumni will make donations, come to events, serve on advisory boards, and refer the next generation of students. It's an altogether new and exciting vision to imagine alumni coming back to lead — for our graduates to take the helm of a college or university with their unique perspectives of having once been a student at the institution they lead. What might it look like if your most esteemed alumni were serving on your leadership team? What are you doing to endear your students and alumni to you so powerfully that they might someday be willing to do as Dr. Frederick has done at Howard by trying to "pay back" a debt of gratitude through profound and unprecedented service?*

Dr. Frederick's story is one that resonates with different leaders in different ways. His conversation with us helped us to appreciate how difficult the job of university or college president truly is, and he got us thinking about deeply committed acts of service from alumni. He said to us:

> "Being a cancer surgeon is probably the most rewarding job that you can have. Patients and their families are very, very gratuitous about what you do. They express that gratitude even when you take difficult news to them — they display a courage and a nobility that's unbelievable. Being a university president is difficult. You have many different constituents and nobody's happy."

We know that last quip was somewhat tongue-in-cheek. It made us smile, and we knew it would connect readers with their own stories of working under difficult circumstances where, sometimes, your efforts fall short of making everyone (or anyone!) happy.

NASA researcher, cancer surgeon — you can find just about anyone in the university president's office these days, as long as their background gave them broad perspectives on learning and stakeholder service ... as long as they're proven leaders and tireless advocates for the people and purpose they serve. Dr. Michael Torrence, President of Motlow State Community

College in Tullahoma, Tennessee, has expertise in technology and eSports, in addition to his expertise in higher education and social equity. During Dr. Torrence's interview with *The EdUp Experience Podcast*, EdUp co-founder and *Commencement* co-author Dr. Joe Sallustio reacted to Dr. Torrence's background in technology and innovation by saying:

> "What I believe the president of the *future* looks like for a college or university isn't what necessarily — in some respects, not all — the current college and university president looks like. I look to someone like you and go, wow. This to me speaks to the college and university president of the future (and of the right now) because of the technology expertise, the interest in training, in innovation and thought, and in marketing and digital. That's where colleges and universities are headed, in my opinion."

You can find just about anyone in the university president's office these days, as long as their background gave them broad perspectives on learning and stakeholder service … as long as they're proven leaders and tireless advocates for the people and purpose they serve.

Dr. Torrence got the wheels turning in our minds when he summed up the way his interests and work align with the needs of higher education in this way, saying:

> "The vertical integration of technology to improve the human condition — that's my research question probably for the rest of my life."

As for how current and future higher-education leaders might be bringing a very different focus and skillset to the leadership table, Dr. Torrence said:

> "When we don't evolve, we fall behind. We should be respectful and honor the past leadership that has gotten us to this point. We've

gone through the agrarian age and the industrial age and we're in a technological era — and we're about to move into Industry 4.0, to Industry 5.0, to Web 3.0. So, all these wonderful options are raising their heads specifically with the use of AI, and higher education ought not be the *last* one at the table to take a piece of that pie. I think we should be leading these efforts and not simply being siphoned off of to be managed by third-party entities. All the subject-matter experts that I know work at institutions of higher education. And those are the people that we lean on."

What Dr. Torrence is talking about here is how college and university leaders can go from *having a vision* (which in the past was all about prestige and reputation) to *being visionary* (taking big risks, making big changes, engaging the imagination). When I began working as a higher-education consultant, I had the opportunity to interview several presidents, deans, provosts, and chancellors during the intake process for institutional rebranding efforts. And I often joked with my colleagues that interviewing a higher-education leader was easy and required almost no preparation on my part because, "I can just walk into their office and say, 'So, tell me about your vision for the university,' and they'll talk for the next hour while I take notes." It was true. Having a vision is important, but most visions — and most leaders who articulate those visions — aren't particularly "visionary" in the active, roll-up-your-sleeves way that disrupts industries or changes the trajectory of entire institutions.

Having a vision is important, but most visions — and most leaders who articulate those visions — aren't particularly "visionary" in the active, roll-up-your-sleeves way that disrupts industries or changes the trajectory of entire institutions.

In the 2020s, it's becoming easier to find academic leaders who are true visionaries — who are unafraid of constant change and who are more focused on the future than on preserving the traditions of the past. Lee Lambert, JD, Chancellor and CEO of Pima Community College, told us:

> "Leaders shape the future. My job isn't just to be a key caretaker — do the ceremonial things, make sure the lights are on, and ensure the students are taught. My job is really to be paying attention to where our industry of higher education is going. How can I play a role in helping shape that reality, especially in light of Industry 4.0, the Four Superpowers,[35] and all those kinds of realities?"

Defining leaders as "insiders" and "outsiders" is not entirely clear-cut. Some people who serve on a president's cabinet (including those in presidential roles) spend decades in technology, finance, marketing, or other functional areas before sharing their professional expertise with the next generation by becoming a part-time educator. And it's in the *classroom* where some former "non-academics" fall in love with higher education. No matter how you choose to think about the difference between higher-education leaders who are "home grown" and those who came to the academy from the outside, it's important to consider the value of both perspectives — the fresh ideas that higher education can glean from other industries and the way in which higher education should continue to understand and draw upon its roots. Dr. David Harpool, Former President of Northcentral University, talked to us about how Northcentral was thinking about "insiders" versus "outsiders" on its leadership team, saying:

> "Our cabinet is not typical in the university structure sense. We don't take votes; we reach consensus. We disagree and we don't stop talking until we agree. And in that model, we're about 60% female and we're about 40%, right now, diverse, which represents our student population almost exactly. And I try to set a goal that at least 50% of everybody in our university leadership grew up in the institution and around 50% come from the outside, because I think you need other perspectives."

---

35 The Four Superpowers of technology are generally agreed upon to be mobile technology, the cloud, artificial intelligence (AI), and the internet of things (IoT).

" Your school is only as strong as your Board of Trustees. **"**

Richard W. Schneider, PhD

President Emeritus, Norwich University,
and Rear Admiral, U.S. Coast Guard (Retired)

Having an intentional balance of insiders and outsiders on a cabinet or leadership team can help strike the appropriate balance of maintaining shared governance while innovating with speed. Those who don't fully understand their boundaries will imagine new possibilities while those who understand some of the higher-education shackles will provide context. Somewhere in the middle, innovation really can take place.

As much as we have been inspired by leaders coming into the higher-education leadership ranks from other industries, we are equally impressed by higher-education lifers who know the academic landscape forward, backward, and upside down. When we spoke to Dr. Philomena Mantella, President of Grand Valley State University, she shared an interesting story about college leaders who are trained up through higher education. Dr. Mantella has spent 30 years in higher education, and she told us:

> "I started on the service side — working in enrollment, financial aid, and student affairs — and then broadened into academic innovation, adult and continuing education, and digital education at the end of my career at Northeastern University, before I joined Grand Valley."

While many presidents come from a financial background (working in fundraising/advancement or in finance), the respondents to the *Commencement* survey told us that the #3 most important type of experience for academic leaders, particularly presidents, is "expertise in marketing, enrollment, and brand." We asked Dr. Mantella to speak to the unique opportunities of going from an enrollment-management expertise to a presidency and she said:

> "I think that the benefits of the background in enrollment management is it starts with the *market*. And I believe education has to take what I call an 'outside in' look versus an 'inside out' look. So, we have things we offer, and we want to push them out to the universe or to the public. The question is: What do people *need*? How do they *learn*? And I think true enrollment management is really about understanding the learner and understanding the markets.

> "That's how you do it. It's not by 'What of set of gimmicks can we do or who can do more visiting and have more giveaways?' It's really about those two fundamentals — [the needs of learners and markets]. And

then being honest with yourself as an institution about what we do well and what we don't do well and how to *align* those interests or *change* the way we do our work in order to work toward what is important for learners.

"And so I found it a really helpful background because it *does* lay a foundation for strategy, without a doubt. It's about marketing. It's about learners. It's about how you make choices around those things and optimize for your institution and for the students. It's about having a graduation mindset, not an enrollment mindset. So those kinds of values are really important."

A graduation mindset instead of an enrollment mindset. So much of what motivated Dr. Joe Sallustio and me — with significant contributions from our dear friend and professional collaborator Elvin Freytes — to write this book comes down to the opportunity to play a role in an industry-wide "mindset reset." Collectively, the 125 presidents we interviewed and the 136 higher-education leaders we surveyed for this book offered a giant bouquet of fresh ideas — they gave us permission to think about things in new ways as we embark on a future with new goals and new imperatives.

Collectively, the 125 presidents we interviewed and the 136 higher-education leaders we surveyed for this book offered a giant bouquet of fresh ideas – they gave us permission to think about things in new ways as we embark on a future with new goals and new imperatives.

Such goals (and initiatives and strategic plans) can be difficult to execute if you don't have stable leadership. President Emeritus of Norwich University in Northfield, Vermont, Dr. Richard W. Schneider, RADM, U.S. Coast Guard (Retired), talked to us about the all-too-common challenge of short tenure among college and university presidents. A few years ago, the average president was staying at the helm for 6.5 years, representing a downward trend that has consequences across the organization. And many of us can point to examples of presidents who have stayed for three years or less. President Schneider said:

> "The biggest organizational problem is these presidents who stay four years and leave. My God, it takes you two years to know your school well enough to *write* the long-range plan, let alone know if anybody will *believe* in it yet. And when they leave, then the cycle starts again."

Even when we have a good plan and a stable leadership team to guide us through it, we often don't have the hours in the day or the people on the payroll to execute all the initiatives outlined in the plan. And, let's be honest, many institutions aren't holding themselves accountable for executing the strategic plans they make; they're celebrating the completion of the *plan* without planning the completion of the *work*. Dr. John Porter, President of Lindenwood University, told us:

> "Most universities don't have a PMO — project management office. We've got these six strategic initiatives, and we want to make sure that we've got dashboards built, that we're doing what we say we're going to do. I tell my team 'Bullets on paper mean nothing. It's all in the execution.' And unless we see results and can see the metrics, we don't know whether we're making progress. So, putting a PMO in place is important. We have a project management office at Lindenwood. We have a project manager who is driving all the action items in a software package called Cascade, using technology in a way that ensures we can make progress. We've also made the technology available to our Board of Trustees. So, they now can sign in and they can go to our dashboard, and they can look to see where they're red, yellow, or green in each of our six initiatives."

There are few things more inspiring to me than seeing academic leaders roll up their sleeves to focus on the daily work of running a thriving college or university. It's work that's an honor and a privilege, but it's still work — sometimes very *hard* work. And in the end, it's *important* work. Dr. Thomas R. Bailey, President of Teachers College at Columbia University in New York, New York, said to us:

"Higher education is important. From an *individual* perspective, it's very important for individuals to be able to get additional education, because that gives them more opportunities. And as a *society*, we need a strong, effective system of higher education. In higher ed, we've got problems, but we've got a very important job to do."

So how, exactly, do we perform those important jobs and make the difficult, interconnected daily decisions that are required of us? It all comes down to the overall culture and a shared institutional approach to decision-making. During the initial days and weeks of the pandemic, college and university presidents who were in crisis-response mode quickly learned that, per the modern business adage, culture eats strategy for lunch. Those who found themselves at the helm of institutions that were collaborative in nature, where the relationship between the president and the board chair was rock-solid, where the organizational chart was flat (or easily flattened), and where decision-makers were confident and nimble — those presidents had a much easier time doing their jobs during exigent circumstances. Governance structures and cultural norms are everything in a crisis. Dr. Christopher Roellke, President of Stetson University in DeLand, Florida, took the helm during the early days of the pandemic and spoke to us at the height of it all (during the summer of 2020). He told us that good culture is what was allowing him to accomplish a great deal — to hit the ground running as a new president during unprecedented times. He had a five-month onboarding process before the previous president stepped down, and Dr. Roellke said of his initial impressions of Stetson:

"I really liked what I saw. I saw tremendous commitment to the institution. I saw thoughtfulness, kindness, humanity. All the good stuff that you would hope for in a higher-education context was certainly true in my initial experiences at Stetson. So, although [a pandemic] certainly is not the context that I anticipated coming into, I have a superb team around me and we're going to do the very best we can to make sure that our students can pursue their degrees."

Governance structures and cultural norms are everything in a crisis.

Stetson University also did something quite wise in orchestrating a five-month overlap of the outgoing president and the incoming president. We all talk about real-time, immersive learning for college students, but rarely offer such immersion experiences for new leaders. Dr. Roellke told us during the mid-summer of 2020:

> "I feel very grateful … that the exiting president, Dr. Wendy Libby, who served Stetson so well for over a decade, did engage me quite fully back in February when the pandemic really started to take root in the United States. So, over the last four or five months, I've actually been immersed in the Stetson community in terms of its planning and its preparations.

> "We sort of joke that we were wonderful dance partners: she was fully respecting the fact that I was the incoming president and I was fully respecting the fact that she was the outgoing president, and I feel so grateful for that experience. I got a chance to meet senior leadership in real time. I got a chance to speak with faculty and students and several other important constituents of our university. So, I feel very grateful in many ways. The typical kind of 'learning and listening tour' that a new president would do? I was immersed in it quite authentically."

One of the first relationships a college or university president makes when they are hired into a new institution is with the board. The trustees/directors are the leaders who hire the president and the relationship, from day one to day last, is vital. President Emeritus of Norwich University in Northfield, Vermont, Dr. Richard W. Schneider, RADM, U.S. Coast Guard (Retired), told us:

> "The most important relationship on campus is between the president and the chairman. If that is not solid as a rock — where they can both share their concerns and share their joys at the same time — the whole school grieves. When the chairman doesn't trust the president, or the president doesn't trust the chairman — and that's essential to get through an emergency — this is a national crisis for higher ed like you have never seen. And if we don't have strong boards and great relationships between chairmen and presidents, we are doomed. You cannot get yourself out of this."

I look back upon a distinct moment in my career and wish that President Schneider had been there to advise my colleagues on this matter. Count yourself lucky if you have never lived through what my colleagues and I experienced when the phone rang with a call from the FBI. They were calling to tell us that they believed we had been the victim of a fraud. Our board chair, along with other co-conspirators on the board, had embezzled more than a million dollars from our university, had been involved in a money-laundering scheme with our assets, and had duped our leadership team into believing that a sudden influx of cash into the university was an "anonymous gift." The FBI showed up to take files from offices (including mine) and we were advised not to let on — to any of our constituents and especially to the board — that we knew what they had done. Our commencement ceremony was the next week, and our president was forced to share the stage with a corrupt board chair, handing out diplomas and keeping a stiff upper lip. The Friday before our graduation ceremony, our president did something he'd never done — he sat down in my office and put his head in his hands. And he asked me, "How could they have done this to us?" — looking heartbroken and so disappointed. The board was political and corrupt and had been the root of so many issues on campus for so many years. And we had trusted them and done nothing to question them. The following week, we asked every member of the board to resign ... and we started over.

Leadership matters. When it's bad, everyone suffers. When it's strong and trustworthy, everyone benefits. And now is the era in which we are shining a bright light on leadership — who we need at the top, how to restructure our institutions for improved governance, and how to support the worthy new leaders who have stepped up to guide us through unprecedented times and unparalleled opportunities.

> **Reflection Question:** *How solid is the relationship between your President's cabinet and your board? What can you do to build and nurture those high-level relationships for the benefit of your students and other stakeholders?*

Making Education Your Business with Dr. Joe Sallustio

Measuring Your Leadership

A little over a decade ago, I had the displeasure of working for some of the worst leaders I've ever encountered in my 20+ years in higher education. And I worked under these bad leaders all at the same time!

Let's play a game of "what if." Imagine that, in a time of transition, your university hired a new president. Now imagine that the person hired into the presidency chose to work from a conference room on your campus for *four months* without introducing themselves to staff. Are you picturing it? Hmmm. Yeah. What kind of uncertainty do you think this situation might create for employees? Might some of them find it completely unbearable as questions of job security and the future presented themselves when they weren't ready to consider them? Of course.

Then, on top of such a scenario, imagine working for a boss (not that evasive president but yet another layer of dysfunctional leadership) who would email their employees several times between the hours of 4:00 a.m. and 6:00 a.m. with a list of demands or requests for reports "ASAP, when you wake up" — for weeks and months on end. And imagine that, while all this was happening, you were in the middle of buying a house for your spouse and new-born baby.

Now ... stop imagining and be thankful that it happened to me, and not you. (Whew!)

From that moment on, I made a commitment to operate with what I considered to be the three most important leadership traits and the ultimate measurement lens. My three A's — approachability, authenticity, and accountability. The measurement? What do my employees' spouses or significant others think and say about me? Do my employees go home and complain about me to their families, or do they go home and say that they enjoy their current employment situation? I've always kept this top of mind because it was my wife — when I was being poorly led and when I was working to be an admirable leader myself — who became my sounding board and helped me realize my value.

Perhaps the three A's (approachability, authenticity, and accountability) might help you assess (and inspire) yourself and your colleagues in new ways. And I challenge you to really think about the management lens: What do your direct reports say about you when they go home at night? And how might you make more fans among the families of your most critical team members?

We were so pleased, during the research phase of writing this book, to discover overwhelming evidence that — despite higher education's reputation for being too bureaucratic and hierarchical — that a fresh crop of leaders, across the sector, has begun to tackle the topics of inefficient structures and governance, power distance, and organizational politics. When I was a medical-university communications director, every decision I made — every single day — had to be filtered through worries about whether the leadership team would think I'd "overstepped" (a term I heard a lot during those years) and whether a project I was overseeing would highlight turf wars between competing deans and directors. I was constantly wondering whether my careful words and authentic relationships across a large organization (where I had many friends and supporters) foretold alliances outside my assigned silo and might ruffle feathers with my vice president. And I lost sleep over whether there was anything I could do to ensure my projects weren't sidelined by unnecessary sign-offs or dozens of competing priorities and concerns from committees and boards who were privy to my work. I said it then and I'll say it again: If you work in a traditionally managed higher-education institution, you couldn't possibly be working in a more political environment unless you actually worked in ... well, politics.

🔆 **EdUp with Elvin**

Practical Tips and Frontline Insights from Elvin Freytes

So, what makes a good leader? It's a complicated topic, which is why we've devoted an entire chapter to it here. But at the most *practical* and *human* levels, the answer to the question "What makes a good leader?" is simple: Don't be an asshole!

That's right — don't be a tool, a jerk, a … you get the point. **Want to know how to avoid being an asshole?**

Here's how:

1. **Smile**. Smile when you're passing someone and catching eye contact. Smile when you're listening to someone talk about something that excites them. Smile while you talk. It's time to reject the old, faulty notion that you can't be nice *and* be respected. Smiling is a trait of great strength.

2. **Connect**. Say hello and get to know people you don't already know — at your institution and in the wider community. Seek them out and introduce yourself with a smile.

3. **Learn**. Ask questions and genuinely listen to the answers. Don't do the "look around the room while someone is talking to you" move — not cool! Intently focus on them and ask follow-up questions to learn more. If eye contact doesn't come naturally for you, practice this skill. It gets easier with time.

4. **Trust**. Trust that people were hired for a reason and should be given a chance to prove their competency before being second-guessed, criticized, or micromanaged.

5. **Invest in integrity**. Don't tell little white lies to make yourself look good/better, even if you're stressed or just trying to cover yourself (CYA!) during a shitstorm. People can easily determine that you're full of it (or full of yourself).

6. **Collaborate and serve**. Don't make the mistake of thinking that people work for *you*; always remember that you work for *them* (for your team, for your peers, for your students, for your faculty and staff, for your community, for your alumni). Oh, and please don't send an email, text, or voicemail saying you want to see someone or talk to someone "ASAP" without giving a reason — that scares people. Focusing on collaboration and servant leadership will help prevent those kinds of communication missteps.

7. **Be humble and inclusive**. Stop saying, "I did this" and "I did that" and "This was made possible thanks to me." Start using "we" and "us" or "they" when appropriate. As a leader, it can be too easy to feel the weight of the institution on your shoulders and to feel like the bright light is shining on you alone. Do your best to distribute praise and accept blame.

8. **Read the room**. Do your best to customize (and pivot) your communications and behaviors in accordance with what's happening around you — in the boardroom, during a team meeting, and from the front of a classroom or lecture hall. If you're talking and no one cares (you may be able to tell by observing facial expressions and body language), stop and check in with the audience. Learning to read the room can be hard but is a critical skill to develop. And once you can read the room, respond accordingly. Because only a real asshole would take note of a disengaged, frightened, confused, or angry audience and keep right on trucking.

9. **Be gracious**. Always, always, always say "hello" and "goodbye," make use of important phrases like "please" and "thank you," hold doors open for others, give kudos to folks when they deserve it, and never make anyone feel like they're wasting your time (by checking the clock) or you're not interested in what they have to say (by looking over their shoulder or multitasking).

10. **Avoid the busywork**. I think you know where I'm going with this one ... Never ever call a working group a *committee*!

Enter the 2020s and a fresh opportunity for dynamic new leaders (many of whom paid their dues for decades in the old-fashioned cultures of academia) to shake things up — to humanize cultures, flatten organizational charts, accept responsibility, and distribute praise. One leader we spoke to about reimagining bureaucracies was Dr. John Swallow, President of Carthage College in Kenosha, Wisconsin, who told us:

"I think things are different than they were in the past — things are changing. And so, I've really wanted people to see that — over and over — we might have a function under one person, one vice president, for example, but then we might move it. I want people to feel that that's okay — that we can be dynamic. We all have a lot we could do, and we all want to be rewarded and we need to be given permission to go ahead and do things, but this is as far from silos as I can possibly get it. It's also about not having too many steps along the way. Sometimes we feel like we need a lot of committees in place — sometimes because we're just so worried that something might be wrong. But, in fact, what we *want* to do is do a *lot* of things and we know we won't get them a hundred percent right. (Or at least not the first time.) And we want to enable that, and we want people to feel rewarded and excited every day they come to work.

"So that's how I start. One thing that follows from that is that people's titles might change and what they *do* — from year to year — might change. That's not to say we don't have a lot of standard functions, but we don't want the boundaries to be fixed. We're not trying to organize around those boundaries. We're trying to *move* the boundaries or have *permeable* boundaries. And that means lots of teamwork. That means people just need to get in and not wait for the committee meeting — not wait for a whole lot of structure — but just decide 'How do they think it should go?' and then get *going*.

"The truth is that you don't need hundreds of people on campus all to approve — or even know about — everything that everyone does. That's a recipe for taking too long. One of the reasons we've been able to do so much is that lots of people are activated and excited to do different things. ... And it's important to be giving people permission maybe *not* to know or not to *worry* that they should know and then letting them be most excited about the things they're doing within their group."

I honestly can't think of a better gift that the leadership of any organization could give to their people than the gift of permission not to need to know everything — *not* to have to serve on every committee or attend every meeting. Imagine being able to serve the students and other stakeholders without having to give and receive a million updates every day, where the organizational culture focuses on trust and confidence. I have always believed that most "status meetings" are a great way to waste time when we could actually be doing work on behalf of our stakeholders. Status updates can be posted on a wiki or project portal, and communication across groups and hierarchies can happen efficiently and asynchronously. During our interviews for this book, many presidents talked about the power of transparency and trust as the driving forces of a higher-education culture. Dr. Roellke at Stetson University told us that he's committed to transparency as a way to build trust as a leader. He said:

> "I think the word *transparency* is important. It's a word that's hot right now in higher-education circles. And what I think it really is about is *trust*. I think people are smart and they are proactive and they're intelligent. And if they're given the information so they can understand who made that decision and why — [if you offer] transparency about where resources are allocated and why — you build trust. Because I think everyone recognizes that there are a limited amount of resources. There are difficult decisions that have to be made, but if you can be honest and open and candid, I think you're going to build trust between administration and faculty, between administration and students, between administration and alums, local government agencies, et cetera. So, I view transparency as important to building trust.

> "How do you pull that off? I think that you have to also, as a leader, be willing to listen and be willing to be honest about why you made a particular decision and, frankly, sometimes raise your hand and say, 'I didn't get that one right.' In other words, what I'm suggesting is I think good leadership also involves allowing yourself to have some vulnerability. None of us are perfect in this work. We all have the best of intentions, but we make mistakes here and there."

Vulnerability, transparency, trust, confidence — they're key to a high-functioning organizational culture. What *else* goes a long way? *Empathy*. Dr. Mary Papazian, Former President of San José State University in San Jose, California, talked to us about how she was keeping everything in balance — the responsibilities, the COVID-19 crisis, and the thousands of stakeholders. She told us:

> "You have to have a great *team*. I know we always say that and it's another buzzword, but honestly, in moments like this, it's really, really true. I have an amazing leadership team working together — there's a lot of support. Together, we've been able to create that sense of a shared *commitment* and, I hope, some *trust* that we have the best interests of everyone at the forefront of our minds.

> "It's just about, I think, listening a lot, being thoughtful, and frankly expressing empathy — recognizing that people are going through so much (some of which we know and, honestly, some of which we don't). And so, we just have to be empathetic, and we have to be patient. We have to be open. We have to listen in a real and genuine way. And then we have to be clear about — *really* clear about — what we're trying to do. And frankly, what we don't know."

What we heard from leaders like Dr. Papazian was that — when it comes to creating a culture that works on behalf of all its stakeholders — communication counts. And one of the most important things we communicate about in higher education are issues that require a decision. Not surprisingly, the challenge of nimble, smart decision-making surfaced in many of the interviews for this book. Dr. Melody Rose, formerly the Chancellor of the Nevada System of Higher Education, talked to us about decision-making in higher education, and how we can quickly get "out of the emotions and into the facts" (a term I often use to describe what she touched upon). She told us:

> "I'm very much focused on this notion of driving decisions with two things in mind: One is student interests and centering the student experience in every business decision that we make. And two is focusing on metrics, targets, and data, because, as the old business adage goes, 'If it's not measured, it's not managed.' And so, I think that a focus on outcomes and performance creates transparency and

When any leader truly leads from a place of values, only good things happen.

Lisa Honaker

Former Sales Executive at FedEx Office,
Director of Expansion Sales at Highspot,
and Recurring Guest Co-host of
The EdUp Experience Podcast

therefore creates trust. And if you get everybody to the table, it's also creating inclusion."

It's not only difficult to make the *right* decisions with the right support, but it's also more important than ever to be making decisions *quickly*. Dr. Summer McGee, President of Salem Academy and College in Winston-Salem, North Carolina, talked to us about the degree to which higher-education leaders must be tireless and energized because the work marches on — the decisions need to be made now so we can get busy making *tomorrow's* decisions. She said to us:

"Accreditations wait for no one ... new academic programs wait for no one."

Make the decisions. Do the work. Keep going.

Nimble decision-making regarding complex problems was the topic that surfaced when we asked Carthage College President Dr. John Swallow to tell us about how his background — as an accomplished mathematician and a former English professor — prepared him for a higher-education presidency. We were fascinated by his left-brained/right-brained strengths, and he explained his talents and his higher-education passion in this way:

"I like to contemplate and work on very complicated problems and issues. I have a deep respect for beauty, but also know that things can get really quite complex.[36] And I think over the course of my career, that problem-solving aspect of me has driven me every day. First, I was spending lots of time teaching and then wanting to have an impact teaching English or humanities. And then over time, I was wanting a bigger and bigger scope for the things I did. And so, as you can imagine, these days, there are a lot of really complicated things to think about in higher education. Now, at this later point in my career, I'm glad to have a larger impact on more and more people. It's great to

---

36 Dr. Swallow once devoted nearly five years of his life solving a mathematics problem so complex that no one else had even come close in 25 years. Learn more about "beauty and complexity" and what this college president's life looked like years before he took the helm at Carthage College: https://www.charlotteobserver.com/entertainment/article224180820.html. Swallow's story is a reminder that every college president brings a unique set of skills and talents to the president's office, and the very best institutions find ways to apply those skills to solving the problems of modern-day higher education.

prove something that takes you years and a hundred people worldwide can appreciate it [i.e., mathematics proofs], but it's really much more deeply satisfying to affect the lives of thousands of people."

Dr. Swallow talked to us about one of our very favorite subjects — the kinds of mindsets it takes to lead in higher education. He said:

"It really is quite complex, because you're thinking about people at a very important time in their life. You're thinking about the *choices* they're making — financially and also educationally. And then you're thinking about the *outcomes* that they achieve. Higher education enrolls a very diverse set of people; that's a wonderful thing. But when you start talking about finance, it's easy for some people to forget that much of the actual tuition people pay is discounted — it's indexed to their academic profile and/or their financial profile. Then there are different retention rates and graduation rates. And the system — and this is really important — the system of people we put in place and how we interact with our *students* really does determine a lot. And so that's *psychology*. That's *education*. That's *sociology*. All those pieces come into play."

I walked away from that conversation feeling a little better. It felt validating to hear Dr. Swallow talk about higher education in the context of its layered complexities. No wonder the work that we do — the work that *you* do — is hard. It's hard because it's incredibly complex. And yet here you are — 4,000 institutions strong (in the U.S. alone) with hundreds of thousands of faculty and staff, choosing every day to wake up and keep chipping away at the complex problems of higher education because you care enough to solve the challenges before you. Because you care enough about the students. In a conversation with Dr. Daniel F. Mahony, President of the Southern Illinois University System, he told us that, as higher-education leaders:

"We need to look at the way we do things — our policies, procedures, processes — and ask ourselves: 'Are they truly fair? Are we considering how this might impact people who are different from me?'"

Dr. Mahony told us that he sought out leadership roles to help solve these problems — to challenge the status quo and to make a difference for students. He said:

> "One of the reasons I wanted to be in leadership roles is that I thought we could do a better job in meeting the needs of all of our students and being more equitable."

And that's exactly why any of us should seek out leadership roles and positions of authority — because we aim to contribute even more than we've been honored to contribute so far ... because being a leader is not about a title or a sense of power, but because it's about an opportunity to do more for others.

Leading in an Industry You Love

It used to just be about doing what the leader before you did — maintaining the status quo, keeping the faculty and staff from getting upset, keeping groups of students walking in the door each fall and crossing the commencement stage each spring. Presidents who made waves didn't fare well. If your predecessor was credited for increasing your spot in the third-party rankings, it was your job to hold steady or earn additional or more prestigious accolades. It was all strategic plans and board meetings and blue business suits.

But today, more academic leaders are bringing their whole selves to the work of leading colleges and universities. They care as much (or more) about the students than about the faculty and fellow administrators. They are working to "right" the wrongs of previous generations — by doing away with exclusionary practices, retiring racially insensitive team mascots, and fixing other shortcomings that have long hurt the institutions and their people. They're forging stronger relationships with students and with community partners, making themselves approachable, and no longer shying away from personal traits like humility and vulnerability, but embracing them as workplace strengths. They're asking the tough questions and creating space for innovative and creative thinking. They're finding a way to fund what matters and let go of what no longer works. In a word, today's most effective higher-education leaders *love* what they do.

President Schneider at Norwich University, when reflecting on his long career in higher education, told us:

Our nation is blessed with a rich spectrum of colleges and universities – 4,000 of them out there. And while I'm biased, I think those colleges and universities (and their associated programs) are our nation's greatest asset. "

W. Kent Fuchs, PhD
President, University of Florida

"I would do it all again in a minute. I love it. And I think devoting your life to future generations of leaders is an unbelievably wonderful thing to do."

Dr. Elsa Núñez, President of Eastern Connecticut State University, was yet another leader who told us she loved her job. She said to us:

"I'm ready to retire. I've had a wonderful career. I thank God every day — I have a wonderful family and I couldn't have had a better career. And I think, 'How lucky am I? How lucky am I that I did this work?' Here I am, leading a public institution, making a difference in the lives of a lot of people, giving them a quality education. And I feel really proud about that."

It's important for a higher-education leader to love not just the industry but the institution in which they lead. Dr. Philomena Mantella, President of Grand Valley State University, talked to us about making a sort of "love connection" between leader and institution, just as students should be seeking the right "fit" when they choose a college for themselves. Dr. Mantella said of her entrance into the presidency at Grand Valley:

"When I came to find the university and know it, it was everything that I had hoped for. And I knew that I had to be extremely passionate about the place where I would lead. The president's life is absolutely 24/7, and I knew that I had to live and breathe — and *wanted* to live and breathe — the work of an institution I truly believed in. And so that brought me here."

Loving what you do becomes apparent in so many ways. Dr. Stephen Spinelli, President of Babson College, demonstrated his passion for helping others as a way of creating a better world. We could hear, in his voice, his love for higher education when he said to us:

"If we can teach people to continually assess how they're adding value to people's lives, I think that makes a better world."

And that "better world" requires leaders with a sense of humor and a sense of duty. When we talked to Dr. Anthony Jenkins about having started his presidency at Coppin State University at the height of the pandemic crisis (in May 2020), he evoked one of my mom's favorite phrases when he joked:

> "Anyone who wants to be a university president is a glutton for punishment anyway."

Indeed. And it takes a deep, authentic love to sign up for the rigors of a presidency, even in the best of times.

Redefining Leadership

In this book, we've explored the many ways in which the college and university experience for today and tomorrow's students is less and less like the experience of previous generations. This book is about the beginning of a new era in higher education. And it's not just new (and improved!) for *students* … it's also calling upon the entire industry to think anew about *leadership*. We can't change the student experience without first changing ourselves. What, then, does the higher-education leadership skillset of the future look like?

We're so glad you asked. Through 125 presidential interviews and in a survey with 136 higher-education professionals, we asked industry insiders to help us build a new "job description" for higher-education leaders. In the final, following pages of this chapter, we offer you three assets that we think will help you refine your *own* leadership strengths and that might help you to mentor, hire, and support future leaders at your organization. So, buckle up for:

1. **Survey Says!** An infographic that illustrates the key findings of our industry survey, which contains lots of statistics to guide your work.

2. **What Do You Want to Be Known For?** An inspiring essay by Dr. Joe Sallustio on the five elements of a rock-solid presidential brand.

3. **The Higher-Education Leadership Skillset of the Future:** A data-driven "job description" for what college and university employees are requiring and preferring when it comes to the character traits of their current and future leaders.

SURVEY SAYS!

Higher education is currently led by a collective team that is neither too junior nor too senior. More than 48% of higher-ed professionals have been leading for 10 years or less, and 16% have been leading for more than 20 years.

How Long They've Been Leading:

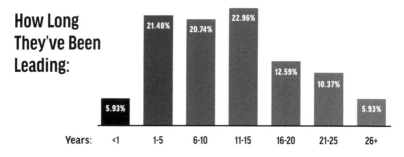

Years:	<1	1-5	6-10	11-15	16-20	21-25	26+
	5.93%	21.48%	20.74%	22.96%	12.59%	10.37%	5.93%

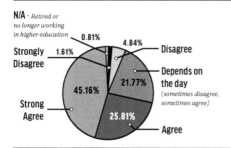

N/A - *Retired or no longer working in higher-education* 0.81%

Strongly Disagree 1.61%

4.84% — **Disagree**

Depends on the day *(sometimes disagree, sometimes agree)* 21.77%

Strong Agree 45.16%

25.81% — **Agree**

71% of higher-education leaders say they really enjoy their jobs.

To what extent do higher-educational professionals agree with the following statement: **"I really enjoy my job as a higher-education leader."**

57% of higher-education leaders intend to stay in higher education for several more years or until retirement. The remainder are telling us to watch out for another wave of resignations in the academy and to be mindful of culture, because a lot of people are on the fence about whether to stay or go.

We asked survey respondents: **"Where do you envision the future of your career?"**

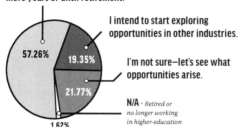

I intend to stay in higher-education for several more years or until retirement. 57.26%

I intend to start exploring opportunities in other industries. 19.35%

I'm not sure—let's see what opportunities arise. 21.77%

N/A - *Retired or no longer working in higher-education* 1.62%

The Pandemic Effect

More than 56% of higher-education professionals say the pandemic significantly changed their sense of job stability.

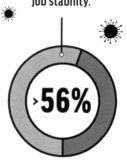

>56%

Most higher-education leaders consider themselves to be very risk-tolerant and innovative. On a 10-point scale in which 10 is "extremely risk-tolerant and highly innovation-focused," survey respondents had a weighted average of 7.76.

Nearly 62% of leaders assessed themselves as being very strong risk takers and innovators (with a score of 8-10)

1/3 of higher-education leaders anticipate the future of higher education will look vastly different from what we know it to be now.

The Future of Higher Education Will Be...

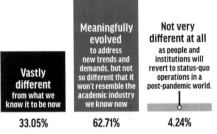

Vastly different from what we know it to be now	Meaningfully evolved to address new trends and demands, but not so different that it won't resemble the academic industry we know now	Not very different at all as people and institutions will revert to status-quo operations in a post-pandemic world.
33.05%	62.71%	4.24%

Twice as many higher-education leaders think we're in for an *evolution* as those who think we're on the verge of a *revolution*.

More than  of higher-education leaders think their institution is in trouble, when considering the looming demographic shift and their institution's current operational health.

45% of higher-education leaders say their institutions are currently exploring (or considering the exploration of) a merger, acquisition, or significant strategic partnership to ensure their institution's viability and to improve quality and access for prospective learners.

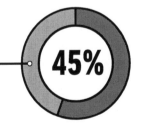

"Survey Says!" data was derived from an anonymous online survey of 136 higher-education leaders, conducted in the summer/fall of 2022. More than 45% of respondents were high-level leaders, such as presidents, chancellors, chief academic officers, or vice presidents. Overall data also included insights from board members, provosts, deans, department chairs, faculty members, senior-level consultants and service providers in the higher-education sector, and other higher-education professionals. Respondents represented the full spectrum of institution types: 45.93% from private colleges or universities, 18.52% from public/state colleges or universities, 11.11% from community colleges, 2.96% from technical colleges, and 21.48% from other types of institutions (like consultancies, ed-tech companies, higher-education associations, industry-associated nonprofits, secondary schools, and foundations).

Making Education Your Business with Dr. Joe Sallustio

What Do You Want to Be Known For? Five Elements of a Rock-Solid Presidential Brand

Higher education is on the precipice of a new normal. It has been brewing for some time, but the pandemic hastened its arrival. This new normal — or, rather, new future — will be defined by institutional innovation and consumer response, and successful university leaders will need to rise to the occasion. We have some tips to help you do just that.

Higher education has had to evolve to meet the needs of students, while addressing the public health crisis during the early 2020s, and it must continue to innovate to serve digital natives who have now fully experienced online learning.

Those at the top of the academic enterprise must also evolve to serve in a world where transparency, trust, and visibility of leaders enhance or dilute their institutional brand. The student consumer expects to see more than degrees, educational quality, internships, or rankings — they expect to "see" university leadership at the highest level, out there in a visible (and audible) way, communicating the value proposition of the brand and standing by the "product."

At some institutions in the United States, undergraduate enrollment has been down by as much as 15% over the past few years, and student acquisition costs are rising. It's no wonder many haggard leaders are stepping down after an intense era of pandemic-related crises — an era marked by worry and uncertainty about staff, students, and financial viability.

Boards, executive search firms, and search committees must take notice. There are five traits that every next-gen higher-education leader will need to possess or quickly amass.[37]

---

37 Further along in this chapter, we provide an outline for the "leadership skillset of the future." The five traits explored in this sidebar are a subset of that larger skillset. Here, we focus on building and maintaining a rock-solid presidential brand.

1. **Expertise in Marketing, Enrollment, and Brand:** The digital frontier is where colleges and universities must deliver their value proposition to potential students. If there is any doubt about this, refer to Google's digital ad revenues, which are consistently hovering above 50% each quarter since the pandemic began. Leaders at the highest levels need to understand the deepest intricacies of digital spend, yield, and efficiency to effectively run their institution. Someone like Claire Foster, Executive Vice President for Enrollment Services at Regent University, is a good representation of the next generation of higher-ed leadership. She's savvy and poised and operates with a student-first mindset underpinned by her expertise in data-driven enrollment and marketing.

2. **Entrepreneurial Mindset:** Institutions are facing many internal and external factors that contribute to enrollment difficulties. Many forces are challenging the way we think about traditional education: questions about the overall value of a college education, demands from the marketplace for clear communication about the return on investment graduates can expect, and more options for non-degree credentialing blurring the lines. Leaders positioned well for the future will strategize around students as "consumers," have a testing/experimental mindset, and take risks to achieve evolved levels of operational and program efficiency. They'll challenge the status quo, all the time. Educational leaders can take lessons from ed-tech innovators like Tom Woolf, founder and CEO of EdAid, who partners with colleges and universities to offer fair and affordable funding opportunities beyond the traditional options. Taking risks, particularly those that improve access, is a must-have for next-gen leaders.[38]

---

38 Our research shows that most higher-education leaders think of themselves as extremely risk-tolerant and highly innovation-focused. Whether those personal perceptions translate to actual risk-taking and innovation activity may be something else entirely.

3. **Social-Media Savvy:** Future leaders will leverage their personal brands by nurturing, growing, and engaging with a social-media audience. If a college or university president today thinks they can avoid social-media participation because they serve adult students, consider this: the Pew Research Center, as of 2021, shows that 72% of adults over the age of 18 use at least one social media platform consistently. A leader's personal brand will be intertwined with the college or university brand if done correctly.
Dr. Daria J. Willis, Former President of Everett Community College and new President at Howard Community College, is a model of the personal/professional representation. Scroll through her Twitter posts and you'll see her successfully and authentically blending her personal and professional identity, from celebrating a workout, to highlighting what she is doing to expand educational access, to a candid photo of her family. Potential and current students get to know Dr. Willis personal and professionally — she doesn't code-switch.

4. **An Open Mind to New Functional Structures and Operating Models:** The 21st-century leader must be willing to consider that the way of operating and staffing post-pandemic will be fundamentally different from how we operated prior to 2020. As of this book's publication, employees have spent two and a half years adjusting to remote work and its benefits. The traditional-aged student has experienced the flexibility of online learning, and leaders like Dr. Jon Bauer, President of East Central College, are balancing the difficulties of operating in a rural geography with the opportunity to reach more students via online learning. Geography has become a variable and is no longer the *defining* variable.

5. **Authenticity:** Future university presidents have been seen at their best, their worst, and everything in-between during impromptu Zoom meetings. In the past, authenticity

may have had negative consequences because it exposed opportunity for judgement. Now, we are more mindful, empathetic, and accepting of the reality that we all face in balancing work with our home lives and health priorities. A leader must be authentic and accessible. Being real is vital to building a presidential brand that people can trust and gravitate to. This creates next-level networking opportunities, and the relatability students want to see in a brand they select. Authenticity comes in the form of inspiring messaging and believability from leaders. Take Dr. Emily Barnes, previously the Interim President at Cleary University and now Provost and Vice President of Academic Affairs at Siena Heights University. The first sentence of her LinkedIn bio reads, "I see what higher ed can be; I also see what it's not...YET. I want to boost and rebuild it, to truly make the higher education journey a valued place of passage for those seeking more than they were given." This message is personal and shows authentic passion that will resonate with students.

Creating a personal/presidential brand that enhances institutional communications and overall college/university brand is a prerequisite for the future of higher-education leadership, but not every higher-ed leader or governing board understands the importance of this. As the new normal and new future come into focus for higher education, so too must the vision of what an executive-level university or college leader must bring to the table to navigate the contemporary landscape. A new wave of presidential candidates will ascend and boast a 21st-century skillset that will be much less traditional than those before them. Institutions, governing boards, and search committees should be prepared to adapt with the changing times for the progression of their institutions and learners.

"Upskilling and Reskilling" for Higher-Education Leaders: New Requirements for New-Age Leaders

Welcome to a bold new world in higher education, where a PhD and some "time served" in the academic ranks are no longer the only core job requirements of a college or university president. Climbing the collegiate ladder just got a lot harder. (And the results — for students, alumni, staff, faculty, and others — are getting a lot better.)

Throughout the research for this book, we had several conversations with higher-education leaders about the skillsets and character traits that have served them (and others) well in the leadership ranks — everything from being a leader who is selfless, devoted to others, and exhibiting less ego than in the past, to leaders who are passionate, inspired, collaborative, comfortable in volatile and ambiguous situations, and have the perspectives of having worked on the student-services side of higher education in their earlier careers. And we have conducted survey research to dig deep into the higher-education "leadership skillset of the future" — determining what higher-education insiders most value when it comes to the personalities and credentials of their leaders. It turns out that the skillsets that were acutely necessary during the pandemic have set a new expectation for the remainder of the 2020s and beyond.

It turns out that the skillsets that were acutely necessary during the pandemic have set a new expectation for the remainder of the 2020s and beyond.

We asked Marvin Krislov, JD, President of Pace University in New York, New York, about the challenge of leading during a pandemic, and he said:

> "I want to be both empathetic, but also help people feel that there's someone who is taking care of them and will help lead them to a stronger tomorrow."

President Krislov also talked to us about being humble enough to say, "We don't know all the answers" — a sentiment echoed by Richard L. Dunsworth, JD, President of the University of the Ozarks in Clarksville, Arkansas. President Dunsworth told us, about leading during uncertain times, that:

> "Sometimes 'I don't know' is the right answer. And sometimes it's the most *authentic* answer. Yet I also understand that sometimes 'I don't know' can cause people to feel unsure. Many people want assurances — they want to hear 'It's going to be okay.' Well, I believe it *is* going to be okay. But there are things we just don't know yet."

Being willing to admit you don't have all the answers is a modern leadership strength, but a position or overall ethos that many of us were previously told — perhaps decades ago — was decidedly *not* presidential or authoritative. Now we understand that honesty and humility are key. President Dunsworth told us that it's not enough just to admit that we sometimes don't have all the answers; sometimes, we need to admit we were wrong — that we made a mistake. And that we're sorry. He said:

> "As we've been working through a lot of these questions and challenges [associated with operating during a pandemic], what I've told our campus constituents — as well as the public — is, 'Hey, we're going to make some mistakes. When we do, we're going to say we're sorry. We'll make additional decisions, and we'll keep moving. Let's build an organization that's based on action.' And with this complex organization that we have, there are going to be a lot of times where we go 'I don't know,' but that's not 'I don't know and I'm not going to figure it out.' It's usually 'I don't know. Let's figure out who does, or let's put that question on the wall for another day.'"

It's about being nimble and committed to solving the complex problems of higher education — in real time, with humility and with utter devotion to the people we serve. And it's about doing so forever — long after the acute pain of the pandemic is years or even decades behind us. I have had the benefit of working in many sectors — in higher education, in small business, in a cross-section of technology and the media, in healthcare, and in banking. And the challenges of a volatile, uncertain, complex, and ambiguous (VUCA) environment were a common topic of conversation in every sector ... except in higher education. In higher education, we often chose to believe that our industry was static, traditional, predictable, and clear. We didn't have to be nimble; we didn't have to be comfortable with risk; we didn't have to be innovative. Our world was knowable. The pandemic, however, taught us that *everyone* works in a VUCA world, and — if we're honest — our stakeholders have been telling us for long before 2020 that some of that old "static, traditional, predictable, and clear" approach to the way we served them just wasn't working. It's time to go from rigid and immovable to flexible and nimble. Dr. Emily Barnes, previously the interim President at Cleary University and now Provost and Vice President of Academic Affairs at Siena Heights University, told us:

> "Higher education has to become *extremely* adaptable. And adaptability is going to require leaders to put down their forms, put down their expectations, their norms, and the things that create comfort. It's going to require them to stay in a state where they know that change is happening all day, every day."

It's about being nimble and committed to solving the complex problems of higher education — in real time, with humility and with utter devotion to the people we serve.

Dr. Summer McGee, President of Salem Academy and College, echoed that need for flexibility and for the ability to thrive in a VUCA world when she told us:

> "As every college president knows, no two days are alike."

Being adaptable and flexible — and ready for a tomorrow that is unlike yesterday — requires that leaders also be truly "out there," engaging in authentic relationships, garnering feedback from stakeholders, and finding out what opportunities and problems require an adaptable response. During our interview with Dr. Anthony Cruz, President of Miami

Dade College's Hialeah and Kendall Campuses, guest host Dr. Michelle Cantu-Wilson, former Director of Teaching and Learning Initiatives and Special Projects at San Jacinto College in Pasadena, California, complimented Dr. Cruz on the ways in which he exhibits his love for the students. Miami Dade College's Hialeah Campus has a high Pell-grant recipient rate, and they offer food banks and other wraparound services for their students. Dr. Cantu-Wilson talked about Dr. Cruz loading groceries into students' cars at food-bank events and going to visit students at their homes — and she referred to these activities as "flattening the hierarchy of higher education" and of Dr. Cruz making himself "available and accessible and relatable." This is a powerful concept.

> **Reflection Question:** *What are you and other leaders doing to flatten the hierarchy of higher education? How might you begin to make yourself more available, accessible, and relatable to key stakeholders with whom you don't regularly connect on a candid, unscripted basis?*

Dr. Cruz told us:

> "Leadership has really changed with the times. I think that leaders are really connecting and willing to connect — being much more *authentic* in their leadership. I think community college leaders, in particular, are much more 'down to earth' today and kind of understand what's going on in their communities a lot better [than in the past]. More and more leaders are embracing what it is to be a leader *today* and are being much more 'out there' and authentic. And they're removing that ivory tower facade and being more practical."

Dr. Daria J. Willis, Former President of Everett Community College and new President at Howard Community College, built upon this sentiment by telling us:

> "I think it's important that people can see their leaders as regular people who feel pain and who can see and feel the emotions of their stakeholders, and can relate to what's happening in society."

One of the biggest compliments a student could ever give a higher education leader is to say, "They totally 'get it.'" Conversely, being perceived as a leader who *doesn't* "get it" is difficult to overcome.

Making Education Your Business with Dr. Joe Sallustio

Hey, you — Higher education "search committees" and executive search firms!

Yes, you. I'm talking to you! There is nothing more ridiculous than a job posting or leadership search profile that emphasizes innovation, risk-taking, bold leadership, and/or financial acumen while, at the *same* time, communicating the necessity of teaching experience, a doctoral degree, and a request for the candidate to write a cover letter that could wrap around the world twice.

We still treat the presidency of an institution as an academic appointment, when, in fact, the trend is shifting to hiring practices that consider marketing, enrollment, and financial skillsets. Think "LinkedIn Easy Apply" for the best candidates. Why? Because the fast-moving, innovative candidates are going to see the requirement for a five-page cover letter and think, "Nope, this is a traditional institution. Next!"

Understanding the student is crucial. Dr. Laurie Borowicz, President of Kiswaukee College in Malta, Illinois, formerly served the industry as a vice president of student services. She knows several peers who also were trained up from student services to presidencies. She told us that:

> "Working in student services prepares us to understand the whole student."

And it's the whole student who benefits when their leaders truly see them, understand their needs and aspirations, and step up to make the educational experience invigorating, enjoyable, and effective.

My co-author, Dr. Joe Sallustio, responded to Dr. Borowicz's comments about former student-services leaders ascending to the presidency by saying:

"It's almost borderline ridiculous how narrow the pool has been for college presidents. If we look at a higher-education presidency in a traditional path, you're a teacher or professor and dean and provost and president ... I think that is *one* way to get there. But if we don't open up other pathways, we are going to fail to serve the consumer of the future. Because you must have different ways of looking at things. Technology is becoming ever more important. Student services are critical."

So, how do we widen that pool for college presidents? We redefine the job description and we adopt a new understanding of the skillset that makes modern-day, future-proof presidents successful.

Students benefit when college and university leaders truly see them, understand their needs and aspirations, and step up to make the educational experience invigorating, enjoyable, and effective.

The Higher-Education Leadership Skillset of the Future

A data-driven "job description" for what college and university employees are requiring and preferring when it comes to the character traits of their current and future leaders.

Leadership roles inside colleges and universities — from presidents to chief information officers to VPs for student services — are mission-critical opportunities to individuals in senior positions to run a complex enterprise for better or (as is all too often the case) for worse.

Research we conducted in 2022 helped us develop a fresh skillset for modern higher-education leadership.

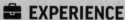 **EXPERIENCE**

Required (in this priority order in terms of candidate's strengths):

1. Financial acumen
2. Extensive experience working in higher education (15+ years in progressive roles)
3. Expertise in marketing, enrollment, and brand
4. Customer/constituent relations expertise
5. Experience as a department chair, dean, VP, or provost

Other experience considered beneficial:

- CEO experience (in any industry)
- Experience as a faculty member
- Experience working with elected officials, lobbyists, and government agencies
- Experience working in student support areas, like IT, ed-tech, or student services
- Fundraising experience
- Leadership skills and management experience
- Experience in building or transforming enterprises
- Skills in leading for diversity, equity, and inclusion to transform systems that produce equitable outcomes

BONUS: Special consideration may be given to candidates with mergers & acquisitions, or strategic partnerships, experience. Likewise, internal candidates with distinct knowledge of our institution and its stakeholders may be given special consideration.

☺ CHARACTER TRAITS/DISPOSITION

Required *(in this priority order in terms of candidate's strengths):*

1. Open-mindedness to new structures and operating models
2. Strong communications skills
3. Comfort operating in volatile, uncertain, complex, and ambiguous (VUCA) environments
4. Data-driven mindset for decision-making
5. Transparency and trustworthiness

Other traits, values, and dispositions considered beneficial:

- Authenticity
- Collaborative spirit
- Entrepreneurial spirit
- Humility
- Tech-savvy
- Visibility/accessibility
- Social-media savvy
- Vulnerability

BONUS: Special consideration may be given to candidates with demonstrated engagement with equitable thinking and behavior, compassion for students, and emotional intelligence.

✎ EDUCATION/CREDENTIALS

PhD or EdD preferred. Candidates with JD, MBA, MD, and other leadership credentials will be seriously considered.

BONUS: Special consideration may be given to candidates with a degree credential from our institution or with experience as a student in an institution type similar to our own.

> **Reflection Question:** *How does this skillset validate the ones you've been hiring for? In what way does it reflect some key shifts that you should be paying attention to?*

Well, that's a juicy job description. And not every job candidate is going to check all the boxes. So, we wondered, if the higher-education leaders who helped us develop this "skillset of the future" couldn't have it *all*, what experiences and attributes would they select as *most important*? We had them look at the "top 3" leadership qualifications/experiences they had chosen on their surveys and narrow it down to just one. And we likewise had them look at the "top 6" critical traits/attributes they had selected and narrow it down to just one. *Survey says …*

The #1 most important leadership qualification:

Extensive experience working in higher education (15+ years in progressive roles)

The second most important qualification was customer/constituent relations experience, and the third most important qualification was CEO experience, in any industry.

> Leading in higher education requires a deep understanding of the industry, a deep connection to students, and a proven ability to lead from the very top.

The #1 most important leadership trait or personal attribute:

Open-mindedness to new structures and operating models

The second most important trait was comfort operating in volatile, uncertain, complex, and ambiguous [VUCA] environments, and the third most important trait was entrepreneurial spirit.

> Changing times require change-makers at the helm. Innovation is the only way forward.

As you can see, our survey produced fascinating results. The skillset that revealed itself can be boiled down to one big challenge: Higher education's leaders of the future need to have extensive experience working in higher education (15+ years in progressive roles) *and* have open-mindedness to new structures and operating models. We need "insider" experience and "outsider" mindsets. Though it may sound like an oxymoron or even common sense, we must remember that today's aspiring leaders are experiencing a time of mergers, acquisitions, closures, financial difficulties, declining enrollment, and social disruption — all while the world watches on social media. If ever there was an environment for innovative leaders within higher education to create change, it's now.

CHAPTER 8

KEEPING THE LIGHTS ON

The Financial Realities of Contemporary Higher Education

I n the previous chapter, we explored what strong, modern leadership
looks like in higher education — what it takes to be followed and
respected, how hard it can be to lead during crisis and other exigent
circumstances, the vital parts of leadership that are never in the job
description, and the fascinating and varied paths taken on the way to
academia's C-suite. In our survey research, we asked higher-education
professionals to identify the top three types of experience critical for
leaders — especially for presidents. They ranked financial acumen as #1.

Show Me the Money: Leading with the Balance Sheet in Mind

Whether you like the terminology or not, and even if you're uncomfortable with the reality of it all, colleges and universities are *businesses*. And even if you're a nonprofit institution with a mission-driven,
student-centric (i.e., customer-focused) culture, you're a business. Take
your eye off the balance sheet, and your college or university won't be
meeting its mission for much longer.

We wondered, when we began the interviews and quantitative research for this book, whether college and university presidents would be comfortable talking about the money. Not only were they comfortable, but they were also usually the ones who brought up the financial realities of higher education in the first place. Surely, the economic crisis that resulted from the public health crisis of the pandemic gave us all new stresses and opportunities as it related to the way cash flows in and out of our organizations, but we quickly discovered that most higher-education leaders have been tackling the money issues — rising tuition, discount rates, student debt, operating costs, philanthropy challenges, state funding, and more — for a very long time. Dr. Hal L. Higdon, Chancellor of the Ozarks Technical Community College System and President of OTCC Springfield Campus in Springfield, Missouri, told us:

> "I know the faculty are tired of hearing me talk about finance, but without finance, we don't stay open."

And it's not sufficient to simply *talk* about the financials — leaders must *understand* them and have the will to *act* upon them, sometimes swiftly and boldly. Having financial acumen should be table stakes for a presidency (or any leadership role in a college or university, if you ask me), but far too many academic leaders lack experience overseeing profit and loss. Too few have expertise in finance, accounting, or economics and not nearly enough have launched or scaled a business. As such, we were not surprised to discover that some of the industry's most dynamic leaders have expertise in higher-education recruitment or fundraising or that they're officially or unofficially "quants" — loving and living by the numbers. Dr. John J. Rainone, President of Mountain Gateway Community College (formerly known as Dabney S. Lancaster Community College) in Clifton Forge, Virginia, told us:

> "My role before I became president was as a fundraiser. I was the chief advancement officer for a community college in Maine. And I quickly learned that fundraising makes a *good* college a *great* college."

On our survey about the future of higher education, while we included "financial acumen" as a type of experience or trait that survey respondents could choose when helping us build the higher-education leadership skillset of the future, we still received several write-in responses for the "other" option that read, "fundraising, fundraising, fundraising."

Vision without resources is hallucination.

Richard W. Schneider, PhD

President Emeritus, Norwich University,
and Rear Admiral, U.S. Coast Guard (Retired)

How, then, do we balance vision and resources — money and mission? Too much focus on the bottom line, and we might lose our grip on providing meaningful educational services at a fair price ... and on providing high-touch wraparound services for learners. Conversely, being "all in" on mission without realistic and specific attention to the financial realities can leave a college or university in peril. While your mission and your stakeholders are the heart and soul of your institution, the resources are the lifeblood. You can't live without either. Dr. Arthur Keiser, Chancellor of Keiser University, whose flagship campus is in West Palm Beach, Florida, talked about how his own career path changed when he observed his former colleagues in the public sector — where institutions are limited by tax dollars — getting the "money vs. mission" equation out of balance. He told us:

> "I taught in the public sector and all we talked about were *budgets*, not students. In fact, the professor I worked for had a great line. His line was, 'It would be a great job if it wasn't for the students.' That's one of the reasons we opened our school, because it just drove me nuts ... because I wanted to *teach,* and I wanted to help students *grow.* And I didn't find that where I was teaching [previously]."

Ultimately, higher-education leaders must understand and care about the financials, but not more than they care about the students. If you work in a primarily tuition-driven institution, you probably spend a lot of time focusing on enrollment numbers and retention. Unless, of course, you work for the kind of *elite* tuition-driven school where the affluent student body is willing and able to keep the lights on for you even if you never diversify your revenue streams. Or maybe the numbers don't keep you up at night if you work for an institution where the hedge fund managers who oversee your endowment make more money than the entire faculty combined (we're not naming names!). But as we move — as an entire industry — to a commitment to making higher education accessible and flexible, we have to find ways to comfortably tolerate when students stop in and stop out during their journey, or when students take just one class at a time instead of three or four or five, because they're "earning and learning" — they're working (full-time or part-time) each academic term to pay that term's tuition, and they must look at their educational experience one *course* and one *paycheck* at a time. If we were to ask our readers to raise their hands on the following question, we wonder how many would choose the third bullet (or know enough to select it in the first place).

+ Who works for an institution where it feels like "mission without money" — where you love and care for your students and your people but are struggling with ever-shrinking budgets and where you're sure you're being grossly underpaid for work you love?

+ And on the flip side, who works for an institution where it feels like "money without mission" — where you have one or several cash-cow programs and where you can afford to add a water park to the student union and another Starbucks to the science building's lobby, despite the curriculum being a little outmoded and your wraparound services needing some work?

+ Who works for an institution that effectively balances "money and mission," where students are served well, resources are robust, employees are committed, and there is a long-term sustainable financial plan?

Mission without money vs. money without mission — both are problematic. So, how do we address that from the leadership ranks?

If we have leaders who have strong financial acumen or financial-management experience, we also need those same leaders to have a relentless focus on generating revenue through program development and increasing enrollment. These leaders must understand and care about the financials with mindfulness of the balance needed to serve students and employees. The balance of *generating revenue* through increasing enrollment and improving retention while also *managing expenses* though cost cutting (when necessary), recognizing inefficiency, and sunsetting academic programs that are draining the coffers is a unique set of skills and knowledge. I was particularly struck by the honesty and empathy we heard when we interviewed Dr. Mary Schmidt Campbell, President Emeritus of Spelman College in Atlanta, Georgia, who acknowledged that the only way to tackle the affordability challenge in higher education is to be looking for ways to diversify the revenue streams. She said to us:

> "The median income for African American families is something like $56,000. When you think of the fact that, at Spelman, our tuition, room, and board is $50,000, we have to begin to think, 'At what point do we become unaffordable to the very demographic that we were designed to serve?' We have taken a look at several ways that we can

approach this issue. One is just raise more financial aid. Just keep our prices exactly where they are and just go out and full-blast, just raise tens of millions of dollars. That's one solution. Another solution is to take a look at all the component parts of college and say, 'How can we make each of them more affordable?' So, take books, for example. Well, it turns out if students don't have to purchase textbooks (which are unbelievably expensive) — if they can get them through either some open-source comparable text or they can rent them or otherwise lower the cost of getting their textbooks — that's one way to make college more affordable. If you can give them options to be able to bring in credits like their AP credits or their international baccalaureate credits, that helps. You can perhaps shorten their time to degree or maybe they can take summer school courses in your college that are deeply discounted. That will be cheaper — and again, shorten time to degree … maybe three and a half years or three years.

"So, there's *affordability*, and then there is the actual looking at your business model and saying, 'Well, what alternative sources of revenue can I bring in so I don't have to depend on tuition … and *raising* the tuition every year?' Over five or 10 years, the tuition has gone up considerably. 'What can I do to maybe subsidize the operations, and provide more financial aid through bringing in alternative revenue sources?' Spelman is looking at every single one of those options."

Getting creative about helping students afford college while also keeping the lights on at your institution is necessary for long-term sustainability. And if you believe in your mission — which most people in higher education do — your sustainability matters. Leaders like Dr. Campbell care about the financials because they care about the students. Capping off our discussion of affordability, she reminded us that, "Spelman College produces more black women who complete PhDs in STEM fields than any other college or university in the country." The mission matters. And therefore, the money management is crucial.

That balance of money and mission is perhaps one of the most important criteria for managing a college or university program. And program development — when you get it right — attracts a lot of revenue. But how do you think about legacy programs that enroll small numbers of students or departments that must be bootstrapped by others because they're not breaking even? Resource management in higher education is, in a word, hard. We talked about this very issue with Dr. Jorge Haddock, Former President of the University of Puerto Rico, and he offered this advice:

> "Don't try to be all things to all people. Be strategic. The thing that you have to focus on is identifying what would be the programs that would make you *competitive*. That said, I think there's still going to be a number of courses or programs that we ought to maintain ... because it's the mission of the university. I think that there are some programs for which you cannot see them in terms of the cost effectiveness, but you have to see them as the mission of the university — something that you need to provide to society and, in our case, the island.
>
> "As we have these budget cuts, we have to be more cost conscious and we have to be more strategic in terms of what programs we create, what programs we maintain, and what programs we may eliminate or transform."

Sage advice: Always be assessing your program offerings because competitiveness is about the "products" you offer. We discussed program relevance in a previous chapter and it is a theme that continues its thread throughout this book. Dr. Haddock said something that struck a nerve for me: "eliminate or *transform*." Too often, when something isn't working optimally, we double-down on keeping it because we have an emotional attachment. We see our options as "maintain the status quo" or "kill it" — when there often is a third option: transform it. True transformation, however, is also difficult. Transformation demands open-mindedness to change. And change is even harder — for many in higher education — than managing resources effectively.

Reflection Question: *What academic programs at your institution are currently floundering or even weighing you down — financially and logistically? And which of those programs — if you put on your thinking caps and got truly creative and innovative — could be transformed into truly excellent programs? What might your college or university look like if you embraced the possibility that there's a third option in addition to "keep the program" and "sunset the program?" What if you could transform the program?*

Making Education Your Business with Dr. Joe Sallustio

Transformation!

Think about the multiple ways you can transform academic programs. First, consider modality. Can you move a program that is fully on-ground or fully online to hybrid? Can you move a hybrid program to fully online? What about the academic calendar? If your institution is operating programs on the standard academic year, consider moving to non-standard terms. Sure, standard academic-year calendars allow for intersessions, but non-standard term enrollment allows for increased intake periods, multiple tracks, reduced break schedules, and ins-and-outs that students are clamoring for.

Get close with your institutional instructional designers (IDs). There may not be a more important position in higher education as we discuss what the future holds. IDs can help you to change course lengths, while maintaining all the course outcomes, to allow for academic-calendar flexibility. Some institutions allow students to begin courses every single week. Eliminate pre-requisites where you can. Share courses between programs.

Innovation exists. Some time spent on the internet searching for innovative models in higher education will equip you with ideas to upgrade programs, models, and delivery. "That won't work for us" must be eliminated from our psyches in higher education. Accreditors are *looking* for innovative institutions, not *limiting* them.

Six of One, Half Dozen of the Other: Different Kinds of Budgets and Bank Accounts

We've just begun our discussion of higher-education financial realities and already, we're sure that some of you are thinking "But it's different at our school ..." And you're right. When it comes to budgets and bank accounts, cash flows and endowments, the higher-education industry is a vast spectrum. There are institutions who have almost no cash to spend on brand marketing or enrollment marketing; and there are others who spend millions of dollars just on the search-engine marketing ... for their graduate programs (because the undergraduate programs spend a ton more than *that*!). It's expensive to be competitive.

When it comes to budgets and bank accounts, cash flows and endowments, the higher-education industry is a vast spectrum.

When I was working in the MBA market, we had rather efficient marketing and our open houses had a 50% "closure" rate for converting inquiries into students. But as the marketing director, I was always thinking about the money I had spent to get people to those open house events. By the time a prospective student showed up for their MBA Preview, I had spent $5,000 on them. It was a reasonable investment if I could turn half of those prospects into students and get each student to spend $36,000 or more. But we couldn't squander the investment. My marketing colleagues and I would remind our admissions counterparts that the worst thing they could do at an open house was stand near the hors d'oeuvres and talk to each other. Engaging the prospects was critical. We'd tell them, "Imagine we just went out onto the street and handed someone $5,000 in cash to come to this event. Treat the attendees tonight how you'd treat them if they had our $5,000 in their pockets. Know their worth."

The cost of being competitive is, any many ways, steeper for *online* education, where you're competing with institutions across the country and around the world. Dr. John Porter, President of Lindenwood University in St. Charles, Missouri, told us:

> "If you look at the online education space, it's a very, very, very competitive market. I think the differentiator, though, is how you market the product."

Higher-education marketers have a steep hill to climb. With competition being so stiff and the cost of mindshare being so high, colleges and universities need to capture reliable ways to become and remain top of mind and differentiated in the eyes of the prospective student and their influencers. They need to be endeavoring to deliver the prospect's first online tour and to be the first school that responds to the student's inquiry. It's vital to be first and then to be best. And to do that also requires sophisticated brand development on social media. Dr. Porter told us that:

> "Understanding the metrics around what drives students to enroll is *critical*. Metrics and marketing are critical."

With competition being so stiff and the cost of mindshare being so high, colleges and universities need to capture reliable ways to become and remain top of mind and differentiated in the eyes of the prospective student and their influencers.

 Pro Tip: *If the people at your organization who are responsible for sales (your admissions team, your corporate-education sales team, etc.) are only working Monday-Friday 9-5, then you're closing down your cash register for 128 hours each week.*
Today's prospective student wants to reach you when it's convenient for them. *The first step toward an improved bottom line might be hiring and scheduling enough people to cover all the times when your customers need you — days, nights, and weekends.*

Making Education Your Business with Dr. Joe Sallustio

Acquisition!

So, what should institutions spend on marketing? Well, that depends on how strong you think your brand is. Some institutions, particularly in the online space, budget their marketing spend to be at or around 20% of gross revenue! Yes, you read this right.

Some institutions today will go as high as 30% on their marketing spend. It's a lack of marketing awareness and spend that has many of the smaller private four-year institutions in trouble. Perhaps an institution wants to recruit 500 students in its next recruiting cycle. Let's say, for arguments sake, that the cost of acquisition is $2,500 per student. That is a $1.25 million marketing spend.

A simple question: Does your institution or its leaders value your marketing function appropriately? Asked another way: Does the person who leads marketing have a seat at the table for the most important institutional decisions? At an American Marketing Association meeting in 2019, one of the keynote speakers asked this question to a room full of thousands of marketers: "How many of you believe your leadership truly understands the value of marketing?" Only a few hands went up. A few months later, the pandemic hit and, well, life changed.

Fast forward a few years — to where we stand as we approach 2023 — and the question that keynote speaker asked is still relevant.

At its core, higher education can only succeed if the educational *product* it offers has value to the students. And with changing cultures and work-place needs — with new professions (especially in STEM and healthcare fields) cropping up at Mach speed — a college or university's old play-book might be getting out of date. You might have an amazing Classics

Department, but do you have demand for that major? Viability in higher education is largely about program relevance (there it is again). So why does higher ed struggle so much with offering new programs — with innovating the product — and doing so quickly? We asked Don Kilburn, CEO of University of Massachusetts Online (UMass Online), and he told us:

> "In the modern university, resource allocation is difficult. Times are — for many institutions — tough around resources and no one wants to say, 'Let's start this new program over here and let's close this program down over there.' Those are really difficult conversations to have around resource allocation and how to do things. So, I think schools struggle with new program development, which sometimes also requires accreditation and quite a bit of faculty review and faculty senate review."

The mention of the faculty senate gave me chills. I've been working on the outside of higher education long enough now to really appreciate the way in which the faculty senate sometimes operates like a ruling class on some campuses. While change is necessary in many institutions, many changes end up being presented to the faculty senate, faculty council, or similar faculty involvement groups. The entire cycle of change and innovation in higher education is designed to be considered and discussed to death in the black hole of Robert's Rules. As institutions get "back to normal" in 2022 and beyond, some are becoming normal in the exact same ways that *created* the criticism that higher-education institutions move too slowly. Institutions at the mercy of their faculty are, generally, averse to change. Why? Because personal relevance becomes central to decision-making. "What about me and my class?" becomes the central question. "What about the students?" becomes a secondary question.

Institutions at the mercy of their faculty are, generally, averse to change. Why? Because personal relevance becomes central to decision-making.

🔆 EdUp with Elvin

Practical Tips and Frontline Insights from Elvin Freytes

Now let's be honest. It is absolutely impossible to keep the lights on — at any institution of higher education — without faculty! There would be no such thing as education if it weren't for teachers/faculty. If you *really* want to keep the lights on at your college or university and make those lights shine even brighter, then you have to ensure the faculty are happy!

How do you take good care of the faculty? Here's how:

1. Make the salary range in the job posting transparent and competitive, and make the job description and qualifications realistic based on the salary range.

2. Shorten the duration of the application-to-hire process — everyone will appreciate this.

3. Pay your faculty what they are worth! I am talking about all faculty, including adjuncts.

4. Make sure they all have kick-ass benefits packages.

5. Provide them with professional-development opportunities.

6. Give them tools that will help them provide learning experiences that are beyond excellent for all learners.

7. Support their research opportunities and side gigs. Faculty are multi-talented — encourage and celebrate their activities and achievements.

8. Highlight the faculty as much as possible (without making them do extra non-paid work to receive that limelight).

9. Never tell them they must do something when there's an opportunity to *ask* them if they want to participate.

10. Get rid of useless faculty committees so the faculty can focus on what they love to do: TEACH!

> This whole "faculty versus administration" battle has got to stop! Focus on and invest in making faculty happy and your lights will continue to shine brighter — it's a no brainer!

Yes, change and innovation are difficult. Nobody has the time for program development, and nobody has the heart for program cessation. Our most painful moments in the institutions where I worked were when we were birthing or killing an academic program. Can you relate?

Nobody has the time for program development, and nobody has the heart for program cessation.

When it comes to the financial realities of "keeping the lights on" in higher education, one of the most fascinating interviews we conducted for this book was with Dr. Creston Davis, Founder and Director of The Global Center for Advanced Studies (GCAS) and Chancellor and CEO of GCAS College Dublin. GCAS is "the world's first global, debt-free, accredited college co-owned by faculty and graduates." Yes, you read that right. We talked to Dr. Davis about new ways to think about institutional overhead, budgets and funding, and even the currency that flows between a higher-education institution and its stakeholders. The story of GCAS is like no other that we have heard (yet). Dr. Davis told us:

> "We can be very lightweight — we don't have a lot of overhead. Our model is blended and is low residency and located in different locations around the world."

So how does a relatively new institution with centers around the world generate interest? How can they compete with the "big spenders" in the academic advertising realm? Dr. Davis explained:

> "There's no way we can compete with the traditional universities that spend $10,000 or $20,000 a month on advertising their programs. We

spend hardly any money on marketing. Our marketing strictly comes from word of mouth — through different events that we hold. We had a conference in Athens, Greece, a couple of years ago where we had a couple thousand people show up. That was for free. We do a lot of free events. Part of our crypto economy that we have is really a tracking system and it rewards students who are in GCAS College who will advertise and spread the word of mouth — so they're rewarded accordingly. Instead of us paying for a marketing firm to advertise for us, we run it through our own people, our own community. And we've been growing, and we have a lot of applications, a lot of our researchers. That's what we call our students — "researchers" — because we're all searching and researching and searching again for who we are ... a better world, better insights, new innovations. And the way we do that is through each other."

The cost of building new facilities, updating/renovating old ones, and keeping a physical campus running is monumental. So, colleges and universities that find ways to be more "lightweight" in terms of overhead are tackling the *expense* side of the financial equation. Often, the investment in fancy campuses with well-groomed quads keeps the CFO chasing their tail in an endless loop of "How are we going to pay for this all?" And a trip to various types of post-secondary education facilities in the United States might leave you wondering why there's so much investment in the amenities at state universities and liberal-arts colleges but not at technical or vocational schools. Dr. Arthur Keiser, Chancellor of Keiser University, posed this important question during our conversation with him, saying:

"Because the industry wants to invest so much in the *graduate* schools and so much in the big universities — they've done more building at schools like Florida State in the last 10 years than you can believe — they haven't made the investment in the voc-techs and in the career colleges. Yet, you know, try to get a plumber today. Try to get an electrician, try to get a truck driver. I mean, it's expensive now because of the shortage. There is a role for those kinds of institutions and students and graduates."

Indeed, there is a role for every kind of post-secondary education institution today, yet they're not operating on a level playing field. They don't all have giant endowments or loyal donors. They don't all have a lightweight overhead model. They don't all have A+ bond ratings or self-sustaining bank accounts. And the ongoing operating costs can be exorbitant at institutions with tenured faculty, large senior leadership teams, generous fringe benefits, and lots of amenity "extras" that attract people during the recruitment phase but don't pay for themselves. We talked to Dr. Christopher Roellke, President of Stetson University in DeLand, Florida, about endowments and salaries, and what senior leadership teams can do to start making meaningful and even symbolic strides toward cost control. We asked him about the rumor that when he became Stetson's president, he took a 15% salary reduction from day one — voluntarily. He took over the presidency at Stetson at the height of the pandemic, when the financial pressures were unprecedented across the industry. He told us:

> "It wasn't a hard decision for me at all. It was a rather obvious one to make, given the financial landscape that many higher education institutions are confronting. I think it's important when you have financial challenges that the leadership — who are typically better compensated than others — lead the way. I think it's just absolutely critical that you lead the way in the reductions that might be necessary, all with the intent of trying to make it possible for our students to continue through and have deep engagement with faculty and make advances toward their degree.

> "Here at Stetson University, we are almost entirely tuition and room-and-board dependent. We do have an endowment of $250 million, which is nothing to be ashamed about. That's a very helpful endowment, but we certainly have rules about how much we can draw from that endowment because we want that endowment to serve generations to come of Stetson students. So, I think it's critical that senior leadership take the lead when difficult decisions have to be made."

Money decisions are certainly the most difficult decisions to be made in any organization, and those decisions are especially complicated in colleges and universities — where the customer base can be hard to maintain, where the employees deserve to be fairly compensated for their work, and where the sales (admissions) cycle is long and complex. I'll never forget a moment in my career when I truly felt the power of making the right financial decisions for the benefit of the people who run the institution. I was a few years into my tenure at Rosalind Franklin University as the director of communications when our human resources office announced that we'd be doing a staff-wide "benchmarking" of salaries. It was the first effort of its kind in the university's 100+ year history. At first, it was just a lot of paperwork to write a detailed, comprehensive abstract of our true job descriptions, then getting those write-ups approved by our bosses. I had a team of three at the time — brilliant marketing and communications professionals who were making far less money than they deserved. And then the benchmarking decisions came out, and I was asked to share salary decisions with my team. One of the most incredible days in my professional life was the day I brought my dear friend and brilliant writer, Sara, into my office and showed her the salary adjustment we were about to make — a written promise to more than double her salary on the next pay period. She started to cry. And so did I. Within weeks, I was helping her to move *out* of a tiny studio apartment in a subsidized housing project — where she felt unsafe and alone — and *into* a two-bedroom apartment in a trendy suburb, with friendly neighbors and a beautiful view. Like it or not, money makes the university go 'round. That was a "money decision" that was life-changing for Sara (and for hundreds of other staff members who received raises)[39] and created staffing sustainability for the university. As of the publishing of this book, that moment was 16 years ago ... and Sara is still a loyal employee of that very same university.

Money decisions are certainly the most difficult decisions to be made in any organization, and those decisions are especially complicated in colleges and universities — where the customer base can be hard to maintain, where the employees deserve to be fairly compensated for their work, and where the sales (admissions) cycle is long and complex.

---

39 I can't claim to be the best boss or an entirely selfless person, but I'm proud to say that after meeting with all my employees and sharing the new salary data (two employees got big raises and one was kept at his current salary), I went home so overjoyed ... having completely forgotten to inquire of my boss whether *my* salary was being adjusted. (It was. And it was just icing on the cake of my managerial pleasure at finally compensating my team for their distinct contributions.)

Making Education Your Business with Dr. Joe Sallustio

"Sales?" What do you mean, SALES?

Here is a question that will cook your bacon. Why are our salespeople (yes, I said sales) paid at entry-level or lower salaries within higher education? Look at other industries, and you'll see that the salesforce is paid at much higher levels compared to other organizational functions — because organizations value those who generate revenue. Somehow, within higher education, the job of an admissions counselor, enrollment representative, or similar professionals, historically have not been valued in the same way. Yes, I'm very aware of the incentive-compensation regulations (I worked in for-profit colleges), but that doesn't mean that a higher salary and promotional pathways can't be achieved. Watch this as a trend that will change in the coming years as successful institutions invest in marketing and enrollment to supercharge their brands.

I have no idea what that benchmarking process ended up costing the university — surely, it was millions of dollars on an ongoing basis. But overnight, it resolved an epidemic of disgruntled employees and it skyrocketed productivity and high-quality student services. It's a difficult balance figuring out how to keep costs down and tuition rates fair while also giving people, programs, and processes their just due. This is especially true in tuition-driven institutions. One of my favorite higher-education stories to tell at cocktail parties is the story about an MD student who came to my office, seeking permission to use the university's logo on some T-shirts he and his classmates had designed. He was part of a community-outreach program that provided walk-in clinic services in neighborhoods with high rates of poverty. He had a T-shirt design with the university seal on the front chest and the words "Let's Play Doctor!" emblazoned across the back. I laughed, shook my head, and said, "No way." He started pacing around my office, giving me a piece of his mind, and ended his diatribe with, "I pay your

#$@$$$!!! salary!" I responded, "You're not wrong ... But you're also not putting this esteemed university's logo on that T-shirt." And I showed him the door.

> **Reflection Question:** *"I pay your salary!" a student once screamed at me. Has anyone ever said that to you? If you work in an institution with high tuition (and ever-increasing tuition) — especially if you don't have diversified revenue streams — you can probably relate to that power struggle between the student body (i.e., the customers) and your college or university's staff, faculty, and administration. It's hard to serve students who are understandability upset about what they feel to be a mismatch between the cost of their education and the value you're delivering. While students have the biggest stake in wanting education to be more affordable, the higher-education workforce is also often extremely invested in wanting the cost/value equation to be perceived as fair.*

All the higher-education stereotypes notwithstanding, no two colleges or universities are entirely alike. In addition to the curriculum differentiators, the educational delivery method, the geographic and lifestyle differences, and the institutional brand positioning differences, you can't forget how tax status divides the industry into two large groups. I was cutting my teeth in higher education when there was a broad perspective that nonprofit schools were intrinsically "better" than for-profit schools; today, I don't believe that at all. In fact, the nonprofit institutions are — in many ways — scrambling to replicate the processes and programs that the for-profits mastered long ago. And with accreditors ensuring parity in terms of educational quality across the entire sector, it's high time we admitted that, from the student and the employer's perspective, a college is a college is a college ... and their status with the IRS is really irrelevant. During our interview with Dr. Arthur Keiser, Chancellor of Keiser University, my *Commencement* co-author and *EdUp Experience Podcast* co-founder, Dr. Joe Sallustio, asked Dr. Keiser to talk about the evolution of nonprofit/for-profit politics, and whether he thinks for-profits have gotten a bad rap. Dr. Keiser told us:

"In a recession, our schools [for-profit schools], which have elasticity in terms of enrollment, grow very rapidly, whereas public institutions are limited by tax dollars and are shrinking during a downturn and the public nonprofit schools tend to limit enrollment. We get a bad rap because we're growing when everybody else is not. And that makes it a very uncomfortable competition among the sectors of higher ed. So yeah, I do believe we've gotten a bad rap. I think there is a rationale behind it — whether it be unions not liking us because we're not unionized (for the most part), or whether it be the fact that the public education doesn't like the comparisons because our graduation rates and placement rates (which they don't even count [typically]) are higher. Yeah, you could say I'm passionate about this higher education sector known as the 'for-profit sector.'"

Joe responded by saying:

"It's tough because you pour your heart into helping students. And then somebody on the outside says, 'Oh, well, you guys don't care as much' and you've devoted your life to helping people. It's hard to accept that."

All the higher-education stereotypes notwithstanding, no two colleges or universities are entirely alike. In addition to the curriculum differentiators, the educational delivery method, the geographic and lifestyle differences, and the institutional brand positioning differences, you can't forget how tax status divides the industry into two large groups.

Making Education Your Business with Dr. Joe Sallustio

Imitation Is the Highest Form of Flattery

If anyone thinks for a minute that nonprofit universities across the U.S. aren't trying to replicate the processes of for-profit universities, they're being naïve. For-profits were doing intrusive student advising, reducing speed-to-lead times, selling against competitors, building lead-nurturing campaigns, and creating elaborate retention campaigns long before many nonprofit schools were even thinking about these things. There is a reason why the University of Phoenix had nearly 500,000 students.

Were there some bad actors in the sector? Yes. Did the sector shrink partly due to incredible regulations? Yes. Closures and bad actors aside, there were incredible educators, administrators, and operators in the for-profit sector (and still are). Another question to ask yourselves: Where did all these for-profit employees go? The answer may surprise you. If they're not still teaching or leading on the for-profit side of the industry, they have gone to innovative *nonprofits* or online program managers (OPMs). These for-profit employees, which many in the nonprofit sector still look down their noses at, are college presidents or other C-level roles across the higher-education organizational spectrum. Why? Because they are really good at running businesses, which higher-education institutions happen to be. I spent 15 years in for-profit education and I'm proud of every single minute. In the end, I received a general business education within the context of higher education ... from institutions with sharp leaders overseeing practices worth imitating.

Too Much Tuition Now and Too Much Debt Later

We could write an entire book on the problem of tuition (and others *have*). Here, my co-author, Dr. Joe Sallustio, and I aim simply to address the largest tuition-related issues at hand — to trigger conversations at your institution and mindset shifts for yourself. Dr. Mary Schmidt Campbell, President Emeritus of Spelman College (a private, historically black women's liberal-arts college) talked to us about the degree to which higher-education has, in the past, ignored the tuition issue altogether. She told us:

> "When I was a member of the board, some 20 or 30 years ago, at a well-endowed liberal arts college, I recall the admissions director stood up at a board meeting and said, 'What makes you think that even the wealthiest families in this country are going to continue to pay the rising cost of tuition to send their children to elite private schools?' He asked that question of a rich college three decades ago. So here we are three decades later. And in fact, those rising tuition rates have made it a challenge — not just for black families, but for families across the board — to consider costs when they're making a choice of where to send their son or their daughter to school."

The issue of tuition is simple, and yet it's so complex. During our conversation with Dr. John Swallow, President of Carthage College, we spent a lot of time talking about the financial realities of the business of higher education. Dr. Swallow said:

> "You *could* say higher education's really pretty simple. Revenue comes from tuition. It comes from room and board. It comes from contributions. There may be a few other things, but those are the main ones. But when you dig into to tuition, particularly, and how different *people* are paying different *rates,* and *succeed* at different rates, it becomes very, very complicated. And another thing that's often forgotten, particularly when I talk to folks in the business community, is that we have a very long sales cycle. I could talk to a friend who's selling the same thing every single day, and so what's happening in the marketplace for that product and service, you get a lot of signals all the time. But in higher

> **From an economic perspective, you should expect to be able to afford to go to school without having to go into debt.**

Akiba J. Covitz, PhD
President & CEO, Foundry College

education, we spend — for our undergraduates — basically a whole year talking to them before they decide to come. And so you spend *four* years *delivering* on the promise and you spend *one* whole year recruiting the people who will come and you know as well as I do how fast things are changing today. So, you only have so many changes you can make from year to year, and the impacts could be enormous."

EdUp co-founder Dr. Joe Sallustio, whose own expertise includes deep insights about enrollment management, responded to Dr. Swallow with the following:

"Let's talk about the discount game. I don't want to call it a game because it's a strategy; but it's a strategy that can be abused in higher education. You could price something really high and then it's discounted at 80%, if you want to. And it gives this allure sometimes of elitism though what students actually pay is different. But students are becoming much more financially aware of how debt affects them. What's the sense from students that they're just going, 'Okay, wait a second. What is my ROI here? How does this really affect me in the future? What kind of job am I going to get?' What's the awareness — financially — of today's students?"

Dr. Swallow responded:

"Well, there's quite a bit of variation, but the essential point is that students today know that they're making a very large financial commitment over several years. That's absolutely the case. Some have more anxiety about it than others. Some *should* have more anxiety about it. The issue of tuition is incredibly complicated for your college-going family to understand: the amount that's going to be contributed by state or federal government, that might be contributed through loans, that would need to be contributed through the family's own resources and the student's too. And we did feel here at Carthage that it was time to stop with this idea that an ever-higher sticker price was somehow the signal. We know that over 60% of families don't realize that private institutions discount at all. And if we're really about enrolling students from every background possible and providing them an education, we need to remove these obstacles to even getting here in the first place. So that was why we, in 2019, undertook the first significant tuition reset in Wisconsin and lowered our tuition 30%. I want to be very upfront and honest about it — it didn't change, on average, what students *paid*, because we adjusted financial aid too. But the point was that we were pricing ourselves *much* closer to what many families are actually paying. And that helps people — particularly those who haven't been involved in the higher-education system with their parents or grand-parents — start to understand that it *is* accessible and it's affordable, and allows us to be in conversation with them."

A tuition reset is about attraction of new prospects — about helping prospective students and their families or other influencers understand what the *real* price of a college education is at any given institution. By and large, consumers understand that the "sticker price" on a car (at least before the pandemic-era microchip shortage in the auto industry!) is rarely what the driver pays for the car. As such, people have learned not to be afraid of sticker prices on cars. But most people don't understand that this same principle applies to college tuition as well. Institutions that have announced "tuition resets" often find that their prospect pool suddenly gets much larger, and that the institution is able to serve more students from a broader range of socio-economic backgrounds.

Across every tax bracket, Americans are saddled with student-loan debt — sometimes for decades or entire careers or lifespans. As we were writing this book, federal student-loan forgiveness measures were making head-lines, and people in the U.S. — as well as across the globe — were having reinvigorated conversations about the cost of higher education and how student-funded education is perhaps a seriously flawed model. During our interview with Dr. Creston Davis, whose institution — GCAS College Dublin — has low tuition and a unique model (which includes financial aid for 100% of students, flexible payment options, ownership shares in the college for its graduates, and a proprietary cryptocurrency for paying down tuition), we were inspired to think about tuition and debt in new ways. We asked Dr. Davis, *"Shouldn't education be something that elevates students instead of hurts them, putting them in debt that's crippling?"* He replied with another question:

"Isn't the society's basic responsibility — if it really cares about its citizens — to foster the most innovative possibilities there? And I think that by putting our young people into massive debt — to the tune now of $1.6 trillion and growing every second — that, to me, doesn't seem like a society is fostering the conditions for really elevating genius levels of innovation, identifying who are the folks who can really think across and against the grain of hegemonic understandings of what it means to *be*. And that's where you're going to get *advancement*. That's where you're going to get *leaps*."

Dr. Davis went to the Army after high school, where he suffered a serious injury and then began reading voraciously — which opened his mind to new possibilities for himself. He ultimately pursued higher education (at Duke, Yale, and UVA) and fell in love with the idea of opening doors for other people who reminded him of himself — having come from a working-class family, not initially being able to afford college, not having the grades for college, and having been told he wasn't good enough. When he finally found himself in a tenure-track teaching position at a liberal-arts college, he suddenly realized how the tuition and debt situation in the U.S. was impacting the students he was committed to serving. He told us:

"My students — who I cared for and I loved — were going into debt and they couldn't find jobs. And here they were, crushed. At 23 years old, their dreams were crushed. And for me, I couldn't handle that. Like if I went into this profession to open doors up and I was actually part of a system that would crush even *more* students in their lives and their prospects — and we're talking about students who don't have the privilege of the 1% — we're talking about the majority of Americans and I couldn't be part of that. So, I started to really think through a different model."

Student loans, it should be said, are not universally a bad thing — they enable education and a better life and career for many people. What is in need of reconsideration (and perhaps drastic overhaul) is how we introduce such debt to students, how we fully inform them of how the interest works on student loans, and how loans are serviced in the long run. Dr. Ward Ulmer, Former President at Walden University, said to us:

"I got an undergraduate degree from a private school and a master's degree from a private institution. I got a PhD from a private institution and another PhD from a public institution. So, when it comes to debt, I *lived* on student loans while I was in school, even after

I was married and had kids. But I did that knowing that it was going to give me a better life — it was going to give me the ability to go get a better job. And I took that on knowing full well what I was doing."

Student loans, it should be said, are not universally a bad thing — they enable education and a better life and career for many people.

I have my own student-loan stories — none too tragic and none all that rosy either — and I feel strongly that we can do better, as an entire industry, in the ethical stewardship of the financial-aid relationship. We can show prospective students "truth in lending" figures and amortization schedules. We can explain how different types of loans work in different ways, and we can surely do a better job explaining capitalized interest. Because for every person who looks back on their educational debt experience and says they fully understood what they were signing up for, I'd wager there are 100 others who had no idea how long it would take or what it would really cost (and what emotional and practical tradeoffs they'd have to make in their lives in order to live with that debt). I strongly believe that taking on student loan debt should require a type of "informed consent" — like what we'd expect in medical/surgical treatment. But, of course, such informed consent might translate into plummeting yield rates at colleges and universities across the country. And the impact on *society* would be greater still, if even fewer individuals could ultimately access a college education. Glossing over the "Are you sure you can afford this?" conversation with would-be students and their families helps admissions professionals close a lot more deals. But at what cost to the very people we purport to serve … and to society at large?

In Chapter 4, we talked about student-centric cultures and giving more "power to the purchaser" in higher education. But an empowered consumer creates financial challenges for the institution. Last-minute "no, thank yous" and "goodbyes" can be hard to project and even harder to plan for. Whether students "melt away," slow down their program progression by taking fewer classes at a time, take an academic term or two "off," or otherwise leave you with less tuition revenue than you were counting on, building and evolving an institution to be student-focused requires that you have a plan for scaling or for diversifying your revenue so you don't find yourself in tears over the balance sheet.

This is an important issue, especially as more institutions are building out significant online-program capabilities. Dr. Bill Pepicello, Former President of University of Phoenix, tells it like it is (which is why we appreciate him so much!). He told us:

> "From my experience, online students don't hang around very long if they're not happy with the product. They just disappear. And they can do it with impunity."

When it comes to the institution's bottom line, student retention is just as important as student enrollment. Institutions who truly understand, in a data-driven way, what causes their students to leave and what helps them to stay are the institutions that will thrive for the ages. Dr. Melody Rose, Former Chancellor of the Nevada System of Higher Education, told us:

> "We need to be asking ourselves, 'What are students telling us with their behavior?' We know that students vote with their feet, and we need to be looking at what they are doing ... and reading those tea leaves to be guided to the right outcomes. And I think we need to be not afraid to follow what students — by their behavior — are telling us they need."

> **Reflection Question:** *Is your institution conducting regular focus groups and surveys with students who take long breaks or stop out completely? What about prospects who don't finish the admissions process? Or those who get accepted and never commit? Or those who commit and melt away before showing up for classes? The student you lose can often teach you more about your institution than the student who stays. And a little research goes a long way.*

Keeping an eye on your institution's financials requires you to get up close and personal with many dilemmas. If you're honest about loans and debt, you'll lose some customers before they even convert. Once you have the students enrolled, it can be hard to keep them enrolled if you truly acknowledge their busy lives and the fact that interruptions happen in higher education. And the piece that barely anyone talks about is the fact that if your students graduate, they stop paying. Increasing speed to degree leaves you scrambling for new monies.

The piece that barely anyone talks about is the fact that if your students graduate, they stop paying. Increasing speed to degree leaves you scrambling for new monies.

During our conversation with Dr. Chuck Johnson, President of Vincennes University in Vincennes, Indiana, we asked: *"What's keeping you up at night, Chuck? And what keeps you coming back the next day?"* Dr. Johnson replied:

> "Well, the enrollment is always a focus, especially if you have programs that turn as quickly as we do. We've had some great success in improving our on-time graduation numbers. And that is really wonderful. We're very pleased with that. We've been very *intentional* about that, but it also comes at a cost. That means you have to bring more people in — more often — because they're leaving you faster than they used to. So, we have to make sure we have the sustainability of those numbers because of the turns that we have."

Who Pays? A Complicated Quagmire of Funding Sources

Fortunately for today's learners, rarely is it true that the student pays 100% of a college's sticker price, without the tuition being subsidized in some way. And luckily for many institutions, tuition isn't the only lever we can press when seeking revenue for our colleges and universities. But bringing various "buyers" to the table in higher education can be complicated. So, who pays?

📝 Pop Quiz!

Who and What Keeps the Lights on at Contemporary Universities?

There are many ways to pay the bills at a college or university. Which of the following sources of income is your institution taking fullest advantage of (and conversely, where are you leaving a lot of money on the table)?

❑ Tuition dollars, paid by:

> ❑ Students
>
> ❑ Families
>
> ❑ Banks (private loans)
>
> ❑ Federal student loan programs
>
> ❑ Donors and foundations that underwrite scholarships

❑ Investment/endowment returns

❑ State and federal governments

❑ Foundations that provide program and initiative grants

❑ Philanthropists/donors

❑ Organizations like the National Institutes of Health, which provides "indirect" funds to the institutions that house NIH-funded researchers

❑ Real estate (through rental income and student housing, plus room rentals for community organizations and corporations, renting out the dorms and athletic spaces in the summer for sports camps, and even the leasing of incubator spaces and labs on your campus to start-ups and other enterprises)

❑ Other

When it comes to who pays the bills at a college or university, the model is fundamentally flawed at many institutions. Listen closely, and you'll hear higher education's leaders talking about how government is doing less and less, how rising tuition helps institutions but causes affordability/accessibility issues for the community, how many institutions have become too reliant on the use of loan money that flows to them from banks and governments and is repaid by the students, how debt financing with big bonds for capital projects are adding up, and how the only sustainable way forward is through diversifying revenue streams.

In our conversation with Dr. Michael A. Baston, Former President of Rockland Community College in New York, and now President at Cuyahoga Community College in Ohio, we talked candidly about the broken funding model in higher education, especially as it relates to non-degree credentials. Dr. Baston said:

> "The federal government does not provide short-term Pell grants, so even if you had the shorter-term credential that ultimately would give somebody access to the world of work to get into hot fields, they can't afford it. Particularly if you're a student who comes to the community college with some economic fragility issues. You may not have a whole lot of money, but you are able to come to the community college, but only if you go full-time. Well, if you go full-time and … you've got to work and you've got to take care of your family, can you *really* go full-time? So that's why so many students who come to the community college go part-time, but you're only going to get part-time Pell. And if you're going for the shorter-term credential that can get you right into the workforce and ultimately get you a higher wage, well, the federal government doesn't support that from a financial-aid perspective.

> "So, if poor people who could have access to programs that are shorter term — that lead them to a family-supporting wage and then allow them to come back at a later point in their journey for the longer-term credential that would lead them to even higher wages — that would make a huge difference. But right now, they can't."

The solution that community colleges offer to this challenge is embedding certificates, badges, micro-credentials, and short-term skill-building into the associate's degree curriculum so that you can get financial aid and you can stop out at pre-determined junctures where you have already also earned an industry-recognized credential or "micro-credential." Pursuing a degree in this sort of serialized, bite-sized way helps combat the funding challenges. But it's still confusing and complicated for institutions and learners alike.

Dr. Baston reminded us that internships are a great way to give students competitive advantage in the job market, and many of today's internships are paid. Think about universities whose differentiators include their robust internship programs — like Northeastern University's co-op culture, where students are taking one, two, or three co-op assignments for six months at a time (often with very healthy wages). I've had the opportunity to talk to Northeastern students who have used the co-op/internship opportunities to earn money to pay their tuition and then walk out of the institution with a degree and a job offer from one of their co-op employers. Hard as the financial calculus is in higher education, there are definitely shining examples of win-win models.

Dr. Bill Pepicello, formerly the president at University of Phoenix, talked to us about the problematic business model for higher education, saying:

> "The current business model for higher education is very simple. You've got state funds, you've got federal funds, and you've got private funds (tuition, and if you're lucky, an endowment). That's not a sustainable model anymore. State funds are drying up and in some states are basically gone. Federal money depends on who's in power. And we can't fit that third leg on the student's back with tuition. So that business model is simply not very viable."

Viable models can be seen through recent merger and acquisition results: the Purdue/Kaplan[40] model, the Grand Canyon University and Grand Canyon Education relationship, University of Arizona's purchase of Ashford University, the University of Arkansas acquisition of Grantham Education, UMass's expansion through Brandman University, and several others. Institutions that have experimented with online program managers (OPMs) in revenue share or fee-for-service models represent another evolution of the business model in higher education.

---

40 Purdue University acquired Kaplan University in 2017, creating a new institution called Purdue University Global.

Making Education Your Business with Dr. Joe Sallustio

Revenue Share or Fee-for-Service?

When discussing online program managers (OPMs), many higher-education professionals ask questions about how OPMs operate. Historically, there have been two ways of doing business.

1. **Revenue Share** — The OPM puts up the marketing spend, enrollment operations, and retention services, and, as a result, commands up to 70% (in some instances) of the revenue generated by each student. Federal and accreditor regulations prevent the OPM from providing most of the academic services. Institutions that questioned their ability to create the infrastructure to grow their online education units typically outsourced to OPMs with mixed results. These relationships started with long contract terms, often up to 10 years.

2. **Fee-for-Service** — To avoid scrutiny from state and federal legislators, some OPMs have shifted from a revenue-share model to a fee-for-service or à la carte service model. This means that an institution can choose marketing and enrollment services only, on a monthly, quarterly, or yearly fee and are paid at the standard rate no matter how many students were recruited. Fee-for-service models result in OPMs avoiding criticism (to some degree) and allow for shorter contracts and less dependency for the institution on the OPM.

Dr. Pepicello said to us, referring to new partnership models that are beginning to bear fruit:

> "People seem to think that those kinds of relationships — for-profit corporations providing services to nonprofit universities with an online program management (OPM) firm added to the mix — that somehow

that stands in opposition to traditional higher education. My take on things like Kaplan Purdue is that we're seeing the evolution of the next model of higher education. It's going to be a model that is responsible — not just academically, but also financially."

Dr. Elsa Núñez, President of Eastern Connecticut State University, also talked to us about a higher-education funding model that's just not working. She said:

"Regarding the future of higher education, states are going to have to fund it the way it was when we had the GI Bill. The GI Bill was created so men could go to college, right? Mostly white men came out of the service, and they could go to college. That was a good thing. Otherwise, those men could not have gone to college.

"You've got to do that again. If you want an educated workforce, you have to invest in it. You can't say to an Eastern, 'Okay. out of every $10 you spend, only $3 can come from the state and $7 has to come from tuition' because eventually parents and students can't keep funding those raises. So, I think you're going to see some really serious discussion — state by state — on funding of the public universities."

We also spoke with Dr. Jon Bauer, President of East Central College in Union, Missouri, about the challenging issue of managing the influx of funds (or lack thereof) in higher education. He said to us:

"Because of the pandemic, we've gone through a period of 'How do we manage over the next few weeks?' and 'How do we manage *now*?' We had to reset the horizon. I think, especially with the stimulus packages and the funds coming to higher-ed institutions like mine, we begin thinking now about how to use those resources to have the most *lasting* impact. So nationally, we're thinking *beyond* the horizon."

Dr. Bauer brought up such a critical point — that higher-education leaders are no longer counting on tomorrow and, as such, are motivated to be different/better stewards of financial resources.

So, if we can't count on government funds and we can't rely on ever-increasing tuition, where do we turn? We continued this important

I think the money from the federal government (the CARES Act funds, etc.) and also the ability to borrow money on low-interest loans has given the industry a couple more years of breathing room. But there's a lot of financial distress out there among a lot of institutions right now.

Don Kilburn

CEO of University of Massachusetts Online (UMASS Online)

conversation with Dr. John Rainone, President of Mountain Gateway Community College. He said to us:

> "I think that there are still some publics who think that their state government's going to bail them out. And that hasn't been the case for 20 years. So, I do think that fundraising — donor relations — is going to have to step up. But I certainly hope that the pandemic has maybe awoken some giant from the legislature that we can really be able to sort of get the funding and maybe much more of the *equity* funding.
>
> "And I use the CARES Act as an example for community colleges, as well as sort of higher ed in general. When higher ed is truly talked about, I think a lot of people don't include community colleges; they think about the four-year schools. So I've committed to being in this space — in two-year colleges — for 30 years and I'm expecting at least another 10 or so before I retire. So, I just continue to fight for our share."

Just as educational attainment has its "haves" and "have nots" in terms of the learners who can access a post-secondary education — especially a degree program — the institutions themselves fall into categories of "have" and "have not," privilege and challenge. It was important for us to hear leaders like Dr. Rainone talk about the need for community colleges and other institutions to fight for their share of funding in a crowded marketplace where even governments and foundations don't fully understand the industry enough to treat higher-education institutions with equal respect and financial generosity.

Resource allocation at any institution of higher education is complicated — because the institutions themselves are complex. Dr. Bill Pepicello, whose experience leading one of the largest universities in the United States has equipped him well to talk about the business model, said to us:

> "The future requires transforming the business model of higher education. Right now, traditional higher education is based on students in seats. The business model is based on how many students you're going to have and how long you're going to keep them. It's about keeping the brick and mortar open. Some institutions have gone online more and more — and some of them are major ones like Arizona State, as well as MIT and Harvard even with an online presence. As that happens, the smaller institutions — those without good endowments — are simply

going to have to find ways to adapt to virtual education environments if they're going to survive.

"For the business model to change, institutions of higher ed are going to have to understand that they need help. They need partners. That's it in a nutshell: The way traditional institutions are going to have to survive is to look for partners."

Dr. P. Wesley Lundburg, President of San Diego Miramar College, reminded us that funding of colleges and universities comes down to full-time equivalencies (i.e., full-time students or full-time course loads) — that 12 credit hours is the definition of a full-time student, which has financial implications for learners and institutions alike.
Dr. Lundburg said to us:

"The evolution of higher education all comes down to economics. How we're funded is going to drive things, and hopefully what society values will drive the way that legislators fund higher education — whether it's private or public. But nothing's going to change without that changing."

New Ways to Think About the Money: Partnerships, New Models, and Cost Efficiencies

Capturing lightning in a bottle for higher education's future will come down to two things: providing true value to learners and finding a way for institutions to attract the revenue necessary to maintain and build upon that value. My previous book, *Think Like a Marketer*, was all about how to maintain a virtuous cycle of *creating* value for the customer and *capturing* value back to the organization. Give away too much for too little, and you'll struggle and fail. Give away too little and charge too much, and the customers will start fleeing — ensuring that you fail. In any industry, it's a balancing act. But in higher education — where the leaders often lack financial acumen, innovation mindsets, customer-service philosophies, or a team willing to follow them into the breach when big changes are warranted — mastering the financial model is especially difficult.

In higher education – where the leaders often lack financial acumen, innovation mindsets, customer-service philosophies, or a team willing to follow them into the breach when big changes are warranted – mastering the financial model is especially difficult.

But there are new ways to think about the money in higher education, and surely partnerships are key. When we surveyed higher education leaders (anonymously), 45% of them told us they were seriously considering or actively pursuing a merger, acquisition, or significant partnership to ensure their institution's future. I tend to think that institutions that are not well-partnered — like standalone law schools, medical schools, and business schools — may be a dying breed. It's expensive to run an institution without a natural pipeline (i.e., without K-12 schools sending you their graduates, or without your own undergrads sticking around for graduate degrees through 3+2 programs). And it's likewise precarious to run a college or university that operates without sister programs to offset "down" years. When one program or one degree/credential offering is all that you've got, that's a lot of eggs in one basket. Running a nursing school when nurse burnout has people reconsidering the profession would be a lot easier if you also have a thriving physical therapy program, a medical technician program, or a podiatry college.

Partnering wisely — with K-12 institutions, with other colleges and universities through shared service or consortia arrangements, with area businesses, and with other nonprofit organizations — can take you from good to great.

Dr. John Porter, President of Lindenwood University, knows a little something about not putting all your eggs in one basket. He moved into higher education after a career at IBM and he's been innovating in academia ever since, diversifying revenue streams and giving students what they need. Dr. Porter told us that it's important to develop and hone your risk tolerance and that the future of higher education requires breaking with the status quo. He said:

> "There are some things with our strategic plan that we're going to do that are non-traditional for higher education, but that's really going to diversify our revenue streams, which I think is going to be the root of some great things for us going forward."

The current revenue model at Lindenwood is what Dr. Porter calls a "40-40-20 model" —whereby 40% of revenue comes from on-ground education (tuition, room and board), 40% comes from online education (tuition), and 20% comes from auxiliary revenues. An example of auxiliary revenue at Lindenwood is their LindEngage for-profit venture that will offer level 1 and level 2 support for technology products. Other auxiliary revenue examples could include rental income, athletic sales, and student fees.

My co-author, Dr. Joe Sallustio, once said on *The EdUp Experience Podcast*:

> "Going down a consortium path or having some type of affiliation or shared services agreement is one path toward being financially sustainable. Such partnerships create an advantage, which means you can take your resources and time and *go serve the students*."

Yes! #MicDropMoment

Let's end this chapter by talking about pipelines and the concept of "meeting students where they are" — something we explored in Chapter 4 and elsewhere. During our conversation with Linda Garza Battles, Regional Vice President of Western Governors University (WGU) South and Chancellor of WGU Texas, we talked about the idea of vertical integration — about covering the entire pipeline. Western Governors University has WGU Academy, a bridge program that helps students get in, and first take non-credit courses that could turn into credit-bearing courses. WGU Academy allows for the "dip your toe into the water" student — who may not be ready for higher ed completely but walks in hoping you can serve them. WGU also has WGU Labs, which is an innovation hub for what the future of higher ed could look like and working with employers and so on and so forth. Dr. Joe Sallustio asked Battles, *"How do you at WGU Texas intersect with Labs, with Academy, and so on?"* She replied:

"With WGU Academy, we have a pilot program for transfer. It's called the Onward with Learning Transfer Pilot Program where we are working with three community college districts in Texas, which are the largest: Lone Star College, Austin Community College, and Tarrant County College. We launched these programs recently. Through the program, we reach out to students who just are newly enrolled at the partner college [Lone Star, etc.] and we ask if they would be interested in participating in this pilot project. If they complete all the program requirements, when they achieve their associate's degree and are ready to transfer to WGU, they will get automatic admission plus a $900 per term scholarship for up to four terms. And then, of course, their credits from the community college will be applicable toward one of our degrees.

"Part of the WGU Academy piece is that they're required to take these courses through the Program for Academic and Career Advancement, which is an experiential learning curriculum that helps students discover what's most important for them, what's holding them back from achieving success, and how to address those challenges. So, it boosts their confidence and so it helps retain them not only at the community college, but then also helps them complete their two-year degree and then be successful at WGU. It's also *beyond* that program, students can enroll in that if they're not quite ready to succeed in higher education. They don't have to come to WGU when they complete the program at WGU Academy. They can go on to any other institution. It's a low-cost way to get college ready. It's $150 a month and students can complete in as little as two months, and WGU Academy does provide scholarships for low-income individuals."

This was the first I had heard a higher-education leader talk about a high-school-to-college bridge program that didn't require the learner to ultimately enroll at the college that sponsored the bridge program. Remember what I said earlier in the book about my belief that higher education should be endeavoring to provide "Outcomes for Everyone?" This is a great example.

We asked Battles to tell us about one of their other innovations, WGU Labs. She told us:

" Money is the root of all academic excellence. "

Richard W. Schneider, PhD

President Emeritus, Norwich University, and Rear Admiral, U.S. Coast Guard (Retired)

"In Austin, we are working with a hybrid college to onboard a cohort of a few students to see how well they would do in being provided with wraparound services — an in-person place to take WGU courses. We provide them with a private space with a computer, access to the internet, and all that good stuff. So, we're going to see how well that works. If the results are great, then we're going to look into it and try to expand. But we will pivot if it *doesn't* work. WGU Labs is constantly looking at different ways to improve student outcomes, which makes WGU the most innovative institution, I believe, in the country."

The idea of creating space for your institution's students at another institution's campus addresses the overhead or real-estate problem in higher education. If your students would benefit from a brick-and-mortar space with college/university-provided amenities and you want to keep costs down, just take a look at all the empty spaces at other colleges and universities. Hearing Battles talk about the wraparound services proof-of-concept project got me thinking — it's like the business world's co-working concept applied to learners in higher education. I, for one, can't wait to hear how it works!

Keeping the lights on (literally or figuratively) in higher education is no small matter. And the solutions are already being tested around the world. Innovative partnerships, new strategies regarding real estate and online education, and altogether new philosophies on funding and spending are sure to revolutionize the industry.

Money makes the academy go 'round. So how we earn it — sufficiently and consistently, ethically, fairly, creatively, and sustainably — is higher education's question of the moment. Because in the end, there is no value creation without value capture ... and no value capture without value creation. The cycle waits for no one.

Money makes the academy go 'round. So how we earn it — sufficiently and consistently, ethically, fairly, creatively, and sustainably — is higher education's question of the moment.

CHAPTER 9

OLD SCHOOL VS. NEW SCHOOL

The Growth and Continual Adoption of Technology Solutions and Retail Mindsets

In subtitling this book, we dared to propose that we're entering *a new era in higher education* — that what's old is *not* new again, that the status quo is killing us, and that even the most time-honored traditions shouldn't be perpetuated ad infinitum. Traditions change, modes of communication and educational delivery change, and the needs and expectations of the very learners who higher education *serves* have changed — drastically. So, how do you take a long, hard look at your college or university and begin the important work of going from "old school" to "new school" — in your mindsets and in your management of existing and future programs and operations?

We suggest you start by looking around you — taking to heart (and owning up to) your institution's strengths and weaknesses and considering the forward-thinking approaches at your peer institutions. If Dr. Joe Sallustio, Elvin Freytes, and I have done our job in writing this book, then we've offered hundreds of inspiring and thought-provoking examples — "best practices," if you will — of what's really happening at colleges and universities across the U.S. and around the world. Examples we hope you'll use to make your own big plans for the future.

So, what's "new" in higher education? Almost everything, and the most pivotal changes involve technology adoption and retail mindsets. The future of higher education is a story of "high-tech meets high-touch."

Online, On-Campus, and Hybrid ... Oh, My!

If you've been looking to get into the "online vs. on-ground" debate in this book, now is your moment. By virtue of having conducted the research for this book during a global pandemic, we were able to talk to more than 100 institutional leaders who knew a little (or a lot) about online education. Those who knew a little were learning at crisis speed, because even the institutions whose models had previously been 100% face-to-face and campus-based were suddenly trying to serve their students — safely — at a distance. *Everyone* was online (though not everyone was thriving). As many institutions learned during the pandemic, distance education is equal parts art and science. We observed that, when it came to effective technology utilization during the early months of the pandemic, colleges and universities fell into three big groups: those organizations that were purpose-built for the pandemic moment (already fully online and finding that the crisis didn't interrupt their operations one bit); those institutions that were forced to make major pivots to go online (that ultimately communicated success stories in how they stepped up to the moment); and those for whom "going online" in March of 2020 was disastrous for the institution's students (as well as for faculty, staff, and administrators). Wherever you sit on the spectrum of acceptance and experience in online education, you're not alone.

Through our conversation with Dr. Ward Ulmer, Former President of Walden University, we got a glimpse of what it's like to work inside an organization that was pioneering in the distance-education space long before "online" was a thing. And we got his take on the marketplace's acceptance of online education in this new era. Dr. Ulmer told us:

> "We're an institution that has been doing online for a long time, even when online wasn't the thing to be doing. While you could certainly make the argument that *today* people believe that online is not going to deliver the same learning outcomes, I think that most of that has really started to transition. Walden's been doing correspondence for

50 years. We've been doing totally online for 25 years. And when we started doing this, we had a lot of traditional institutions — land-grant institutions especially — think 'You cannot get the same student learning outcomes from online learning.' But over the years, we've seen that paradigm shift a little bit and really what's happened is that since March of 2020, now every institution that was really talking about moving online because they realized that was the future is finally moving that direction. Every institution that realized that online was something that had to be done if they wanted to compete — if they wanted to stay open — (like a lot of the smaller liberal arts universities) have really started to come to terms with that. But since March 2020, when the wheels really fell off of our society, things changed. Everybody is now embracing this, and it's not just at the higher-ed level; it's at the K-12 level as well."

There is, of course, a difference between begrudgingly moving forward with an online strategy and doing so with the right planning and training in place. We talked to Dr. Ulmer about the legitimate complaints from students and parents regarding how some institutions "went remote" during the pandemic, and he told us:

"There are a lot of institutions that believe they are doing online well — who feel like that if you take a syllabus or an assignment and email it to a student and that student completes the assignment and sends it back, that's online education. And then there are institutions that believe that if a faculty member knows how to log into Zoom and have a session with students in the clas, that that's just absolute rockstar status in 'teaching online.' It's very sad."

There is, of course, a difference between begrudgingly moving forward with an online strategy and doing so with the right planning and training in place.

Not all online education is created or executed equally. And we must hold the industry to high standards for online education because learners deserve high quality *and* convenience/accessibility — they shouldn't have to choose one or the other. In fact, students are demanding both. Dr. David Harpool, Former President of Northcentral University, told us:

> "Technology is developing in higher education at such a pace that you cannot ignore it. You cannot just say 'We're going to continue to do things the way we used to do,' because the students who are coming in the next 10 years aren't going to put up with a lack of technology."

So, where is the industry going on the coming years? Frankly, no one agrees exactly – but everyone we spoke to agrees that the "online/on-campus/hybrid" discussion is fundamental to the future of the industry.

So, where is the industry going on the coming years? Frankly, no one agrees exactly — but everyone we spoke to agrees that the "online/on-campus/hybrid" discussion is fundamental to the future of the industry. Dr. Michael Horowitz, President of TCS Education System, which is home to six institutions, including The Chicago School of Professional Psychology, is betting on a hybrid standard with mass customization of experiences for students. He said to us:

> "I think higher education — in the coming years — inevitably has to move toward more of a hybrid model. There's so much that can be done very effectively, sometimes *more* effectively, in an online environment. And we have to be sophisticated about it. It's not a matter of turning on the Zoom camera. It's having faculty and instructional designers who will make the technology — the courses — really come alive, really be meaningful.

"And then we have to mix it with face-to-face education because there are certain things we cannot do online that can replace that human contact. I'm really proud of our law school, which a number of years ago said 'We want to reinvent the JD program. And make the *best* program, not specifically just an *online* program.' And they came to a model that's 70% online and 30% face-to-face in a low-residency model. That's what I'm hoping for the future of higher ed — that faculty and administrators would think together: 'How do we create the best education for the future, rather than resting on our laurels?'"

That "best education for the future," it would seem, puts learners in the driver's seat as never before, which challenges institutions to cede a lot of control to the customer. Understanding the "people imperative," as we have come to call it in this book, is something that's at the forefront for Dr. Melik Peter Khoury, President of Unity College in New Gloucester, Maine. He told us:

"We try to be location and modality agnostic, trying to give students as much control about *how* they want to learn, *where* they want to learn, and *when* they want to learn."

That "best education for the future," it would seem, puts learners in the driver's seat as never before, which challenges institutions to cede a lot of control to the customer.

Yes! My previous book was based on five principles of "thinking like a marketer," one of which was "Be strategy-religious and tactic-agnostic." Suffice it to say, Dr. Khoury is speaking my language. And while it's *important* to give students as much control as possible, it's not always easy to implement and maintain. An inflexible, rigid, "old-school" academia is where we have *been* but it's not where we're *going*. When we chatted with Dr. Philomena Mantella, President of Grand Valley State University, she got us thinking about how "new-school" flexibility increases access and expands the mission. Allowing students choice in the modality through which their education is delivered is part and parcel of equity and inclusion. Dr. Mantella told us that, in thinking about the future of higher education, the three areas she would focus on are:

> "Let's bring the best of digital forward. Let's bring the best of face-to-face forward. And let's try to get out of this supply-chain mentality and allow people to flex so more can be included."

The idea of multi-modal higher education was one that came through — loud and clear — during the research for this book. Dr. Ulmer at Walden University echoed the sentiments about student control and tailored, customized learning experiences, which we heard about from other presidents. Dr. Ulmer said:

> "I think it really comes down to tailoring — the ability to deliver efficient and effective education in the way that a student wants it. Whether it's on an iPhone or a tablet, on a computer or in a classroom, you're going to have to be able to hit all those delivery modes and do it in a way that doesn't violate the academic integrity of what you're trying to deliver."

Perhaps the best places for us to learn about delivering an engaging online experience with high academic integrity is to look to the institutions that have taught hundreds of thousands of learners in an online format. That's why we were sure to interview leaders from Walden University, University of Phoenix, Southern New Hampshire University, Western Governors University, Purdue University Global, and UMass Online, just to name a few. In our conversation with Dr. Bill Pepicello, Former President of the University of Phoenix, he said:

> "When the worldwide web really got hot in the mid-1990s, the University of Phoenix knew everything there was to know about online learning at that point. And what we had to do was adapt what we knew to web-based instruction. So, we were way ahead of the game, and that's what allowed us to expand quickly because no one else had any idea how to do any of this. And we didn't have a *great* idea, but we had a better idea than anyone else."

" Competition is creating a need for us to continue to innovate and transform ourselves. "

Jorge Haddock, PhD
Former President, University of Puerto Rico

> **Reflection Question:** *In what area of education does your college or university have "a better idea than anyone else?" What space could you dominate if you really tried?*

In talking about what it takes to "go online" for a college or university, we inevitably addressed the need for institutions to spend hard on marketing and infrastructure, engagement of instructional designers, and training for faculty. Going online isn't something you can do and just expect your old marketing strategy to work. (If you build it, they will *not* necessarily come.) And going online isn't a trade-off of high-touch student engagement for something that's less human by virtue of being high-tech. Quite the contrary, Dr. Pepicello argued:

> "There's sometimes a false dichotomy between high-touch and high-tech. High-tech also means you *have* to be high-touch. Because if you're not always in real time, you can't always see your students or your faculty, you need to have a whole different approach to the art of teaching. It's not the same. The art of teaching face-to-face is completely different from connecting with students online. And that takes an investment of money because faculty and students both have to be integrated into this new digital ecosystem in which they're going to live."

Going online isn't something you can do and just expect your old marketing strategy to work. (If you build it, they will not necessarily come.)

When asked whether he thinks higher education is ready for competing in this new normal and spending in this new normal, Dr. Pepicello replied: "No. I don't think higher education is ready."

We asked that loaded question in the fall of 2020, and the industry has admittedly begun to flex its new muscles and pivot in new directions since then. Higher education is getting more and more ready every day.

Making Education Your Business with Dr. Joe Sallustio

The M-A-R-K-E-T in Marketing

The marketplace of higher education. Commodity, customer, price, value, return-on-investment, competition, speed, delivery, monetize, and margin are just a few of the business terms administrators within higher education need to become comfortable with as they move into the online learning space. This space — where a Google keyword ranking means more, at times, than your institutional reputation — requires a more entrepreneurial way of thinking than many of the traditional marketing and recruiting tactics (like "setting up a booth") that work for the first-time, full-time freshman.

When you come to realize that a student — particularly an adult student — will select an institution that meets certain criteria (like cost, speed-to-degree, and accessibility), communicating product relevance through differentiation becomes a critical component. Are you competing regionally, nationally, or glob-ally with your online education offering? Does the marketing budget match the intent? Even if you do all the above, there is a retention piece for online learners that's vastly different compared to face-to-face or hybrid learners. A few of the presi-dents we've interviewed have mentioned intrusive advising, nudging, high-touch contact, and predictive analytics as neces-sary practices to retain online adult students. Bottom line: Engage the students in every single possible way or the students will feel disengaged, and cite a lack of contact or community as the reasons they don't complete.

While pandemic-related government relief assisted with budget deficits or logistical expenses for institutions forced to move online (staving off more closures), the secret to sustainability — for institutions without self-sustaining endowments — will be in their ability to market their products to consumers at scale.

My co-author, Dr. Joe Sallustio, continued the conversation with Dr. Pepicello, suggesting that one of the ways in which higher education has lacked readiness for what's to come (and what's already here) is an outdated sense that higher education is different from other businesses and that students, therefore, are vessels to fill … not customers to serve.

One of the ways in which higher education has lacked readiness for what's to come (and what's already here) is an outdated sense that higher education is different from other businesses and that students, therefore, are vessels to fill … not customers to serve.

Dr. Pepicello agreed and added:

> "Education has always been looked at as a public good. And we've always said it's above the fray. It's not really part of the business of the United States. However — especially as we have become more technologically advanced — education is not just a public good … it's also a commodity; it's a service. And higher education still sort of fights that. And that's part of the reason that some institutions are in trouble."

You might recall from our "Survey Says!" section in Chapter 7 that more than 58% of higher-education leaders think their institution is in trouble, when considering the looming demographic shift and their institution's current operational health.

Many of our research participants came right out and told us that their institution's precarious position is a result of wearing blinders when it comes to the adoption of technology to advance the business and serve the students. We even heard from an information technology professional whose job — which focused on tech support for online learning — was eliminated when their campus re-opened after the height of the pandemic because, in their words, "online learning was no longer relevant."

Education is a business and students are consumers. If you don't understand that, you've already lost.

Joe Sallustio, EdD
Senior Vice President, Lindenwood Global & University Strategic Enrollment Management, Lindenwood University

How each institution approaches its balance of online/on-ground/ hybrid will be driven by many factors — hopefully, the needs and preferences of their student body will be chief among those considerations. But leadership perspective plays a sizable role in technology adoption (as it also does in whether your university's $85 million gym expansion includes a 500-foot "leisure river" — we're looking at you, Louisiana State University). And right now, leaders are somewhat mixed on whether technology is friend or foe, and whether educational commoditization and students as consumers are a step forward or a step back. Dr. Creston Davis at GCAS College Dublin told us:

> "As for the future of higher education, I think it's going to get back to the Amazon model. The bigger you are, the bigger your endowments are, the more real estate you can buy up, the more fancy 'lazy rivers' you can put in, the more students you're going to get. So, I think that's the track of higher education in America, which is really sad indeed. So, I think that's the future of higher education. It's more commodification — it's more technology-based rather than human based."

Don't let his criticisms fool you. Dr. Davis's college has its own proprietary cryptocurrency — GCAS College Dublin is working to strike the right balance between high-tech and high-touch, as are many institutions. The things we can learn from businesses like Amazon — lessons about customer service, ease of use, ways to be relentlessly focused on a retail mindset — can, have, and will continue to influence higher education. Because the person who is shopping online with "one-click" purchases with an expectation for quick, free shipping is the same person shopping for higher education. Technology, when it's puts to use to connect people and ideas and when it's used to predict what your stakeholders need (so you can then give it to them) is not at odds with humanity, but in support of it. Dr. Saúl Jiménez-Sandoval, President of California State University Fresno, argues for a hybrid approach to education that serves our human needs above all. He said to us:

> "The future of higher education must have — in its core — the experience of who we are as humans. And that experience of who we are as humans can cannot, in my mind, be fully replicated in the online virtual modality. We can have a hybrid approach, but I do believe

that being present — being at the campus — does provide us with that opportunity to grow both emotionally and academically with the talents that we are given. So, the future of higher education *does* include virtual, it *does* include online, but I do advocate very strongly for that experience of being present or that experience of being with each other and figuring things out as a community."

Surely, most of the presidents we interviewed for this book felt confident that online education won't ever entirely replace face-to-face education. Dr. Khoury at Unity College told us:

"I think that higher education got the false dichotomy of online versus face-to-face wrong. That false dichotomy of you're either in a classroom or in your basement with a laptop is some of the rhetoric that is stopping real innovation from happening."

In the end, educational delivery modality is just that — it's the way the learning is delivered, but it's not the learning itself. Education still needs to be excellent and engaging, and it can be *both* in a variety of modalities. Dr. Arthur Keiser, Chancellor of Keiser University, talked to us about "online vs. on-campus," saying:

"Well, I think the future is still good for higher education ... I believe there will be a need for educational institutions that provide a structure and a platform for students to learn. So that platform may be becoming increasingly multimedia — both in an on-campus and in an online environment, whether it be hybrid, online, or even in the classroom using social media and all kinds of different devices to get the material and to make it more interesting, more exciting, and more usable for the students."

I appreciated Dr. Keiser's perspectives about the future. He was one of many presidents who reassured us that most colleges and universities won't flounder or die in the coming years — they'll adapt. But perhaps your institution is on the precipice of adaptation and you're wondering, "How will we get from point A to point B?" You'll do it with others showing you the way.

Dr. Martha Dunagin Saunders, President of the University of West Florida, acknowledged that going online — for institutions that are just starting out with robust virtual learning — is not easy. She said:

> "You use a different set of pedagogical muscles."

Talented instructional designers have those muscles. And muscles can be built. We asked Dr. Gregory Fowler, President of Southern New Hampshire University Global Campus,[41] to talk to us about his best advice for new players in the online space. He immediately acknowledged the complexities of trying to build out bureaucracies and infrastructures in the online space if you're starting from zero. He said, addressing colleges and universities that are looking to go online in new, larger, and more deliberate ways:

> "Don't try to boil the ocean. You see and hear about all these institutions out there doing amazing things in the online space and there can be a temptation to say, 'If we're going to do *any* of this, we've got to do *all* of this big stuff.' But you can't do it all. You don't have the time and you haven't had the opportunity.

> "Emergency remote learning is not the same thing as an online learning environment that has been built up over time. In a crisis (like the pandemic), focus on 'lighthouse moments.' If you're trying to see through this darkness right now, the light is not going to be this big explosion in the sky. It's really going to be that lighthouse that you're seeing off in the distance. And you should know that it's the simple things that will allow you to help your students find their way to shore."

Start small when moving forward. Do what you do best and support your students through the moment. You don't have to become a fully online institution, nor do you need to build out an online capability that is truly innovative or massive in scale — at least not yet. Go toward the light. Seek what Dr. Fowler calls the lighthouse moments ... the glimmers of hope for a changing industry, and the rays of vision that connect students to your colleges and universities, in convenient ways powered by technology.

---

41 Since our interview, Dr. Fowler has become President at the University of Maryland Global Campus.

Place-based education is important and it's here to stay. And during the pandemic, everyone jumped into the pool to learn how to teach and learn online. And now we have the opportunity to create what a 21st-century education is ... and to use technology — without bias and without politicizing it — to think about what creates the best pedagogical experience for our students.

Daniel G. Lugo, JD

President, Queens University of Charlotte

Among the many presidents we spoke to who gave online education its just due while also telegraphing that they don't believe that online education will take over entirely was Dr. Joseph Marbach, President of Georgian Court University in Lakewood, New Jersey. He told us:

> "The future of higher education is similar to what its past has been. Higher education has evolved in the United States in a way that really is the envy of the world. It *remains* the envy of the world. Students are still going to learn in groups and in person ... it's a social activity."

Dr. Marbach's comment counters the naysayers who worry that fully online education is too solitary and lacks the interaction of face-to-face classrooms. Ask any recent college graduate or current student whose institution has an online platform for interaction with professors and classmates, and they'll tell you that the threaded discussions took on a life of their own (and took a lot of their time and social energy). They'll tell you that modern technology allows them to interact during class time in multiple ways — listening, raising their hand to contribute, helping or posing questions in the chat room, jumping into breakout sessions for problem-solving with their classmates. When done well (and many, many colleges and universities do it well), online education is often more robust, compelling, interactive, and sticky than the kind of learning that typically takes place in brick-and-mortar classrooms.

When done well (and many, many colleges and universities do it well), online education is often more robust, compelling, interactive, and sticky than the kind of learning that typically takes place in brick-and-mortar classrooms.

Dr. Dwaun Warmack, President of Claflin University in Orangeburg, South Carolina, summed it up perfectly when he said:

> "The future higher education is about re-imagining the use of technology."

One of the titles we initially considered for this book was *Re-imagining Academia* (a title that is admittedly not as cool as *Commencement*, but one that made the short list because Dr. Warmack is right — where we are and where we're headed in higher education is all about *re-imagining* what is possible, what matters, who we serve, and what the future might hold). And the creative and transformative use of technology is a key piece of that re-imagination. Technology used in new ways is changing our industry — ed-tech has moved from the geeky fringes to the forefront and eventually will be so ubiquitous that the idea of higher education that's *not* technological at its core will seem foreign.

Where we are and where we're headed in higher education is all about *re-imagining* what is possible, what matters, who we serve, and what the future might hold.

Dr. Emily J. Barnes, who was serving as Interim President and Provost of Cleary University when we interviewed her for this book and has since gone on to become Provost and Vice President of Academic Affairs at Siena Heights University, was matter of fact in speaking to us about technology in higher education. She said:

> "Technology in higher education is here to stay. None of us can do our jobs (or attend to our educations) without tech.

> "What happens when we get to the day when there's not anybody left who knew education *prior* to e-learning or prior to online? Eventually we'll get to the place where it's no longer a before and after, or now versus later. Online learning will simply be what we all experienced. Eventually the question of 'online or on ground' will just outdate itself. It will expire."

Making Education Your Business with Dr. Joe Sallustio

Capitalize on Disruption

Back in the "old days," when you wanted to watch a movie on a Friday night with your family, you'd all get in the car and head down to your local video store and pick up the new release on VHS. Eventually, the smaller and higher-definition DVD came onto the scene (laserdiscs were in between) and an upstart company thought it might be convenient for you to *not* leave your house and instead receive your DVD in the mail. Like me, you probably loved the idea of this mail-delivered movie, and you stopped going to the video store. Have you heard this story?

Then, technology advanced again and, in the early 2000s, we experienced the proliferation of the internet, the evolution of the iPhone, and, you guessed it, streaming video. The company that was sending you DVDs in the mail cannibalized that business and went "all in" on streaming, while the video store company doubled down on their traditional business model.

Any idea what companies I am referencing in this story? Yep, you guessed it. Blockbuster and Netflix. It's a classic story of embracing disruption, adopting emerging technology, and taking calculated risks.

What will be the story of higher education 10 years from now? More important, what will the story of *your* institution be 10 years from now?

At the onset of the pandemic, Cleary University found itself ready because technology was already deeply and meaningfully in play as part of their culture and their educational experience. Dr. Barnes told us that it took Cleary just four hours to transition from on-ground to fully remote when the campus closed due to COVID-19. She explained:

"At Cleary, the content is already built *online* so that on *ground*, the faculty can focus on engagement. They can focus on activity, hands-on application, or discussion. They're not delivering content as much in person. So, when the time came [in March 2020], it was a quick meeting with the faculty and I said, 'All right, we're ready. We're going to transition to remote learning this weekend' and they took it, and it was done. No hiccups."

What a refreshing concept that — if executed well —does away with synchronous and sometimes snore-worthy face-to-face lectures. To what degree is your institution embracing the idea that the initial *learning* can be done online, and the *engagement* and *application* is what happens in person? Dr. Barnes closed out our conversation with the kind of optimism the entire industry can use, telling us:

"I think the future of higher ed is expansive and creative and innovative and exciting. And the fact that I think many of us are wondering about the future is exciting. And I think it *has* to be that way for us to lean into it and to keep going."

Today's students are digital natives. Someday, the entire faculty, staff, and administration will be too.

Today's students are digital natives. Someday, the entire faculty, staff, and administration will be too.

You might be reading this chapter and thinking, "Yes, technology is critical in higher education. But my institution is behind. And catching up costs a lot of money." And it does. When I left the insider ranks of higher education in 2012, our registrar was managing class lists by hand, on paper, using a pencil and eraser to update the records as students added or dropped courses. Considering opportunity costs and errors, what does *that* kind of process cost?

It was important to us, when conducting the research for this book, that we talk to leaders in ed-tech — leaders who have insight into what's happening at hundreds or even thousands of colleges and universities, and who are helping academic leaders achieve their missions through the thoughtful application of technology. As such, we spoke with Jim Milton, Chairman and CEO of Anthology, Inc., and we spoke with Laura Ipsen, President and CEO of Ellucian. We also spoke with other technology leaders, like John Farrar, Director of Education at Google. And their insights paint a bright future of higher education.

The flip side to the cost/investment of innovative technology in higher education is the value such technology brings — to the students and to every other player in the enterprise. Laura Ipsen at Ellucian told us:

> "I think simplification and streamlining is what every institution's looking to do. It's about delivering this new value for students. And absolutely, many institutions are really hurting as it relates to resources. And there has to be some rationalization around cost, but it's really about the *value creation*. So, simplification is mandatory. And the way that we're building it with our open SaaS platform is through the power of integrations, integrating everything. Any application that an institution wants to use can be fully integrated with that student information system and with the ERP (enterprise resource planning system) — so that you have a one-stop shop for all the data and the analytics, so that no matter who you are across an institution (the student, the faculty, the administration, the president), there's one source of truth."

Your institution has great ideas. *You* have great ideas. And yet, great ideas without the ability to execute on them is a dead end. This is where a lot of institutions are right now — with small technology budgets, home-grown systems, and IT teams that are operating for yesterday and not today. ed-tech is as important to today's higher-education institutions as the right overall strategy and the right people. And imagining and implementing meaningful technology nearly always comes down to vital partnerships; partnerships are everything. When it comes to who you want to be as an institution, you can't just believe in value — you must *create* it. And creating it can be hard work.

> " What is central to quality higher education is faculty/student engagement, regardless of platform – regardless of delivery method. Online is just a modality. "

Frank J. Dooley, PhD
Chancellor, Purdue University Global

# EdUp with Elvin

Practical Tips and Frontline Insights from Elvin Freytes

Going from "old school" to "new school" equals change ... and most people don't like change. One of the hardest things to do is to change your routine, especially at work. Imagine if you and your team worked with a certain system or platform for years then suddenly you are forced to change and learn a new one. Ugh.

Let's be honest — learning a new technology sucks! So how do you make it not suck? Here's how:

1. Find out what would make a user's life easier with your current system.

2. Ask them if they have any recommendations for a *new* system.

3. Let everyone know — very early on — that the exploration of purchasing a better (not "new," but *better*) system is under way. And let them know *the reason why* this idea is being considered.

4. Make sure the users who will work with the system daily are part of the workgroup (see what I did there?) that will search for and demo the potentials.

5. Allow all users to vote on the top three potential systems. If possible, try to be transparent with budget realities.

6. Make a decision and let everyone know which system will be implemented — with the expected timeframe (be realistic and let them know that the timeframe is fluid) and the reason why (this should be constantly reiterated). Then provide resources in audio, written, and video form for users to so they can prepare for the transition.

7. Allow a group of daily users to join in on the implementation process, and empower them to provide crucial feedback on components that are needed and not needed (this one is key, as sometimes having all the bells and whistles only causes frustration).

8. Start training users in small, targeted groups. The key here is to have them *drive* so they can experience the system and set up their new routine. Try to keep language from the old system in the better one — learning a whole new language with a ton of acronyms sucks.

9. Provide a customer-service phone number, email, chat, and webpage to open a ticket — to all users — along with audio, written, and video resources to continue learning the better system. Continue to provide small-group trainings until users don't need them.

10. Committees suck. But *change* doesn't have to!

Continuing our conversation with Laura Ipsen at Ellucian, we asked: *"Do administrations understand how important technology infrastructure is?"* She responded:

"I have more and more conversations lately with presidents who are talking about their CIO — with presidents who are excited about digital transformation. And quite frankly, the crazy part of this is that I had as many customers moving to the cloud *during* COVID as I had the year before, because they now need to transform how they work in order to do one thing, which is to deliver a more powerful and wonderful experience for their students. And students are the *consumer*, and the consumer is voting.

"Students are looking for something different, and these are amazing institutions that have tremendous value on their campuses. They're beautiful. They have amazing labs. They have incredible sports teams, and nothing will replace that. But I think the smart institutions — and I see *most* of them doing this — are saying 'There is something new out

> there and we need to go after it because the student consumer is voting and there's a net new opportunity to expand the impact that we have and provide wonderful learning opportunities to more learners. And that's what online represents. This is a transformational time in digital and I'm super optimistic that there's a new relationship being built between the presidents, the CFOs, and the CIOs to reimagine the future of higher education ... to reach out in new ways."

Ipsen touched on some of the very insights that emerged in the research we shared in Chapter 7 regarding the presidential skillset of the future. The leaders we need today and tomorrow are precisely the leaders who are operating alongside their CIOs and CFOs, as Ipsen suggests — they're presidents with financial acumen and the requisite open mind to exploring new ideas, models, structures, and technologies.

That open-mindedness is emerging in individual universities and in entire pockets of the higher-education sector, but we're still collectively behind the times. Dr. Nathan Long, President of Saybrook University, shared with us:

> "One of our trustees made the point of saying, 'You know, higher education has a real sense of itself that it's on the bleeding edge of online, and yet it's still using technology that's 30 years old.'
>
> "Institutions looking to new models are asking themselves, 'How do you let go of some of the old trappings of the past and recognize that new ways of doing the *business* of higher education have great value — not just for faculty and administrators, but for the students, for the learner, for those who are seeking a leg up in the world to advance themselves?'"

Dr. Rowena M. Tomaneng, President, San Jose City College, is another leader whose institution is constantly investigating ways that technology can transform the student experience and the value the college brings to the marketplace. In addition to their traditional academic transfer disciplines, San Jose City College has a Google IT apprenticeship and a Microsoft Pathstream. Student services and student communications involve interactive text messaging and a chatbot for counseling, admissions, and records, and the college is focused on training faculty and staff to lead the way when it comes to technology utilization. Dr. Tomaneng told us:

"Regarding the future of higher education, I definitely think that we have changed in terms of technological readiness because of the pandemic. So many institutions across California and across the nation who were reluctant to embrace online educational modalities — even hybrid modalities and other technological tools — are more ready. Our faculty, our administrators, and our classified professionals have all enhanced their training and their skillsets.

"One of my faculty members recently did an op-ed piece in *The Mercury News* and he talked about how one of the challenges for instruction is that because we have improved and increased our skills in the *online* environment during the pandemic, we have to step it up in the *in-person* instruction. The way that we're going to do that from my perspective is that we have to increase cultural-responsive curriculum across the disciplines, and we've got to increase cultural-responsive pedagogy so that we can really have faculty in higher ed *practice* those strategies of connecting, care, and nurturing so that all our students can thrive and be successful … There's a lot of work that we have to do, but it's *exciting* work, and I know we have the energy to do this. I'm very inspired right now by the opportunities that lie ahead for all of us."

Data-Driven Decision-Making in Higher Education

Much of the opportunity that lies ahead for academia is about the thoughtful and transformative application of data in the delivery of value to students and others. Dr. W. Kent Fuchs, President of the University of Florida, told us that the ways in which Silicon Valley can collaborate with higher education on key initiatives "is a wide-open frontier." He said:

"Using data to benefit students — while carefully protecting their privacy, of course — is probably the largest opportunity for the future in enhancing education."

President Don Kilburn at UMass Online talked to us about how to use data in an ongoing way to improve student success and student experience, saying:

"It's a world rich with *data*, but not as much *information*. And I do think that there will be a lot more usable information in the future that will allow us to figure out where students are succeeding and failing, what kind of interventions we need to do, and how we can continuously improve programs to actually get more students to where they want to go."

Institutional introspection can be the jumping-off point for beneficial evolutions and revolutions.

Getting your hands on the correct data to make the right (timely) decisions is easier now than ever before, especially if you have robust technology systems in place — and if you're starting at the prospect stage in gathering key intel (as Elvin Freytes keeps reminding us to do in his practical *EdUp with Elvin* sidebars). Your students and alumni are offering up data to you all the time; whether you capture it, analyze it, learn from it, and implement meaningful measures informed by that data is the million-dollar question. Data-driven decision-making is the best kind (and, in my opinion, the only kind) of decision-making; shooting from the hip and spending institutional resources on guesswork and hunches is reckless. Don't know how to move forward on something because you don't have the information you need? *Go ask for it.* Send out a survey or call your stakeholders to update key data fields; host focus groups and listening sessions and town-hall meetings. Institutional introspection can be the jumping-off point for beneficial evolutions and revolutions. Dr. Daniel F. Mahony, President of the Southern Illinois University System, told us:

"There are a lot of things I think we can do better in higher education. But we need to first look inward. I think often — in higher education — we make the mistake of always looking outward and being critical of everybody else and what they're doing and not taking a deep dive into our own ways of doing things.

"
Our approach is to think about what the world actually needs and then ask, 'How can we be part of providing it?'
"

John Swallow, PhD
President, Carthage College

> "I think it's important to measure. When we don't measure things, they
> end up not being important. In fact, we had a meeting of one of our
> system-wide taskforce subcommittees on Monday, where we looked at
> benchmarks and metrics and we have about a page — single-spaced —
> of metrics for which we want to be constantly assessing ourselves and
> holding ourselves accountable to … at all levels of the institution."

Introspection matters, and data makes introspection actionable. As you
look to the future, keep looking inward. The answer may be in your roots
— in your origin story or your historical trajectory — and it may be in your
current strengths, your culture, your struggles, and, of course, your data.

"New-School" Cultures

Innovation at your institution — in any form but especially when it
comes to technology adoption — requires culture change and
cross-departmental collaboration. Change adoption is the real challenge
… the technology itself is easy. We talked to Anthology Inc. Chairman and
CEO, Jim Milton, about the complex matter of rolling out technology innovations at colleges and universities where students are eager for changes,
but staff, faculty, and administrators are standing in the way. Milton told
us that institutions of higher education need to "skate to where the puck
is going." The puck is going to an expectation from students for single
sign-on and seamless integration of everything they need — from course
materials to financial aid to tuition billing to Microsoft Teams meetings —
the Amazon experience, if you will, of seamless customer experience. Yet,
Milton tells us:

> "There are still institutions that can't move in that direction. They've got
> to break down the silos that exist — organizationally, technologically,
> and from a data perspective — and start to have that single holistic
> view of that student in order to be able to react and deal with them and
> personalize and tailor their interactions with that student. So, there's a
> lot of work still to be done by institutions. But I'm very optimistic that
> many are moving in that direction."

What we learned from Jim Milton and other ed-tech experts (as well as
from our own harrowing experiences of major tech transformations at
colleges and universities where we've worked) is that you can't just buy

new software or technology systems and be transformed. Structure and culture will make you or break your initiative. Jim Milton told us:

> "Behind the deployment of technology — especially a new system or one that is replacing something that didn't exist or something that's fairly antiquated — there's almost always transformation and/ or business process re-engineering behind that for it to be deployed effectively and consumed and adopted and for real change to occur. So, I view the processes and the change management as critical components to accelerating forward with new technologies in this new world."

Moving forward requires experienced change agents and the personal will to change your mind. Dr. David Harpool, who was President of Northcentral University at the time of his interview for *Commencement*, talked to us about higher education's historical dearth of change agents. He said:

> "The majority of higher ed has been a story of very slow change, of defending the status quo at all costs. I'm unfortunately old enough to remember that when we went from Monday, Wednesday, Friday classes to Tuesdays and Thursdays; that was controversial. And then they went to evening; that was controversial. Then they went to weekends and that was controversial. Then they went to what we call extended learning or extended campuses, and that was controversial.

> "So higher education has not had a track record of what I would call 'quick adoption.' And I think the real story of higher ed is going to be when we come out of this crisis. Was the pandemic a blip that made people reevaluate and made some people solidify what they were already doing, or is it going to be a life-changing event in the history of higher ed?"

Moving forward requires experienced change agents and the personal will to change your mind.

📝 Pop Quiz!!

Understanding Where Your Roots Are Holding You Back

True or False?

___ We should continue speaking, acting, and operating in a way that pleases legacy families, VIP alumni, and major donors, even if doing so compromises our better judgment about our programs, practices, and brand.

___ College or university traditions should be forever honored, and never challenged or changed.

___ We can't just suddenly put new stakes in the ground and announce big changes, because it might ruffle some feathers — internally and externally. It's better to stay under the radar.

___ Our faculty's academic freedom is more important than student engagement, academic success, or career outcomes.

___ Our faculty and staff can't innovate with new courses, programs, and initiatives on a nimble basis — we need a committee for that, and probably cabinet and board approval.

We titled this chapter "Old School vs. New School" — a phrase we borrowed from Dr. P. Wesley Lundburg at San Diego Miramar College — because forward-looking schools are starting to look less and less like the colleges and universities of yore. And it's not just about online instruction, technology innovations, and the smart use of data. New-school operations are also about better collaboration (internally and externally), nimble operations, dynamic curricula, inclusive practices, flexibility, accessibility, and affordability. Lindenwood University President Dr. John Porter, in a quote we featured on the section divider for the second half of this book, said:

> "The aperture has got to open for higher education. We must be open to new ways of thinking and doing things. We need to integrate the

technologies as best we can. We see the speed at which corporations move, and there really is no reason why higher education can't move at that same speed. We can't be the laggards. We can't be afraid to make moves. We can't be afraid to fail. If you don't try, you don't know where the success is going to come from."

Leaning into the future and being willing to dispense with the past is something we heard about from many leaders, including Dr. Emily Barnes, who said:

"We have to determine between what's really essential and what can be let go. What's tradition and what's culture. What's critical to keep, to maintain that wholesomeness — that value of your institution.

"Just because it worked today or yesterday doesn't mean it's going to work tomorrow."

Dr. Stephen Spinelli at Babson College talked to us about being entrepreneurial with the curriculum itself, proposing a dynamic curriculum rather than a responsive one. He said to us:

"Education has to be a dynamic process of constantly adjusting curriculum. And that's super hard. But I have found that when you get faculty in a room together to collaborate, the sparks fly like crazy in very positive ways. And they make dynamic decisions around the curriculum."

What else needs to change? According to Dr. Michael Cioce, President at Rowan College at Burlington County, the schedule needs to go. He said:

"We need to get away from this agrarian calendar of 'Fall: 15 weeks. Spring: 15 weeks. and Summer: maybe.' We need to allow students to start when they're ready to start."

Dr. Bruce Kusch, President of Ensign College, talked to us about the difficulty of letting go of the way we used to do things — about how hard it is to swallow our pride in favor of elevating the needs of students and other stakeholders. We're all comfortable with the status quo, but the paradigms need to shift. Dr. Kusch said to us:

"I admit I've made fun of these dazzling PowerPoint presentations that faculty have made. And, you know, they've got the lecture notes and the jokes just in the right place. And you've got to be willing to set that aside. It takes a great deal of professional humility to set that aside and say, 'No, this is going to be a student-focused experience. Despite all my wonderful stories to tell, it's not about me as a teacher. It's about them as the student.' And that's hard. That's a big, big paradigm shift. It's time to set aside the standard trappings of higher education and academia to say, 'We're going to be very student focused."

> **Reflection Question**: *Every institution says they're student-focused but very few really are in a way that students would agree — there's no common definition of student-centric. Imagine if someone could do a survey of all the college students in the world and ask them how well their school is performing in its efforts to be student-centric. On a scale of 1-10, how well do you think your institution would perform?*

When we asked Dr. Kusch about his outlook on the future of higher education, he said:

"If we learned anything in 2020 and 2021, it's that we must be flexible, we must be adaptable. The elite institutions will probably continue to do okay. But the small private institutions are a disappearing breed. If we were just a private institution and didn't have the funding and the backing that we do,[42] I'm not sure we could weather this storm either. I think that institutions have to look at why they exist, what they do, and how they really add value. They're competing for the educational dollar and they've got to show people that they're adding value. I think there are some challenging times ahead."

One of the other elements of "new-school" thinking is the mindset shift necessary to bring higher education to scale — to truly make post-secondary education accessible to everyone. Frank F. Britt, who was CEO of Penn Foster Education Group during his *EdUp Experience*

---

42 Ensign College is a faith-based institution that is sponsored by and affiliated with The Church of Jesus Christ of Latter-day Saints, and operates in a consortium model with other sponsored organizations like Brigham Young University.

interview (and took an executive position with Starbucks before this book went to press), said quite plainly:

> "One of the challenges of the education system is that it doesn't function at the right scale to help enough people."

This is woefully and heartbreakingly true. During a recent medical appointment, my neurologist told me that "Higher education isn't for everyone" and that made me shake my head. Higher education *should* be for everyone. No, not everyone wants to study philosophy or English or mathematics, and most people can't devote four years of their lives to a college education, but we should all have the chance to learn and try new things — robotics, nursing, pipefitting, music, business. My co-author, Dr. Joe Sallustio, once said:

> "The only way to really achieve social impact at scale through education is to give everybody a chance to access it."

Access — which we explored significantly in Chapter 4 — is critical to moving from "old-school" to "new-school" mindsets. Old school vs. new school isn't just about doing away with antiquated traditions — it's about doing away with exclusivity to throw the doors wide open and welcome all the learners. Right now, even the most accessible institutions are still apt to hide behind big gates and fancy entrances, coming up short in inviting the entire community into a meaningful engagement. Think about your local community college, then think about how many thousands of people in that college's service area have never so much as stepped foot on campus to attend a public lecture, concert, art exhibit, or improv show.

Open minds serve more people. Jim Milton at Anthology Inc., which is based in Florida, talked to us about the technology solution they have implemented in Maharashtra, India, that is impacting literally millions of students. Milton told us:

> "Our raison d'être is to help colleges and universities transform lives and transform *more* lives. It's even more acute when you go around the world and you're transforming a life, you're transforming a community, and you're transforming a nation."

Open minds serve more people.

We've focused most of the conversation in this book on the higher education system in the United States, so we asked Jim Milton at Anthology to talk to us about what kinds of innovations are happening elsewhere, especially in emerging markets. He told us that while hybrid education plays a critical role in the U.S., other areas of the world are focusing right now on overall quality — not on delivery innovations. He said:

> "In the emerging markets around the world, there's a lot of focus on *quality*. There's been a gap in terms of quality. Interestingly enough, a lot of these countries have studied the United States and looked at our accreditation models and, in many cases, use accreditors from the United States to help with development of their quality initiatives and programs. Online and hybrid education, in many countries, hardly exist at all. So, I think there's a tremendous opportunity."

Where else does higher education need a "new-school" mindset shift? We need to ease up on our tendency to make things complicated and "academic" rather than user-friendly or customer focused. Dr. Julie White, President of Pierce College Fort Steilacoom, told us — when we were talking about buzzwords like "stackable certificates" and "badges" and "unbundling," that we need to go out of our way to stop making it all so complicated. She said:

> "The history of higher ed is actually one of exclusion. And at community colleges, we're supposed to be the inclusive colleges, but we're built on that *history* of exclusion. And so, when we make it more complicated, we just continue that exclusion. So, I think that while it's unintentional in many cases, complicated terminology and complicated processes make it harder for people to access what they need. I think we just need to be aware of that risk. It's good to be clear."

Making Education Your Business with Dr. Joe Sallustio

Complicated!

And higher education *is* complicated, isn't it? The Carnegie unit, the difference between list price and net costs, standard-term calendar, non-standard term, financial aid, need-based aid, retention, persistence, etc. We sometimes forget that the student — our customer — has *no* idea what to expect or how to navigate complex systems like class registration. Studies have shown that cumbersome enrollment and financial-aid processes deter students from the higher-education journey.

My favorite question to those I consult with or offer advice to:

"When is the last time you enrolled at your institution?"

Inclusion, as we explored in Chapter 4, is a vital new imperative. So is a customer-service mindset or what some might call a "retail" mindset. And so is affordability, flexibility, and relevance. At the beginning of this book, we suggested that higher education is currently trying to answer the call for "more" — for no longer being "this or that" but being "this *and* that" … for operating in an age when stakeholders want to have it all and will find someone else to provide their education if you can't provide it in the way they need and want it.

> **Reflection Question:** *In what ways is your institution answering the call for more? More options, more styles, more choices, more formats? Where can your institution step up to the era in which "either/or" is not enough … to an era in which the answer your stakeholders are looking for starts with "Yes, and …?"*

All that is not to say that colleges and universities cannot and should not have unique identities, bringing their mission to their unique set of students — often in a unique geographic region — in unique ways.

We loved hearing stories from academic leaders about the special ways in which they were standing out from the crowd, like how Leeward Community College in Hawaii puts an institution-wide emphasis on environmental sustainability. Leeward Chancellor Dr. Carlos Peñaloza told us that:

> "Leeward became the first University of Hawaii campus that became net zero in terms of producing our own electricity."

During our interview with Peter Cohen, who was then President of theUniversity of Phoenix, we asked him to talk about what he sees on the horizon for higher education, and he told us:

> "Unfortunately, it will change more slowly than any of us would like it to. I think that the market for higher education will continue to disaggregate. There will be universities like ours that are focused on career adults. There will be universities that are focused on research. There will be universities that focus on those who want a liberal arts degree and simply want to go along and continue in education and not necessarily go outside of the field of education. There will be universities that are highly technical and focused on helping students get into technical areas and vocational areas.

> "I think that the diaspora of education opportunities and the need for a wide variety of universities will continue. You shouldn't have one university trying to be all things to all people. It's just really hard to be good at that. But I think universities will continue to specialize, and that you'll see more consolidation in higher education among those who have not specialized in the past. And they will sort of gather together and aggregate their resources because scale allows for efficiency in any type of organization or operation — and that includes higher education. So, you will see some universities get larger and smaller ones find niches where they can be experts and grow by becoming the best in their niche."

Indeed, as this book goes to press at the end of 2022, there is a sort of "then and now" paradox that's facing higher education. Colleges and universities feel simultaneously drawn to stick to the status quo — to operate within the timeframe in which they were founded and keep older alumni happy that things are still as they remember them — while also

In 1965, we decided in America that every student deserves an education, but took a model only designed for the 1% and tried to mass produce it.
And it's failing.
And we're surprised.

Melik Peter Khoury, DBA

President, Unity College

balancing that urge and that impetus with the need to operate our institutions in the "here and now" for modern students, a modern workforce, and a drastically different perception of what a college education can be. Not an easy task, but one that the industry is rising to tackle.

Did You Know ...

That *EdUp* asked many podcast guests to tell us "What's your entrance music?" If you imagined that a song played every time you walked into a room or onto a stage, what would it be? And while the question aims to break the ice, go deeper in revealing the guest's personality and humanity, and to offer some levity in the midst of serious conversations, something fascinating happened when we started looking at the answers we got from college and university presidents. As it turned out, some of our favorite responses were songs about transformation, evolution, revolution, and blazing new trails — just as so many higher-education professionals are trying to do right now. Songs about better days ahead are, in our opinion, the perfect entrance songs for higher-education leaders today. What's *your* entrance song?

 "Don't Stop"
By Fleetwood Mac

Entrance music for Dr. Summer McGee, President of Salem Academy and College

"Open your eyes and look at the day

You'll see things in a different way.

Don't stop thinking about tomorrow.

Don't stop, it'll soon be here.

It'll be better than before ...

Yesterday's gone, yesterday's gone."

 "Wake Up Everybody"
By Harold Melvin & The Blue Notes, featuring Teddy Pendergrass

Entrance music for Daniel G. Lugo, JD, President of Queens University of Charlotte

"No more backward thinkin' — time for thinkin' ahead

The world has changed so very much

From what it used to be   ...

Wake up all the teachers — time to teach a new way ..."

*Lyrics for "Don't Stop" were written by Christine Anne McVie, and lyrics for "Wake Up Everybody" were written by John Whitehead, Gene McFadden, and Victor Carstarphen.

YOU in a New-School Industry

At this point in *Commencement,* you are likely seeing what we see — how all these key themes are converging ... how issues like online vs. on-ground, accessibility, inclusion, financial acumen, student-centric cultures, affordability, the power of partnerships, serving new populations of students, applying pandemic lessons, improving educational flexibility, increasing higher education's value, and developing innovative programs are inextricably linked. The overlapping and interdependent issues can feel overwhelming if you think about them as problems or complications, but the moment you see the intertwined themes as drawing your institution tighter toward a reinvigorated mission that will take you boldly toward your next 100 years, the overwhelm subsides. You have the power and perspective to take institutions that are in trouble and get them back on track. You have the ability to reset your own mindset about critical issues in higher education so you can do your job more effectively and leave a legacy of progress. You have the chance — in an industry riper for change than ever before — to make your mark and to make a difference in the lives of your stakeholders.

You have the ability to reset your own mindset about critical issues in higher education so you can do your job more effectively and leave a legacy of progress.

We hope this book, for you, has been full of motivation to move forward — a sort of permission from the presidents (who our foreword author Francisco Marmolejo called "the protagonists" of higher education's story) to apply your talents and your big ideas to higher education's next chapter.

Speaking of "next chapter," you're about to turn the page to Chapter 10, the last chapter in this book and our final opportunity to offer you some value to take back to your work and your life. Gear up for some honest debate on higher-education stereotypes (most of which we're ready to shatter) and for some final inspiration to see the industry — and your career — anew.

SHATTERING THE STEREOTYPES

Seeing Higher Education Anew

My very first job in higher education, if you don't count the years I worked as a cashier at a community college bookstore, was on the English faculty — where I spent a lot of time helping students unlearn the five-paragraph essay. And one of the lessons I taught to hundreds of freshmen was the meaning of "revision." It's a lesson I teach even now, to the authors I coach and to the corporate-education groups who take my communications workshops to help them be more successful on the job.

I write it this way on the dry-erase board — or a PowerPoint slide shared via Zoom:

RE-VISION

I ask the students to help me define it. What does "vision" mean? I never have any college provosts in my classes, so no one has answered with something like, "It's our ambitious goal for the institution's future state ..." What I *do* hear is "the ability to see." *Yes!* And what does the prefix "re" mean? Silence for a moment and then someone chimes in "to do something a second time," "to repeat," "it means *again*!" *Yes.*

Revision is the act of seeing something again — taking a closer look, a second time, to see something anew. Revision isn't about adding a few pretty sentences to your essay for English 121, and it's definitely not about fixing spelling errors (that's editing and proofreading, respectively) — it's about stepping back to look at the whole thing with fresh eyes. *Revision* requires that you challenge your own arguments, dismantle your original thesis, and re-organize the content in ways that better serve the reader. The best revision often generates a new draft that looks almost nothing like the original.

The entire impetus for *The EdUp Experience Podcast* and for this book, *Commencement*, was our collective belief — among Joe, Elvin, and eventually myself — that higher education deserved a chance to be seen anew. Since the beginning of 2020, more than 500 people have stepped up to the microphone to share their thoughts about higher education — its strengths, its opportunities, its success stories, and its failings. The first 125 presidents to contribute to that conversation, plus 136 higher-education professionals who responded to our survey, created an ensemble of voices — here, in this book — that sang a hopeful tune about the future of post-secondary education. Together, they helped us all to see higher education anew, and now it's your turn.

Building Beyond the Stereotypes

When it comes to higher education, the stereotypes all contain at least a kernel of truth (or they did at some point in the past).

→ We're overly bureaucratic, and we move at a snail's pace.

→ We sell an over-priced product without any guarantees regarding quality or outcomes.

→ All our good ideas go to committees to flounder and die.

→ We're isolated from the real world, without meaningful connections to businesses and other external entities.

→ Faculty and administrators just don't "get it" when it comes to student needs.

→ The only path to the college or university presidency is through traditional academic roles (i.e., faculty, dean, provost, president).

- We're risk-averse.
- We don't know how to market.
- And we tend to operate for the time in which we were founded instead of the era in which we currently serve.

Higher education is a time-honored tradition ... but traditions change.

Higher education is a time-honored tradition ... but traditions change.

Now it's time to shatter the stereotypes that hold us back, to retire the practices that are no longer serving us, to defy expectations, to be bigger and more differentiated than we previously dared, and to redefine higher education for a new era. **Are you ready?**

Reclaiming Our History

Much of what will make the *future* of higher education so remarkable is how we will let go of the past. But there are some fundamentals of higher education that are tried and true, and that we should seek to hold onto or rediscover. First, it would behoove us all, as we heard from many college presidents, to keep learning at the core — to never lose sight of the fact that we're in the primary business of *education* ... not all the other things that modern colleges and universities do. It's too easy for a college student's multiple non-academic priorities to render them "spread too thin." But if you strip away party-school culture (what TCS Education Group President Dr. Michael Horowitz calls "the pervasive culture of drinking") at many undergraduate universities, and rethink athletics and other extracurricular activities, it becomes much easier for students to graduate in three years instead of four. And for those students who are planning to go to graduate school, a faster path to an undergraduate degree can mean beginning a career with a graduate degree in hand just four or five years after starting college. So, that got us thinking: What if we "unbundled" education from sports, fraternity parties, lazy rivers, and other activities that, while a potentially meaningful social component of the traditional coming-of-age undergraduate experience, are making it harder for students to graduate in a timely manner?

Not many of the presidents interviewed for this book mentioned trends in collegiate sports — a notable exclusion given the fact that we spoke with many leaders whose institutions have highly competitive athletic teams. But Dr. Creston Davis, President of GCAS College Dublin, made me bite my lip and nod when he said that his college differs from many schools in the United States because:

> "We're not commoditized by the NCAA, which is a corporation that's taking over the universities."

There's something to be said for running a college or university where students choose you because they believe in the curricular model and want to learn. Dr. Davis also lamented the loss of private liberal-arts colleges — what he calls "the heart of American higher education." Because liberal-arts colleges are competing with "elite universities with billion-dollar endowments," the liberal-arts colleges are struggling (and, interestingly enough, adding a lot of new sports to attract more students). Dr. Davis said:

> "These liberal-art colleges — they're gone. They're going. They're dying."

The sadness we all feel when we hear about another small, private, independent college closing its doors is the same sadness we feel when mom-and-pop retail shops or small, neighborhood grocery stores go out of business. The rise of the mega-institution is something we see happening in other sectors, like retail (with huge outlet malls, online giants like Amazon and Wayfair, and combined grocery/department stores like Super Walmart) and even places of worship (e.g., mega-churches, mega-mosques, etc.). There is worry in the higher-education sector about burgeoning institutional sizes and even marketplace monopolies. Dr. John Rainone, President of Mountain Gateway Community College in Clifton Forge, Virginia, told us:

"I think there's a place for everyone. In the future, the industry is going to look very different, yet there is a place for the smallest institutions. I certainly hope that we do not become mega-universities — whether it's virtual or on campus — because I think that would prevent a number of people from going to college."

Dr. Rainone reminded us that many students can't see themselves in a lecture hall of 200 students; for them, 25- or 35-student classrooms are where they're going to be comfortable. As such, community colleges and small liberal-arts colleges have a vital place to maintain.

There are other stereotypes that we must be careful not to play into, like the belief that online and on-ground are mutually exclusive and that more digital emphasis in higher education replaces a focus on humanity. Dr. Mary Papazian, President of San José State University in California, talked to us about the importance of staying true to certain elements of higher education:

"I think institutions that are looking to cut their liberal arts or their humanities, I think it's a mistake, certainly in this world and this fourth digital-technological revolution. *This* digital world and digital economy needs humanists more than ever — to work in partnership with our scientists and our engineers and our data folks. If I'm creating artificial intelligence, I want somebody who's going to think about what impact that has on our community. And so it's the application of these things from a human perspective, from a community perspective — if you don't have the humanities, if you don't have the social sciences there, as part of that conversation, it's not happening. This integration of learning is ultimately what we really need."

Right now, as the higher-education industry looks to strip away unnecessary components to re-reveal its essence, there is a fear that significant closures and mergers/acquisitions will leave us with a higher-ed landscape that is barren in key ways. In speaking with Dr. Arthur Keiser, Chancellor of Keiser University, we had the opportunity to consider the possibility that too much contraction in the industry will have consequences, and that myriad types of institutions and programs are relevant and important, now and in the future. Dr. Keiser said to us:

"I've always had the belief that the doctoral-level institutions hate the master's level, the master's level hate the baccalaureate-degree schools, the baccalaureate-degree schools hate the community colleges, the community colleges hate the voc-techs, and everybody else hated the career schools — the for-profit schools. So, it was this kind of downward progression of faith in what people do. A career college, like Southeastern[43] and like others, play a critical role — even the voc-techs and the public side of it. The fact is that we need air conditioning mechanics, and it doesn't require a four-year degree. You want to be an HVAC person — to learn the sheet metal, to learn the motors — and it doesn't take the four-year degree. It doesn't take the general education courses. An auto mechanic, a diesel mechanic, I can go on — there's so many levels, a vocational nurse for that matter — that don't require an associate degree or a baccalaureate degree."

Dr. Keiser introduced us to a quote from the book *Excellence: Can We Be Equal and Excellent Too?* We agreed that it helped make his point — and a critical point at that — and so we're sharing it with you here.

"An excellent plumber is infinitely more admirable than an incompetent philosopher. The society which scorns excellence in plumbing because plumbing is a humble activity, and tolerates shoddiness in philosophy because it is an exalted activity, will have neither good plumbing nor good philosophy. Neither its pipes nor its theories will hold water."

John W. Gardner, *Excellence*

Focusing on what you do best — and the place you hold in the higher-education ecosystem — can take shape in many ways. As we think about a "back to basics" or "focus on core competencies" approach to running our educational institutions, we inevitably must look at (and often reclaim) our histories — institutionally and personally. Richard L. Dunsworth, JD, President of University of the Ozarks in Clarksville, Arkansas, talked to us about reclaiming our history and about his institution's "Renewing Our Place" strategic plan. He told us:

---

43 Southeastern College was previously named Keiser Career College.

"Our institution is called to serve a vulnerable population. We were founded when this was the frontier. This was the Indian Oklahoma Territory. The state lines hadn't been drawn yet. There are great stories of our first campus, which was burned as different armies were going through during the Civil War. We moved to this physical campus location in 1891. So, when we talk about serving challenging, vulnerable populations, we've been doing this from the beginning. It's our space."

President Dunsworth was the first man in his family to graduate high school. He hadn't realized that until recently, and now he has reclaimed that story — owning it and what it means to him, and sharing it with the colleagues and students all around him. He said:

"When you think about the kinds of stories we have and when we think about reclaiming our history — what I've invited our faculty and staff to do — we can own our stories and there's power in it. There's power in that narrative. If we own it, then maybe that first-generation student for whom college is only a dream can take a look at us and come in and go, 'Okay, I see somebody like me. I hear a story like mine. What might happen if I stay for a second semester or third?'

"We tell our freshmen what we want as it relates to retention.[44] We've almost doubled our four-year graduation rate. We're in the mid-forties. We're 52% for a five-year graduation rate for our student profile. That's amazing. But what we said to our students is, 'What will it take to get us to a 70% four-year graduation rate without changing who we recruit?' What would it take if schools like ours said, 'You know, students who are vulnerable can graduate too?' and that we not accept the old standard that only the students at really, really wealthy schools — that only students who both of their parents have graduate degrees — can graduate at a rate of 90% in four years? What would it look like if we said, 'No. Vulnerable students can graduate in four years too?' *We* have to change, as opposed to them changing."

---

44 This is a refreshing alternative to institutions that still boast their exclusivity and their "weeding-out" process when they tell students during orientation some version of the "Look left, look right. One of you won't be here at graduation" story.

The University of the Ozarks is but one example of how reclaiming your history — how looking to the past — can reinvigorate your commitment to modern imperatives, like access. Dr. Wayne A. I. Frederick, President of Howard University, talked to us about how his HBCU's history informs its passion and commitment to social justice today. He said:

> "Howard's very birth was a paradox because while it was born out of giving freed slaves an opportunity to be educated, we are now training future presidents and we have our alumna, Vice President Kamala Harris, in the White House. And that just goes to show you just what Howard is about. In between there, you've got a 154-year history of a caravan on its way to social justice, picking up people along the way, giving them opportunities."

> **Reflection Question:** *In what way can you fuel your current strategies and achieve your future goals by tying them back to your origin story? What part of the past can ignite the future? And what parts of the past can you let go, evolve, or build upon?*

As we are busy moving forward in higher education, it's helpful to take a moment to analyze where we have, perhaps, gone a step too far — to ask ourselves whether there are ways in which we might need and want "to go back." This topic came up in our conversation with Dr. Jorge Haddock, then President at the University of Puerto Rico. He said:

> "In education, we are at a crossroads — in America and in the world — as there are many factors playing out. And I think that what we are going to see is a reverse in one of the major trends that we've seen for decades. I think we'll see a reversal in *undergraduate* degrees in highly specialized programs. That specialization should be left, I think, for the master's degree or PhD degree, which was the intention at the beginning."

Dr. Haddock makes a fascinating point. Higher education, in the beginning, was about a general education — about producing broad thinkers and strong leaders ... refined citizens and people we might refer to as "well-rounded individuals." But today, you can pursue an undergraduate degree with a very specialized focus — like cybersecurity or civil engineering or French literature. As time has marched on, undergraduate degrees have become less general and more specific. Have we gone too far? Might there be value in rethinking higher education simply as grades 13 through 16 — revising the K-12 system to be K-16, producing more mature graduates with strong general life and work skills that can be applied to any career (i.e., any field for which a specialized education can be pursued at the graduate level or in a post-undergrad certificate program)? When I think about the people in my own family and friend group, and remember what they studied in undergrad, I'm left thinking that Dr. Haddock may be onto something here. I have a cousin who initially was a neuroscience major; he's a K-8 school principal. I have a friend who was a biology major; she's a mortgage underwriter. I know someone who studied forestry; he works in public safety. I have a friend who studied finance; she's a nurse. Who among us knows well enough what we want to specialize in when we're just 18 years old?

Committing to Agility and Speed

There is perhaps no more embedded and universal stereotype of higher education than the overarching belief that colleges and universities move slowly and less than gracefully when it comes to change, innovation, and responsive operations. But we don't *have* to be clumsy snails — there are plenty of institutions that are proving the exception to the rule when it comes to agility and speed. Dr. Martha Dunagin Saunders, President of the University of West Florida, told us:

> "We're not the oldest university in the state, we're not the biggest, and we're not the richest, but we are the most agile. We are absolutely the most agile — we can turn on a dime. And part of that is just that there is a spirit here. I think there's a lot of trust. I call it the frontier spirit, but other people call it an entrepreneurial spirit. Agility is part of the culture."

In higher education, we used to value tradition and prestige above all else. Every day, we're coming closer to being an industry that — while it respectfully honors tradition and brand elitism — aims to build upon the past with an eye toward what I call "outcomes for everyone" ... meaningful results for all the learners who seek access to our institutions.

Speed and agility — a new kind of nimbleness — is critical to achieving that new vision. Innovation is, by its very definition, speedy and ahead of its time. But higher education has been lumbering along through the swampy status quo for hundreds of years, and it takes a certain kind of will — and a new kind of leadership — to put the industry into hyperdrive. We talked to Dr. John Porter, President of Lindenwood University in St. Charles, Missouri, about agility and flexibility, and here's what he said:

> "If there's anything I was told when I came to higher ed, it was, 'Just know that it's going to be slow. It's going to be very, very slow.' And I would just say, 'It doesn't have to be.' We can make decisions and we can execute. I'm not going to accept that paradigm that everything moves at a snail's pace in higher education. We're just not going to do that here. We're going to make informed decisions, and then we're going to go execute.

> "And here's my perspective. There's nothing outside of the box that we can't consider as a team here. That said, we're not going to be all over the place; we're going to really be focused. But I encourage my team, 'Challenge me — rightfully and professionally. Just because I've laid something down doesn't mean we can't have discussion around it.' And so I try to keep an open mind and try to be agile. That's one of the things I really want my team to be: Flexible. We'll consider things. And once we agree, we're going to go forward — we're going to go execute on it."

Innovation is, by its very definition, speedy and ahead of its time. But higher education has been lumbering along through the swampy status quo for hundreds of years, and it takes a certain kind of will — and a new kind of leadership — to put the industry into hyperdrive.

Making Education Your Business with Dr. Joe Sallustio

Speed as Differentiation

Time. We never have enough of it, and it constantly slips through our fingers. However, the information age allows us to redefine our expectations of time. Our expectations and realities align in never-before-seen ways. When is the last time you hailed a taxi rather than scheduling an Uber? And if you scheduled an Uber and it was not going to arrive within 10 minutes, how many of you hit the back button to reset — to see if a car could come sooner? The last time you had to make a change to your travel arrangements, how many of you just did it online versus spending the time to call the airline? And when you think about speed within the business context of higher education, how many leaders out there are accessing real-time (or near real-time) dashboards or receiving automatic reports to your email so you can understand your business "at the speed of business"?

If we can't get *what* we need *when* we need it, how could we possibly run the business? Now take this same question and view it from the student's perspective:

➜ If I can't get my transcripts reviewed when I need them, why would I go to school here?

➜ If I can't enroll and get accepted easily, why would I think this institution is the one for me?

➜ If I can't get IT service 24/7 as an online student, how am I going to get my work done at night?

➜ If I don't hear from my instructor/professor in the next few hours, how will I complete my assignment?

I've said it at least once, and I'll say it again — speed of service will become a more significant differentiator in higher education

> than nearly all else. Speed has a cousin: ease. If it's fast and
> easy to navigate, your chances of landing a new customer will
> be increased drastically. You don't accept slow delivery in your
> personal life. Why do we accept it for students?

I previously mentioned that when I worked at Lake Forest Graduate
School of Management, my CMO, Curt Wang, told me that his "bias is
toward action" — meaning that he wanted me, as a director, to feel
empowered to keep the work moving, even in the absence of his input or
signoff. Reporting to someone like Dr. Porter (and like Curt) makes for
a great experience working in higher education — where you can actually
be part of design thinking and ideation, and get big, exciting things done.

Agility might be something that comes to you quite naturally. But how do
you create an agile organization? It's easier said than done. Taking risks
and being nimble isn't a one-time event. Embracing adaptability and flexibility — to create long-term sustainability for our institutions of higher
education — requires a wholesale culture shift. Managing and even spearheading change is a mindset and a culture, not a process or a structure.
Dr. Emily J. Barnes, who was Interim President & CEO and Provost at
Cleary University at the time of her interview for this book, told us:

> "Whether for programs or for systems, when we have a structure
> and an implementation methodology behind something that is
> very relational-based and individual [like employee mentoring and
> student services], those structures will crumble in chaos. They work
> when everything is fine and everything is standard and everything
> is normal — but among chaos, it will crumble. I feel that way about
> change models and leadership models, and because they're designed
> for assumptions and predictability and even an algorithm, when those
> things are off the table, good luck. Because the world is constantly
> volatile, it's ambiguous, and it's uncertain at all times. As far as leader-
> ship goes, we need to be asking ourselves, 'How do you do something
> every single day — or inconvenience yourself every single day — to
> make sure your institution is adaptable and flexible, and that you're
> creating a culture within your employees and your upcoming leaders
> and your peers in which we collectively know that: *Yes, this is hard. Yes,*

It's a somewhat fair critique of higher education that we are very tradition-bound. And so it really requires a lot of care and conversation among stakeholders to have these bold conversations about 'How do we need to change?'

Melody Rose, PhD
Former Chancellor, Nevada System of Higher Education

there's going to be change every day. Yes, it's stressful. Yes, it's chaos. And we're going to lean right into that because it isn't going away."'

Becoming Risk-Takers

"Playing it safe" — it's a stereotype and an accusation often made of higher-education leaders. So, we were surprised to discover through our research that 62% of such leaders think of themselves as being strong risk-takers and innovators. (We wonder whether their colleagues and employees would agree.) The future of higher education hinges on such risk and innovation.

We talked about big, risky (and highly rewarding) initiatives with Dr. Summer McGee, President of Salem Academy and College in Winston-Salem, North Carolina, where an institution-wide transformation was underway at the time of her interview. Dr. McGee told us:

> "We're doing a complete transformation, not just of our curriculum, but also of our student experience. We're infusing health and opportunities to *learn* about health and wellness — incorporating wellness as a component of our leadership-development curriculum. It's my firmly held belief that you can't be a successful leader if you're not well across all eight of our dimensions of wellness, whether that's financial health or mental health or organizational health. And so, we are really taking a look at every single aspect of our incredibly beautiful and historic campus, asking ourselves, 'How do we make our student experience focus on health and wellness and developing leaders?'

> "We laid out a goal that more than 50% of our entire curriculum — all of our coursework — would be focused on health-related topics and leadership development for health by the end of this year."

Our conversation with Dr. McGee wasn't the first time we'd spoken to a leader whose institution — regardless of the majors they offer — was weaving a theme or value into everything they do. Health/wellness, environmentalism/sustainability, entrepreneurship/leadership. Suddenly, it's not just about choosing a college with your major, but about choosing one with a mindset and cultural vibe that matches your own. The possibilities for "fit" between higher-education institutions and learners are evolving.

> **Reflection Question**: *What if the next time that
> you or someone you care about is shopping for
> a higher-education experience (whether it's a degree
> or a certificate or some other experience), you could
> identify institutions with values and themes that align
> with your own? What if your college cared about what
> you care about?*

Many colleges and universities are telling us about the *new* things they are doing (e.g., new programs, new buildings, new sports, new wrap-around services) but very few talk about what things they are going to *stop* doing. You can't keep adding without also subtracting. I appreciate that Dr. McGee's vision for the future of the industry acknowledges the need for higher-education professionals at all levels to make "stop doing" lists along with "to do" lists. Dr. McGee explained:

> "I think the future of higher education is about finding your niche —
> no longer being everything to everyone. I think it is so important, and
> what I have been so excited about here at Salem is that we are planting
> our flag. We have determined how we're going to be distinctive, and
> we're going to pursue that doggedly. We will continue to have broad
> appeal to a wide range of students but will have a very unique and
> specific identity. And I think particularly for small liberal-arts colleges,
> we have to find ways to differentiate. And that also means *stopping*
> doing some of the things that we historically have done. It's about really
> being very disciplined and being focused. That's one of the things I see
> for the future of small, private liberal-arts institutions — as well as for
> other institutions around the country. I think we all must find our own
> unique identities."

Making a "stop doing" list requires that you be not just nimble, but ruthless.

Dr. Emily J. Barnes, when she was Interim President & CEO and Provost at Cleary University (she has since taken the role of Provost & VP of Academic Affairs at Siena Heights University), talked to us about encouraging faculty, staff, and administrators to be risk-takers and innovators. She said of Cleary University:

"We have a reward system based on innovation and trial-and-error because that's what we want to create in our *students* is that skillset — the ability to problem-solve and that critical thinking. And we want them to embrace trial and error. And if they don't see that through *us*, then we're not doing our jobs."

Letting Go of What No Longer Serves the People We Serve

When it comes to the old trappings of higher education that are no longer serving the students (nor the faculty and staff, for that matter), there was no topic more popular in our research than the agrarian schedule — long semesters, with possible summers off, and courses measures in Carnegie units (credit hours). Richard L. Dunsworth, JD, President of the University of the Ozarks, suggested that we dissolve arbitrary ideas and barriers, like semesters and the agrarian calendar. He said:

"Let's ask ourselves: How do students learn? How do faculty want to teach? Let's find the marriage of the two of those things and remove all the structural barriers that prevent us from making those changes. I think higher ed, ultimately, is going to be a lot more fluid, and that we might be having graduation ceremonies every month, as opposed to every May and December."

Interestingly, there are plenty of institutions that are only having a commencement ceremony once a year and many of those schools are still putting the next May's graduation date on diplomas for alumni who completed their degrees the previous December. There are a lot of things we're doing — and force-fitting our students into — that simply don't work.

Dr. Michael Horowitz, President of TCS Education System, weighed in on this issue as well, saying:

"The American higher-ed traditional calendar dates back to when we were an agrarian economy and students would go home for the summer to work. And it's ridiculous. And we find that more and more

I want to see a disruption of higher education – a world without credit hours and without a belief that it takes 50 minutes, three times a week, to learn a particular subject or skill. I say that not to disrespect where we have been, but we cannot keep on with those archaic, traditional things.

Daria J. Willis, PhD

President, Everett Community College

students are interested in 'Keep me on track. I want to do something worthwhile the entire time.'"

Overhauling the academic calendar is about value, efficiency, and focus. Education should be about education, and learners should be able to learn continuously if they so choose.

All this is not to say that any "schedule" — even a new-and-improved one — should be force-fitted for all learners. Prescribed timing (like "two-year degrees" and "four-year degrees") is another old habit worthy of breaking. Dr. John Rainone, President of Mountain Gateway Community College, shared his thoughts on why we (perhaps erroneously) consider "speed to graduation" a form of success, as well as his thoughts around the life situations that can make going to school complicated and difficult. He said:

> "We are serving predominantly first-generation college students ... who have two and three jobs (part time). They have family to take care of. They may be a single parent and they're trying to get ahead through education. I mean, I just look at some of them and I'm just amazed at them. And I think some of the reporting and the *disincentives* around the federal government [are problematic], where from an institution, for a two-year degree, it should take you three years. Anything above three years, from the Department of Education — from a reporting perspective — is a failure. Well, I don't consider that.

> "I know students who I met the first year I came to [Mountain Gateway]. They graduated this year — it took them seven years. I think we should *applaud* people like that. Even *more* so than the students who had the ability to go for just two years and finish their degree. If nothing else, it was the stamina and their commitment — because maybe they could only take six credits a semester. I don't consider them a failure. And I don't consider the *college* a failure at all, but from a reporting perspective, you know, it's a negative mark."

This wasn't the first time we heard an academic leader talk about the higher-education infrastructure as being out of touch with the way students actually need and want to pursue an education. It should take as long as you need or want it to take — seven years or 10 years or your entire adult life. Isn't it curious that we all believe in "lifelong learning," as long as that means you can finish in four years?

I have a friend who reminds me a lot of the "philosophers and plumbers" quote shared earlier in this chapter; he enjoyed a successful career as a union plumber and also spent several years taking classes at two elite institutions. If you call him on a random Sunday and ask what he's doing, he's just as likely to tell you he's reading Machiavelli as he is to say he's headed to the grocery store. He's a scholar in the truest form. One of the institutions where he took classes (and where he even lived in the dorms) doesn't consider him an alumnus — because he didn't "graduate" with a degree. Never mind that he gave them more money than the average student and that he loves their institution. The other institution he attended — where he spent much less time and less money — gave him a certificate for his studies and held a program-completion celebration (which I was honored to attend). College A is stuck in "old-school" thinking about "class years vs. social-class years" and University B (which, for the record, is an old school — founded in 1890) is embracing "new-school" thinking and treating their learners with the respect they all deserve. Guess which institution my philosopher-plumber friend is most loyal to?

Isn't it curious that we all believe in "lifelong learning," as long as that means you can finish in four years?

New-school thinking is about "degree at your pace" — or no degree at all … just come, learn, grow, and expand. And, the next time we have an educational offering that appeals to you again, come back. *That* is "lifelong learning."

☀️ EdUp with Elvin

Practical Tips and Frontline Insights from Elvin Freytes

So, what does the future of higher education look like? Here's the answer that nobody likes: No one knows!

Sure, there are some people who might know what one component of the immediate future could look at their institutions (e.g., every degree will be paired with a certificate). And there are others — like myself — who have theories on what they want the future of higher ed to look like (e.g., institutions will become centers of lifelong learning).

But the truth is that the future is unknown. So, **all we can really do is prepare for an unknown future.** How can we do this? Here's how:

1. Keep educating yourself — always have a lifelong-learning mindset.

2. Listen to podcasts almost daily. Might I suggest *The EdUp Experience Podcast*?

3. Read educational books on topics that interest you and from authors you trust. (You're reading this one right now, so you already have a head start!)

4. Choose educational content within all your social media platforms so their algorithms continue to give you value.

5. Network to grow your contacts by attending conferences and other online or in-person events of interest whenever possible. We hope to see you there!

6. Create content via your preferred platform, as this exercise forces you to continue learning.

7. Join a Mastermind group, if possible, so you can learn from others and share your knowledge.

8. Have a "LinkedIn first" mindset. Whenever you come across a person or business that you want to learn more about, try to find them there so you can connect with them and follow their content. (LinkedIn should be your preferred social media platform, in my humble but experienced opinion.)

9. Ensure that you always remember to have a mindset that will allow you to be confident and curious. These two pillars will prepare you for anything!

10. Stay away from committees and always look for working groups that get shit done (GSD).

I hope you have received some value from these *EdUp with Elvin* sidebars — and maybe even a few laughs along the way.

Now, go forth and GSD!

Oh, and let's connect on LinkedIn. :-)

Taking risks in dissolving the old trappings — shattering the industry stereotypes — not only requires that we look at things like the academic calendar for students, but that we also deliberately begin to break down internal silos and flatten organizational charts to reduce the bureaucracy that is slowing us down. Dr. Nathan Long, President of Saybrook University, says his institution — which offers master's and doctoral degrees and professional certificates — is doing that in an interesting way. Dr Long told us:

> "We are a university with multiple colleges and schools focused in the humanistic philosophy. Humanistic psychology and philosophy is all about working together in journey toward one's education and towards one's mental health and wellness. It really looks to democratize the educational experience — to create an opportunity for the students and the faculty to work together in collaboration, as opposed to what might be considered the typical hierarchies of graduate education."

When I look back at my years spent working in higher education, I can clearly see that the daily stresses of my job had nothing to do with the students or the process of education — with our core business and purpose — but what ultimately made the career untenable for me was the way the "old-school" thinking was preventing me from fully operating in the best interests of our stakeholders. Silos and bureaucracies, internal politics, and big egos can destroy an institution. Our research for *Commencement* showed that 19% of higher-education employees are actively looking to leave academia, and another 22% are considering a near-term jump to another industry. How might flattening your organizational chart, rethinking the hierarchies, and empowering your employees to do their jobs without "death by committee" help those employees with one foot out the door choose to stay?

The most rewarding part of writing this book was the opportunity it gave us to discover that — without a doubt — today's higher-education leaders are breaking their own stereotypes and are redefining higher education for a new age. It takes will — consistently applied over time — to move from old-school operations to new-school innovations.

Making Education Our Business

If we are ever to escape the "ivory tower" mindsets of our predecessors in higher education, we need to learn to be critical of ourselves and our outdated processes. The most rewarding part of writing this book was the opportunity it gave us to discover that — without a doubt — today's higher-education leaders are breaking their own stereotypes and are redefining higher education for a new age. It takes will — consistently applied over time — to move from old-school operations to new-school innovations. During our mid-pandemic conversation with Dr. Laurie Borowicz, President of Kishwaukee College, we were reminded that tough times and tight budgets are no excuse to rest on our laurels. When our

" Retention should mean graduation with a viable degree and proper knowledge, not just – as our K-12 system is often accused of – passing people through. "

Hal Higdon, PhD
Chancellor, Ozarks Technical Community College System

students are moving fast, we need to be moving with them. Dr. Borowicz told us:

> "Technology is front and center. It *has* been (pre-COVID) and, oh my — it *really* is (post-COVID). We have invested heavily in technology at Kish. When I arrived, we weren't even doing electronic transcript requests! I mean, we were very far behind. We really weren't using technology for anything.

> "And I became a president in Illinois after the first semester of their two-year budget impasse. So, with no state aid coming in and not having made a lot of changes as an institution, we found quickly that the only way we were going to be able to do what we had to do — to serve our students with less staff — is to invest in technology."

One of the key lessons learned during the research phase of this book is that institutions that are truly focused and that get nimble and optimistic while "doing more with less" are the very institutions that eventually are able to "do more with more." A crisis (like a pandemic or a budget shortfall or the undergraduate admissions cliff, which some institutions are already teetering atop) is no time to double down on the status quo. It's time to get moving, get more entrepreneurial, get comfortable with risk and speed, and new ways of operating.

A crisis is no time to double down on the status quo. It's time to get moving, get more entrepreneurial, get comfortable with risk and speed, and new ways of operating.

📝 Pop Quiz!

Late one night, when we had nothing better to do, Joe, Elvin, and I brainstormed a list of common stereotypes about higher education and the people who work in higher ed. We believe — and we hope you do too — that confronting (and shattering) the negative stereotypes will allow us to build remarkable new cultures and processes for the future. Which of the following stereotypes ring true for your organization and your observations of the higher-education industry as a whole? Check all that apply.

Extra credit! Put a star next to the stereotypes you're already working to bust and/or are committed to shattering at your institution and beyond.

❑ Champions of the status quo and strongly attached to time-honored traditions.

❑ Operating more for the time they were founded than the era in which they currently serve.

❑ Very, very slow to enact change or embrace innovation.

❑ Many leaders are promoted from within and often prove the Peter Principle, rising to the level of their incompetence.

❑ Tuition is too high and there are too many hidden fees (and the loan culture is disastrous).

❑ "Collegial" cultures, relatively cushy jobs at the top, excellent fringe benefits for employees, predictable cycles of work.

❑ Tenure system is often unfair and sometimes protects faculty who don't deserve protection.

❑ Inaccessible to minoritized populations in terms of students, and also not enough diversity in leadership or faculty.

❑ Sometimes the priorities and goals of academics and athletics are at odds.

❑ Many operations teams are under-resourced in terms of staff and budget.

❏ Overall, institutions are too reliant on tuition income.

❏ There's a big divide between institutions with large endowments and those without.

❏ Delivery method (online, on-ground, or hybrid) might impact quality.

❏ "Ivory tower" cultures make higher ed out of sync with the real world.

❏ Adjunct faculty and teaching assistants (TAs) teach all the courses.

❏ There's no student support outside of business hours.

❏ Higher ed is not flexible or agile, often exacerbated by internal barriers like unions and tenured faculty.

❏ Bureaucratic structures favor hierarchy, create silos, and foster political divides.

❏ Curriculum is old, outdated, and not connected to the real world of work.

❏ Way too many acronyms.

❏ Way too many committees.

❏ The only path to a college presidency is through the traditional academic infrastructure – faculty, Dean, Provost, President.[45]

❏ Institutions are over-confident about their program quality.

❏ Other (please specify): _____

---

45 We couldn't resist the urge to set the record straight on this dying stereotype. Though this still may be a viable pathway toward a college presidency, there are many examples of institutions/boards who have intentionally changed the hiring profile as a response to address the challenges facing institutions today (e.g., declining enrollment, tuition dependency). Take, for example, Western Governors University's Dr. Scott Pulsipher, who was a retail/tech executive prior to higher ed; Grand Valley State University's Dr. Philomena Mantella, who has a student affairs and enrollment-management background; Pima Community College's Lee Lambert, JD, who has a legal affairs background; William Peace University's Dr. Brian C Ralph, who has an enrollment-management background; and Lindenwood University's Dr. John Porter, who was a big tech executive prior to leading in higher education. See Chapter 7's "leadership skillset of the future" for more on this trend.

" Higher education is going to change dramatically. It is changing now. And over the next five to ten years, it will be *completely* different. **"**

Stephen Spinelli, Jr., PhD
President, Babson College

Higher Standards for Higher Education

Throughout this book, we have presented many stories and perspectives about the role of trust inside higher education, with particular emphasis on a recent perceived loss of trust from students, influencers, and the community in general. One of the best ways to regain trust, we were told, is to "give it to them straight" — to be honest and fair in all your dealings with stakeholders like students, admissions candidates, alumni, staff, faculty, and others. Richard L. Dunsworth, JD, President of the University of the Ozarks, gave us an example of something we should all put on our "stop doing" list: trying to convince everyone to choose our institution even when we know we're not the right fit. President Dunsworth gave us a great example of truly consultative admissions. He told us:

> "Several years ago, I asked our admissions staff the question: 'How often do you recommend to a student that they go somewhere else?' And I had the director of admissions look at me and say, 'I don't have the authority to tell somebody to go somewhere else.' And I said, 'What do you mean?' He said, 'Well, if a student's admissible here, I have to recruit them.' So, I asked, 'Joey, have you ever worked with a family where you knew — darn good and well — we weren't the right school?' And he said, 'Sure.' And I said, 'Well, how about, moving forward, if you don't think we're the right school for somebody, you tell him that? But you have to then give them a recommendation of where they should go. You can't just say, 'We're not a good school for you' because that sometimes is code for discrimination ('you don't fit us'). No. You say, 'Hey, it's lovely meeting you, Mark. You're amazing. You should be at ...' and you tell them what school is the *right* school. And I think that as you start to build real relationships — you get as transparent as possible and you get brutally honest with people — I think we'll see some of that trust coming back."

During an interview with a college president, my co-author, Dr. Joe Sallustio, said:

> "There are all sorts of ways that you can offer a platform *beyond the traditional* that becomes something that somebody wants to come back to. And I think that's the secret, right? Isn't that the secret for

higher ed in the future — when a learner wants to change something, whether it's upskill, re-skill, or increase their knowledge capacity — that you in higher education want loyalty from the student? You want them back every time they think of upskilling or reskilling. That's the holy GRAIL."

 ## Making Education Your Business with Dr. Joe Sallustio

Loyalty Programs

I don't mean to get philosophical here, but it *is* half my book, so I'll do what I want to. One of the questions that nags at me all the time is: Why hasn't higher education figured out the loyalty program yet?

During my 15 years in the for-profit education sector, I worked for a career college (12 years) with 11 campuses across nine states. For 11 of those 12 years, I travelled 50% of the time. When I moved on to a regionally accredited, publicly traded for-profit university with 42 campuses, I travelled about 40% of the time for another three years (by the way, I did get to ring the closing bell at the NASDAQ in 2017; it was basically amazing). All that travel netted me a Marriott Rewards Titanium Lifetime Status. I get points for credit card purchases with my Marriott credit card, and I receive 50% bonus points on any stay, with free breakfast, free access to the concierge lounge, free parking, and other benefits — for life!

As of the publishing of this book, I've stayed in Marriott hotels 1,273 nights or almost three-and-a-half years. Sad, I know, but that is not the point. The point is that I will do whatever it takes to stay at a Marriott hotel when I travel alone or with my family. Every time I stay, it gives me something back. Same thing with United Airlines — where a Marriott membership gets you a level on United.

Your credit card probably gives you cash back and you probably receive points or credits of some kind on other buying accounts that you have. Retail organizations and service organizations agonize over how to build customer loyalty. They create elaborate systems to reward customer loyalty and create the lifelong customer. Marriott has me already. What can higher education learn from organizations that think about the second, third, or tenth sale?

The imperatives for higher education in the 2020s and beyond are myriad and meaningful. Achieving them all won't be easy. As we spoke with college and university presidents, we noticed that almost no one is settling for "good enough" these days. If their graduation rate is improving, they want to improve it *more*. If they're beginning to be truly student-centric, they want to set the bar for student services — *delighting* the students at every turn. If the career outcomes of their leaders are impressive, they want to all but *guarantee* that kind of ROI.

Dr. Mary Schmidt Campbell, President Emerita of Spelman College, brought that kind of high-standards thinking to our conversation. She told us:

> "The thing that matters most to us at Spelman is that we become that place where every single woman who enrolls here graduates. And that she doesn't just walk out of here with a degree, but she walks out of here with a pathway for the rest of her life — a pathway for lifetime learning, for lifetime work, for lifetime connectedness to community."

At the time of Dr. Campbell's interview, Spelman had a 75% graduation rate; she told us: "We will not stop until it's 100%."

High standards in every nuance of college and university operation are the order of the day. In a conversation we had with Peter Cohen, then President of the University of Phoenix, he talked to us about "truth in advertising" and integrity in higher-education marketing, saying:

> "All universities, regardless of what type they are — taxable or tax-exempt — should be held to a high standard and should be held accountable for the quality and accuracy of what they say. We support that 100% in our marketing programs. We do not market, nor

do we have one word that goes out — either over the airways or on Facebook or that our enrollment representatives say to students — that isn't reviewed by our legal department to make sure that what we say is verifiable and is backed up by facts and can be substantiated. I cannot say the same for some of our nonprofit competitors who don't seem to have that same kind of legal scrutiny before they make claims in the media."

> **Reflection Question**: *When your institution writes radio scripts or billboard headlines, when it produces admission brochures and when it gives talking points to admissions managers and tour guides, do the claims you'll be making to prospective students, families, guidance counselors, and others get scrutinized by your legal team or your institutional research department? Or are marketing and admissions folks allowed to say whatever they think most resonates with their audiences?*

In a world of fact-checking and where trust is the greatest currency of all, higher education's accountability, honesty, and integrity matter.

When we asked — more than 100 times — "What's the future of higher education?" we got two kinds of answers (both of them valid). Sometimes the answers were about how institutions of higher education will change (because, surely, they must). And sometimes the answers hinged on how the *students* are the future of higher education. The answers we heard from college and university presidents — which were overflowing with optimism and respect for the students — got us thinking: What if it's all about *them*, and not about us at all?

Administrators might be the protagonists of this book, but students are the heroes of higher education's story.

Administrators might be the protagonists of this book, but students are the heroes of higher education's story.

Dr. W. Kent Fuchs, President of the University of Florida, told us:

> "I'm an eternal optimist about how higher education across this nation
> continues to evolve. And I believe that if we, as a nation, are going to
> make progress on issues of racial equity and all the things that we care
> about, it's got to start within our colleges and universities and with our
> students. Because our students are going to be the ones who are going
> to go out and make the breakthroughs and make our nation great.
> They're going to make our world an amazing place for everyone."

In order for higher education to enable our students to be amazing for the
world, we must first be amazing for *them*. And when there's something we
can't yet provide for our learners — like enough diversity in our faculty
ranks — we can educate our students to *become* those faculty members. In
our conversation with Dr. Melody Rose, former Chancellor of the Nevada
System of Higher Education, she shared a brilliant insight about higher
education becoming "self-sustaining" in this way. To address the completion gap even when a college population is diverse requires hiring faculty
and staff who are diverse, and if there aren't enough people of color or
women in certain disciplines, the best way for colleges and universities to
solve that problem is to *produce* those professionals. Dr. Rose told us:

> "We know that in certain disciplines, the representation of women
> and people of color is still lacking. So, in some ways, we have to think
> upstream about growing our own. We have to think about 'What are
> we doing in our masters and PhD programs to grow those populations
> of professionals — to invest in them — so when it's time for us to hire
> faculty and staff, we're actually looking at a growing pipeline that is
> more representative of America?'"

In an industry that's been full of excuses, we're suddenly full of solutions
and new kinds of accountability. We're setting higher standards for higher
education. And, in the end, colleges and universities are solving the
world's problems by producing the thinkers and leaders who will create
the solutions.

Time and again, we heard higher-education leaders talk about complex
paradoxes to solve and chasms to cross. We heard them talk about the
ways we must come together to bridge our divisions and dismantle our

silos. Dr. Thomas R. Bailey, President of Teachers College, Columbia University, brought up one such paradox when he asked us:

> "Does higher education actually address equity and make the society more equal, or does it actually exacerbate inequities? One could argue that the students who have the most means often go to the institutions that have the most to spend on them. I think that's an issue."

Dr. Bailey is not wrong. Not only does higher education have a lot of work to do and a lot of problems to solve, it also inadvertently creates new problems — deepening divides and complicating matters. But here's the rainbow after the storm: For the first time in perhaps two centuries, higher education is shining a bright, scrutinizing light on itself, ready to see its shortfalls and get to work on being better.

Here's the rainbow after the storm: For the first time in perhaps two centuries, higher education is shining a bright, scrutinizing light on itself, ready to see its shortfalls and get to work on being better.

Surely, a book like this could not have been written 50 years ago or even 10 years ago. The industry was too entrenched in its own "right fighting" about "the way we do things." In decades past, it would have been impossible to bring more than 100 college and university presidents to the microphone to talk candidly about real issues (without their public-relations directors signing off on every word). No one would have stepped up to the conversations and the moments the way they did in the 2020s. The tide is turning. The revolution is underway. The challenges are no longer as frightening because the solutions are at our fingertips. They say that "the first step in overcoming a problem is admitting you *have* a problem." Collectively, we're admitting it ... then rolling up our sleeves to execute on the solutions. Dr. Bailey pulled no punches when he said:

"There's no question that higher education faces *really* difficult challenges. Cost is a huge issue. Equity is an issue. There's the question of the value of higher education; what's the return on investment? And there are even political issues. In some parts of the country, controversies are brewing about what gets taught and *how* it gets taught. For example, how do we teach the history of race in this country? So those are huge challenges that we, as institutions, are facing.

"Now, we can't solve these challenges alone. These are societal questions, but we need to do the best we can as institutions working together, working with policy makers, to try to address those issues. Now while we're facing these problems as institutions, the *need* for higher education is that much greater. The skills that are required — the broad skills that help us adapt as things change. We're facing huge problems ... climate change, equity, the advancement of medicine and science."

The tide is turning. The revolution is underway. The challenges are no longer as frightening because the solutions are at our fingertips.

The bigger the dilemmas, the stronger the need for higher education. Will the industry rise to this occasion, ready to serve and lead and solve societal problems? Yes. It's *already* rising to meet the challenge. In this book, we've told hundreds of uplifting stories about how colleges and universities are setting (and meeting!) higher standards for higher education.

Blurring the Lines, Dissolving the False Distinctions

Perhaps more so than any other industry, higher education has been ruled by its dichotomies. And our inability (until very recently) to bravely dissolve false distinctions and blur the lines that divide us has led to the industry's most acute areas of pain.

📝 Pop Quiz!

Which of the following dichotomies do you think need blurring — at your institution and/or in higher education in general? How are some false distinctions, such as these, limiting opportunity for you or your students?

❑ Arts/sciences

❑ Degree/non-degree

❑ Undergraduate/graduate

❑ Full-time student/part-time student

❑ HBCUs-HSIs-etc./PWIs (historically black colleges and universi-ties, Hispanic-serving institutions, etc. vs. predominantly white institutions)

❑ Public/private

❑ For-profit/nonprofit

❑ Faculty/staff/administrators[46]

❑ Residential/commuter

❑ On-campus/online

❑ Traditional/non-traditional (adult)

❑ Traditional colleges/career colleges

---

46 When I worked at the medical university, I spearheaded an employee survey initia-tive that revealed a great deal of important and actionable data. But when I was presenting the strategy and research methodology to the President's Cabinet prior to the survey's execution, I used the word "employees" to describe anyone on the payroll — faculty, staff, and administrators. The president got very flustered (and downright hostile with me) when he "caught me" calling faculty "employees." He didn't think the faculty should participate in the survey at all. He said, "Faculty are not employees!" I asked, "They *do* collect a paycheck from us every two weeks, yes? And don't you think that faculty are a key population within our overall culture, whose insights we need?" In the end, faculty did participate in the survey (and were happy to do so).

❑ Other: _____

What's the opportunity here? How can you help blur some lines in meaningful ways? _____

_____

_____

_____

"We are more alike than we are different." It's something you've probably said when talking to your students or your children. And it's something we ought to consider when operating within the sometimes-arbitrary rules of engagement regarding higher-education dichotomies like "traditional/non-traditional," "degree/non-degree," or "for-profit/nonprofit." That last one sparked a powerful conversation with Peter Cohen, who was then the President of the University of Phoenix. He said to us:

> "People try to differentiate universities based on their tax status. You have those universities that are considered to be nonprofit, simply meaning tax exempt, and those that are considered to be for-profit, meaning they pay taxes (taxes that support our federal government and support all our programs, which support education). And yet we have different rules for each group. But when you look at the fastest-growing universities in the United States right now, they happen to be tax-exempt organizations considered to be nonprofit. Their marketing approaches are identical to the marketing approaches used by the taxable universities, and they use the same partners, the same marketing teams, et cetera. *They* buy on Google the same way *we* buy on Google. *They* advertise on TV the same way *we* advertise on TV.

> "*Every* institution is trying to grow its enrollments and ensure that it is viable for the long term. *Every* institution has to figure out what it is that attracts students and builds their brand and, in order to do so, they have to *communicate* to those students. Some universities do it by having a great football team and they get free TV time by being on national television. Some do it by buying businesses, and some do it by marketing and the media. So, I think that these kinds of false distinctions between tax status for a university and trying to define how they attract their students is antiquated and inaccurate."

Dr. Mary Schmidt Campbell, then President of Spelman College, talked to us about the limitations of false distinctions in the curriculum. She said:

> "I think we make a false distinction between the arts and sciences. Really what you want is a creative thinker, and that creative thinker can function in a lot of different spheres. We think it's extremely important to have the benefits of a full liberal-arts education."

At Spelman, they teach art to STEM majors and data science to arts and humanities majors. They have a computer-science course that's required for all students and an arts course that's required for everyone.

YOU and Higher Education

When Dr. Joe Sallustio and I sat down to write this book, we had no idea how remarkable the journey would be — who we would meet, the ways in which we would be inspired to help and serve, the stories we would hear, the lessons we would learn, and the opportunities that would open up as we got honest (and hopefully what you would consider generous) in the way we presented this conversation. We leave this book-writing odyssey more determined and committed than we entered it — Joe in a new leadership role at a dynamic university in a new zip code, and me about to go "all in" on higher education as my key industry. We know that the past few years have been tough for higher-education professionals across the ecosystem, at every level, and in every role. It's not easy being a financial-aid director, or a business professor ... an IT help-desk specialist, or a cafeteria manager. It's hard enough to keep up (much less innovate) in enrollment marketing, ed-tech adoption, curricular change, strategic partnerships, physical plant improvements, financial management, and student services. And it's harder than ever to serve on a President's Cabinet. As such, it's vital that we take care of each other — and renew our collective commitment to higher education — so we can take incredible care of our learners for the foreseeable future.

As we wrapped up a conversation with Dr. John Swallow, President of Carthage College, we asked him to share some advice — a pep talk, if you will — for higher-education professionals. He acknowledged that with all the disruption — with the demographic changes and the demographic cliff — it's more powerful than ever to make a personal choice to work and lead in higher education. He said:

> "Higher education, for me, is deeply meaningful and needed for the future of our society. And yes, we have more pressures than we've had in decades; that doesn't make the work any less valuable. In fact, it opens up more possibilities to find ways to do higher education better. That's what motivates me each day — to try to find more pathways, to improve retention, to design ourselves for the students who are *coming* (who are *not* the same as the students who were here 30 years ago).
>
> "And so in terms of advice for people and their careers, there will always be a place for faculty and staff who are absolutely committed to that and are committed to being creative, trying new things — not simply waiting to go to a conference and hear what some other institutions did a few years ago that was *probably* a good idea.
>
> "To really understand the students, you have to understand what they face — to understand how to provide the education (and the entire environment on a residential campus) better. I'd say there's even more opportunity than there was before. Because before, sometimes being creative meant challenging a lot of the status quo and people were very comfortable with the status quo. I think that today a lot of us are *not* comfortable with the status quo, because it just doesn't look like it's going to result in a good decade ahead. And so people at any level who embrace that and who provide that value — and can inspire their colleagues to the same thing — they'll definitely have long and productive careers in higher education."

And that is our wish for you.

📝 Final Exam!

Respond in essay format. This exam constitutes 90% of your final grade. Be creative. Be bold.

What do *you* wish for? You know the past, the present, and the problems; now, what of the future? On the other side of every challenge is an opportunity and an aspiration.

What do you hope for higher education? If you could control the future (and in many ways, you do), what will higher education look like in the 2020s and beyond?

_____

_____

_____

_____

_____

As you close the pages of this book (hopefully, well-worn and marked up with ideas of your own), we urge you to ask yourself: What's *your* vision for the future of higher education? And what are you going to do to make that dream a reality?

The beginning of a new era in higher education begins with YOU.

Epilogue

This book, like all good and beloved things, must come to an end. And in our final moments inside this book with you, we think it's only appropriate for us to finally answer the question we've been asking everyone else for the past few years: **What is the future of higher education?**

In Chapter 10, Elvin Freytes correctly declared that nobody knows. But answering impossible questions is precisely what we have promised to do, so here goes.

A Great Awakening
By Dr. Joe Sallustio

The Beginning of a New Era in Higher Education — that is what this book posits about the post-pandemic years for students, teaching, and learning for post-secondary education. After interviewing college and university presidents from every sector of education, from every size of institution, across the world, I feel confident in the thoughts and ideas I present to you here in this epilogue. In short, I believe higher education in on the precipice of a great awakening.

A "rousing from inactivity or indifference" — that's how our friends at Merriam-Webster define an "awakening." And in truth, it's been an almost universal indifference to change among higher-education professionals that created the predicament many colleges and universities see themselves in today. The rousing of activity that will take place (and that has already begun) will bring new innovation and a resurgence in the positive public perception about the value of degree-based post-secondary education.

However, barriers to change still exist. Just weeks before publishing this book, I had a conversation with a colleague and current provost who is experiencing incredible resistance moving faculty from embedded face-to-face instruction to hybrid and online learning. While such resistance might seem strange in a post-pandemic world (given the crash course we all took in online learning in 2020), resistance is still incredibly common. Administrators, faculty, and staff all should rally around the fact (and it is a fact) that higher education has lost its leverage over the student consumer. Decisions to change should reflect the demands of the student — don't be Blockbuster, be Netflix. Emerging staff and faculty will be from the digital-native generations, where there will be an expectation of technology for teaching and learning.

In the coming years, I expect to see an incredible expansion of competency-based learning as institutions continue to attract the new traditional student — the working learner. Competency-based education allows the traditional constant of "time to degree" to be significantly disrupted, and the working learner (with responsibilities for job, kids, and life) will be increasingly interested in getting what they need as fast and as flexibly as possible. Micro-credentials and skill stacking will increase in importance for this population of students, but soon, momentum will swing back to degree achievement. Why, you ask? Yes, tech companies and others are dropping degree requirements for their employees, and this trend will continue. Perhaps, like Google, tech companies will offer their own credentialing for current and prospective employees. Soon, there will be thousands, if not tens of thousands, of potential hires with similar credentials ... which will lead employers back to the degree as a differentiator for employment.

At some point, the employers will ask themselves why they aren't in the degree business in a more significant way, leading to "degrees powered by" well-known brands/employers as a differentiator. Think about it. Online program managers came into existence when for-profit colleges and universities were on the decline. OPMs offer marketing and enrollment services to higher-education institutions looking to fill their pipelines. Aren't large organizations the ultimate sleeping OPM giant? Imagine a human resources graduate degree "powered by" Amazon in agreement with XYZ University. This will be the next potential evolution of the employer/institutional relationship, particularly as both organizations and institutions see how they can optimize the model rather than rely on career opportunity platforms that have emerged, like Guild Education.

I expect to see the disintegration of the college ranking systems. The *US News & World Report* rankings have long dominated higher education by communicating elitism rather than social mobility. Elitism will become a "bad" word in higher education. The pandemic revealed the vast inequities that exist within higher education in a way not seen before. While super-brand institutions, like those in the Ivy League or those in the Power 5 conferences, will move on as (mostly) normal due to their self-sustaining endowments, athletics earnings, and media exposure, the majority of institutions will strategize how to reposition their brands to serve a student not guaranteed to succeed academically without significant assistance. From the institution's perspective, this is a riskier student — but from a societal perspective, this is also a student who, when they succeed, will change the trajectory for their family for generations. This student will help remind us why we work in higher education in the first place — because we are in the business of changing the lives of individuals for the better, through education. Education for *all*.

We work in higher education because we are in the business of changing the lives of individuals for the better, through education. Education for *all*.

The many changes I expect to see throughout the industry will prompt significant change in the hiring profile of a college or university president. Business savvy — particularly in finance, recruiting, and building business-to-business relationships — will become critically important. Long has the traditional path to a presidency been through academics; this will still happen for some, but boards will look to other areas for future leadership both inside and outside higher education. Mergers and acquisitions, rather than being a consequence of poor performance or declining enrollment, will become part of a growth strategy for innovative institutions, further diversifying the future presidential leadership profile.

Over the past few years that I've been recording *The EdUp Experience Podcast* with EdUp co-founder Elvin Freytes, I've spoken with leaders across the world, and there is one thing I am absolutely sure about. The passion of those leading our higher-education institutions is incredible. It has been one of the great honors of my life to meet, learn from, and develop friendships with these incredibly passionate and talented leaders.

Outcomes for Everyone
By Kate Colbert

In 2021, I was attending a garden party on the lawn of a college president's campus-based home. When I was telling that president about this book — the vision we had for it and the podcast episodes that were making it possible. And I was mid-sentence, explaining that Dr. Joe Sallustio asks every guest on *The EdUp Experience Podcast* — "What is the future of higher education?" the spouse of that president walked up and asked, "*Is* there a future for higher education?" I choked on my chardonnay. We all laughed uncomfortably. And I was surer than ever that the world needed this book.

Until this past year, I've been fortunate to be known in several industries as a marketing and communications expert who helps organizations and individuals "Be Meaningfully Different." I've never chosen one industry as my "home," though higher education and healthcare have always been my areas of strength and passion. I was, for lack of a better term, industry agnostic. But after spending 15 months — seven days a week — listening to the voices of (and then writing about) higher education's brightest and most influential leaders, I've made a big decision. And you heard it here first: I'm so confident about the future of higher education that I'm going "all in" on higher ed as my industry of exclusive focus for my speaking, consulting, research, and writing projects from now until retirement. It's time to build a new website! (And get some comfortable shoes for all the walks I plan to take across flowering quads and through campus buildings with hard floors and lots of stairs.) I'm betting big on higher education. And I hope you are too.

Why am I so confident about higher education? Because the changes that are underway or on the horizon will revolutionize the post-secondary education experience for learners of all types, at every juncture in their lives. Finally, higher education is facing a reckoning ... and a recognition that while it's nice to offer an *experience*, it's more important to offer a *result*. And while it's nice for a higher-education system to help improve the social mobility of *some* citizens, it's imperative that it do so for *all* citizens. The goal, in the end, is outcomes for everyone. The work that is being done — the work *you* are doing — is going to impact every industry, every town, and every family on earth. I believe in higher education because I believe in you.

Finally, higher education is facing a reckoning ... and a recognition that while it's nice to offer an *experience*, it's more important to offer a *result*. And while it's nice for a higher-education system to help improve the social mobility of *some* citizens, it's imperative that it do so for *all* citizens.

So, what will those evolutions and revolutions look like?

Prediction #1: *Programs and institutions that pull away from the old pack will meet the previously unstated and pent-up demands of a changing population of learners.*

Sure, we'll always have some demand for coming-of-age residential college experiences for families who want to send their kids off to become well-rounded (and learn how to do laundry, make friends, be accountable, etc.) — but these programs will serve fewer people. Traditional colleges and universities will continue to attract wealthy consumers accustomed to access, as well as students and families who are looking for a flexible and "comprehensive" (all things to all people) bridge/gap between high school and career[47]. What was traditional in higher education will still have its place, but that place won't serve as the foundation of the entire industry anymore, nor will it be a standard or touchstone for all colleges and universities. Institutions doing brave new things — like Foundry College and GCAS College Dublin — will disrupt the marketplace in revolutionary ways that will put more traditional institutions on notice. Whether these upstart disruptors will hold on and become forces to be reckoned with — or whether they'll simply pave the way for other well-funded institutions to take the industry by storm — remains to be seen. Whether you're higher education's Napster or Pandora, you're changing the game forever and you're making history.

We'll soon stop hearing small, private, liberal-arts colleges refer to themselves as "comprehensive" as they get clear about their unique opportunities and stake their claims in specific niches. I predict that college students and the population in general will — in the next 10-20 years — be able to easily identify which institutions serve which target audiences. "Oh, Johnny ... if you want to study mechanical engineering in the Midwest and also play lacrosse, these are the only two schools you should look at!" Websites will be clear about whether a college or university is "New England's premier institution for young adults wanting to get their start in STEM fields" vs. "The world's only online university for experienced adults seeking to level up their clinical healthcare expertise with public health and healthcare leadership chops," etc. There will be fewer and fewer "all things to all people" institutions. And nobody will proudly call themselves a "best kept secret anymore" — it's time to be known (for something specific) or be obsolete. Brand will continue to matter, but not in the "college rankings" or "winningest football team" way. Students (and higher education's employees, for that matter) will choose institutions

---

47 Going into the military will always be a strong option for that young-adult experience as well.

based on their unique curricular offerings, established cultures, faculty brands,[48] and learning/teaching models.

Prediction #2: *Higher education will start operating in the "real world," once and for all, because the real world is counting on them to do an immensely important job. (And the real world — including big corporations and local and national governments — will start supporting higher education as it deserves.)*

I predict that higher education will finally begin to understand and capitalize on the lifetime value of its students, and — selfishly — I look forward to my four alma maters doing better by offering lifelong learning opportunities that might re-engage me. I think "stop in and stop out" will become *the* way to think about career and life skills — professional and personal skills. All institutions will have online offerings but not all colleges and universities will be "online schools." Immediacy of support and on-demand learning will become the norm. Trade schools, aviation schools, police academies, and military academies will be fully welcomed into the higher-education industry, and we'll stop asking our kids if they "want to go to college *or* want to go into the trades." The questions that we should be asking young adults who are shopping for a college/learning experience are: "What do you want to *do* and who do you want to *be*?" — then "Which group of educators, trainers, and experts deserve the honor of helping you get there?"

Community colleges — perhaps the only institutions that can viably remain "comprehensive" in the future — will reign supreme in industry partnerships and the development of future-ready workforces. Our terminology will shift — community colleges will no longer be simply "junior colleges" and we'll do away with terms like "traditional students" and "nontraditional students" and even "two-year degree" and "four-year degree" as competencies replace time as the constant. We'll make huge strides in equity to the point that "underrepresented students" will no longer be underrepresented, and we'll have such good bridge programs

---

48 I chose my first graduate program based upon one professor (a famous author I wanted to study under). I had teaching-assistantship offers with higher pay elsewhere, but Illinois State University had David Foster Wallace, which was something that no other institution could compete with.

and wraparound supports that we no longer need to call out "1st genera-tion" or "1st in family" students ... because everyone will feel seen and will be leveled-up, no matter how "college-ready" they are when they arrive. What's good for minority or at-risk students will be good for all students.

Semesters and agrarian schedules will die; states will fund institutions in a way that makes sense for the *students*; campus politics will continue to dismantle themselves with less protection for the tenure track and more pay and respect for adjunct[49] instructors. Research institutions will emerge that are think tanks and research only — signaling that while some universities thrive with research functions and even hospitals attached, there's no need for regional science incubators and other such places of discovery to always be inside of universities. Researchers will research. Teachers will teach. Sometimes those functions will overlap. But neither imperative will suffer at the detriment of the other.

Traditions that distract faculty from excellent teaching will be reimagined or set aside; "publish or perish" will die and paid sabbaticals will become a relic of the past. Business leader/practitioner faculty will become the default preference — for students and for the institutions that hire those faculty. Why on earth would someone — in the 2020s and beyond — pay $30,000 a year to learn accounting from someone who hasn't been entrusted to manage a corporation's taxes in the past 20 years or ever? Or take theatre classes from someone without a SAG card? Or take commu-nications classes from someone who has never headed up the communi-cations division at a major organization? Or learn auto mechanics from someone who doesn't work in a service department or a mechanic's shop?

Overall, the calculus of higher education is going to change to benefit the student. Prices are going to come *way* down – institutions will seek to earn repeat business (by offering true lifelong learning) rather than continuing to focus a big, giant one-and-done per customer with a huge tuition bill. $10,000 MBAs and $3,000 certificates are paving that way now. Lobbying for federal and state legislation overhauls will bear fruit. IRS tax code section 127, which has limited employer tuition reimbursement to $5,250 since 1986, will be adjusted (finally) because society will insist upon it.

---

49 A term I've always hated. By definition, adjuncts are "connected but not essential." Part-time faculty have always been essential, and should be treated (and labeled) as such.

Collectively, we will no longer tolerate post-secondary education continually becoming more expensive while financial supports for students stagnate or decrease. Companies that employ the millions of working adults who are taking college classes will need to put more skin in the game — and the tax code might incentivize them to do so.

Collectively, we will no longer tolerate post-secondary education continually becoming more expensive while financial supports for students stagnate or decrease.

I hope we'll see other terminology changes — like "post-secondary education" instead of "higher education" and "learners" instead of "students," and higher education will become welcoming instead of exclusionary. Access, affordability, and flexibility will continue to be the goals of educators — not with "pie in the sky" visions but with practical changes that create low-friction, "come as you please" education options for everyone. Competition for today's colleges and universities will include publicly traded corporations, like Google, and venture-backed companies ... not just traditional, accredited institutions of higher education. As such, the accrediting models around the world will need to be revolutionized.

Outcomes/results/ROI will become expected from higher education, just as they are for any other high-price, high-involvement purchase. I won't buy anything from Amazon without reading the reviews and checking the star rating — and higher ed needs to be held to these same consumer standards. For prospective learners and their families on the hunt for the right program, we need to offer standardized dashboards/scorecards so it's easier to compare the many choices. Experts from industry — people with start-up and turnaround experiences and those with online expertise and customer-experience knowhow — will partner with collegiate leaders to transform the post-secondary education experience (the buying experience, the educational experience, and the career/life experience after completion of the learning). Some schools will close entirely (but not a huge percentage of the marketplace), and mergers and acquisitions will allow institutions to scale better, to share resources, and to grow.

And while parents love to complain about all the brochures arriving when their kid is "just a sophomore," society will do a better job of talking to kids (from as early as pre-K) about careers and learning and we will, at every socioeconomic level, begin to see ourselves as capable of achieving — as being "college-going" people, whatever that means for future generations.

Higher education will throw the gates wide open to welcome all students. The "look left, look right" weeding-out stories of yesteryear will be shunned, not bragged about. Other industries want their customers to be happy and to succeed; higher education needs to do that very same thing. It's our *job* to get the learner to their goals. Accessibility for students with physical disabilities (like blind students) and learning or interpersonal differences (like learners with sensory processing differences) will improve radically. Education will become more practical from day 1 and curriculum will rise to the challenge; in the future, it's not just about teaching theory and then hoping a local company will translate that to practicality if they get a student as an intern or a recent graduate as an employee.

Arbitrary, elitist practices and cultures will be rejected; teachers and students will be respected and supported; and learning experiences will be dynamic. We will not, another hundred years from now, be looking back and bemoaning the fact that the industry hasn't kept pace since the 2020s. Higher education — like technology and retail — will strive to stay one step ahead of its customers ... instead of 20 steps behind.

That's a lot of "what ifs" and "I hope." And I might be wrong about some — or even all — of these predictions. But one thing is for certain: I'm going to stick around to find out. The only thing that's as wonderful as being a student for the rest of your life is committing yourself to work on behalf of students for the rest of your life. So, I'm not going anywhere.

And while I usually enjoy having "the last word," I'm going to give it to Dan Lugo from Queens University of Charlotte.

"I think this is an important moment.
If we don't screw it up — and if we don't get complacent in reminding the world,
and especially in reminding our state governments and our federal government,
that the real changemakers in society are the higher-education institutions —
I think **the future of higher education is really very bright.**"

Daniel G. Lugo, JD
President, Queens University of Charlotte

"We've got to do everything that we can in the United States to invest in our people. The truth is: The better that folks are educated, the more innovative they can become, and the more money they can make — which will allow them to contribute to society so that other people will have future opportunities. And that's what makes the entire country competitive."

Michael A. Baston, JD, EdD
President, Cuyahoga Community College

RESOURCES, ACKNOWLEDGMENTS, AND ADDITIONAL INFORMATION ABOUT *COMMENCEMENT*

Your 100+ College and University Presidents

Commencement: The Beginning of a New Era in Higher Education was made possible because of the contributions of more than 100 higher-education leaders who were interviewed on *The EdUp Experience Podcast* during the research phase of this book. It is with profound gratitude that we share their names here.[50]

Patrick G. Awuah, Jr., MBA
President & Founder, Ashesi University

Kenya Ayers-Palmore, PhD
President, Tarrant County College Northeast Campus

Irma Becerra, PhD
President, Marymount University

Thomas R. Bailey, PhD
President, Teachers College, Columbia University

Emily J. Barnes, EdD
Interim President & CEO and Provost, Cleary University
Provost & VP of Academic Affairs, Siena Heights University

Michael A. Baston, JD, EdD
President, Rockland Community College
President, Cuyahoga Community College

---

50 To the best of our ability, we have endeavored to present leader names, credentials, titles, and affiliations accurately. Titles and affiliations shared here reflect positions held at the time of the leader's podcast interview. In the event that we were made aware of a leader having changed positions between the interview date and the release of this book in late November 2022, new title and/or affiliation are listed in a third, italicized line. We regret any errors or omissions.

Jon Bauer, PhD
President, East Central College

Joseph Bertolino, EdD
President, Southern Connecticut
State University

Leah L. Bornstein, PhD
President & CEO, Aims Community College

Laurie Borowicz, EdD
President, Kishwaukee College

Carrie Brimhall, PhD
President, Minnesota State Community
and Technical College (*M State*)

Frank F. Britt
CEO, Penn Foster Education Group
*Chief Strategy and Transformation
Officer, Starbucks*

M. Christopher Brown, II, PhD
President, Kentucky State University
*President & Managing Partner,
The Chicora Boxwood Group*

Mary Schmidt Campbell, PhD
President, Spelman College
President Emerita, Spelman College

Carlos Campo, PhD
President, Ashland University

F. Javier Cevallos, PhD
President, Framingham State University
*President-in-Residence, Harvard
Graduate School of Education*

Michael Cioce, EdD
President, Rowan College at
Burlington County

Peter Cohen
President, University of Phoenix
President Emeritus, University of Phoenix

Ryan Collins
President, Bethel School of Technology

Daniel P. Corr, EdD
President, Arizona Western College

Akiba J. Covitz, PhD
President & CEO, Foundry College

Anthony Cruz, EdD
President, Miami Dade College –
Hialeah Campus
*President, Miami Dade College –
Hialeah & Kendall Campuses*

Robert O. Davies, PhD
President, Central Michigan University

Creston Davis, PhD
Founder & Director, The Global Center
for Advanced Studies (GCAS), and
Chancellor & CEO, GCAS College Dublin

Sean Decatur, PhD
President, Kenyon College

Frank J. Dooley, JD, PhD
Chancellor, Purdue University Global

Sandra Doran, JD
President, Bay Path University

Richard L. Dunsworth, JD
President, University of the Ozarks

Wade Dyke, PhD
President, American Public
University System
*Former President, American
Public University System*

Jackie Elliott, EdD
President & CEO, Central Arizona College

Susan Engelkemeyer, PhD
President, Nichols College
Former President, Nichols College

Tracy Y. Espy, PhD
President, Mitchell College

Marcheta Evans, PhD
President, Bloomfield College

David Finegold, PhD
President, Chatham University

L. Dean Fisher, EdD
President, College of Southern Idaho

Kristie Fisher, PhD
President, Iowa Valley
Community College District

Gregory Fowler, PhD
Global Campus President,
Southern New Hampshire University
President, Unversity of
Maryland Global Campus

Wayne A. I. Frederick, MD
President, Howard University

W. Kent Fuchs, PhD
President, University of Florida

Angélica Garcia, EdD
President, Berkeley City College

Jorge Haddock, PhD
President, University of Puerto Rico
Professor, University of Puerto
Rico Río Piedras

Merodie Hancock, PhD
President, Thomas Edison State University

David Harpool, JD, PhD
President, Northcentral University
Acting Associate Vice President, Online &
Graduate Programs, Newberry College

Marjorie Hass, PhD
President, Council of Independent Colleges

Kathleen Hetherington, EdD
President, Howard Community College
Former President, Howard
Community College

Hal Higdon, PhD
Chancellor, Ozarks Technical
Community College System

Michael Horowitz, PhD
President, TCS Education System

Thomas M. Huebner, PhD
President, Meridian Community College

Laura Ipsen
President & CEO, Ellucian

Mathew Jacobsen, DProf
President & Founder, Dūcere
Global Business School

Anthony L. Jenkins, PhD
President, Coppin State University

Marc Jerome, JD
President, Monroe College

Saúl Jiménez-Sandoval, PhD
President, California State University
– Fresno (Fresno State)

Chuck Johnson, PhD
President, Vincennes University

Larry Johnson, Jr., PhD
President, Guttman Community College

Debora Kayembe, HND
Rector, University of Edinburgh

Arthur Keiser, PhD
Chancellor & CEO, Keiser University

Melik Peter Khoury, DBA
President & CEO, Unity College

Don Kilburn
CEO, University of Massachusetts
Online (UMass Online)

John C. Knapp, PhD
President, Washington & Jefferson College

Marvin Krislov, JD
President, Pace University

Bruce C. Kusch, PhD
President, Ensign College

Mark La Branche, DMin
Chancellor, The University of
Tennessee Southern
Special Assistant to the President,
University of Tennessee System

Lee Lambert, JD
Chancellor, Pima Community College

Paula Langteau, EdD
President, Presentation College

Brian A. Lenzmeier, PhD
President, Buena Vista University

Nathan Long, EdD
President, Saybrook University

Daniel G. Lugo, JD
President, Queens University of Charlotte

P. Wesley Lundburg, PhD
President, San Diego Miramar College

Daniel F. Mahony, PhD
President, Southern Illinois
University System

Christine Mangino, EdD
President, Queensborough
Community College

Philomena Mantella, PhD
President, Grand Valley State University

Joseph Marbach, PhD
President, Georgian Court University

Francisco Marmolejo, MBA
Higher Education President,
Qatar Foundation

Miguel Martinez-Saenz, PhD
President, St. Francis College Brooklyn

Summer McGee, PhD
President, Salem Academy and College

Stanton F. McNeely, III, EdD, MBA
President, University of Holy Cross

Jim Milton
Chairman & CEO, Anthology

Jason Morrison, EdD
Chancellor, Southern Arkansas
University Tech

Terry Murrell, PhD
President, Western Iowa Tech
Community College

Mel Netzhammer, PhD
Chancellor, Washington State
University Vancouver

Elsa Núñez, PhD
President, Eastern Connecticut
State University

Jack Paduntin, DBA
President, Pacific Oaks College

Mary Papazian, PhD
President, San José State University
Executive in Residence,
San José State University

Carlos Peñaloza, PhD
Chancellor, Leeward Community College

Bill Pepicello, PhD
Former President, University of Phoenix
Chair of the Board of Trustees,
American InterContinental University

John R. Porter, EdD
President, Lindenwood University

Scott Pulsipher, MBA
President, Western Governors University

John J. Rainone, EdD
President, Mountain Gateway Community
College (Formerly known as Dabney
S. Lancaster Community College)

Brian C. Ralph, PhD
President, William Peace University

José Luis Cruz Rivera, PhD
President, Northern Arizona University

Félix V. Matos Rodríguez, PhD
Chancellor, City University of New York

Christopher Roellke, PhD
President, Stetson University

Mark Roosevelt, JD
President, St. John's College

Melody Rose, PhD
Chancellor, Nevada System
of Higher Education
Principal, WittKieffer

Mike Rounds, MS
President, Williamson College of the Trades

Christina Royal, PhD
President, Holyoke Community College

Yves Salomon-Fernández, PhD
President, Greenfield Community College
SVP for Operations Planning, Southern
New Hampshire University

Luis P. Sanchez, JD
President, Oxnard College

Martha Dunagin Saunders, PhD
President, University of West Florida

Richard W. Schneider, PhD
President, Norwich University
Rear Admiral, U.S. Coast Guard (Retired)
President Emeritus, Norwich University

Claudia V. Schrader, EdD
President, Kingsborough
Community College

Lillian Schumacher, EdD
President, Tiffin University

Ronald Shape, EdD
President & CEO, National
American University

Mikhail Shneyder, MBA
President & CEO, Nightingale College

Bradford L. Sims, PhD
President, Capitol Technology University

Christine Sobek, EdD
President, Waubonsee Community College

Stephen Spinelli, Jr., PhD
President, Babson College

Roger Stanford, PhD
President, Western Technical College

Kurt T. Steinberg, EdD
President, Montserrat College of Art

David Stout, PhD
President, Brookdale Community College

John Swallow, PhD
President, Carthage College

Jack Thomas, PhD
President, Central State University

Rowena M. Tomaneng, EdD
President, San Jose City College

Michael Torrence, PhD
President, Motlow State Community College

Ward Ulmer, PhD
President, Walden University
Co-President, West Coast University

Robert H. Vela, Jr., EdD
President, San Antonio College
President, Texas A&M University – Kingsville

Reynold Verret, PhD
President, Xavier University of Louisiana

Dwaun Warmack, EdD
President, Claflin University

Steven Weiner, MBA
President, Menlo College

John Weispfenning, PhD
Chancellor, Coast Community
College District
Former Chancellor, Coast
Community College District

John W. Wells, PhD
President, Emory & Henry College

Julie White, PhD
President, Pierce College Fort Steilacoom

Daria J. Willis, PhD
President, Everett Community College
President, Howard Community College

Jermaine Whirl, EdD
President, Augusta Technical College

Julie E. Wollman, PhD
President, Widener University
Professor of Practice, University of
Pennsylvania Graduate School of Education

Frank Wu, JD
President, Queens College

Acknowledgments

From Kate Colbert, Dr. Joe Sallustio, and Elvin Freytes

This book was a labor of love and the creation of an entire community. There are so many people to thank.

First, and most importantly, we would like to acknowledge and thank **the listeners of** *The EdUp Experience Podcast.* If not for your support, there would be no podcast — and certainly no book based on the podcast interviews with our first 100+ college and university presidents. The notes that Joe and Elvin have received via LinkedIn or email — telling them that you've enjoyed listening — have kept them going in moments of stress and doubt.

Thank you to **The EdUp Experience partners,** including **Google, The Charles Koch Foundation, Unmudl, the Alliance for Innovation & Transformation (AFIT), Leadsquared, Advance360 Education, Fierce Education,** and **MDT Marketing.** MDT Marketing's Founder and CEO, **Mitch Talenfeld**, was the show's very first partner and stayed true to the partnership even back when we were still figuring out how to hit the record button!

It goes without saying that we are immensely grateful for **the 127 leaders whose insights formed the backbone of this book.** We have endeavored to acknowledge everyone by name in the preceding section of this book, and we look forward to speaking your names and sharing your insights for years to come. This book is as much *your* book as it is ours.

We'd like to thank and acknowledge all the EdUp co-hosts who have helped us contribute to the conversations with higher education's movers and shakers. Those co-hosts include: **Elizabeth Leiba, John Farrar, Lisa Honaker, Ryan Stowers, Dr. Amardeep Kahlon, Dr. Vistasp Karbhari,**

Linda Battles, Dr. Michelle Cantu-Wilson, Dr. Kurt Steinberg, Dr. Bill Pepicello, Dr. Eric James Stephens, Erika Liodice, Geoffrey Roche, and so many others.

Thank you to the Silver Tree Publishing team for bringing this book to life — to **George Stevens** for lending his distinct talents to the cover design and the interior layout of *Commencement*, and to **Jessica Gardner** for her eagle-eyed edits.

We'd like to extend a special thank you to **Eric Williamson** for introducing Joe and Elvin to Kate, sparking the conversation that lit the fire of *Commencement* — the "extracurricular project" of our lives. *Commencement* commenced with that first conversation. We've never looked back.

To our **colleagues**, **families**, and **friends** for their patience while we spent every spare moment — for 15 long months — working on the research and writing for this book.

To the neurosurgeon who saved the day (*and* this book!), **Dan S. Heffez, MD, FRCS**, for his impeccable care with a scalpel in restoring Kate's nervous system function, and to the remarkable nursing team (Sarah, Tom, and Mike) at Froedtert and the Medical College of Wisconsin. And to **Ceilia Boyce, PT, DPT, NCS**, and **Stephanie Pizzala, PTA**, for delicately balancing their best clinical judgment with Kate's stubborn insistence that she return to work immediately after spinal-cord surgery. The medical care and life hacks offered by this dream team are a gigantic part of this book's backstory.

Finally, and most wholeheartedly, we'd like to thank our spouses — **Antonella Sallustio, Olga Freytes, and Robert Colbert** — and our children, **Gemma, Giulio, Olga**, and **Jackie**, for being our inspiration, now and always!

Don't let the conversation end!

Listen to *The EdUp Experience Podcast*

New episodes every week, featuring the brightest and most influential minds in higher education.

Commencement: The Beginning of a New Era in Higher Education contains insights from more than 100 college and university presidents from across the world who were first interviewed on *The EdUp Experience Podcast*. Keep listening! Start listening! Share the insights with colleagues and friends.

Tune in for more gems of knowledge and to remain a part of *The EdUp Experience Podcast* movement.

Visit EdUpExperience.com to experience America's leading higher-education podcast.

500+ Episodes …	**The who's who of higher education,**
and counting!	*at your fingertips!*

The EdUp Experience Podcast brings the most important, relevant, and innovative thought leaders to the microphone for honest and organic conversations about the challenges and successes of operating in higher education today.

Listen now on your favorite podcast app!

About the Authors

KATE COLBERT

A former higher-education insider and current world-renowned marketing expert, Kate Colbert conducts complex market-research endeavors for colleges and universities and develops institutional brand stories that are meaningful to the prospective student and measurable on the balance sheet.
She has overseen brand and enrollment marketing, public relations, and alumni relations at two Chicago-area graduate schools. Kate has additional expertise in corporate education, university crisis management, and faculty relations. She has consulted for Northeastern University, UC San Francisco, Carthage College, Tulane University School of Law, Babson College, The University of Tulsa College of Law, Bradley University, Medical College of Georgia (now Augusta University), Viterbo University, and the University of Wisconsin – Platteville.

Kate has spoken at conferences for the American Association of Medical Colleges, the Council for the Advancement and Support of Education (CASE), and Education Dynamics. She is a six-time recipient of CASE District V's annual awards for excellence in marketing and communications. She contributed to the book *Net Proceeds: Increased Revenue from Enrollment and Advancement* (Moore and Abrahamson) and authored the acclaimed 2018 book *Think Like a Marketer: How a Shift in Mindset Can Change Everything for Your Business*. Kate has served as a faculty member at Illinois State University, the College of Lake County, Loyola University Chicago, and Lake Forest Graduate School of Management. She holds graduate degrees in English and business administration, and has served on advisory and governing boards for colleges and social-services agencies.

Having consulted for industries including healthcare, financial services, professional services, and retail, Kate's first — and forever — love is higher education. Co-authoring this book was the opportunity of a lifetime. Kate lives in Southeast Wisconsin, near the shores of Lake Michigan, with her husband Robert and a pack of beloved dogs. When she's not reading, writing, attending a board meeting, or conducting market research, you'll find her on a travel adventure ... usually via cruise ship.

JOE SALLUSTIO, EdD

Dr. Joe Sallustio is one of the world's foremost higher-education experts and recognizable voices. He is part of a select group of higher-education executives with expertise in the critical verticals of operations, finance, and academics. Having led teams in every function of university operation — in nonprofit universities and for-profit colleges — he brings essential knowledge necessary to scale and operate institutions in the 21st century. With more than two decades of experience in higher-education operations, Joe has led teams in marketing, enrollment, finance, financial aid, student services, student affairs, human resources, accreditation and compliance, business-to-business relationships, and product strategy. Specifically, his expertise in marketing, enrollment, and mergers and acquisitions within higher education has driven the success of the institutions in which he has served.

Joe is the co-founder and host of America's leading higher-education podcast, *The EdUp Experience*, which interviews higher education's brightest and most influential leaders from across the globe. Joe's combination of influence and experience has made him a sought-after keynote speaker, moderator, and facilitator. He holds an undergraduate degree from the State University of New York – Oneonta, a master's degree from Regis University, and an EdD in Organizational Leadership from Northcentral University. At home, Joe enjoys being a devoted husband to his wife, Antonella, and father to his kids, Gemma and Giulio. They currently reside in Weldon Spring, Missouri.

ELVIN FREYTES

Elvin R. Freytes is an esteemed higher-education professional and co-founder of *The EdUp Experience Podcast.* He holds a graduate degree in student personnel administration from Teachers College, Columbia University in New York and an under-graduate degree in communication studies from Northeastern University in Boston.

Elvin has worked for several institutions, including Michigan State University, University of California Berkeley, Columbia University, Boston University, Northeastern University, New York Academy of Art, Mildred Elley College, Touro University, and the Manhattan School of Music.

Elvin brings to bear a global perspective on his work in higher educa-tion. He has taught English and worked as a college consultant in China, and has traveled extensively throughout China, Australia, Italy, England, Brazil, Egypt, and Chile.

Elvin has 20 years of experience in the higher education field and brings a wide range of expertise, such as international student recruitment, admissions, college consulting, housing, financial aid, academic affairs, and student affairs.

Elvin lives in New York City, with his wife, Olga, and daughters, Olga and Jackie, where he absolutely loves to spend as much time as humanly possible with them!

Go Beyond the Book

Invite Kate, Joe, and/or Elvin to:

- → Deliver a keynote or breakout session at your higher-education conference, or serve a panelists or moderators.

- → Bring an onsite podcast studio to your special event, to interview your attendees and leaders about hot topics in higher education.

- → Conduct a book-signing at your campus or conference.

- → Facilitate a leadership retreat, workshop, or professional development session about the future of higher education or any of the key topics explored in the book.

- → Host a "guided book club" in which your people discuss *Commencement* with the authors and pick their brains about how to apply the book's principles to your institution's challenges, in real time.

Get the conversation started with an email to:

Kate@SilverTreeCommunications.com, JKSallus2@Gmail.com, and/or **ERFreytes@Yahoo.com** … or fill out an inquiry form at **CommencementTheBook.com/Connect.**

Keep in Touch!

Learn more about the book and link to other resources:

www.CommencementTheBook.com

Send an email:

Kate@SilverTreeCommunications.com
JKSallus2@Gmail.com
ERFreytes@Yahoo.com

Find, follow, and share on social media:

LinkedIn.com/in/KateColbert | Facebook.com/KateColbertAuthor
LinkedIn.com/in/JoeSallustio | JoesSallustio.com
LinkedIn.com/in/ElvinFreytes
Facebook.com/Groups/CommencementVIPs

Listen to the podcast that started it all! Tune in to *The EdUp Experience Podcast ...*

The EdUp Experience is America's leading higher-education podcast. Higher education is changing rapidly and the thoughts, ideas, and insights from today's brightest and most influential educational minds from across the globe are brought to you via *The EdUp Experience.* Co-founded by Dr. Joe Sallustio and Elvin Freytes, *EdUp* brings a down-to-earth conversational approach, making dry and complex educational topics more engaging and fun to explore. Pulling on over 40 years of combined experience, the *EdUp* team has a goal to inspire and educate people to pursue a lifelong learning mindset, no matter the path you choose. We make education YOUR business.

Listen at EdUpExperience.com or play the more than 500 episodes on your favorite podcast service.

AN ENTIRE PODCAST NETWORK FOR YOUR LISTENING AND LEARNING PLEASURE:

Beyond the flagship podcast, The EdUp Experience, *listeners can explore EdUp Network podcasts with topics ranging from international education, legal education, higher education leadership, K-12 learning, and more! We make education YOUR business.*

📖 **To order books in bulk and learn about quantity discounts:**

Visit CommencementTheBook.com to learn about discounts on book orders of 25 or more copies of *Commencement.*

Interested in placing a large order of books (500+) for your association, campus, or conference? Be sure to ask us about custom-edition books that feature your branding and a foreword by your institutional leader. Inquire at Kate@SilverTreeCommunications.com.

Made in the USA
Middletown, DE
04 December 2022

17041282R00309